Moving Together
Theorizing and Making Contemporary Dance

Rudi Laermans

D1264132

Antennae
Valiz, Amsterdam

Moving Together
Theorizing and Making Contemporary Dance

Rudi Laermans

Contents

Preface

Looking Back at the 'Flemish Wave'

In several respects, this book reflects an individual journey through the world of contemporary dance that started somewhat unexpectedly more than thirty years ago. My artistic trip now and then brought me to Berlin, Paris or Vienna, but Flanders has been the locality where I attended the most performances and regularly spoke with upcoming dance makers, already renowned choreographers, befriended critics, or programmers who were keen to receive some feedback on the show I had just seen. Renaat Braem once mockingly called Flanders 'the ugliest country in the world', but this is the kind of hyperbolic statement one can expect of a modernist architect who abhors the ribbon development that dominates the Flemish landscape. For a contemporary dance enthusiast, the Dutch-speaking northern region of Belgium tends to coincide with the cities of Antwerp, Brussels, Ghent and Leuven because they are home to the most important venues programming 'dance beyond ballet'. Particularly Brussels, the official capital of both Flanders and Belgium (and the unofficial capital of the European Union), has been a real hotspot for contemporary dance for some time now. My move from Leuven to Brussels in the 1990s was partly inspired by the city's vibrant dance culture, which is still going strong these days.

The Flemish dance context has profoundly shaped my personal views on contemporary dance's possible aesthetic or socio-political stakes, its recent histories (in the plural, indeed) and probable promises for the near future, or the policies that might benefit this art world. When my journey took off in 1982, 'dance beyond ballet' was almost non-existent in both Flanders and Belgium. Around the mid-1990s, however, things looked entirely different: contemporary dance had rather rapidly become an established discipline whose artistic raison d'être was taken for granted by a meanwhile substantial audience and official funding bodies. Also, some epoch-making performances had at that time already announced a fundamental renewal that would turn over the Flemish — and broader: the Western European — dance landscape, with various effects that can still be felt today. A few words on these changes and, more generally, on the main stages in my more than three decades long rambles through contemporary dance, seem appropriate. Besides offering an introductory background, they may already shed a bit of light on issues that will be further elaborated in the next chapters. As I will clarify below, this book's overall composition is indeed loosely inspired by the successive developments I witnessed within 'contemporary dance made and/or shown in Flanders' since the beginning of the 1980s.

When one evening in 1982, I walked into the Stuc theatre in Leuven to attend, somewhat offhandedly, a staging of *Fase*, I did not have the slightest idea that a long artistic journey was about to commence. After its Brussels premiere, some Flemish media covered Anne Teresa de Keermaeker's second debut as a 'must see' (in 1980 she had shown *Ash*, but this partly theatre, partly dance production was only performed a couple of times in Brussels). Although I was somewhat acquainted with the minimalist music of Steve Reich, which directly inspired the choreography, I did not really know what to expect of the work — except that the reviews made clear that the performance was definitely not 'a Béjart'. In those days, Maurice Béjart and his Ballet of the Twentieth Century, also the in-house dance company of the Brussels opera La Monnaie/De Munt, indeed still framed the social imaginary of contemporary dance within Belgium with considerable impact. Despite a few incidental Brussels performances by American dance companies during the 1970s, the line going from Martha Graham to Merce Cunningham, and further on to Judson and to minimalism, was by and large unknown in this country. The same was true for the tradition of German *Tanztheater*, which Pina Bausch had vastly renewed during the 1970s. All in all, contemporary dance equalled contemporary ballet, which had become synonymous over the years with the often spectacular, more then once athletically flavoured mass choreographies of Maurice Béjart. The attendance of a Béjart production had in fact been my only contact with dance prior to *Fase*. I must have been 16 when, together with my classmates, I boarded a bus that one hour later stopped at the entrance of Forest National/Vorst Nationaal, a huge concert hall at the outskirts of Brussels with a capacity of about 8000 seats. From far away, I saw little brawny men making all sorts of movements on the massive stage, with much gymnastic bravura, accompanied by bombastic music and an impressive light show. Together with thousands of other adolescents I participated in a free obligatory performance that my classmates and I above all enjoyed as a welcome break in the dull school routine. At the end of the show, I applauded for something — was it *The Firebird* or perhaps *Petrushka?* — that I could not really make sense of.

Attending *Fase* did not suddenly ignite a deep passion for contemporary dance. The repetitive, quasi-mechanical character of the piece mainly intrigued me in the sense of a mathematical model: everything looked right, up to the point that the performance created a self-enclosed 'world within the world' that made further musings over the dance's possible meanings superfluous. In this way, *Fase* raised the vague presentiment that perhaps within dance a match existed for the abstract fine art I had already come to appreciate. My personal intimation would have remained a speculative conjecture if the critical success of *Fase* among a younger audience had not encouraged some artistic programmers of up-coming Flemish venues to show contemporary dance on a relatively regular basis. Michel Uytterhoeven of the Leuven-based Stuc — actually the abbreviation of 'student centre', now STUK — even decided to recalibrate the already existing bi-annual arts festival Klapstuk (which literally means 'Highlight') into an event solely devoted to 'dance beyond ballet'. From 1983 until 2005, Klapstuk effectively showed an international, highly varied sample of current dance practices every two years in the month of October, thus providing a transnational context for the Flemish dance scene that emerged during the 1980s.

The first editions of Klapstuk had an overtly pedagogical purpose and were of great importance for all those novices who, like myself, had been quite charmed by *Fase* but lacked an elementary roadmap for contemporary dance. With their intended mixed bills, they aimed 'to give an overview of what is relevant within the art of dance: Merce Cunningham and American postmodern dance, the emotionality of German dance theatre, the cultural shock that Japanese Butoh-dance effects, the young vehemence of the new French or British choreographers' (this could be read in the introduction to the programme book of Klapstuk '83). Re-reading these lines more than thirty years later, I am particularly struck by the words 'the art of dance'. The expression indirectly indicates that contemporary dance was at that time indeed still everything but aesthetically evident in Flanders. Hence the necessity to emphasize that the choreographic appropriation of apparently easy to make everyday movements, such as the ones informing De Keersmaeker's score for *Rosas danst Rosas* (which premiered at the Klapstuk 1983 edition), was truly artistically valid. Combining instruction and legitimation was also the hallmark of the early contributions on dance in *Etcetera*, the Flemish periodical that also started up in 1983 and continues to cover the main trends in the performing arts within and outside Flanders until this day. I can still vividly remember eagerly reading in one of the first issues of *Etcetera* an article on the general principles underlying Cunningham's work or on the main differences between modern and postmodern dance. It all sounded definitely interesting, yet the great thing was that Klapstuk provided the opportunity to become directly acquainted with the work of historical figures such as Cunningham, Trisha Brown, Susanne Linke, or Lisa Nelson and Judson-legend Steve Paxton (their duo-improvisation concluded the Klapstuk 1987 edition).

Klapstuk and the dance programme of the new Flemish arts centres, such as Kaaitheater (Brussels) or Vooruit (Ghent), turned a considerable number of Flemings into steady enthusiasts for contemporary dance. I am one of them, and like with many of my regular companions the initial appetite for the genre had much to do with the shared excitement that we were discovering new terrain. Something genuinely novel was happening in artistic Flanders – and we were the privileged spectators that saw it come into existence. Two other crucial tendencies aggrandized the thrilling avant-garde feeling of directly witnessing a cultural transformation with a possibly long-lasting impact even more. On the one hand, the surging interest in contemporary dance was part of a more general renewal of the performing arts in Flanders. A whole new generation of daring directors, such as Guy Cassiers, Jan Decorte, Jan Fabre, Jan Lauwers, Luc Perceval or Ivo van Hove, challenged the ruling theatre establishment with growing public acclaim. Like myself, many of the new dance enthusiasts were also eager to attend the innovative kind of theatre that was shown in the very same venues embracing contemporary dance. It all added to the feeling that at least artistically, we were part of a broader evolution propelling Flanders into another cultural era at a high speed. The 'we' in question were a faceless group of twentysomethings constituting an anonymous audience that preferred not to attend the well-made plays in the well-subsidized theatres. 'We' were a non-organized collective of art consumers collectively supporting, by their actual behaviour, what around the mid-1980s became known and promoted as the 'Flemish wave'.

On the other hand, the contemporary dance we had started to appreciate was not a belatedly discovered artistic object that had already received a definitive shape in America or Germany.

At stake was a lively and multi-faceted practice that was currently being renewed within Flanders itself. The then much talked-about 'Flemish wave' was not a homogeneous affair, quite the contrary. De Keersmaeker started in a minimalist vein but visibly incorporated many aspects of German expressive *Tanztheater* in her 1984 production *Elena's Aria* (although containing several unisons, this dark and rhythmically slow meditation on female pangs of love came as a shock to many a spectator who expected gradually shifting movement patterns set to repetitive music again). Whereas Alain Platel also drew on the work of Pina Bausch or Susanne Linke, Marc Vanrunxt — who never enjoyed an international breakthrough but is to this day a core figure within the Flemish dance scene — rather combined the modernist stress on the medial autonomy of dance with a particular sensibility for the scenic presence of the human body. Jan Fabre took yet another path: he critically addressed the ballet tradition and its built-in tendency towards physical discipline and docility. By contrast, his former collaborator Wim Vandekeybus immediately made a name for himself with the joyful, highly energetic exploration of various sorts of physical risks in *What The Body Does Not Remember* (1987).

The remarkable heterogeneity within the all in all modest 'Flemish wave' had much to do with the absence of an established tradition in 'dance beyond ballet' within Flanders or Belgium (it also explains to a certain extent why artists without a formal education in dance, such as Fabre or Platel, felt attracted by the medium of choreography). This freedom from binding historical references, even from a profound second-hand knowledge of previous developments, indeed created a unique situation. Overall, *the 'Flemish wave' partly demonstrated that 'not knowing dance' could be a productive artistic force because it was an invitation to explore the physicality of the body in novel ways.* A particular boldness, reminiscent of the days of punk, therefore characterized the first works of, for instance, Fabre and Vandekeybus. We, the also not-so-knowledgeable new Flemish dance audience, happily sided with 'our' artists in their provocative ventures into 'dance beyond ballet'. Several of them rapidly turned into internationally successful artists, which evidently added an extra flavour to the personal experience of being a direct observer of 'contemporary dance made in Flanders'. Seen from a more distant perspective, we were in fact witnessing, first, the proverbial birth and, subsequently, the settling of a 'glocal' art world, one in which local events were intrinsically connected through sometimes difficult to decipher relationships with artistic decisions made in Berlin (for instance with regard to co-production money) or New York (such as honouring De Keersmaeker or Vandekeybus with a Bessie Award), the regular import of foreign dance productions, and recent transnational choreographic trends or artistic renewals.

From Conceptual Dance to Collaborative Dance
With the benefit of hindsight and the concomitant risk of practising 'Whig-history', the beginning of the 1990s may on several grounds be dubbed a crucial period for the then future of the Flemish landscape of contemporary dance. The first ground is of a contextual nature: in 1993, after some years of political strife and manoeuvring, the Flemish parliament voted in favour of an umbrella Decree on the Performing Arts. It replaced the existing regulation on theatre dating from 1975 and explicitly acknowledged both dance and the new arts centres as policy categories in their own right. The decree at once symbolized and furthered *the institutionalization of contemporary dance as an autonomous artistic field* within Flanders (a similar evolution occurred in several other European countries). Besides a definitive emancipation from the ballet tradition, this multi-layered process was roughly synonymous with the development of a specialized production and distribution circuit or, in sociologist Pierre Bourdieu's terminology, a restricted cultural market on which various actors primarily vie for symbolic recognition. At least in Western Europe, the viability of such a market directly or indirectly depends on government money. The new Flemish regulation effectively created autonomous budgets for contemporary dance and its immediate sparring partners, the various arts centres. A basic differentiation was made between structural funding, guaranteed for four consecutive years, and incidental project subsidies. The latter were – and still are – a crucial policy instrument in most Western European countries for flexibly calibrating the claims for financial support and symbolic appreciation by upcoming dance makers.

We, the nameless Flemish collective already hinted at, of course wholeheartedly welcomed the official recognition of contemporary dance. The new government money not only guaranteed the future chances of 'dance beyond ballet' but also had some direct side effects, such as the general material improvement of the settings in which performances were shown. Austere wooden benches might be ecologically sound, but it was definitely more pleasant to observe a dancer standing still for about ten minutes when seated in a somewhat comfortable chair. However, the crucial keystone completing the institutionalization of an autonomous artistic field was still lacking: an educational curriculum to transfer the specific competences needed to be active within this very cultural market. It is the only way of securing the steady input of creative newcomers who challenge the temporary canon or reigning orthodoxy. In 1993 and 1994, in Brussels some people were busily setting up a school that would primarily focus on contemporary dance. The project materialized in September 1995, when the first generation of P.A.R.T.S. students was welcomed on the premises of the Rosas company outside the centre of Brussels (P.A.R.T.S. is the acronym for Performing Arts Research and Training Studios). Structural funding was not yet guaranteed, but Anne Teresa De Keersmaeker, the school's principal initiator, betted on the probable conversion of her symbolic capital as internationally renowned choreographer in longer-term government support. The wager rapidly became a success story, from an artistic point of view as well: many P.A.R.T.S. graduates became acclaimed choreographers or sought-after dancers.

Also in the beginning of the 1990s, a performance premiered at Klapstuk that announced a paradigmatic shift in 'contemporary dance made in Western Europe' and prefigured a future rift within the anonymous 'we' or Flemish dance audience. *Disfigure Study,* the 1991 debut of American choreographer Meg Stuart, who would later opt for Brussels as her principal base of operation, immediately caused a stir. The performance superseded the somewhat cliché opposition between expression and formality through a keen fragmentation of the familiar figure of the purposefully controlled dancing body. Not only I had the sentiment that Stuart's innovative choreography implicitly resonated with key ideas of poststructuralism, particularly the work of arch-deconstructivist Jacques Derrida that was quite trendsetting in intellectual and artistic circles at the time. *Disfigure Study* was also a critical dialogue with contemporary dance's cultural environment – read: with the existing web of constraining significations interpreting the human body as 'naturally gendered', normally behaving or deviant, attractive or rather repulsive, et cetera. Stuart's debut forcefully demonstrated that choreography could be a genuine medium for reflection and was able to bring to the fore, in a stimulating way, ongoing key issues, such as the status of the body within 'the society of the spectacle' as depicted by Guy Debord. Whereas contemporary dance primarily gained artistic recognition during the 1980s, the genre now also became intellectually more respectable. Evidently, choreography had already been articulated as a mode of public criticality in its own right before (witness the *Tanztheater* of Pina Bausch, to which the work of Stuart may be linked in several respects). Yet, during the 1990s, a markedly vaster number of young dance makers started to question, through choreography, the seemingly evident gender identities and other cultural meanings that constantly transform the body, in often unnoticed ways, into 'scripted matter' or a readable text.

Stuart's second work *No Longer Readymade* (1993) further explored and deepened the basic features of *Disfigure Study*. At least from a Flemish perspective, both productions marked a crucial moment in *the twofold trend towards the intellectualization of contemporary dance, its increasing positioning during the 1990s as a medium for both critical cultural reflection and artistic self-reflection.* Indeed, several sections in the two performances not only addressed the body's dominant culturalization, but also questioned the prevailing definitions of the medium of dance. Can, for example, the sustained crawling of an arm over a back be legitimately called dance? Through the consistent choreographing of isolated parts of the body, the pieces invited the spectator to rethink both the hegemonic significations grafted onto human physicality and dance as a specific artistic genre. Though it is perhaps a bit of an overstatement, Stuart's first works therefore signalled a decisive turn within the Flemish dance world. They paved the way for those further exercises in medial self-reflexivity that became increasingly associated with the labels 'conceptual dance' and 'performance' towards the closing of the millennium. French artists such as Jérôme Bel, Xavier Le Roy and Boris Charmatz, whose work was rapidly picked up by Flemish venues, sealed this tectonic shift, which keeps on informing dance practices today. So-called conceptual dance, an expression that most dance artists linked with it firmly rejected, stretched the idea of the danceable so far that some critics and spectators alike began to doubt the actual artistic identity of the staged reality. 'Non-dance' was the disclaimer, 'performance' the more cautious category to assign the new mode of contemporizing dance in a self-reflexive manner.

Conceptual dance inadvertently created an already alluded to rift within the new audience for contemporary dance: 'we' became divided. Part of the audience behaved inquisitive and accepted the artistic invitation to experience, evaluate and think about dance or choreography differently. The other part held to notions such as physical virtuosity or emotional expressivity, or formal beauty and harmony, and eventually dropped out of the renewed world of contemporary dance. Yet another unintended effect of the conceptual wave was its strengthening of the emerging link between current performance practices and deconstructive or critical theorizing. The intellectualization of contemporary dance particularly stimulated the breakthrough of dance studies as an autonomous academic discipline within Western European universities. There indeed existed an elective affinity between conceptual dance's self-reflexive leanings and the tendency within dance studies to embrace rather speculative modes of theorizing when clarifying the specific stakes of a singular performance or general trend in choreography.

Most Flemish venues and other actors that were directly involved in the production and mediation of contemporary dance approached the twofold intellectualization of the field with an open mind. The sustained engagement with the artistic merits of current dance practices spilled over into a sometimes difficult attempt to convince as many spectators as possible of the aesthetic, cultural or political value of works that apparently only quasi-nihilistically undermined the idea of dance. In brief, the ethos of constant renewal or avant-gardism and the related stance of trying to catapult the marginal into the centre of attention, which had been the prime reason of these actors' existence in the 1980s, continued to inspire their functioning. Hence the relatively central position of so-called conceptual dance practices within the Flemish dance world around the year 2005. To a certain extent, they were the new canon and considerably determined the general framing of, and discourse on, contemporary dance. However, another distinctive notion had meanwhile also gained currency among choreographers and dancers.

Collaboration was the new, omnipresent buzzword when dance artists were 'talking dance'. Various connotations were (and are) involved, such as the political ideas of equality and democracy, or the belief that making dance together in a less hierarchical way offers all participants more effective chances for self-expression, thus producing a heightened personal engagement that positively colours the end result. Artists associated with the conceptual wave originally formulated the new work ethos of collaboration as part of their comprehensive institutional critique of the dominant modes of producing and mediating dance. *Collaborative dance indeed emerged within the practice of conceptual dance but rapidly changed into a generally valued mode of commonly creating dance, whatever its more specific stakes.* As an implicit poetics of artistic self-reflexivity not wanting to endorse its explicit name, conceptual dance chiefly addressed the reigning preconceptions of what dance is and might be. By contrast, collaborative dance practices do not as such imply a particular aesthetic stance. They first and foremost exemplify a cooperative mode of artistic creation that precedes a public performance without necessarily marking its observable features (though this may of course be the case). Much conceptual dance was (and is) collaboratively brought forth but certainly not all of it; conversely, several instances of collaborative dance do not explicitly commit themselves to the overt kind of self-reflexivity characterizing conceptual dance.

Writing on/Researching Contemporary Dance
Somewhere in 1991, Guy Gypens, then company manager of Rosas, approached me with the friendly worded request to write an essay on De Keersmaeker's work, for a planned book. Although the publication did not materialize, I effectively penned a longer text. The writing demanded a serious effort: for the first but not the last time, I had to face the notable differences between watching dance (live or recorded), thinking over a singular choreography (or parts of it), and 'textualizing dance'. Besides my known acquaintance with contemporary dance as a regular audience member, the essays I had already published on the bewitched entwinement of the body and consumption culture probably inspired the commission. Others heard of it, which resulted in new invitations by Kaaitheater and Klapstuk to engage with the work of Jan Fabre and Meg Stuart respectively. I indeed commenced to write on contemporary dance, and also on current theatre practices, because others were convinced that I was able to do so. From around the mid-1990s onward, I regularly contributed to *Etcetera* (even becoming a member of its editorial team for some years) and occasionally published on contemporary dance or theatre in English books or journals. By definition, writing forces one to articulate and structure

initially loose thoughts on the subject at hand. Vague intuitions have to be substantiated with preferably clear arguments, which proves not always possible. The same goes for teaching when this activity does not just equal the social transmission of pre-cooked information. In my various attempts to think dance, I have benefited substantially from the open theory classes I now and then teach in P.A.R.T.S. since the school's inception in 1995. Although contemporary dance was never the direct topic of my teaching, the overall context – and certainly the students as well – again and again invited me to link this concept or that line of reasoning with specific performances or more general developments in current dance practices. Ideas professed during a P.A.R.T.S. class, often in an impromptu mode, looped back into my writing on dance, which in turn regularly inspired my teaching at the school.

Except for my personal viewing experiences and a broad background in social and cultural theory, nothing really qualified me as a potential dance critic or theorist. For several years, I truly was a *bricoleur*, or tinkerer, who tried to make sense of the discussed work or oeuvre by selectively combining 'the sensory' and 'the conceptual', descriptions of specific works and more abstract insights that were mostly borrowed from the authors making up the canon of post-structuralism and critical theory. The word 'essay' aptly describes my at times laborious endeavours to construct somewhat convincing textual configurations in which the difference between the particular and the general was never superseded and rather acted as an epistemological fault line that had to be overtly acknowledged. I use the past tense, yet the 'dialectics without reconciliation' alluded to still greatly informs my writing on art works and, consequently, this book. Especially in the first part, 'Theorizing Contemporary Dance', the kind of interpretative analysis of individual performances for which anthropologist Clifford Geertz coined the term 'thick description', is constantly alternated with conceptual moves of the more abstract sort. The latter are always anchored in the first, yet I deliberately foreground the unresolvable tension between the usually detailed descriptions of single dance works and the sometimes cautious, at other times straightforward theorizing of 'the general in the particular' – read: of the abstract problematic that a work of dance unfolds through the temporary creation of a sensory force field consisting of always singular affects and percepts. Taking such a problematic seriously asks for its conceptual isolation and consistent elaboration, with the evident risk of now and then producing heterogeneous flight lines in which the discussed work, or even the however defined reality of professional theatre dance, only vaguely resonates.

Between my initial essays on contemporary dance and this book stands my growing acquaintance with the still expanding field of dance studies. From around the turn of the millennium onward, I started to read scholarly publications on the history of dance and its present outcomes in a more systematic fashion. I enjoyed reading most of the work that sails under the flag of dance studies and have greatly benefited from it. Several books or articles acted as inspiring examples of how one can write, with an always singular voice and conceptual interest, about dance through a hermeneutical lens without disregarding its peculiar performativity or materiality. Nevertheless, my training and professional activity as a sociologist also inform this book in several respects. One visible influence is the regular invocation of concepts and insights stemming from social systems theory, particularly the work of Niklas Luhmann. Even when not explicitly referred to, Luhmann's conceptual framework functions as a main theoretical source of inspiration. Neither systems theory nor Luhmann's oeuvre is widely read in the humanities, let alone in dance studies (also within the social sciences, systems theory is today overall a marginal paradigm because of its abstract nature and its at times difficult to master conceptual technicalities). Since my Luhmannian leanings are free from the kind of theoretical orthodoxy that is mostly unproductive, I loosely combine, throughout the book, theoretical notions or intuitions borrowed from Luhmann's work with insights forged by authors who are by now established names in dance studies, such as Jacques Derrida, Gilles Deleuze or Giorgio Agamben.

My background in sociology also partly frames my personal curiosity and scholarly interest in contemporary dance, which of course both vastly inform this book. How does a choreography critically suspend or theatrically question ingrained cultural significations? What kind of relationship with the audience is actively performed through the succession of the countless temporal events making up a dance work? These and related matters recurrently guide my sensory attention as an individual spectator, yet not exclusively and without perhaps being truly specific for a theoretically minded sociologist. Whereas they frequently surface in the book's first main part, the second one testifies to the 'typically sociological interest' in the divergent social factors or cultural meanings that condition contemporary dance's functioning as a singular art world. Already in the mid-1990s, I ethnographically studied the practice of making dance together through several months of observation within the Rosas company. Around that time I also supervised empirical research by Pascal Gielen on the institution-alization of contemporary dance into an autonomous artistic field within Flanders. After the turn of the millennium, this research activity was continued in the coaching of policy-oriented stud-ies on the fields of contemporary fine art and cultural heritage, which were at that time in Flanders the subject of intended official regulations, and on the Flemish audience for the performing arts. As said, my sociological interest in the various social contexts pre-ceding or enveloping a dance performance takes the lead in the book's second section, 'Making Contemporary Dance'. It opens with a more general chapter on art's social aspects in which the tendency toward sociologism, or the kind of social reductionism typifying quite some studies within the sociology of arts, is explic-itly criticized. This stance directly relates to one of the principal stakes of this book: the deliberate combination of a mostly single-work-centred approach, inspired by dance studies, with a context-oriented sociological perspective on contemporary dance in the first and second part respectively.

The principal distinction underlying this book's two main sections is the latent double meaning of the notion 'work of art', which points to a decisive split that is constitutive for every ar-tefact deemed art. The notion of art work predominantly refers to an autonomous object or product; in the case of dance, this is a temporal quasi-object that not only unfolds through time but also re-articulates this medium by means of, for instance, the spe-cific rhythm that frames the performing of a particular series of movements as well. Yet every art work also necessitates a however minimal productive effort or 'art-work', now in the sense of artistic labour. Within dance and the other performing arts, the labour is often notably cooperative both during the creation or rehearsal pro-cess and in a public performance. In 'Theorizing Contemporary Dance', the product-oriented meaning of 'work of art' prevails: I describe and interpret in depth singular works and discuss at length the general questions they raise. By contrast, in 'Making Contemporary Dance' the principal focus shifts towards making dance together in the semi-collaborative mode. This labour regime visibly honours the current stress on co-creation among dance artists but nevertheless implies important differences in artistic decision-making between the cooperating choreographer and dancers. In focusing on both significations of the word 'work of art', I partially question the boundaries still distinguishing the 'internalist', text- or aesthetics-centred traditions in the humanities and dance studies or dance criticism from the 'externalist', context- or socially oriented approaches dominating within sociology and most other social sciences. At the same time, through the book's two distinct parts, this general dividing line is all in all willingly re-affirmed.

Several arguments legitimate the book's somewhat dual nature. The principal ones are spelled out in detail in the fifth chapter, in which I contend that the 'internalist' and the 'externalist' modes of observing art come with two contrasting vocabularies that not only exist within art worlds themselves, but also effectively allow the construction of two divergent epistemological objects involving distinct 'regimes of truth'. The sometimes manifest, more often latent struggle between the humanities and the social sciences in the study of the arts, is therefore rather pointless. I advocate *a consistently symmetrical approach in studying art practices that focuses by means of divergent conceptual frameworks on both text and context, product and production, 'the aesthetic' and 'the social'.* The hope to detect always singular interfaces in which these two dimensions actually meet, also motivates this position. Besides, a symmetrical stance explicitly corrects the active forgetting of the various kinds of art-work-as-labour, commonly associated with the notion of aesthetic fetishism, when concentrating on the specificities of an art-work-as-artefact.

'Theorizing Contemporary Dance'

The first part, 'Theorizing Contemporary Dance', exemplifies a more general position on the relationship between theory and current dance practices. At least within the humanities and the social sciences, the notion of theorizing indicates an interpretative activity that, through the always singular blending of conceptual thinking and argumentative writing, is often practiced in the absence of a self-enclosed Theory that only needs application. This also holds for the field of dance studies. An all-compassing Theory of Contemporary Dance is impossible if one subscribes to the idea, as I do, that a genuine theoretical framework consists of a series of abstract concepts that refer to each other and therefore offers a fitting conceptual model of the observed 'reality'. Generalizing statements on dance's present condition or main characteristics, and by definition their hypothetical combination into one umbrella model, cannot take into account the sheer heterogeneity of practices claiming to be artistically contemporary. This incomparable plurality makes it impossible to use the same notions or insights for an analysis of, say, the work of Anne Teresa De Keersmaeker and most performances of Jérôme Bel. Furthermore, due to the many possible or virtual relations between the divergent positions that currently constitute the dance world, a totalizing or God-like view is a theoretical chimera, not to say a phantasm. In truth, there exists only a still growing, but necessarily fragmented body of generalizing propositions on contemporary dance and choreography that are in fact nearly always anchored in particular exemplars, which are selectively magnified by means of concepts. This is not a deficit that must be deplored or remedied but a symptom of *the structural impossibility of an encompassing theory of contemporary dance because of the objectified field's internal heterogeneity, which in turn conditions the possibility of an active but unavoidably multiple theorizing, vainly in search of the ultimate object it discursively addresses and co-constructs.*

The actual route taken in 'Theorizing Contemporary Dance' consists in focusing on the more abstract problematics that single oeuvres, niches or trends within contemporary dance put to the fore through singular dance works. Given their highly divergent nature, thinking through these general issues stimulates and even requires the deployment of different theoretical viewpoints and the use of often specific concepts or ideas. Inspired by my personal journey, I focus on three particular artistic sub-worlds. Whereas so-called pure dance emphasizes, at least on first sight, the formal qualities and medial autonomy of dance as 'the art of human movement in time and space', dance theatre foregrounds the difference between the performers' physical presence on stage and the partly imaginary, partly symbolic transformation of the human body with an always non-representable 'left-over' — the famous Lacanian Real — into various representations in both culture and the relationship with the audience. By contrast, so-called conceptual dance makes observable, in a mostly deconstructive mode, the many parameters that co-determine any performance shown within the regulating framework of the modern theatre dispositif, including the socially dominant definitions of dance and non-dance. These three sub-worlds are of course ideal-types, constructions selectively highlighting some aspects or particular features at the expense of others. They do not have a robust referential value but primarily function as heuristic devices in dealing with contemporary dance's heterogeneity.

Personal interest and the selective experiential or cognitive familiarity this implies are the decisive reasons for discussing only three sub-worlds. The practices and problematics corresponding with the labels of 'pure dance', 'theatre dance' and 'conceptual dance' repeatedly engaged me when attending performances; I therefore acquired a somewhat reliable and durable firsthand knowledge of them. Hence the conspicuous negation of, for instance, the niche of dance improvisation or the reality of dance-as-spectacle, whose actual importance within present dance I do not deny. My already mentioned 'journey' also provides the principle rationale for both the overall trajectory in the book's first part and the choice of the analysed works or oeuvres. I first comment De Keersmaeker's 'pure dance', indeed a category in need of several qualifications, because it marked the beginning of my wanderings through the landscape of contemporary dance. About a decade later, Meg Stuart's debut and her subsequent works invited me to address the specific issues raised by the less controversial notion of dance theatre. Although *Disfigure Study* also announced the conceptual wave, later produced works did much more directly articulate its stakes, especially those created by French choreographers such as Jérôme Bel or Xavier Le Roy. In selecting performances by Vincent Dunoyer, Etienne Guilloteau and the collective deepblue, I not only wish to honour the Brussels dance scene as my primary artistic biotope when it comes to 'dance beyond ballet'. The discussed works first and foremost obliged me to think about dance and choreography differently, and, not in the least, about the nature of the self-reflexivity co-defining conceptual dance.

Like the second main part of the book, 'Theorizing Contemporary Dance' starts with a chapter, titled 'The Virtual Nature of Dance. Basic Assumptions and Hypotheses', that sets the scene for the subsequent ones through the clarification of some general issues, insights and concepts. In congruence with the composition of all chapters, it consists of two sections or 'movements', subdivided into paragraphs, and concludes with listing the bibliographical sources mentioned or alluded to throughout the chapter. In using the word 'movements', I of course deliberately hint at the world of dance. Yet this expression also connotes the idea of thought movements, which fits the notion of theorizing that underlies this book (in his scant but influential musings on dance, Paul Valéry famously emphasized the direct affinity between human bodily movement and the difficult to tame agility of thinking). 'First Movement: Dance and the Danceable' opens with a discussion of Jérôme Bel's *Le Dernier Spectacle* as a somewhat bewildering instance of contemporary dance (indeed of the conceptual sort) and then puts forward an explicitly medium-centred approach of dance that is grafted on the difference between movement and non-movement. Dance's medium involves a vast, impossible to represent potential that every historical dance culture restricts and structures, which results in an at once contingent and binding definition of the legitimately danceable.

The 'first movement' is rounded off with some speculative thoughts on 'the contemporary danceable' and is followed by a second one that takes up some works by the legendary Judson collective of the 1960s as the starting point for a universal characterization of contemporary dance. This may come somewhat as a surprise since I stated that every attempt to formulate a Theory of Contemporary Dance is an imaginary undertaking doomed to fail. In fact, this not only has to do with the plural nature of the relatively broad spectrum of practices making up the implied art world. The very notion of contemporary dance also acts as a truly performative category co-defining, even co-producing a dance work's contemporaneity. Relying on art theoretician Thierry de Duve's incisive remarks on 'the Duchamp moment' in the fine arts, I argue that the term 'contemporary dance' (or indeed 'dance') is in essence an empty name that is situationally applied, or not, with an always particular perlocutionary force in relation to performances, artists, the programmes of venues, et cetera. Contemporary dance is therefore a reality at once co-constructed through and conditioned by the repeated, socially validating use of the name apparently only representing the state of affairs it helps to create.

In the three remaining chapters of 'Theorizing Contemporary Dance', I follow the already outlined route and successively discuss so-called pure dance, theatre dance and conceptual dance through a focus on single choreographers and some of their singular creations. The 'first movement' in 'Making "Pure Dance" Impure. Notes on the Work of Anne Teresa De Keersmaeker & Rosas' zooms in on two early works of

De Keersmaeker that have been Rosas repertoire pieces for some time now, *Fase* (1982) and *Rosas danst Rosas* (1983). Notwithstanding the evident minimalism underlying *Fase*, I particularly stress the specific dialectics between choreographic structure and a partly unintended, partly theatricalized bodily expressivity that comes to the fore during the work's performance. In this way, the piece's liveness vastly undermines the 'ideality' or 'purity' of the Platonic body presupposed by every instance of 'written dance' or choreography. I try to give that latter notion some more substance via the concept of 'the choreographic', defined as the virtual space in which in principle repeatable (series of) movements or non-movements are both recorded and rationalized. My discussion of *Rosas danst Rosas* highlights how making ordinary movements scriptable within 'the choreographic' greatly transforms their status. Yet the quoted and frequently echoed everyday actions are often also markedly feminine. Their recitative identity, thus I argue in line with Judith Butler's views, precisely mimics the at once imitative and reiterative nature of the male and female genders we continuously embody within the confines of the dominant heterosexual script.

In the 'second movement', I analyse at length the 2001 production *Rain*, which is often considered as testifying to De Keersmaeker's choreographic mastership. After discussing the importance of bodily phrasing and its immanent relationship with singing in De Keersmaeker's work, I deploy the concept of temporal self-referentiality as forged by Niklas Luhmann in order to grasp the specificity of the relationships among separate movements or poses in a choreography such as *Rain*. The same notion is subsequently used to deconstruct the experience and idea of presentness. Later on, I put presentness once again critically into perspective and unfold the thesis that every mode of live performance continuously recreates the difference between actual actions or non-actions and the virtual potential of also possible movements or non-movements they unavoidably hint at. Through the repeated staging of everyday actions such as walking or running and their observable contrast with clearly artificial movements connoting 'danciness', *Rain* also positions 'non-dance' as the condition of possibility of 'dance'. This already questions the work's apparently 'pure', medium-centred or modernist character, but of even greater importance is the self-reflexive relationship with the audience that it deliberately constructs. Presumably 'pure dance', thus I conclude, is always rendered impure by the fact that it is being watched: not presence but co-presence grounds theatre dance.

The third chapter too, 'Re/Presenting the Body. Glosses on the Work of Meg Stuart & Damaged Goods', offers in the 'first movement' an in-depth description and interpretation of two early works of the choreographer I focus on here, the already mentioned *Disfigure Study* (1991) and *No Longer Readymade* (1993). Both pieces illustrate in at least a twofold way the idea of choreography-as-construction, thus I contend. On the one hand, Stuart approaches the body not as a self-controlled organism or structured totality but rather as an ensemble of loosely coupled autonomous corporeal zones. She therefore consistently choreographs the specific physical potentialities corresponding with the moving of the hands, the feet, the arms, the back, et cetera. On the other hand, Stuart's early works also excel in the montage of condense body images through the well-considered use of lighting and sound in relation to the shown movements. Referring to the tradition of German *Tanztheater*, I emphasize the paradoxical nature of the created *tableaux vivants*. Notwithstanding their seemingly expressive mode, Stuart in fact recurrently stages physical actions in a neutral or 'de-represented' way: it is the spectators who culturalize or 're-represent' the seen movements through their quasi-spontaneous reading in terms of the associated prevailing meanings. Yet another essential feature of Stuart's work, which again concurs with the common understanding of dance theatre, is the subtle handling of theatricality. After a brief intermezzo on the latter notion, I concentrate on a short solo of Stuart in *No Longer Readymade* wherein she performatively stages her individual failing as a dancer in such a way that theatricality is played out against itself. Moments of failing, or of not being able to realize a movement potential, regularly turn up in Stuart's performances. I interpret them as gestures, in the meaning Giorgio Agamben gives to the word: sometimes uncanny moments in which a medium becomes visible as such – as 'a means without ends'.

The first edition of the *Highway 101*-series, created in Vienna in July 2000, inspires the 'second movement'. Through the substitution of the traditional theatre dispositif for an old workshop, in which the dancers and the audience are often face-to-face, and the frequent incorporation of video-imagery, the performance enhances the impression of liveness and simultaneously deconstructs this still hegemonic framing of the performing arts. *Highway 101* therefore invites one to re-think liveness in a subtle way, beyond the critique of presentness as a mere ideology or phantasm. I argue that the experience of liveness essentially points to the paradoxical entwinement that emerges in the loop between a performer's bodily presence and its unavoidable transformation in a representation of 'being there'. Hence the reality of re/presentation, which *Highway 101* continuously re-articulates through the keen use of video technology and, particularly in the closing section, the remediation of dance by music. In the concluding coda, I once again take up the already conceptualized difference between actually made movements or non-movements and potential ones, but now in direct relation to the dancing body. 'The motioning' (Gerald Siegmund) or the performer's virtual potential to move and to not-move is both singularized in and hinted at within the presently made movements or poses – yet it remains a forever unobservable enigma for the dancers and the spectators alike. I suggest that Meg Stuart's remarkable way of contemporizing dance again and again addresses this unbridgeable difference between presence and absence, actually made movements and the virtual capacity their enactment at once evokes and bars from sight.

The fourth chapter, 'Dance beyond "the Human". Thinking Through Recent Developments in Contemporary Dance', has a somewhat different status than the two previous ones. Here I do not describe, interpret and theorize singular works of a single choreographer-author but discuss three performances created by different dance makers in view of highlighting, first, the principal stakes of so-called conceptual dance and, second, the possible contours of what I term – for lack of a better term – 'dance/choreography in general'. The defining role of video imagery in Vincent Dunoyer's solo *Vanity* (1999) initially brings me to speak of 'videography', but the piece's pronounced self-reflexive character also legitimates the label 'conceptual'. After a brief historical detour on Conceptual Art and a short note on the kind of hybridizing postmodernist dance that was quite successful during the 1980s, I introduce the notion of reflexive dance as a possible alternative for the established and previously used, but also rather disputed category 'conceptual dance'. Reflexive dance deconstructs contemporary dance's material and discursive conditions of possibility through questioning performative gestures. In line with Hal Foster's insightful discussion of the paradoxical relationship between the historical avant-garde and the neo-avant-garde in the fine arts, I argue that instances of reflexive dance, which can also be found in the oeuvre of canonized choreographers such as De Keersmaeker or William Forsythe, often both implicitly rehearse and actively re-articulate, even retrospectively reconstitute 'the moment of Judson' within a significantly different context.

Through an in-depth reading of Etienne Guilloteau's *La Magnificenza* (2006), I first return in the 'second movement' to the problematics of liveness and presentness. Inspired by Frédéric's Pouillaude's perceptive ideas on the subject, I situate performance's performativity in the literal contemporaneity of 'those who do' and 'those who watch', thus again stressing the crucial importance of the co-presence of performer(s) and audience. Guilloteau's work also prompts me to formulate a tentative answer to the pressing question, nearly always raised by so-called conceptual dance pieces, of what it actually means to perform ideas. The ensuing critical thoughts on the prevailing body humanism that still greatly informs the production and reception of contemporary dance are followed by an interpretative description of *closer*, the 2003 production of the Brussels collective deepblue. The work creates a totalizing choreographic dispositif in which the movements of both the dancers and the spectators continuously interact with those of bamboo rods, video images and electronic sound waves. I subsequently coin the concept of 'dance/choreography in general' with reference to performances that, like *closer*, systematically handle human and non-human motion potentials in a symmetrical way. Drawing on the writings of Gilles Deleuze and Bruno Latour, I deploy the concept of assemblage, understood as a force-field made up of intensities necessitating an always specific mode of governmentality, to shed more light on the specific issues this new performance practice has put on the table. However, in the closing coda I underline that 'dance/choreography in general' does not rebut my medial approach of dance in terms of the unity of the difference between movement and non-movement: it only emancipates this potential from the humanist ideology that continues to determine its actualization with considerable effects.

'Making Contemporary Dance'
The most recent performance discussed at length in the first part is Guilloteau's *La Magnificenza*, which dates from 2006 and is therefore not exactly an example of current dance, in the temporal

meaning. Yet precisely around this time, the ethos of collaboration became a central topic in contemporary dance 'made in Europe'. Although this notable shift did not directly inspire the book's second part — I already did fieldwork on making dance together in 1995 — it does in fact ensure a temporal continuity between 'Making Contemporary Dance' and the preceding 'Theorizing Contemporary Dance'. To put it bluntly: 'collaboration' succeeded 'conceptuality' as one of the key signifiers in European contemporary dance, thus solidifying a change in the field's self-understanding, away from performance-as-text or the art-work-as-artefact to performing as collective labour or joint artistic work.

As the opening chapter's subtitle explicitly suggests, I again start in 'Making and Valuating Art. On the Social Nature of Autonomous Art Worlds' with a set of general propositions, this time on art's most salient social features. Together with Pierre Bourdieu's view on so-called restrained markets of cultural production, which stand out because of the primacy of symbolic capital and the conspicuous disavowal of economic matters, Nathalie Heinich's conceptualization of the value regime of singularity inspires the sketched sociological view on art's autonomy, indeed a still hotly debated topic. I continue with broaching artistic fetishism, or the usually flagrant negation of the often hard work invested in an art work when it is publicly enjoyed or discussed. The rather questionable idea of the author-subject partly legitimates this over-looking and also re-centres the production of collectively made art works by attributing their principal merits to one, and only one, person. This individual maker resembles a God-like figure: he or she is truly autonomous and finds the ultimate grounds for creating art in him- or herself. This is clearly a liberal belief that simultaneously points to the widely valued cultural ideal of genuine self-expression.

The 'second movement' unfolds the alternative view: taking art's sociality seriously, but without giving in to the temptation of an over-simplifying, one-dimensional 'sociologism'. We must consistently distinguish the regime of singularity, which prevails in an art work's reception, from the collective or context-oriented regime of 'talking art' that is also frequently invoked by the directly involved actors themselves when art is in the making and mediated. The social nature of art production is then further clarified by means of Howard Becker's thoughtful portrait of art worlds as fluid cooperative networks in which various actors, ranging from for instance choreographers and dancers to lighting or sound technicians and programmers, at once act interdependent and in a joint or collaborative mode.

Because the two last chapters owe much to direct observations made in 'dance capital Brussels', 'Co-creating Contemporary Dance. Paradoxes of the Semi-Directive Mode of Participatory Collaboration' first briefly informs on this specific context. An intermezzo on the precarious socio-economic status of many dancers and choreographers within the neoliberal regime of artistic accumulation paves the way for the detailed discussion of the dominant mode of collaboratively creating dance. I speak of a semi-directive or participatory working relationship because the social difference between choreographer and dancers, especially with regard to artistic decision-making, is not fully cancelled out in most instances of co-producing dance. Dancers enjoy much independence, but within the overall framework stipulated and overseen by the choreographer, who also takes the final decisions regarding the publicly shown result. I therefore introduce the paradoxical expression 'heteronomous autonomy'. The corresponding ambivalences are highlighted on the basis of my ethnographic observations within the Rosas company of the main features underlying the rehearsal process that preceded the premiere of the rather brief 1995 choreography *Erklärte Nacht*. I discuss how the dancers deal with the contradictory expectation to be original and to take into account an assumed Rosas aesthetics when developing material and how they experience 'the choreographer's gaze' in a sometimes constraining, but often empowering way. Overall, the relationship between the choreographer and the dancers resembles a specific artistic attention regime in which the renowned artist-subject legitimately authorizes the collaborators' contributions. Inspired by Marcel Mauss' conceptualization of the symbolic relationship, I put the semi-collaborative working relation further into perspective by interpreting it as an exchange of various gifts within the context of an unequal power balance.

In the 'second movement', the paradoxes framing the practice of participatory collaboration are further spelled out through the minute analysis of twenty long conversations I had with dance artists who mostly have direct links — the others entertaining indirect ones — with the Brussels dance scene. The majority of my interlocutors regularly switch between the position of choreographer and the role of dancer in another artist's work.

One begins a collaboration with a particular choreographer because one appreciates his or her work and/or for reasons of artistic self-development, even self-transformation: a productive working relationship recurrently provokes processes of artistic de- and re-subjectification. In an intermezzo, I briefly clarify a dancer's subjectivity in terms of a virtual potential to move and to think dance that is profoundly structured by a personal dance habitus, or a set of gradually acquired routines, and the dancer's self-image, which is always informed by one or more socially shared definitions of the legitimately danceable. A structure by definition restricts possibilities; within communication or social interaction, mutually stabilized expectations function accordingly, thus states a well-known sociological theorem recently updated by Niklas Luhmann. My conversations show that within the world of contemporary dance, performers expect to be given the chance to say 'I' or to singularize their potentials and to become co-authors in their own right. This is indeed one of the cornerstones of the ethos of collaboration. By way of interim conclusion, I situate this new labour morality within the broader contexts of the current post-Fordist creative economy and the culture of expressive individualism that became institutionalized in the wake of 'the roaring sixties'. Given the precarious status of the majority of artists, who are typical flexi-workers in charge of a highly vulnerable 'Me, Inc.', the question arises if the rather diabolical loop between the desire to be self-expressive and overall meagre material rewards still leaves some space for a genuine criticality.

My in-depth interviews with mostly Brussels-based dance artists also sustain the last chapter, 'The Social Choreographies of Collaboration. Tracing Conditions of Artistic Cooperation and Commoning'. Partly relying again on Luhmann's work, I open the 'first movement' with a sketch of the specific dynamics generating mutual trust and a peculiar sort of quasi-intimacy between choreographers and dancers. Both are essential ingredients of a prolific cooperation and rest on a now and then difficult to manage affective engagement. The sometimes latent, at other moments manifest 'heteronomous autonomy' characterizing participatory collaboration is further elaborated through a discussion of artistic directivity's ambiguities (not 'too much', but also not 'too little') and the various sources of authority that can legitimate a choreographer's binding aesthetic decision-making in the eyes of the cooperating performers. Besides individual charisma, a personal artistic vision and the recurrently confirmed ability to behave at once professionally competent and truly dialogically may greatly 'soften' the structural imbalance in power between a dance maker and those collaborating. I then return to the theme of artistic subjectivity and argue that the choreographer, often routinely regarded by the dancers as 'the subject supposed to know' (Jacques Lacan), in fact directs and decides through an at times failing reliance on a non-transparent self, conceived as a structured potential to move and to not-move and to think dance or to conceive choreography. This perspective is further explored in a rather associative, essayistic mode in the closing intermezzo on 'the intimacy of the dance studio'.

'Second Movement: Composing Commonalities' takes off with some general considerations on the particularity of the act of judging art or dance, which again and again hybridizes the well-known distinction between facts and values, descriptive knowledge and appreciations. After briefly presenting the critical view of conceptual dance voiced by several of my interlocutors, I clarify the main operations underlying the collective negotiation of shared judgments. Discussing the present and future worth of newly created material and its potential is indeed a crucial and continuously re-performed event in artistic collaborations. They can only steer away from a mostly unproductive surplus in social tension or discursive strife by the partly purposeful, partly unintended production of a situational value common, a somewhat stable way of 'talking dance' marked by a collective set of appreciative viewpoints on 'what we are actually doing'. Inspired by Hannah Arendt's and Bruno Latour's framing of politics, I contend that the active and usually zigzagging composition of such a common defines a collaboration's micro-politics. This practice of 'commoning' is grounded in three essential operations: a sustained concentration on the work at hand and its possible outcomes, a genuine pragmatism that opts against lengthy speculative discussions and for the empirical testing of propositions, and an a-personal 'leadingfollowing' (André Lepecki) in which leading also includes following and the latter act constantly passes over into the first. Together with a distinct decentring of the individual in favour of an anonymous 'one' when 'talking dance', these activities also greatly inform the non-directive or flat mode of collaborating, as I show in the subsequent paragraph. In the concluding coda on 'the collaboratory', I first give my observations a general twist and then relate them to the politics of commonalism that is currently taking shape. The end verdict states that each artistic collaboration is in essence a micro-political experiment in democratizing democracy that is valuable as such.

Related to the already signalled difference between an 'internalist' and an 'externalist' approach', 'Making Contemporary Dance' overall unfolds a somewhat different perspective on dance than the first main part. In 'Theorizing Contemporary Dance' I consistently deploy a broad medium-centred approach to dance in terms of the unity of the difference between movement and non-movement; in the second part, this view is not exactly swept aside, quite the contrary, but rather supplemented by the recurrent focus on 'thinking dance' and 'talking dance', both in a reflexive mode, when moving together. This shift in emphasis is of course a direct consequence of the different perspective of the book's two parts. Whereas in the first section the notion of art-as-artefact prevails, the second articulates the idea of art-as-work through a minute analysis of co-creating dance. Every joint performance by two or more dancers also clearly involves acts of 'thinking dance' – without them, the dance would go astray – and often elicits moments, however brief, of 'talking dance' before going on stage. Making dance together during a rehearsal process and performing dance are evidently different practices. Yet the decisive point, which this study admittedly does not address, is that a public work of dance equals dance work, a specific sort of cooperative labour, which the fetishist gaze that only acknowledges the work-as-artefact uncritically negates ('represses' is probably a better term: enjoying a performance is for many a spectator difficult to reconcile with a sustained concentration on the performed labour).

In spite of the somewhat distinct accents in both parts when it comes to the idea of dance, there is a notable theoretical continuity too. Indeed, the intrinsically related notions of virtuality and potentiality function without doubt as the book's key concepts. In 'Theorizing Contemporary Dance', the medium of dance stands for a virtual potential of movements and pauses, selectively actualized by historically fluctuating framings of the danceable and, in relation to one such framework, by singular dance works. Within a single choreography, every movement or pose also opens up a horizon of 'possible possibilities', of actions or standstills that, given the context of previously observed dance elements, could also have been performed (this point is highlighted in the chapter on De Keersmaeker's oeuvre). A convincing dance work succeeds in making the actually produced movements or non-movements more plausible than the virtual ones accompanying them — evidently not in the abstract but in the eye of an always particular beholder. Yet the very same difference between actuality and potentiality also defines dancers' artistic subjectivity, as I argue towards the end of the chapter on Stuart's work and, with more conceptual underpinnings, in the two last ones. Performers literally embody this distinction and especially value those collaborations that offer them numerous chances to explore and deepen their virtual self, the non-representable whole consisting of all actions they may make, through presently made movements. Likewise, every collaborative undertaking at once creates an open set of relational or dialogical possibilities and structures this vast ensemble through socially generalized and situationally specified expectations. Hence the notion of 'the collaboratory', presented at the end of the book: the always contextually embedded, only partially realized and still virtual potential to co-create.

With distinctive accents, the difference between 'what is' and 'what could be', 'the actual' and 'the potential' or 'the virtual' is one of the central theorems in the sociological writings of Niklas Luhmann and in Gilles Deleuze's philosophy. As said, the former are my principal guide in this book, but the latter is also frequently invoked. Moreover, the notion of potential plays a prominent role in the thinking of Antonio Negri and, particularly, of Giorgio Agamben, another author whose name, not by accident, surfaces several times over the next pages. Indeed, the leading theoretical intuition this book consistently articulates, though with shifting emphases and significations, is that *ontology should be practiced in the mode of virtuology*. Or to hint at yet another thinker, whose work now and then loomed in the background while I was writing this book: the Real, as conceived by Jacques Lacan, first and foremost has a virtual nature. Nevertheless, this is not 'a theory book' but an exercise in empirically informed theorizing on contemporary dance. I therefore do not disentangle in detail the major differences between Luhmann's, Deleuze's and Agamben's theorizing of 'the potential' or 'the virtual'. Like the cited or referred to writings of other theorists, their distinct views are primarily used as conceptual resources or heuristic devices when interpreting in depth the general problematic(s) raised by single choreographies or the individual desires, shared expectations and principal paradoxes animating the multi-faceted dynamics of artistic collaboration.

A last and brief proviso. Throughout this book, I have overall refrained from foregrounding my 'self' or any authorial function like I do in this introduction. This stylistic choice is of course debatable, yet it best fitted the writing process. Admittedly, the choice is also partly inspired by the poststructuralist decentring of the subject and, concomitantly, of the traditional view of the author-subject on the one hand, and by the somewhat objectifying, 'one'- instead of 'I'-oriented mode of acting prevailing in conceptual artistic practices on the other hand. One of my main concerns was to write in a relatively condense but simultaneously comprehensible way that deliberately blends 'the academic' with 'the essayistic'. I indeed hope that this book will not only be read by other scholars of contemporary dance, but may be of interest to members of this artistic world.

A Word of Thanks
This book has been a long time in the making. The initial research was started up in 2008, the writing commenced one year later. Due to other professional obligations, the work had to be regularly deferred, which also had a positive side since it allowed me to read not yet consulted resources or just published books and articles that could inspire the writing during in between periods. Ula Sickle was my constant co-pilot once I had completed the first three chapters. She read all chapters several times and corrected my global English without smoothening it to such an extent that I would no longer recognize the text as being self-written. Being a dance artist herself, she also frequently gave feedback that obliged me to reconsider an argument on this dance work or that tendency within contemporary dance. I owe her many thanks. English being only my third language, I was lucky to find in Leo Reijnen a copy editor who at once respectfully and masterly handled the final manuscript.

In conceiving the book's first part, I profited substantially from the publications of many dance scholars. I single out those of André Lepecki and Gerald Siegmund because they were at times direct sparring partners in my effort to make a particular argument. Within Flanders, I benefited — and continue to do so — from the writings of and talks with dance critic Pieter T'Jonck and dramaturge, performer and author Jeroen Peeters; also my scant but intellectually sparkling meetings with former dance scholar and present artist Myriam Van Imschoot directly inspired specific passages. I moreover thank Guy Gypens (previously manager of the Rosas company, now director of the Kaaitheater), Johan Reyniers (former chief editor of *Etcetera*) and Theo Van Rompay (adjunct-director of P.A.R.T.S.) for their long-term interest in my views on contemporary dance and their generous invitations to publicly speak or write on this topic.

As I already indicated, I first tried out or even invented on the spot many of the ideas formulated in this book during my regular guest lectures in P.A.R.T.S. The different generations of P.A.R.T.S. students alternately greeted them with silent enthusiasm and a diplomatically voiced scepticism; I thank them most of all for the second reaction. Several leading ideas in the second chapter were also presented in one keynote and different paper sessions organized by the Sociology of Culture Research Network of the European Sociological Association during that professional organization's bi-annual conferences or the network's interim meetings. I am grateful for the critical comments made on these occasions by various fellow-sociologists.

Academic life tends to be quite stressful because of its heavy workload; nevertheless, my professional home base, the Centre for Sociological Research of the University of Leuven, regularly gave me the opportunity to concentrate on the research and reading activities necessary for this book. I am also grateful to Gabriele Brandstetter for inviting me to take up the Valeska Gert guest professorship in dance and performance at the Free University of Berlin during the winter semester of 2008-2009. Some of the core ideas on re/presentation unfolded in the third chapter took shape in the course of the inspiring dialogue with the students attending the seminar on liveness that I taught in Berlin. The finalization of the book was greatly furthered by a two-month stay as visiting fellow at the Institute for Sociology of the Technical University of Berlin in 2014. I thank my colleague Hubert Knoblauch, then director of the institute, for his kind cooperation in making this leave possible.

I owe many thanks to the dance artists who were willing — actually, no one declined my request — to participate in an in-depth interview on collaborative practices in contemporary dance. The book's second part could not have been written without the often illuminating insights put forward by Alexander Baervoets, Varinia Canto Vila, Claire Croizé, Ugo Dehaes, Andy Deneys, Tale Dolven, Vincent Dunoyer, Alix Eynaudi, Davis Freeman, Nada Gambier,

Domenico Giustino, Etienne Guilloteau, David Hernandez, Mette Ingvartsen, Heike Langsdorf, Agata Maszkiewicz, Lilia Mestre, Erna Omarsdottir, Salva Sanchis and Vincent Tirmarche. As some of the paragraphs in the sixth chapter will amply make clear, my general approach on making dance together is grounded in the fieldwork I did within the Rosas company during the second half of 1995. I thank Anne Teresa De Keersmaeker for allowing me to study *in vivo* the rehearsal process for *Verklärte Nacht* and to join the company a couple of times during tours. My gratitude of course extends to the dancers who were active with Rosas at the time. Marion Ballester, Iris Bouche, Misha Downey, Kosi Hidama, Suman Hsu, Osman Kassen Khelili, Oliver Koch, Brice Leroux, Marion Levy, Cynthia Loemij, Mark Lorimer, Sarah Ludi, Anne Mousselet, Johanne Saunier and Samantha Van Wissen not only tolerated a sometimes intrusive outsider during their work but were also willing to answer at length questions they probably considered to be utterly naïve now and then.

Carine Meulders, herself active in the field of contemporary performing arts as artistic director of the Antwerp based workspace wpZimmer, was once again my most direct 'partner in crime'. Although she disagrees with some of the views expressed in this book, it could not have been written without her personal support and critical input. My last words of thanks go to Astrid Vorstermans, director of the publishing house Valiz, and my colleague Pascal Gielen (University of Groningen, the Netherlands), who supported this research cum writing project in several respects via his part-time affiliation with the Fontys School for Fine and Performing Arts (Tilburg, the Netherlands). If there existed a prize for patiently awaiting a finished manuscript, they would for sure be plausible candidates. Yet without Pascal this book would simply not exist. He suggested to me to write it, knowing that it would be a long journey. At the end of it, I wholeheartedly thank him for the trust he invested in me: our symbolic cycle of giving and counter-giving can at last be renewed.

Brussels, 2015
Rudi Laermans

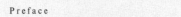

Part 1

Theorizing Contemporary Dance

The Virtual Nature of Dance
Basic Assumptions and Hypotheses

First Movement: Dance and the Danceable

An Evening with Jérôme Bel

Imagine you are in a theatre hall. The auditorium lights are turned off, the performance with the somewhat enigmatic title *Le Dernier Spectacle* ('The Last Spectacle') commences. A man enters the stage, walks up to the microphone, stands at the centre of the proscenium, and says 'Je suis Jérôme Bel' ('I am Jérôme Bel'). He then sets the alarm on his wristwatch, waits, and exits the stage about one minute later, when the alarm goes off. Meanwhile, you had had ample time to observe that the performer is actually not really Jérôme Bel. This does not bother you since it is common in theatre that a performer all too visibly feigns that he embodies a character, be it a fictional or non-fictional one. By naming himself Jérôme Bel, the man indeed simply enacted the basic theatrical convention that the stage delineates a space of fictional representation, a second reality in which nothing or nobody actually is what it, she or he seems to be. The apparent normality of the situation that has just occurred is nevertheless slightly undermined, and also ironically commented upon, during the second scene.

Dressed in white tennis-player attire, the 'real' Jérôme Bel comes on stage and repeats the walk towards the microphone stand; he then states 'I am Andre Agassi', hits a tennis ball a couple of times against the black back wall of the stage, and disappears. 'Will this elementary scene be once again repeated?', you ask yourself — and indeed: another performer walks in, stands by the microphone for a while, and then explicitly hints at the normal theatre situation by declaring, deadpan like the previous performers, 'I am Hamlet', followed by the statement 'To be'. After this brief allusion to the famous line of Act III, Scene 1 in *Hamlet*, he slowly walks off stage, shouts 'Or not to be!', and then calmly returns to the mike in order to deliver the remaining words of Shakespeare's famous line: 'that is the question'. Exit Hamlet, enters a young woman in a white dress with long blond hair, obviously a wig, who announces 'Ich bin Susanne Linke' ('I am Susanne Linke'). Because of her age, you know that she cannot be the choreographer who gained international acclaim as one of the leading proponents of the distinctive kind of *Tanztheater* that emerged in Germany during the 1970s. The pretender moves to the back of the stage, lies down parallel to the stage wall, and starts to dance, for about four minutes, the opening sequence of Linke's 1978 solo *Wandlung* ('Change') on the tones of Franz Schubert's *Death and the Maiden*. After the female dancer has left, her dance act is re-performed by each male performer, in an identical white dress.

Repetition turns out to be the main compositional device in *Le Dernier Spectacle*. During the second half of the show you observe that the four previous acts are rehearsed and simultaneously transformed, displaced, negated. Jérôme Bel enters and says 'Je ne suis pas Jérôme Bel' ('I am not Jérôme Bel'), the female performer states — in tennis dress — 'I am not Andre Agassi', and another performer denies that he is Hamlet. He subsequently takes off his Hamlet costume and, dressed only in white underpants, pretends to be Calvin Klein. After his disappearance Bel walks in again; notwithstanding his white dress, he says 'Ich bin nicht Susanne Linke' ('I am not Susanne Linke'). He does however indirectly perform Linke's piece by mumbling the Schubert tune while listening to a walkman. After Bel's exit, one of the male performers returns with the walkman, places it on the stage floor, turns it on, and leaves. You hear a voice reciting a list of names, and you quickly realize that they are the names of spectators who are present. You were also on tonight's reservation list, so you are not surprised that towards the end of this final scene you hear your own first and last name. End of the spectacle, applause — but what are you actually clapping for?

Le Dernier Spectacle, which premiered in 1998 at the Kaaitheater in Brussels, is without doubt a theatrical show, a series of premeditated events that was actively prepared in view of an anonymous collective of spectators. The performance is therefore also a spectacle in the literal sense, a temporal assemblage of happenings that is meant to be seen — and also to be heard: every spectacle is an audio-visual representation. The show clearly plays an ironic game with the basic ingredients that define the theatrical situation, such as the distinction between personae and performer or the witnessing presence of the spectators. It is indeed a performance on performance, a meta-performance that reflexively engages with the prevailing expectations about theatricality. Yet *Le Dernier Spectacle* was not announced as a theatre show but presented as a dance work: it toured within the circuit for contemporary dance and primarily attracted a dance audience. More than one spectator felt deceived and reacted accordingly. For instance, dance scholar André Lepecki, who attended a performance of *Le Dernier Spectacle* in 1999 in Berlin, within the context of the annual festival

Tanz im August, witnessed some catcalls and a couple of loudly voiced demands for 'Dance'. He also observed 'a huge release of tension' once the female performer started to dance Linke's solo: 'The audience had been close to riotous. But then there was motion at last! Finally, someone following music in the recognizable patters of "dancing!" Flow, classical music, body, presence, woman, femininity, ongoing motion, pretty white dress — one could finally enter into the zone of recognition and relax with the kinetic familiar. But Linke's segment is short, no more than 4 minutes.'

Le Dernier Spectacle not only frustrates with provocative gusto the elementary expectations of the average dance lover in a way that involuntarily reminds one of the gestures of Marcel Duchamp and his countless successors within the fine arts. This idea-based or, as many would have it, conceptual performance also contains some statements on contemporary dance and choreography that are hard to misunderstand. Thus the title hints at the ephemeral character of every dance work. The continual appearance and disappearance of actions positions performance as a permanent 'becoming past': nothing lasts, each movement is the final one. The iterative structure of *Le Dernier Spectacle* corrects this somewhat melancholy reading and relates the performing of a dance work to its repeated re-enactment over a certain period of time. This unavoidably involves a peculiar play of repetition and difference that marks the public showing of all choreographed dance (such as Linke's *Verwaltung*). To perform scored dance is synonymous with its re-performance, first during rehearsals — a telling expression — and then in a live situation. Each reiteration brings involuntary shifts or re-articulations, however small or microscopic. A re-performance therefore does not passively execute an original but actively interprets a 'first time' that only exists as a phantasm, an ever receding imaginary vanishing point haunting every kind of re-doing. 'The same is different': the 're-' in the verb 'to re-perform' at once points to the 're-' in the act of repetition and the autonomous, untameable play of differences that this very operation implies. At the same time, *Le Dernier Spectacle* puts choreographed theatre dance on a par with the recycling of an already existing series of movements. Dance or choreography, in the probably still dominant sense of structured movements put to music, is literally performed within quotation marks, as a recitation of a borrowed assemblage of actions and sounds that was composed two decades earlier. Bel thereby explicitly questions the author-function that the status of the choreographer commonly implies. The maker of *Le Dernier Spectacle* is not an innovative producer of movements and their sequencing but rather behaves as a reader and annotator, someone who creates a new choreographic text out of an already existing one and adds his footnotes.

Something more general is at stake here. Through the repeated Linke-quotation, *Le Dernier Spectacle* implicitly positions present-day choreography as a ghost of the past, thus suggesting that there exists a difficult to bridge distance between 'the contemporary' and 'the choreographic'. What should we make of this proposal? Has a genuine contemporary choreography perhaps become impossible? Can one no longer devise a dance work that is 'up-to-date', no longer create a movement score that puts present concerns into perspective by means of a new vocabulary? Do we indeed inhabit a postmodern era that is also truly post-historical and therefore doomed to rehearse past gestures, to once again re-perform fragments of previous performances with or without self-consciousness? Or is a show such as *Le Dernier Spectacle* perhaps a prototypical instance of contemporary dance precisely because it raises these and related questions? Because the work reflexively meditates on the nature of dance and choreography, and therefore willingly takes the risk of not being regarded as genuine dance or choreography?

The Medium of Dance

In 2002, the Austrian dance critic Helmut Ploebst published the first overview of the generation of dance makers that emerged during the 1990s. *no wind no word*, subtitled 'New Choreography in the Society of the Spectacle', introduces the works and artistic views of Meg Stuart, Vera Mantero, Xavier Le Roy, Benoît Lachambre, Raimund Hoghe, Emio Greco/PC, João Fiadeiro, Boris Charmatz and, indeed, Jérôme Bel. They all became autonomous choreographers following their careers as dancers – or, in the case of Hoghe: as a dramaturge – with various companies. Although their pieces are often presented at the same venues or festivals, these artists do not commit themselves to the same aesthetic credo. There are marked differences between Jérôme Bel's iconoclastic shows, the formally elaborated choreographies of Emio Greco, Meg Stuart's highly particular blend of movement and theatricality, and the semi-rituals staged by Raimund Hoghe. Nevertheless, the nine artists who are brought together in Ploebst's book share an attitude of reflexivity and research: they do not take the traditional parameters of dance or choreography for granted but performatively question, displace and re-define these ingredients. A new generation has meanwhile continued this deconstructive frontier work, which frequently oscillates between a cautious exploration of the supposed boundaries of dance and their playful de-limitation or transgression. Thomas Lehmen, Philipp Gehmacher, Mette Ingvartsen, the choreographic twin deufert&plischke, or the Superamas collective all excel in various modes of what may provisionally be termed reflexive dance (a notion that will be further elaborated in the fourth chapter).

Reflexive dance radically de-essentializes dance by deliberately subtracting elements that are usually regarded as being constitutive for dance. Gerald Siegmund therefore gave his detailed study of the oeuvres of William Forsythe, Jérôme Bel, Xavier Le Roy and Meg Stuart the apt title *Abwesenheit* ('Absence'). One or more common parameters of dance are indeed absent within reflexive dance performances, which at least part of the public experiences as a lack, even as a threatening loss of identity (the hostile reactions of the Berlin public to Bel's *Le Dernier Spectacle* are anything but exceptional). Siegmund discerns, within the performative bracketing of the assumed nature of dance, a more fundamental issue: 'Every decision within the context of a choreographic structure to release through strategic absences the presence of dance (of dance as such, of the dancers' bodies, of dramaturgic phrasings, of structure), inevitably touches upon ... that fundamental absence allowing dance to appear.' The constitutive absence underlying each instance of dance is simply stillness or not moving. This is a recurrent motif in reflexive dance works: they overtly question the still prevalent idea of dance-as-bodily-movement or as the art of 'a measured pace' (dixit the title of Francis Sparshott's lengthy plea for 'a philosophical understanding of the arts of dance').

With *Exhausting Dance*, André Lepecki has accurately baptized the trend within contemporary dance, especially in Europe, to undo movement by doing nothing in the face of the audience's gaze. Halting dance is a critical gesture with wider ramifications since stillness goes against the grain of contemporary culture. Western modernity indeed unleashes an always more restless and meanwhile globalized mobilization of natural and human resources, varying from the forced mobility of labour power to the manipulation of sensory perception by the mass media. 'To the same degree as we modern subjects understand freedom a priori as freedom of movement, progress is only thinkable for us as the kind of movement that leads to a higher degree of mobility', as Peter Sloterdijk observes, adding: 'Ontologically, modernity is a pure "being-toward-movement"'. The 'Copernican making mobile' of ever more faculties and resources involves a plethora of social choreographies that couple objects and subjects, commodities and bodily actions, into assemblages of being-moved and of being-on-the-move. Mobilizing equals activating, putting to work and into movement. This is also the hallmark of ballet and modern dance, as well as of their contemporary successors. 'Dance and modernity intertwine in a kinetic mode of being-in-the-world', Lepecki concludes. 'Thus, dance increasingly turns towards movement to look for its essence. ... Dance accesses modernity by its increased ontological alignment with movement as the spectacle of modernity's being.' Not moving during a performance temporarily suspends this hidden coalition. It is for sure a minimal gesture that apparently seems to lack a genuine criticality in light of the tradition of public engagement and activism. Maybe the staging of stillness hints to a protest politics yet to come, one that prefers the temporal tactics of exodus or exhaustion above the dominant modernist strategy of mass mobilization and kinetic excess?

The opening scene of *The Sound of One Hand Clapping*, a choreography created by Jan Fabre for the Frankfurt Ballet in 1990 (then still directed by William Forsythe), is a striking example of exhausting dance. This versatile artist, who combines a multi-faceted career in the performing arts with being a visual artist, definitively belongs to 'the generation of the 1980s'. Nevertheless, with its stress on repetition and stillness, his relatively small but significant choreographic work preludes two central motifs of the dance makers of the succeeding generations. Fabre primarily addresses the world of ballet, which he stages as a particular regime of physical discipline or the taming of various life forces through their incessant confinement and active regulation according to the symbolic model of the self-enclosed virtuosic ballet body. Thus *The Sound of One Hand Clapping* opened with a twenty-minute scene in which the whole company was on stage, dispersed around a string quartet, but standing predominantly still. It rapidly became clear that the top dancers of the Frankfurt Ballet were struggling to avoid moving for long segments of time. After a while, an instant choreography of micro-movements started to unfold, consisting of trembling corners of the mouth and slightly shaking legs and fingers. The scene demonstrated that even a highly skilled performer is not able to master the autonomous life of the organic body, or to transform it into a smoothly functioning quasi-machine. Fabre's choreography of the unintended may thus be read as a critical exposé of the limits of ballet's civilizing offensive through a simple but effective staging of the kinetic counter-power of 'the human flesh'. The opening scene of *The Sound of One Hand Clapping* can even be interpreted as a choreographic hymn to authentic bodily life, a motif that Fabre himself has repeatedly put forward in interviews and which was also constitutive for modern dance (Isadora Duncan, Mary Wigman or Martha Graham rejected the technique of classical ballet out of the partly primitivist belief in the existence of a natural body and its immanent physicality. 'Movement never lies', goes a famous saying by Graham).

To move from the micro-movements of hyper-trained ballet bodies standing still to the supposed naturalness of the organic body, is to move from the sensible to the realm of Ideas, and ultimately from physicality to a metaphysics of bodily presence. An alternative reading of the long beginning of *The Sound of One Hand Clapping* would focus on the dialectical intertwinement of bodily stillness and corporeal movement beyond the latter's purposive mobilization within the symbolic framework of a set choreography or an improvised dance. Fabre did away with intentional action, in view of a void in which uncontrolled micro-actions could visibly emerge: he created an absence that would signify the presence of dance. The movements produced did not aggregate into an overall figure in which the dancer was inseparable from the dance due to the restless production of self-referentially linked gestures, deliberately foregrounded at the expense of their potential halting. The unintended micro-movements were, on the contrary, profoundly marked by the impossibility of their hinted at suspension: they pointed to that negation of dance that is also 'that fundamental absence that allows dance to appear' (Siegmund).

Silence, John Cage has taught us, conditions the possibility of sound: 'The material of music is sound and silence.' In a similar way, non-movement is the ultimate condition of movement: the absence of dance makes the presence of dance possible. At least as far as human bodies are implied, this negation is a virtual one, a state that a skilled performing body may try to approach but never actually reaches. Since it is nevertheless a constitutive absence, non-movement must be included in the definition of

movement. Emphasized stillness exposes the transcendental structure of dance, that which permits movement and its articulation
to exist. It shows that an action can only surface in relation to
the ever present eventuality of its cessation. The unity of the difference between movement and non-movement therefore defines
the medium of dance. This is certainly not a new insight (and one
that must be qualified later on). Already within classical ballet,
the steps and movement combinations culminated in distinctive
poses. And it was Merce Cunningham who wrote in 1957: 'The
nature of dancing is stillness in movement and movement in stillness. No stillness exists without movements, and no movement is
fully expressed without stillness.' It is impossible to perform the
medium within which dance happens or takes place, appears and
disappears. For one either moves or does not move in a particular
way: *the medium of dance is a merely virtual potential consisting of
all possible movements and non-movements.* Every singular dance
work selectively actualizes and combines some of these medial
possibilities; and each present action or non-action is a singularity,
a peculiar instantiation in time and space — 'now, here' — of the
medium of dance. It is, however, debatable whether the latter is
immanently coupled to the generic human faculty to move and to
not-move. Until today, the notion as well as the practice of dance
is imbued by a seemingly self-evident humanism that, in the final
instance, identifies the medium of dance with the human body.
Only recently, certain strands coming out of contemporary reflexive dance have started to question and actively deconstruct this
underlying ideology (they will be addressed in more detail in the
fourth chapter).

On Potentiality and Impotentiality
'The human' is just another word for potentiality. Life becomes
and remains human thanks to faculties such as the capacity to
speak or to articulate sounds, to sense or to be affected through
the five senses... and also to move and to be moved. Aristotle already discerned two kinds of potentiality, as Giorgio Agamben
points out: 'There is generic potentiality, and this is the one that is
meant when we say, for example, that a child has the potential to
know, or that he or she can potentially become the head of State.
This generic sense is not the one that interests Aristotle. The potentiality that interests him is the one that belongs to someone
who, for example, has a knowledge or ability. Thus we say of an

architect that he or she has the *potential* to build, of the poet that he or she has the *potential* to write poems. It is clear that his *existing* potentiality differs from the *generic* potentiality of the child. The child, Aristotle says, is potential in the sense that he must suffer an alteration (a becoming other) through learning.' Between generic and existing potentiality stand culture and socialization. The transformation of a blank faculty into a developed one involves the intervening power of an always particular ensemble of regulating ideas, values and norms – or a set of meanings – that is imperatively transmitted to newcomers. In this sense, everybody has the generic capacity to move, but nobody moves in a completely arbitrary way. Our existing potentiality to act corporeally is selectively structured through the various body techniques and disciplines that were used in our youth to impart on us how to sit still, walk properly or behave civilized. In a similar way, learning to become a dancer is to acquire a thoroughly cultured body, one whose generic potentiality to move has been changed into an always particular ability to dance. Like every human body, the dancer's trained corporeality is not just an organic bundle of flesh and bones but a materialized discourse, a physicality that repeatedly signifies through its actions the alteration undergone from the general potential to move into a structured one.

Only with regard to an existing potential does it make sense to include the possibility of deprivation or impotentiality in its very definition, such as for instance the ability to not-move. The skilled dance artist has acquired a *hexis*, or a 'having', on the basis of which he or she can also *not* actualize this personal capacity, so not make a movement or – more generally – not compose or execute a dance work. Humans differ from other living beings precisely because not only can they realize particular faculties but they are also capable of practicing the de-realization of these faculties. This possibility to actively negate what one is able to do actually informs the dancers' non-dance. Their stillness intrinsically belongs to their dance potential, which should therefore be grasped as the unity of the difference between the capacity to move and to not-move, either literally (the stillness within a performance) or figuratively (the halt within the trajectory of a dance maker). What is ultimately at stake in the affirmation of both abilities is the medium of dance as well as the root of human freedom: 'To be free is not simply to have the power to do this or that thing, nor is it simply to have the power to refuse to do this or that thing. To be free is, in the sense we have seen, *to be capable of one's own impotentiality*, to be in relation to one's own privation' (Agamben).

Culture is the necessary supplement of human nature, understood as an overall generic potentiality that comprises a variety of more particular faculties. The universality of human nature is realized in various cultures: what makes us one (generic potentiality) exposes itself in multiple actualizations (existing potentiality); what unites us (nature) simultaneously divides us (culture). Culture cultivates nature, thus transforming a blank potential into a genuine capacity to speak and to communicate, to sense and to think, to move, et cetera. An existing potential is therefore by definition marked by a culture's normative codification of some possibilities as truly human, at the expense of others. Indeed, every culture is an exclusionary machine that performatively differentiates between valuable and non-valuable possibilities to act and to not-act. The selection comes down to complexity reduction, and is at once contingent and unavoidable. For no culture, however tolerant, can encompass the indetermination of human nature, its virtual mode of being as pure potentiality or — to borrow another expression from Agamben — as 'naked life'. Modern culture has understood the generic openness of human life predominantly in terms of a possible purity, an authentic mode of existing to which it is always possible to return. Hence the vast series of naturalisms and primitivisms that both exoticized and eroticized singular ways of 'being in the world' and 'being a body'. In this tradition, human nature is interpreted as standing outside of history, as timeless and uncorrupted by civilization. Or, as the cultural sociologist John Jervis writes: 'Nature is the past, but also the future; something to be used, controlled, but also a potential to be realized. "The primitive" offers a challenge to be overcome, but also a hope of escape from the artificial and the over-civilized. ... Romanticism, with its emphasis on the "alter ego", a hidden or "unconscious" self, linked to nature and the primitive, contributes powerfully to these post-Enlightenment strands.'

Modernity's dream of a return to both the purifying and pure potentiality of nature was a constitutive element in the emergence of a distinctive dance tradition that wanted to overcome the mannerist artificiality of classical ballet. 'The school of ballet of today, vainly striving against the natural laws of gravitation or the natural will of the individual, and working in discord in its form and movement with the form and movement of nature, produces a sterile movement which gives no birth to future movement, but dies as it is made', asserts Isadora Duncan in *The Art of the Dance*. Duncan, who is commonly regarded as one of the co-founders of modern dance at the beginning of the twentieth century (the others being Loie Fuller and Ruth Saint Denis), describes the dance school she was dreaming of as free of movement codification and even of culturalization: 'In this school I shall not teach the children to imitate my movements, but to make their own. I shall not force them to study certain definite movements; I shall help them to develop those movements which are natural to them.' The mythical belief in the possibility of a restoration of the lost touch with an at once transhistorical and foundational Reality is symptomatic of modernity's discontent with itself — with the various modes of rationalization, disciplining and control over nature, as well as self-control, that typify modern life. Naturalism points to a peculiar cultural ideal that is actually unrealizable since to be human is to be always already humanized, to affirm a culturally structured potentiality. Such a life form may be restructured but cannot be destructed in the vain hope of making contact with an undefined blankness. No individual human being or social re-arrangement can completely undo the altering transformation by culture of generic into existing potentiality. One may actively try to inhabit several modes of culturalization and effectively become a multicultural human being, but one can never turn oneself into 'naked life'. For one is cultured and therefore hampered by what one has previously learned in one's eventual attempts to unlearn and re-learn, or in the utopian quest to reach the kind of unmarked state of pure potentiality that the founders of modern dance were, and certain strands of dance improvisation still are, looking for.

The /Contemporary/ Danceable
Claude Lévi-Strauss and structuralism have taught us that cultures are binary machines. They include and exclude particular generic possibilities, while simultaneously differentiating between good and bad actualizations, proper and despicable instantiations of what is culturally possible. To categorize and to valuate in a dual way, and thus to create various hierarchies, is the basic operation that every more specific form of culture reproduces. Thus every dance culture delineates and codifies within the medium of dance, usually with the help of distinctive body techniques, a specific realm of the danceable that is sharply distinguished from what it

regards as non-dance. *The contingent distinction between the dance-able and the non-danceable, legitimate and illegitimate movements, defines a dance culture's imperative structuring of the medium of dance*, its production of an effectively existing potential for dance as well as choreography out of the generic human potential to move and to not-move. A dance culture reframes this general medium into a socio-cultural one through technical and aesthetic conventions that actively shape movement possibilities. As far as the human body is concerned, it differentiates between dance movements and movement-in-general by stressing skilled action, often resulting in a cult of virtuosity, and the ability to produce detailed meanings in an articulate way. Choreography further elaborates this distinction by patterning legitimate movements, thus embedding them within the self-defined context of a work of dance. The danceable thereby acts as a normatively binding symbolic order that incorporates one or more body ideals existing within the surrounding culture, together with their allowances and constraints, their do's and don'ts.

Take, for instance, classical ballet. Its mechanically moving upright body originates in the early-modern aristocratic culture of the royal courts, which valued the civilized formality of an artificial posture distancing itself both from work or task-oriented movements and ordinary, functional gestures. At the famous Versailles court of Louis XIV, one did not walk but made strides that honoured the omnipresent gaze of the king, who was considered to be God's representative among the living. The well-considered steps and measured pace of a trained ballet dancer still refer to this 'grace', or the self-conscious and highly polished lifting of the body out of the world of daily movements made by common people. They are corporeal traces of a socio-cultural past and indirectly commemorate a way of living that has meanwhile become a text that is difficult to decipher. Yet the contemporary ballet dancer's body is actually a cultural-historical palimpsest, a *codex rescriptus*. Thus Romantic ballet rearticulated the canon of the danceable by bringing it in line with the new bourgeois view on the differences between the sexes. 'More significantly, the Romantic ballet celebrated the principle of distinct vocabularies for male and female dancers – the dainty and complete footwork, the *developés* of the leg and extended balances for women and the high leaps, jumps with beats, and multiple pirouettes for men. It rationalized the new technique of pointe work, which added a strenuous precariousness to the female dancer's performance. And it encouraged new conventions of partnering that incorporated new codes for touching, of support, and for the achievement of pleasing configurations', as Susan Leigh Foster observes in her essay 'The ballerina's phallic pointe'. Different times, different body ideals, different definitions of the danceable. Witness, for instance, contact improvisation and other strands of 'free dancing' that emerged by the end of the 1960s. Its proponents often understand it as the celebration of a liberated, or even natural body, yet the actual potentiality to move within contact improvisation is strongly codified according to the 1960s ideal of sociality as being together in an informal and smooth way, without conflicts or tensions. This dance culture enacts a core value of what was once an active counter-culture and that presently looks rather like a worn-out utopia of democracy: being always in tune with each other, being endlessly engaged in a harmonious conversation.

Every instance of the danceable necessarily creates a depreciated Other, a realm of aesthetic possibilities that must remain inactivated or non-actualized, in a word: virtual. This is non-dance in the figurative or cultural sense: movements and non-movements that are unworthy of being performed in light of the affirmed artistic and body ideals. Cultural non-dance is not stillness but the symbolic impossibility of realizing particular movements within the context of theatre dance because they are deemed improper or illegitimate. All dance cultures produce such symbolic excrement, which haunts the enacted notion of the danceable as an all too real and dangerous nothingness — as an at once desired and abhorred potentiality, a psychoanalyst might add. The fault line between legitimate and illegitimate movements is both reinforced and justified by the modern idea of autonomous art. Although theatre dance never figures prominently within histories or theories of art (if it is mentioned at all), dance cultures draw a difficult to cross line between 'high' and 'low' movements, and also between permissible and rather unlikely ways to choreograph or combine plausible movements. Contemporary dance is no exception. It houses many styles and various notions of the danceable, ranging from the hip hop and breakdance inspired choreographies of Bruno Beltrao, to Anne Teresa De Keersmaeker's elaborated choreographic dialogues with music and to the kind of overtly deconstructive dance of Jérôme Bel. Much is possible within current dance, but not anything goes. At least within the Western European context of professional theatre dance, it seems rather transgressive, for example, to present as a genuine instance of contemporary choreography a performance based on the kind of expressionistically toned movement vocabulary with which Mary Wigman once created a furore. That much could indeed be learned from *A Mary Wigman Dance Evening*, the truly post-colonial 2009 piece in which Ecuadorian artist Fabian Barba staged a dance recital as it could have taken place in the early 1930s during Wigman's North American tour. This reconstructive re-enactment by a young male performer of the work of a female icon of modern dance telescoped through time, and also 'through gender', a once widely applauded definition of the danceable. Moreover, the work hinted at the countless implicit 'don'ts' of today's practices. Many dance makers consult the archive of dance and choreography in search of inspiration, but its literal actualization produces either a pastiche (such as the Linke-quote in Bel's *Le Dernier Spectacle*) or a reflexively re-performed document that bears the 'Classic' stamp and is thus barred from directly entering the field of 'the contemporary'.

Barba's piece does not stand by itself but signals a broader trend that indicates – in the words of André Lepecki – a 'will to archive/will to re-enact'. In recent years the interest in the reconstruction of past choreographies and the selective re-performance of the plural history of modern dance has indeed significantly increased. This modest boom testifies to the desire to give current dance a genealogy as well as a palpable archive. It can also be interpreted as a solidifying operation that expresses the will to consolidate the artistic autonomy of contemporary dance through the deliberate construction of an imaginary museum, à la André Malraux, which brings some of the highlights of its modern forerunners together with recently created performances. The French choreographer Boris Charmatz adopted this idea when he took over as artistic director of the Centre Chorégraphique National of Rennes: it was renamed into Musée de la Dance in 2009. However practically conceived, a Museum of Dance/Dancing Museum can probably only be thought of as a real place constantly pointing to a virtual space that can be hinted at but never actualized. This space is the contemporary danceable, which differs from the various delineations of the danceable within present dance. Currently existing dance cultures open up new possibilities with each new performance produced within their frameworks. They always act as promises of future productivity and announce, each in their own respect and with heterogeneous accents, dances and

choreographies yet to come. A Museum of Dance/Dancing Museum may infect this future orientation with the selective remembrance of past dance or choreography, thus creating a horizon offering the potential to formulate virtual histories, possible lineages that remained unrealized, historical absences that indirectly inform present dance making and choreographing. Possibilities that could have been actualized but were not, re-articulations of a once existing dance culture that did not occur, or conceivable hybrids that, for whatever reason, did not come into existence, all re-position current dance works as contingent historical outcomes. The corresponding virtual space also obliges us to ask a slightly uncanny question: 'what could dance nowadays be in light of what it could have been?' *The contemporary danceable is present dance haunted by the virtual possibilities that past dance suggests.*

Second Movement: From Judson to Contemporary Dance

Revisiting Judson
The 6th of July 1962 is undoubtedly one of the defining dates that mark the multiple beginnings of contemporary dance: that evening 'A Concert of Dance' was presented in the Judson Memorial Church, located in New York's Greenwich Village. The event consisted of twenty-three dances by fourteen choreographers, several of whom had studied — and sometimes danced — with Merce Cunningham, and was the outcome of a composition workshop given the previous two years by musician Robert Dunn. Inspired by the insights of John Cage, the participants had predominantly explored the use of chance methods in the scoring of bodily movement. Since the initiators experienced 'A Concert of Dance' as a genuine success, they decided to continue organizing weekly workshops at the Judson Church and regular public showings in which the outcomes of their joint undertakings, as well as individual dance works, would be presented. The last numbered concert, 'Concert of Dance #16', took place on the 29th of April 1964 and marked the official end of the legendary Judson Dance Theatre. However, its core members kept collaborating and sharing ideas in the years to follow. Several of them even re-united within the framework of The Grand Union, an improvisation collective that was active from 1970 until 1976. It has therefore become common to speak of the Judson Dance movement, or just Judson. Yvonne Rainer, Steve Paxton, Trisha Brown, Deborah Hay and Lucinda Childs are

probably its best known individual representatives, because they all made distinguished careers within contemporary dance (and in the case of Rainer also within experimental film). The original impetus of Judson was, however, strongly cooperative and interdisciplinary, witness the participation of musicians Robert Dunn and Philip Corner or visual artists Robert Rauschenberg (also a regular collaborator as set designer in Cunningham's performances) and Robert Morris (one of the defining voices in the first wave of American Minimalism).

In her authoritative study *Democracy's Body: Judson Dance Theater, 1962-1964*, Sally Banes equates the overall spirit animating Judson with an 'attitude that anything might be called a dance and looked at as a dance; the work of a visual artist, a filmmaker, a musician not recognizable as theatrical dance, might be re-examined and "made strange" because they were framed as art'. Judson thus redefined the danceable and went beyond Merce Cunningham's earlier undoing of the expressionist tenor of modern dance by means of a series of critical moves that can all be found in a nutshell in *Proxy*, the twenty-three minute trio that Steve Paxton presented at the first edition of 'Concert of Dance'. In the opening section, a dancer entered a square marked off on the floor with yellow tape, sat down, and ate a pear. He was then joined by a second performer who drank a glass of water. The next action showed the dancers walking around the backcloth seven times in large circles. On one of the circuits, a basin outfitted with ball bearings was put on the floor; a performer stepped in it and was then pulled about by another dancer. The two ensuing sections were based on scores consisting of cartoon images, sports photographs, and pictures of people walking, glued onto a large sheet of brown paper. Each dancer selected an image to start from, embodied it, and then worked through the rest of the score, moving from image to image, according to the instructions regarding the order of the succession of the poses and the number of times one had to mimic a particular photograph. In the fourth and final section the performers resumed their walking and picked up the basin with the ball bearings (Paxton would return to walking as a choreographic core ingredient in subsequent pieces such as *English* [1963] and particularly *Satisfying Lover* [1967]).

Walking and sitting, eating a pear, and drinking a glass of water are everyday actions that the then dominant definitions of the danceable — which continue to inform the expectations of the average dance public — rejected as being non-dance. To quote such common movements or doings and to enact them in a factual mode would become a recurrent motif in the work of the dance makers associated with Judson. By the end of the 1960s, theorist Michael Kirby could therefore write, in an essay aptly titled 'Objective Dance', that '"danciness" has been replaced by the muscular dynamics of everyday life'. The blurring of the difference between art and non-art, or crossing the border that seals off the sanctuary of high culture from the realm of the ordinary, was already a defining feature of the historical avant-garde. Futurism, Dadaism and Surrealism viewed the 'dissociation from the praxis of life as the dominant characteristic of art in bourgeois society ... The avant-gardists proposed a sublation of art — sublation in the Hegelian sense of the term: art was not to be simply destroyed, but transferred to the praxis of life where it would be preserved, albeit in a changed form', observes Peter Bürger in his influential *Theory of the Avant-Garde*. The utopian impulse to organize an entirely new life praxis from a basis in art is rather absent in Judson and similar neo-avant-garde tendencies that emerged during the 1960s, such as Fluxus and the Happenings-movement initiated by George Brecht and Allan Kaprow. Works such as *Proxy* do not hint at a future liberation of daily life through the incorporation of the aesthetic potentials already explored by autonomous art. They primarily direct the spectator's attention to the particularities of pedestrian movement, or to the complexity of simple movements that the photographer Eadweard Muybridge had already brought to the fore in the famous picture series he made towards the end of the nineteenth century.

Besides ordinary actions, *Proxy* contained movement poses that were imitations of cartoon images and of photographs of people engaged in sports. They were not ordinary but shared with the enactment of daily doings, the quality of being de-contextualized quotes, or found movements. This *readymade aesthetic of movement appropriation* also reiterated a strategy that was originally devised within the historical avant-garde (it was the Dadaist Marcel Duchamp who codified the practice of the readymade). However, Judson's re-use once again involved a twofold displacement that characterized post-war neo-avant-gardism in general. Indeed, it signalled a moving away from the utopian and 'anarchistic' impulses of Futurism, Dadaism or Surrealism, and towards what later came to be known as institutional critique, or the critical deconstruction of the basic parameters that make up the institution of dance, for instance (such as the distinction between dance and non-dance or the prevailing definition of spectatorship). Judson also vastly reframed the notion of the work of dance and, by implication, of choreography. Thus *Proxy* was clearly a juxtaposition of sections and, particularly within the two central parts, of actions or poses. The consequent use of chance in putting together the photo-movement scores even resulted in the kind of awkwardness that was already present in the work of Merce Cunningham. Judson radicalized this approach through the incorporation of found movement, which not only broadened the pallet of possible material but, in combination with chance-based composition, also enhanced the fragmented character of the choreography. Judson thus reinforced the trend established by Cunningham in the direction of *the open dance work*, one that is no longer a structured totality but rather a scattered collage or montage, a non-totalizing assemblage of all kinds of movements and non-movements.

Intermezzo: Witnessing Everyday Movements
The inclusive stance of Judson towards everyday actions has since become firmly entrenched within contemporary dance. This resulted in a thorough re-articulation of what Jacques Rancière calls *'le partage du sensible'*, the partitioning or distribution of the sensible, or the division between seemingly evident facts of perception within the reigning aesthetic regime of dance and that which is thus excluded or banned from sight. The relative institutionalization of the citation of mundane movements is all but a uniform process, following the divergent lines of existing dance cultures. Therefore walking around the stage is done differently, with various emphases and styles of execution, in a performance of William Forsythe, Anne Teresa De Keersmaeker or Jérôme Bel. Notwithstanding the normalization of 'the everyday' in theatre dance, it may still amaze spectators to witness trivial pedestrian actions, especially when they are executed in a matter-of-fact mode. Dance critics usually counter this astonishment with the argument that this forced 'looking at the overlooked' – dixit the title of Norman Bryson's well-known study of the genre of still-life painting – creates a simultaneously aesthetic and democratic experience in which the viewer starts to unravel the physical complexity of what is commonly considered as banal and therefore not worthy of attention. The egalitarian spirit that levels down the hierarchic difference between highly skilled and ordinary movement is thus

linked to an artistic politics of perception that foregrounds within the spectator's visual field the connections between art and life, the performer's premeditated physicality and the corporeality of the average audience member. However, the bewilderment of the 'naïve' spectator may indicate a genuine difficulty in finding an appropriate viewpoint when confronted with quotidian movements that are performed in an everyday mode but are nevertheless framed as dance. As Carrie Lambert-Beatty argues at length in her study on the work of Yvonne Rainer, looking at factually represented everyday movement in a focused way asks for a detached kind of attention, or 'a spectatorship neither of pleasure nor of revulsion, but of non-involvement'. This kind of necessary curiosity that is not animated by the desire for stunning revelations resembles the objectifying attitude of a scientist carefully studying the micro-movements of bacteria. If spectators can adopt this attitude, which is anything but evident, their attention will primarily go to the materiality of the dancing bodies.

In the process of incorporating ordinary actions, physicality actually became vastly redefined. The widening of the definition of the danceable within Judson, notes dance historian Ramsay Burt, 'led to the creation and performances of movement material that encouraged the dancers to develop focused neuro-skeleto-muscular sensitivities. Such sensitivities would subsequently underpin the development of contact improvisation.' Burt also observes that 'the new dance not only prompted performers to develop new kinds of embodied sensitivities, it also made demands on spectators to acknowledge the physical presence of the dancing body in ways that departed from the spectatorship of mainstream dance'. The dancer who walks or sits down matter-of-factly is first and foremost performing a degree-zero mode of the 'being body' of 'being a performer'. The spectator may come to appreciate the exposed physicality, but there is in any case no edifying message to infer from a performance of common movements that primarily tries to re-enact the normalcy of the quoted state of daily life. Like the well-known simple boxes of Minimalism – the artistic movement with which certain Judson members such as Yvonne Rainer felt strong affinities – the performer embodying 'being a performer' through a marked ordinariness only offers the spectator diverse actions and non-actions that must be taken at face value. They are what they are, and they demand to be watched for what they are, without an evaluating eye.

Performing everyday movements within a theatre context hints at the existence of a generic corporeality shared by the performer and the spectator alike, and demands of the viewer the readiness to activate one's ability to watch in a quasi-generic way, even to look 'beyond culture' when looking. 'What is important now is to recover our senses. We must learn to see more, to hear more, to feel more. Our task is not to find the maximum amount of content in a work of art, much less to squeeze more content out of the work than is already there. Our task is to cut back content so that we can see the thing at all', writes Susan Sontag in her famous essay 'Against Interpretation', which ends with the once much quoted line: 'In place of an hermeneutics of art we need an erotics of art.' Sontag's eloquent plea for a genuinely degree-zero spectatorship was originally published in 1964 and referred, among other things, to the dance work of Merce Cunningham; her essay also captured the then increasingly popular artistic spirit exemplified by many Judson works as well as Minimalist or 'Literalist Art'. But is a truly literalist stance actually possible? Are we able to put off at will the spectacles of culture that structure our perception? This is doubtful. The average spectator of a performance cannot fully undo the act of interpretation but only go against the tendency to read movements, or to transform them into a text, an ensemble of signifiers pointing to possible meanings or signifieds. When trying to weaken or halt the play of denotations (such as 'This is pedestrian walking') and particularly connotations ('The performers do not seem to relate to each other') through the act of distanced looking, one actually unfolds another interpretation: 'it means nothing or almost nothing.' *Negating sense, or trying to do so, is indeed a particular way of making sense.*

Art as a Proper Name

In July 1964, Lucinda Childs presented her new work *Street Dance* within the framework of a summer workshop organized by choreographers associated with the Judson Dance Theatre. The audience gathered at the fifth-floor loft near Chinatown where the workshop took place. After switching on a tape recorder, Childs left the building via the elevator: the dance maker disappeared. On tape, her voice invited the spectators to move to the loft's street-side windows and to watch the dance that would be performed across the street by Childs and Tony Holder. Both intermingled with the general street activity, yet now and then they momentarily punctuated their actions by pointing out surrounding details that the viewers were unable to see, such as the lettering of signs or the content of a shop window. These specifics were described by Child's voice on the tape in the loft, which made linguistically present what was absent in the audience's visual field. In this way, a threefold series of events unfolded: ordinary street movements, bodily indications, and words that clarified the actual referents of the latter. This went on for about five or six minutes, and then Childs and Holder both returned to the loft.

Street Dance self-reflexively addressed the observation that dance is in the eye of the beholder and only exists thanks to an often non-reflexive act of categorization and labelling, raising particular expectations. Judson Dance Theatre had already widened the notion of the danceable by including ordinary movements within a 'concert of dance'; Childs' work demonstrated that this re-evaluation was reproducible outside the theatre and actually depended on a primarily discursive or symbolic operation. Not only could 'the ordinary' be transposed into a dance work performed in a theatre context, it was also possible to define pedestrian movement more directly as dance through the delineation of a viewer position (the loft's windows) and a name (the piece's title) that generated the expectation 'there will be dance'. Insofar as the activities of the two performers blended in with the surrounding street action, there was no genuine work of dance but only pedestrian activity framed as dance and — depending on the viewer's readiness to accept this identification — watched accordingly. At the same time, *Street Dance* played with the difference between that to which the spectators' attention was drawn (the physical indications made by the two dancers) and that which they were able to observe. This perceptive gap was bridged by the words on the tape, which offered the missing information. *Street Dance* was thus a truly audio-visual work in which the viewer had to rely on the listener, and vice versa, in order to make sense of what happened outside. However, why would one be willing to accept the framing of a slice of street life as a dance? Because some genuine efforts had been made to conceive and set up the overall situation? Because one knew that two people were actually performing on the footpath, behaving *as if* they were average pedestrians but actually addressing an informed public? In sum, because there existed that basic agreement between performers and audience that grounds every performance: 'we do what we do because you are there'?

In the same year that Childs created *Street Dance*, the analytic philosopher Arthur Danto published his by now classic essay 'The Artworld' in *The Journal of Philosophy*. Referring to, among other works, Andy Warhol's *Brillo Box*, a staple of silkscreened facsimiles of cartons containing Brillo soap powder, Danto raised the question of 'the difference between a Brillo box and a work of art consisting of a Brillo Box'. His answer was deceptively simple, not to say disenchanting: it all depends on the ideas one has about what is, and what is not art. Art is in the eye of the beholder because that eye's look is thoroughly informed and formatted by a particular discourse on art. 'To see something as art requires something the eye cannot descry — an atmosphere of artistic theory, a knowledge of the history of art: an artworld', writes Danto. 'It is the role of artistic theories, these days as always, to make the artworld, and art, possible.' In this view, the status of a work such as *Street Dance* rests on one's idea of the danceable. Such a dance theory may be very rudimentary and refer to a commonly held view ('dance is skilful movement put to music') or rather idiosyncratic and sophisticated ('dance makes visible the absence of dance as its condition of possibility'). And spectators are willing, or not, to revise that set of ideas in light of a work that obviously does not fit their notion of dance or, like *Street Dance*, or Bel's *Le Dernier Spectacle* and many other works, reflexively plays with the art theory that says that art depends on a theory of art. Yet, is not the view that art (dance) is the performative effect of more or less institutionalized ideas about art (dance) way too 'idealistic', relying too much on the intuition that recognizing artistic artefacts rests on primarily cognitive acts of interpretation?

In *Kant after Duchamp*, the Belgian art theoretician Thierry de Duve offers an alternative. De Duve tries to think through the consequences of Marcel Duchamp's readymades, of which *Fountain* is without doubt the most emblematic one. Notwithstanding the promise that it would exhibit all work submitted, the urinal that Duchamp presented in 1917 as a possible art work was not accepted by the committee that presided over the exhibition of the New York based Society of Independent Artists. Duchamp's gesture initially failed and the original object, signed 'R. Mutt', disappeared (only a photograph by Alfred Stieglitz documents that it once existed). The artefact nevertheless retroactively became, not least through the activities of the neo-avant-garde that emerged by the end of the 1950s, one of the defining works of twentieth-century art. Perhaps it is even justified to say that *Fountain* and, more generally, Duchamp's readymades are at the origin of contemporary art, in a non-temporal or categorical sense. In any case, the work shows that *art is a proper name that can be given to whatever kind of artefact for whatever reason*, so with or without the backing of a theory of art. Baptizing something a work of art is an active operation comparable to the handing out of an identity card that binds a living body to a particular territory. The act as such is decisive, regardless of the underlying motivations or reasons for performing it. Or, in the words of De Duve, who often self-reflexively refers to his own position of individual spectator and art lover in his considerations on Duchamp: 'Just as with Peter, Paul, or Harry, or Catherine, Fanny or Valérie, the name of art is a proper name. This is a theoretical definition, the only one that can be given to the word "art". Here, then is a theory at once extremely simple and terribly meagre. It rests on a single proposition, a single theorem. You must not forget that you have arrived at it ... on the conviction of the certitude (and what is certitude, if not the feeling of knowing?) that you are dealing with art when you express your judgment with the phrase, "this is art." Among certitudes of this sort, the particularly fragile and totally unjustifiable feeling that Duchamp's urinal "contained" a theory of art was the one on which you reflected the most, for this object is the most exemplary, the most paradigmatic of all works of art, inasmuch as it begs you to call it art and does nothing else. With regard to all the other things that convince you that you are dealing with art, of course you could have chosen to express yourself with other formulas, which are apparently not nominative, like "this is beautiful, sublime, extraordinary, sensational, fantastic, tremendous, great, super," with "as art" being implicit. (You could do this with regard to the urinal too, but only after having christened it.).'

To Name and To Not-Name Dance
Since John Austin's *How to Do Things with Words*, we know that a performative utterance simultaneously says and does something. Thus the statement 'I promise to be at your place tomorrow by 7 pm' is literally the production of a promise: to make a promise is to say 'I promise'. 'I apologize', 'I christen this ship "Nijinsky"', 'You are under arrest' or 'Go!' are all examples of performatives. To say of a urinal or whatever kind of artefact 'this is art' is also clearly a performative act with a binding or so-called perlocutionary

force that varies situationally. The doing is constitutive, constructive, world-building: it adds a work of art to the existing world. Without the assertion 'this is art', the concerned artefact would remain a mundane object, or just paint on canvas, or nothing more than a series of movements. Although the phrase only seems to describe an ontological state of affairs that exists independently of the declaration ('this *is* art'), this presumed realness is actually the performative result of the act of naming something a work of art. The operation's effect greatly depends on the social position of the person or institution proclaiming 'this is art'. Everybody can pronounce this simple sentence when faced with an artefact, but its social impact will vary with one's symbolic power regarding art matters. Established artists and critics, or curators and art collectors with a certain reputation, evidently possess more cultural authority, or publicly recognized credentials, than the average museum visitor. If one of them publicly baptizes something a work of art, explicitly or rather implicitly (for instance by writing about the artefact in question or purchasing it for a collection), the chances that others will accept the judgment are higher than when a simple art lover with no institutional backing says 'this is a superb sculpture'. Indeed, this is all quite obvious – but it is also evidence that is constantly negated and forgotten, not to say repressed, within contemporary art worlds. Their members thrive on a 'collective unconsciousness' that at the same time involves an all too visible operation: they simultaneously know what they do – naming (or not naming), for contingent reasons and with a particular perlocutionary force, something a work of art – and yet have difficulties in openly acknowledging what they know.

According to Pierre Bourdieu's influential sociological view, every contemporary art world is a social arena in which the participants constantly struggle with uneven weapons over the symbolic capital to define legitimate art or – once the framing has been relatively widely accepted – to determine an artefact's actual aesthetic value. This sometimes fierce controversy wages to a large extent implicitly. The competing parties or agents deny that they are rivals, sublimate their positional interests into highbrow theories, and cover up their antagonistic relationships with the shared credo that they all act 'for the sake of Art'. Both the struggle for symbolic authority and its ritual disavowals are mainly performed on the basis of unconscious habits and semi-conscious dispositions, without much overt deliberation or latent strategic thinking, Bourdieu

asserts. The net outcome is an always contested divide opposing the possessors of cultural power or consecrated artists and the many inhabitants of an art world's margins. Nevertheless, the powerless are not completely dispossessed: they can always appreciate differently or dispute the existing hierarchies in canonized art and rejected non-art (which Bourdieu tends to negate). Even the most humble visitor of an exhibition of contemporary art may question the prevailing definitions, and say 'this is not art' when stumbling over a Duchamp readymade, for instance. This lasting ability to un-name when it has already been stated that 'this is art' with some perlocutionary force, is a constitutive element of the contemporariness of art. The particular performativity that every work of art presupposes is indeed not one- but two-sided. Again, it involves a potential that includes its own negation or impotentiality: the capacity to name an artefact a work of art comprises the possibility to not-name.

The performative differentiation between dance and non-dance has always characterized the specification of dance's general medium within this or that dance culture. However, contemporary dance is marked – in Hegelian parlance – by a heightened sense of self-consciousness regarding the contingency of this foundational operation. Indeed, *the at once difficult to acknowledge and impossible to negate possibility of self-reflexivity about the contingent nature of the basic act of naming, or not-naming, something a work of dance, co-defines the contemporariness of contemporary dance*. Here, a particular kind of socio-cultural reality is involved, an art world characterized by the simultaneously foreclosed and constantly re-affirmed capacity to recognize that every definition of the danceable is in principle groundless, possible but not conceptually or empirically necessary, and therefore devoid of an ontological rationale. Individuals or institutions may stick to a particular view of dance as representing its undisputable essence, but this stance is constantly belied by the actual social self-reflexivity within the field of contemporary dance. For if the contingency of the act of naming or not-naming a performance a work of dance is eventually 'repressed' on the individual level, it unavoidably returns with each communicative negation of the affirmation 'this is dance, period'. Like every currently existing art world, contemporary dance indeed primarily actualizes its potential self-reflexivity in a social way, not only through thinking or conscious acts but predominantly through public statements.

Someone says 'this is dance' with the conviction of depicting an existing state of affairs; another person asserts the contrary, and a discussion follows. The ensuing debate does not usually settle the dispute: it more commonly highlights the differences in viewpoints and their non-ontological character, thus emphasizing their contingency. More generally, the world of contemporary dance does effectively resemble a site of struggle, à la Pierre Bourdieu, but not only that: it is also a postmodern cultural field, à la Jean-François Lyotard. In such a context, every presumed consensus regarding the legitimately danceable is repeatedly unmasked as an untenable claim and functions as the stepping-stone to once again produce an insoluble dissensus or a 'differend'. 'As distinguished from litigation, a differend [*différend*] would be a case of conflict, between (at least) two parties, that cannot be equitably resolved for lack of a rule applicable to both arguments', stipulates Lyotard. Considered as a discursive universe populated by countless enunciations, contemporary dance illustrates the idea that 'the postmodern' is characterized by clashes and controversies between 'differends' or 'phrases in dispute'. These consist of heterogeneous enunciations pointing to incommensurable framings of the danceable, and also of opposing opinions of dance works that are formed or artists who are active within the context of a particular dance culture. Yet besides harbouring explicit statements on dance, the 'differends' first and foremost involve diverging performances that tend to negate each other's identity.

An Anxious, Undecidable, and Performed Object
Every possible artefact appearing within an institutional context in which art works may be expected also functions as the equivalent of a publicly uttered phrase. It embodies the conviction, commonly ascribed to its maker, that it is a genuine work of art and therefore deserves to be recognized as such. In a non-human language it gurgles: 'I am art'; and sometimes with a hardly concealed desire, witness the various instances of dazzlingly spectacular objects or virtuoso actions, it mutters: 'please say "you are art"'. The sought-after appreciation was already given by the individuals and organizations implied in the artefact's production and public mediation. Nevertheless it remains open whether the statement 'this is art' will be reiterated by individual spectators, critics and other institutional actors, or by artists who may or may not take up the

artefact as an example of good practice. From the point of view of its public reception, the (potential) contemporary art work is therefore – to quote an expression once coined by the American art critic Harold Rosenberg – 'an anxious object', an artefact that is not sure if it will be esteemed an art work or a piece of junk. 'This can only mean that the art object persists without a secure identity', Rosenberg writes. 'Art does not exist. It *declares itself.*' Or not… Every contemporary artistic practice is indeed haunted by the possibility that it is, in the words of Hegel, *'ein Nichtiges, ein sich Vernichtendes'*, 'a self-annihilating nothing'. Nowadays if one is animated by the desire to create a work of dance for instance, one cannot negate the possibility of negation, of a symbolic death that performatively nullifies the artistic worth of one's work.

Contemporary dance is a simultaneously fragmented and unified universe of discourse in which various individual and collective agents repeatedly make mutually contradictory statements about the same artefacts according to the opposition dance vs. non-dance. Of course this social world also comprises many forms of valuating a dance work or choreography, its ranking on the ladder from 'bad' through 'quite good', to 'outstanding' or, in the less overtly discriminating language of today's art worlds, from 'I couldn't really relate to it', to 'it had its flaws', to '(very) interesting'. However, this hierarchic appreciation presupposes the actual recognition of an artefact as being a genuine instance of dance. The fundamental fault line therefore remains the binary distinction between dance and non-dance, the inclusion or exclusion of a potential candidate of dance. The distinction operates as a two-sided code, a directive difference that co-structures the functioning of contemporary dance as a discursive field or communicative system. Yet the linguistic game of differentiating and marking according to the opposition dance vs. non-dance, is also based on a double *tertium non datur* that is mostly overlooked. For on the one hand, a work may be observed as a genuine hybrid or paradoxical object: 'it is both dance and non-dance'. Though this seems a somewhat implausible statement with regard to an overall performance, it is much less improbable when that quasi-object is split up, for instance in terms of a work's fragmentary composition. A spectator can thus enjoy some parts of a show as dance and reject others as 'a self-annihilating nothing' (Hegel). On the other hand, it is also possible to stick to the eventuality that the observed artefact is just a candidate for 'dance': 'this may (not) be dance'. The final qualification remains in suspension: the definitive identification is put between brackets and deferred – or better: virtualized. To say 'this may (not) be dance' not only confirms the status of the concerned work as 'an anxious object'. The sentence also pushes it in the direction of an undecidable object that does not answer Shakespeare's famous question 'To be or not to be?', but deliberately leaves it in a virtual state. The world of current dance practices only rarely ratifies this kind of existence that oscillates between 'being' and 'not-being'. *Observations of contemporary dance tend to exclude the actualization of the 'virtuology' implied by the statement 'this may (not) be dance' that conditions the ontology presupposed by the assertion 'this is (not) dance'.*

There is the overall label 'dance' and the possibility of self-reflexivity about the contingency of the name's use, which characterizes the world of contemporary dance; and then there is the more specific name, 'contemporary dance', which may be explicitly invoked or just assumed when stating 'this is dance'. Contemporary dance has been and will likely continue to be – at least in the foreseeable future – that evident and at the same time rather strange spectacle of publicly observable practices that involve the external designation and self-designation of artefacts, authors, stylistic features, institutions, et cetera, as contemporary dance. Venues, reviews, or spectators use that very label when referring to highly divergent sorts of performances; and individuals who are recognized dance makers create and present works that they themselves identify as instances of contemporary dance. The overall result is a genuine paradox: as an artistic reality contemporary dance is commonly assumed to 'really' exist independently of any kind of performativity, by performances and other practices that assert 'this is contemporary dance'. *The reality of contemporary dance thus primarily consists of the ongoing performative realization of its presupposed realness: like every dance work, it is a performed object.* What is supposed to exist comes into existence thanks to the perlocutionary force of countless actions that are connected to buildings, dossiers and subsidies, social positions and symbolic power... and evidently also to movements and non-movements. They are the stuff contemporary dance is made of, not as a particular artistic genre but as an autonomous art world hinging on a singular name. Like the general label 'art' or 'dance', 'contemporary dance' is actually an empty category or signifier that is repeatedly used in strikingly divergent ways to indicate, examine or contest what is at stake. It is therefore of little use to ask: 'what is contemporary dance — really?' As Wittgenstein has taught us, the meaning of an expression is in its use. Since the corresponding name is applied in divergent ways, contemporary dance as an artistic reality is not one but many things, not a universe but a 'pluriverse', a world that — like a Russian doll — contains many sub-worlds. And what goes for the name of contemporary dance also holds for the more particular labels associated with specific sub-worlds, such as 'pure dance', 'postmodern dance', 'dance theatre' or 'conceptual dance'. Each sub-world is a shifting and volatile network of artists, works, institutions, et cetera, unified by a name plus some very general axioms about the danceable. These basic assumptions are differently articulated within the 'sub-sub-worlds' of a dance sub-world: the widespread agreement on the identifying name once again conceals profound disagreements on its possible referents.

Being Active, Becoming a Name

Deconstruction and post-structuralism have become firmly entrenched within the human sciences and the discourse on the arts, yet overall modern humanism and its sacralisation of the self-conscious subject still prevails. The game of naming and unnaming that characterizes contemporary dance is thus coupled to the activities, purposes or opinions of individual artists and spectators, programmers and critics, or the officials deciding on dance subsidies. Performances, reviews or dossiers are consistently humanized as well. They do not possess a genuine performativity but are viewed as intentional products of human authors: they express individual states of mind, personal emotions, or collectively devised tactics. Thus a dance work never really speaks for itself. Notwithstanding the reigning rhetoric on the autonomy of art, the art work is still predominantly regarded as an intermediary or passive relay between the artist and an individual spectator. Economic and other constraints may influence and fracture the work's message, but this observation only reproduces the basic presupposition that the art work is in principle — or perhaps better: should principally be — a smooth communication channel between a sender and a receiver. However, the dance work is not per definition a neutral operator: it behaves as an active mediator as well. A potential artistic artefact does not only mirror the artist's conscious intentions or unconscious affects, it presents itself to the viewer firstly as an object that desires recognition, that wants to convince or aims to impress. *The art work (the dance work) is an actor that overtakes the actions of its maker (the choreographer), and this autonomous performativity is overtaken by the receiver (the spectator).*

Whereas intermediaries transport meanings or forces without transformation, mediators are modifiers or displacers. Ballet dancers are trained to become smooth intermediaries but contemporary choreographers often consider their collaborating performers as genuine mediators (or, in common parlance: the personality or particularity of the dancer is valued). Yet even a well-executed ballet performance hovers between intermediation and mediation. It is always marked by the untameable play of repetition and difference, the never completely controlled dialectic between the passive reproduction of a choreographic score and the however microscopic deviations from its ideal embodiment (which actually requires impossibly ideal bodies). Moreover, as it unfolds in time, the work as such begins to convince the spectator or not. Of course it is scripted by the choreographer, yet during the rehearsal process he or she was also constantly valuating movements and poses as plausible or implausible agents in their own right. Seeing is interpreting, but in framing and appreciating a series of movements, the dance maker as well as the audience member regularly attributes a genuine agency to the observed movements. They are read as 'powerful' or 'rather bland', as 'forthcoming' or 'hesitating', and so on. All is in the eye of the beholder, and it is the viewer who ascribes the observed qualities and the corresponding purposefulness or agency to the actions as such. This account has a marked effect, even if the interpretation looks highly questionable from the point of view of common sense. The series or work acts — or rather: a movement phrase or a complete choreography seems to act — in an autonomous mode thanks to a particular framing that grants agency to entities through their quasi-humanization. We indeed inhabit a culture that offers us not one but two vocabularies to speak of artefacts. There is the dominant humanistic regime that locates the capacity to act and to not-act exclusively in human subjects because they possess self-consciousness and free will. This general 'human-centrism' backs the notions of authorship, creative genius, skilled craftsmanship, and the other established clichés we mostly use to make sense of art. Nevertheless, there also exists a less elaborated vocabulary that ascribes agency and performativity to the many entities that fall outside the scope of the humanistic regime. This way of speaking or interpreting bestows a genuine capacity to act onto all kinds of objects that are per definition lacking the features of subjects. They may thus immanently convince that they are artefacts deserving to be called art or (contemporary) dance.

Not only art works but also dossiers, announcements, photographs, reviews and other textual or discursive artefacts can be regarded as quasi-actors that are all actively involved, together with human beings, in the artistic game of naming ('this is (good) dance') and condemning ('this is not dance', and also: 'this is bad dance'). They all enact and instantiate – or at least commit themselves to – a contingent definition of dance or choreography, and they all do this with more or less perlocutionary force or persuasiveness. As an art world, contemporary dance therefore resembles a discursive swarm, a heterogeneous multitude of various kinds of actors. The swarm is not an anarchistic mass but partially structured by diverse and often volatile forms of internal organization. Thus, tactical coalitions and strategic assemblages exist to further particular notions of the danceable or, on a more concrete level, to secure the name and value of individual dance makers and their work. If someone or something is already called an artist or an art work, usually in combination with certain qualifications, the initial labelling indeed needs confirmation. For the subject or object of a performative definition unavoidably loses its identity if its name and the accompanying attributes are not continually reiterated. *Identifications require re-identifications within different temporal and social contexts*: the performative naming 'this is (great) dance' demands a re-performative re-naming at subsequent points in time in order to hold. If the reiterations effectively take place, a self-referential chain emerges that consolidates the identification. Repeated by various actors at various moments, the echoed social confirmation creates a social or symbolic fact, a rather difficult to contest identity that has a thing-like quality. One's name as a dance maker becomes firmly established: 'William Forsythe is an outstanding contemporary choreographer'. Or the reputation of a dance work is turned into an indisputable quality: '*Artifact* is a masterpiece'. In addition to time, such a process of stabilization or institutionalization requires countless cooperative efforts from all kinds of actors: from the choreographers, their company members and, not least, the works themselves, as well as from the positive contributions of dance programmers, critics and spectators or, in another register, from well-composed brochures, attractive announcements, and the always difficult to analyse composite called rumour or hearsay. The various human and non-human actors all act with a distinctive symbolic power or perlocutionary force. What matters most, however, is that an ever growing and geographically dispersed swarm of agents move in unison, thus creating a general force line. This peculiar social choreography iteratively unfolds itself without any central coordination: 'making a name' is the partly intended, but overall unintentional, effect of the continual repetition of being positively named within an ever wider territorial network.

Viewed through a sociological lens, one never is a tremendous choreographer but one endlessly *becomes* one through repeatedly being named as such by a plethora of individual actors. The process has a self-propelling nature that makes the is-designation ever more real. From a certain moment onwards, which is always difficult to determine empirically, an artist or an art work 'is really great'. The reiteration of the statement 'this is (great) art', or of one of the many variations of this little phrase, not only confirms what has already been said. It also stands for a dynamic in which the designated subject or object and its qualities seem to gain in ontological firmness. The concerned individual, artefact or institution remains what it was, but possesses more 'being'. This greater solidity is a forceful mirage-effect without much substantiality, since it rests first and foremost upon the presupposition of a socially shared belief. Indeed, a social or symbolic fact such as a famous name always functions to a certain extent as an imaginary *belief object*. At an individual level, the conviction is backed by the unchecked faith that there are countless others who are of the same opinion: 'one believes that William Forsythe is a great choreographer because one believes that one (the many) believes this'. The personal conviction is not necessarily the effect of a passive conformism, quite the contrary, but it is definitely sustained in part by the routinely made assumption of an existing collective belief. The latter is an insubstantial quasi-thing that, not unlike a gender identity for example, is primarily the imaginary effect of the repeated performative act of naming someone, for instance, an innovative contemporary choreographer. Without the continual reiteration of this initial act, which also involves differential shifts and critical displacements, the non-ontological nature of a famous name becomes rather rapidly evident. The 'Big Name' is a performative symbolic construction that is continually re-enacted through countless communications — or it is not, and subsequently the Name loses its currency. It then becomes apparent that *the ontological substantiality of a Name consists in the purely communicative 'being' of 'being reiteratively named'.*

Sources

An Evening with Jérôme Bel

The description of Bel's *Le Dernier Spectacle* is based on personal recollections of the work as performed by Claire Haenni, Antonio Carallo, Frédéric Seguette and Jérôme Bel, during the premiere series in November 1998 at the Kaaitheater in Brussels, supplemented with the information offered by Gerald Siegmund's in-depth analysis of the work in his study *Abwesenheit. Ein performative Ästhetik des Tanzes. William Forsythe, Jérôme Bel, Xavier Le Roy, Meg Stuart.* Bielefeld: transcript Verlag, 2006, pp. 335–344. The quoted observation of André Lepecki on the public's reaction in Berlin during a performance of *Le Dernier Spectacle* stems from his essay 'Choreography's "slower ontology": Jérôme Bel's critique of representation', which is included in André Lepecki, *Exhausting Dance. Performance and the Politics of Movement.* London: Routledge, 2006, pp. 45–64 (p. 61).

The Medium of Dance

Reference is made to the following publications: Helmut Ploebst, *no wind no word. New Choreography in the Society of the Spectacle.* Munich: Klaus Kieser, 2001; Gerald Siegmund, *Abwesenheit*, p. 36; Francis Sparshott, *A Measured Pace: Toward a Philosophical Understanding of the Arts of Dance.* Toronto: University of Toronto Press, 1995; Peter Sloterdijk, 'Mobilization of the Planet from the Spirit of Self-Intensification', in *The Drama Review,* 50 (4), 2006, pp. 36–43 (p. 38); Peter Sloterdijk, *Kopernikani-sche Mobilmachung und ptolemäische Abrüstung.* Frankfurt am Main: Suhrkamp, 1987; and André Lepecki, 'Introduction: the political ontology of movement', in André Lepecki, *Exhausting Dance,* pp. 1–18 (p. 7). Emil Hvratin discusses Jan Fabre's *The Sound of One Hand Clapping* at length in his study *Herhaling, waanzin, discipline: het theaterwerk van Jan Fabre* [*'Repetition, madness, discipline: the theatre work of Jan Fabre'*]. Amsterdam: International Theatre & Film Books, 1994. Martha Graham's credo 'Movement never lies' is borrowed from Susan Leigh Foster, *Reading Dance. Bodies and Subjects in Contemporary American Dance.* Berkeley: University of California Press, 1986, p. 28. John Cage asserts that 'the material of music is sound and silence' in his short essay 'Forerunners of Modern Music', reprinted in John Cage, *Silence. Lectures and Writings by John Cage.* Middletown (CT): Wesleyan University Press, pp. 62–66 (p. 62). Merce Cunningham's statement on 'the nature of dancing' is mentioned in Roger Copeland, *Merce Cunningham. The Modernizing of Modern Dance.* London: Routledge, 2003, p. 115. The characterization of the medium of dance, presented toward the end of this paragraph, in terms of 'the unity of the difference between movement and non-movement' may sound quasi-Hegelian. The definition is actually primarily inspired by how the German sociologist Niklas Luhmann appropriated George Spencer-Brown's logic of forms and Fritz Heider's concept of medium in his later writings. Luhmann himself offers an extensive introduction in several parts of his *Theory of Society. Volume 1.* Stanford (CA): Stanford University Press, 2013; see also Niklas Luhmann, *Art as a Social System.* Stanford (CA): Stanford University Press, 2000. A second source of inspiration is Giorgio Agamben's approach to the notion of potentiality as a 'being able to' that per definition includes its negation, so impotentiality or 'being able not-to'. This view is further elaborated in the next paragraph.

On Potentiality and Impotentiality

The two Agamben quotes stem from the essay 'On Potentiality', in Giorgio Agamben, *Potentialities. Collected Essays in Philosophy.* Stanford (CA): Stanford University Press, 1999, pp. 177–184 (p. 179 and p. 183; italics in the original). Besides Agamben's essay, the following publications are quoted: John Jervis, *Transgressing the Modern. Explorations in the Western Experience of Otherness.* Oxford: Blackwell, 1999, p. 7; Isadora Duncan, 'The Dance of the Future' (excerpt from *The Art of the Dance,* originally published in 1928), in Roger Copeland and Marshall Cohen (eds.), *What is Dance? Readings in Theory and Criticism.* Oxford:

Oxford University Press, 1983,
pp. 262-264 (p. 263 and
pp. 263-264).

The /Contemporary/ Danceable

Claude Lévi-Strauss first set forth the
structural method of decoding myths
and other cultural artefacts in terms
of binary oppositions in the essays
collected in *Structural Anthropology*.
New York (NY): Basic Books, 1974.
Norbert Elias documents in detail
the historical genesis of the civilized
court body that informed classical
ballet in *The Civilizing Process.
Sociogenetic and Psychogenetic
Investigations*. Oxford: Blackwell,
2000. Susan Leigh Foster's essay
'The Ballerina's Phallic Pointe' is
included in Susan Leigh Foster (ed.),
*Corporealities. Dancing Knowledge,
Culture and Power*. London: Rout-
ledge, 1996, pp. 1-25 (p. 4). Contact
Improvisation's broader cultural and
social embedding is highlighted by
Cynthia J. Novak, *Sharing the Dance.
Contact Improvisation and American
Culture*. Madison (WI): University of
Wisconsin Press, 1990. André
Lepecki discusses the recent 'will
to archive/will to re-enact' within
contemporary dance in 'The Body as
Archive: Will to Re-Enact and the
Afterlives of Dances', in *Dance
Research Journal*, 42 (2), 2010,
pp. 28-48. Boris Charmatz' 'Manifes-
to for a Dancing Museum' is reprinted
in Noèmie Solomon (ed.), *Danse: An
Anthology*. Dijon: les presses du réel,
2014, pp. 233-240.

Revisiting Judson

Sally Banes characterizes the overall
spirit that animated Judson in her
insightful study *Democracy's Body.
Judson Dance Theater, 1962-1964*.
Durham (NC): Duke University
Press, 1993, p. xviii. I also rely on
Banes' reconstruction of Steve
Paxton's *Proxy* in *Democracy's Body*,
pp. 58-60. Michael Kirby's essay
'Objective Dance' is quoted by Carrie
Lambert-Beatty, *Being Watched.
Yvonne Rainer and the 1960s*.
Cambridge (MA): MIT Press, 2008,
p. 84. My succinct presentation of
the historical avant-garde is primarily
inspired by Peter Bürger, *Theory of
the Avant-Garde*. Minneapolis (MN):
University of Minnesota Press, 1984,
quoted p. 49.

Intermezzo: Witnessing Everyday Movements

Jacques Rancière summarizes his
ideas on 'le partage du sensible' in his
essay 'The Distribution of the Sensible', included in Jacques Rancière,
*The Politics of Aesthetics. The
Distribution of the Sensible*. London:
Continuum, 2004, pp. 7-46. The
cited publications in this paragraph
are Carrie Lambert-Beatty's *Being
Watched*, p. 103; Ramsey Burt's essay
'Minimalism, Theory, and the Danc-
ing Body', included in Ramsay Burt,
*Judson Dance Theatre. Performative
Traces*. Abingdon: Routledge, 2006,
pp. 52-87 (p. 53); and Susan Sontag's
'Against Interpretation', which opens
her essay collection *Against Inter-
pretation and Other Essays*. London:
Penguin, 2009, pp. 3-15 (p. 14). Also
mentioned in passing is Norman
Bryson's *Looking at the Overlooked.
Four Essays on Still Life Painting*.
London: Reaktion Books, 2004.

Art as a Proper Name

The description of Lucinda Childs'
Street Dance relies on the informa-
tion given by Carrie Lambert-Beatty,
Being Watched, pp. 37-38 and Nick
Kaye, *Postmodernism and Perfor-
mance*. London: Macmillan, 1994,
p. 103. Arthur Danto's quoted article
'The Artworld' is reprinted in Philip
Alperson (ed.), *The Philosophy of the
Visual Arts*. Oxford: Oxford Univer-
sity Press, 1992, pp. 426-433 (p. 432).
Thierry de Duve's cited essay 'Art
Was a Proper Name' is included in
Thierry de Duve, *Kant after Duchamp*.
Cambridge (MA): MIT Press, 1997,
pp. 3-86 (pp. 52-53).

To Name and to Not-Name Dance

John Austin first presented his views
on performative statements in the
William James Lectures he delivered
at Harvard University in 1955; see
J.L. Austin, *How to Do Things With
Words*. Oxford: Oxford University
Press, 2009. Pierre Bourdieu synthe-
sizes his sociological approach of
art in *The Rules of Art. Genesis and
Structure of the Literary Field*. Stan-
ford (CA): Stanford University Press,
1996. The Lyotard-quote can be
found in Jean-François Lyotard,
The Differend: Phrases in Dispute.
Minneapolis (MN): University of
Minnesota Press, 2002, p. xi.

The view on the contemporariness of current art or dance unfolded in this and the next paragraph is partly indebted to Niklas Luhmann's already mentioned *Art as a Social System*.

An Anxious, Undecidable, and Performed Object
Harold Rosenberg speaks of art as 'an anxious object' in 'Toward an Unanxious Profession', which opens his essay collection *The Anxious Object*. Chicago (IL): University of Chicago Press, 1982, pp. 13–20 (pp. 17–18; italics in the original). Hegel introduces the idea of 'a self-annihilating nothing' in relation to Friedrich Schlegel's views on art in his *Aesthetics*. I owe the quote to Giorgio Agamben, who devotes a chapter to Hegel's expression in his book *The Man Without Content*. Stanford (CA): Stanford University Press, 1999, pp. 52–58.

Being Active, Becoming a Name
That non-human artefacts can be ascribed agency is a fundamental axiom of Actor-Network Theory (ANT) as developed by Bruno Latour, who also sharply distinguishes intermediaries from mediators in his synthetic *Reassembling the Social. An Introduction to Actor-Network-Theory*. Oxford: Oxford University Press, 2005. The idea that identifications need future re-identifications in different contexts in order to hold can be found throughout the work of Niklas Luhmann; see esp. the essay 'Identität – was oder wie?', in Niklas Luhmann, *Soziologische Aufklärung 5. Konstruktivistische Perspektiven*. Opladen: Westdeutscher Verlag, 1990, pp. 14–30. This intuition, and the concomitant stress on iteration, also founds the performative approach of gender that Judith Butler unfolds toward the end of her influential study *Gender Trouble. Feminism and the Subversion of Identity*. London: Routledge, 1999, pp. 163–190.

Making 'Pure Dance' Impure

Notes on the Work of Anne Teresa De Keersmaeker & Rosas

First Movement: *Fase* and *Rosas danst Rosas*, or Maximizing Minimal Dance

Re-Viewing *Fase*

On the 18th of March 1982, *Fase, Four Movements to the Music of Steve Reich* premiered in the Beursschouwburg, a venue in the centre of Brussels. The performance was Anne Teresa De Keersmaeker's first full evening's choreography and is commonly regarded as the starting point of the contemporary dance wave that, rather unexpectedly, emerged in Flanders during the 1980s. *Fase*, originally performed by De Keersmaeker herself together with Michèle Anne De Mey, is based on four minimalist works by the American composer Steve Reich, all written between 1966 and 1972: *Piano Phase, Come Out, Violin Phase* and *Clapping Music*. Three of the four sections are duets that alternate dancing in unison with more individual variations of the basic phrase. *Violin Phase*, by contrast, is a solo that De Keersmaeker created already in 1981 in collaboration with the members of the Steve Reich and Musicians ensemble during her study leave in New York at the Dance Department of the Tisch School of the Arts. The most striking feature of *Fase* is without doubt the sustained combination in each section of iteration and variation, sameness and difference. The dance movements are continually divided into short sequences that are both incessantly repeated and gradually altered by way of small shifts. In the course of their reiteration, simple phrases are varied or recombined and thereby forged into longer units.

Piano Phase, the first of the four movements on Reich's music, aptly illustrates the choreographic logic of repetition and difference that is *Fase*'s hallmark. The section opens with the two dancers, each in a beige dress, white socks and shoes, standing still while facing the audience in front of a white background. Their projected silhouettes show them slightly larger than they are, yet there is also a darker silhouette in the middle that blends the contours of both dancers into one, thus producing the slightly uncanny impression of the presence of a third, phantom-like dancer. On the tenth measure of Reich's score the dancers first look towards each other, then briefly gaze at the public again, and subsequently start to dance. The first basic phrase of *Piano Phase* consists of a series of semi-turns, pushing off from one foot and pivoting on the other while simultaneously swinging the right arm forward. Following the momentum of the turn, the arm swings forward, drops down to the side and swings forward again with each half-turn. The body rotates continuously in a clockwise direction, the turning movement accentuated by the rhythmical moving of the dancers' arms and the swaying of their dresses. After a short while the rotation changes into a simple forward and back step along a straight line, punctuated by sharp turns, the left hand held behind the back and the right one swinging freely forward at an angle. Both phrases are combined and alternated for some time. The movement sequences are performed in unison, but with increasingly small differences in tempo that cause the dancers to go out of sync, bringing them for a moment face to face, then gradually back together again into a smooth harmony. At which point they pause, before continuing on in a straight line, one after the other.

After eleven minutes of dancing, the stage suddenly darkens. The silhouettes on the background disappear and the dancers do a couple of semi-rotations in the direction of the spectators, and then continue their movements in a straight line within a lateral stroke of light. The latter shifts a couple of times towards the proscenium, thus bringing the dance closer to the audience. The different light design and the visible fatigue of the dancers both re-articulate the quality of the movements, which continue to vary the initial phrases. The performers' gestures now look more intense and contrasted, at times even charged with a kind of physical power that makes them appear to be striking at the air. In the final part of *Piano Phase*, the initial scenography of the opening section is restored. De Keersmaeker and De Mey once again dance close to the white background, in company of their own silhouettes and a central one that mixes their individual contours into a hybrid body-shadow.

Fase acts as a choreographic totality that is more than the sum of its parts: the selected movements, the use of space and the lighting are embedded in an overall dramaturgy that encompasses the four sections. Thus the choreographic articulation of the stage is based on a small number of basic patterns. In *Piano Phase* the dancing alternates between straight lines and circles (the continuous semi-rotation of the dancers). The dancers also trace circles in *Come Out*, but they are confined to the chairs they are sitting on. The solo to *Violin Phase*, by contrast, makes use of the whole stage, which is transected by circular and diagonal dance lines. The closing part of the duet to *Clapping Music* brings the dramaturgy of the space to full circle: the dance retakes the straight line and lateral light previously seen in *Piano Phase*. In short, the play of difference and repetition not only characterizes the choreography of the movements in every section of *Fase*, it also marks the performance's unity. Moreover, the work embodies a particularly structural view of the relationship between music and dance, sound score and choreography. In the short essay 'Notes on Music and Dance', originally published in 1973, Reich himself advocates a drastic renewal of theatre dance after Judson, based on 'a return to the roots of dance as it is found all over the world: regular rhythmic movement, usually done to music. ... For music and dance to go together they must share the same rhythmic structure. This common rhythmic structure will determine the length of the music and dance as well as when changes in both will occur. It will not determine what sounds are used in the music nor what movements are used in the dance.' The dancing in *Fase* is definitely rhythmic due to the precisely measured, visibly counted pace of the movements, yet none of the four sections follow Reich's choreographic advice.

The music and the dance do not directly mirror each other in *Fase*, quite the contrary: they clearly follow distinct rhythmical patterns that sometimes interfere but primarily entertain a contrapuntal relationship. Music and dance therefore appear as autonomous media, allowing different articulations of sound and bodily movement. At the same time, the choreography unfolds relations of analogy with the music through the selective emulation of some of the basic principles that underlie Reich's compositions. The different sections of *Fase* each transpose one or more of these general axioms into the choreographic score, which may involve the use of space, the nature of the movements, or their overall temporal sequencing. Whereas the circular structure of the solo to *Violin Phase* is anchored in the *rondo*-form of the composition, the percussive use of the piano in *Piano Phase* is reflected in short and angular movements. Each of the four parts of *Fase* also keeps to the principle of gradual phasing that characterizes Reich's minimalist music: movements that are first carried out in perfect synchronization, although apparently continually repeated, are gradually shifted and offset. In sum, various structural similarities link the musical composition to the choreography, but without the first guiding the second.

Minimal Dance and/as Repetition
Dance criticism quickly positioned *Fase* as a genuine instance of the kind of minimal (or minimalist) dance that had emerged as a

distinctive choreographic approach by the end of the 1970s, particularly through the work of Lucinda Childs. Her by-now classic *Dance*, a collaboration with composer Philip Glass and conceptual artist Sol LeWitt, offended conservative audiences so much that they promptly walked out of the performance during its New York premiere series in 1979. The choreography was obviously inspired by the basic principles of minimal music, a vague term that became rapidly popular at the beginning of the 1970s and refers to music that is based on a logic of repetition and variation, which primarily makes use of harmonious consonants and has a clear rhythm. Yet the new dance genre also implicitly re-enacted, within the medium of time, the historical moment of architectural or 'spatial Modernism'. For the reductive stance of minimal dance with regard to the movement vocabulary employed, reiterates Adolf Loos' well-known sentence concerning the decorative ornament as an architectural crime, and moreover brings to mind the famous slogan, commonly attributed to Mies van der Rohe, that 'less is more'. However, the most intimate link between 'danced minimalism' and architectural Modernism, which simultaneously relates the first to certain strands of minimalism within the fine arts as well, is the structural logic of the grid.

The choreographic score of a work such as *Fase* — or, rather, of each of its four sections — is the equivalent of a modernist urban grid that at once repeats and varies discrete components or units (Le Corbusier spoke of 'units of habitation'), according to a serial logic that fuses sameness and difference into a purely structural whole. Such a totality positions the constitutive elements as empty signifiers that receive a formal particularity, yet not a proper meaning or observable content, through the slightly contrasting variations of these very same parts, or the minimal differences with resembling components. In a word, *minimal dance is 'grid dance'*. The genre thus lays bare the underlying temporal premise of spatial Modernism within urban planning. For an urban grid is not a purely topological object but a patterned play of sameness and difference that unfolds in time, one that consumes time in order to be seen or observed. 'Danced minimalism' highlights this temporal premise: its implicit rehearsing of the axioms of architectural Modernism within the medium of dance, brings to the fore the proverbial truth that spacing, however minimal, involves time (simultaneously demonstrating that time 'takes space').

Within the realm of dance, minimalism emphasizes that every choreographed dance work is a temporal object. Scored dance is performed in a now-time that the defining movements and pauses actively construct and structure, define and give shape through their self-referential intertwinement, according to the underlying choreography. Every movement appears and disappears in such a short leap of time that the average spectator often has difficulty remembering them, thus running the risk of only partially grasping the overall patterns that motivate the dancing. Indeed, the ephemeral or fleeting character of a dance's elements works against the more encompassing time-logic of choreography. Or, as Yvonne Rainer remarks in her self-commentary on the famous *Trio A*, first presented in 1966: 'Dance is hard to see. It must either be made less fancy, or the fact of that intrinsic difficulty must be emphasized to the point that it becomes almost impossible to see.' Rainer herself successfully tried out the second possibility. Now considered canonical, her *Trio A* consists of a single flattened out phrase of about four and a half minutes that is not articulated by any differences in energy distribution or movement intensity and that contains a lot of similar movements. Minimal dance, on the contrary, opts for the accentuating, even the ultra-visibility of the defining movements and their choreographic structuring by means of the logic of varied repetition. This type of dance resists the disappearance of momentarily made movements via their (somewhat altered) re-appearance, or their continual re-inscription within the choreographic text. In this way, fleeting movements are solidified and given a durability, which they usually lack within a dance work. In sum, *minimal dance implies an ethics of spectatorship that foregrounds the possibility of continuously looking anew*, which of course also singles out other forms of dance or performance that primarily rely on a logic of repetition. A work such as *Fase* thus partly exempts the spectators from the need to recall the previously seen movements: through its reiterative structure, the performance in a sense does the memory work for them. Every minimal or — more generally — repetitive dance work is indeed a peculiar kind of 'time monad' that creates an autonomous temporality dominated by the law of re-occurrence crossing out momentary forgetting.

A choreographed dance work is also a totalizing temporal object that condenses longer sequences of singular movements made in successive now-moments into a singular performance that, over a certain period of time, is repeatedly re-performed. This iterative instantiation of scored actions in an always particular 'now, here' defines choreographed dance, notwithstanding the small variations every re-enactment unavoidably produces. Minimal dance, à la *Fase*, not only highlights choreography as the reproduction of patterned series of movements and poses, the genre also stresses its prescriptive and repetitive nature, or the fact that in whatever form, choreography implies the existence of a 'dance text' that must be interpreted once again in order to exist publicly. Within the context of an individual work, 'danced minimalism' implicitly stresses this general recitative character of choreography through the visibly scripted accumulation and variation of basic elements such as, in the case of *Fase*, rhythmic stepping, the paced turning of the body, or the swaying of an arm. What is thus put forward is that 'written dance' exists in the mode of the 're' of the 're-reading anew' by one or more bodies: *minimal dance self-reflexively demonstrates the reiterative nature of all choreographed dance.*

Intermezzo: Defining 'the Choreographic'
Through choreography, dance participates in the modern scriptural economy that is a fundamental cornerstone of the various forms of rationalization, or calculated goal-directed action, within the domains of the economy, science, politics, education, and so on. 'What is writing, then?', Michel de Certeau asks in *The Practice of Everyday Life*, and he answers: 'I designate as "writing" the concrete activity that consists in constructing, on its own, blank space (*un espace propre*) – the page – a text that has power over the exteriority from which it has first been isolated. ... The scriptural enterprise transforms or retains within itself what it receives from its outside and creates internally the instruments for an appropriation of the external space. It stocks up what it sifts out and gives itself the means to expand.' The still pure page waiting to be marked delineates a place of production for the self-conscious subject, one that allows the subject to put the observed environment at an objectifying distance in view of its rational control. The space of the page does not know the many ambiguities 'out there' but it is, on the contrary, structurally coupled to the deliberate, strategic use of codified signs that separate and categorize, produce an abstract order and make all sorts of calculative operations possible. 'An autonomous surface is put before the eye

of the subject who thus accords himself the field for an operation of his own', De Certeau observes. 'This is the Cartesian move of making a distinction that initiates, along with the *place* of writing, the mastery (and isolation) of a subject confronted by an *object*. In front of the blank page, every child is already put in the position of the industrialist, the urban planner, or the Cartesian philosopher — the position of having to manage a space that is his own and distinct from all others and in which he can exercise his own will.'

De Certeau's incisive characterization of the modern scriptural economy undoes the ongoing association of writing with the particular use of a codified language and suits the practice of choreographing well. In the dance studio, various movements and divergent poses are first meticulously tested during rehearsals and then tentatively combined into longer phrases. Movements and intervals are archived in the dancers' bodies, selectively recorded and stored on video, and eventually 'textualized' in the strict sense, so graphically noted and written out. Yet video recordings are also a form of discourse to which the dancers can return when in need of a reminder, example or model, once particular actions are definitively inscribed into the choreography. The dance maker effectively writes: he or she retrieves from the exteriority consisting of the dancing bodies and the rehearsed movement vocabulary, certain actualizations deemed proper, and subsequently assembles the selected elements into a linear text made up of a beginning or introduction, sections or chapters divided into different paragraphs, and a finale or closing section. Every choreography indeed resembles a book — and once finished in view of the premiere, it starts to dominate its environment like a law-enforcing text.

Choreographed dance is haunted by the impossible to realize possibility of a perfect embodiment of the enacted dance script, or of a purely literal reading that crosses out every form of individual interpretation, even that of bodily difference. This ideal actualization acts as a transcendental structure, alternately a regulating standard or disciplining norm, informing the empirically observable performance. The choreographic score contains its own perfect bodily realization, both as a kind of Platonic Idea (which is also an Ideal animating the dancing) and as a virtual possibility of which the enactment is postponed indefinitely. William Forsythe once perspicaciously remarked that 'ballet only exists in theory. ... Every dancer must learn that ballet only knows a virtual existence. Nobody can dance an absolute, correct arabesque. All a dancer can do is to move with his individual body and his capabilities through the figure of the arabesque as through an empty form.' Yet the endless deferral of the impossible to realize ideal of a literal interpretation of the elements of a 'dance text' does not prevent it from exercising power over the dancers via the imperative injunction of an embodiment as close to perfection as possible. Although this disciplining Platonism is predominantly associated with the practice of ballet, the disembodied idealism of 'written dance' marks most choreographed performing.

Choreography is rationalizing, or selecting and fixing the most efficient means in view of an overall objective, which may vary from visual beauty and bodily grace (the ballet tradition), over emotional and narrative expressivity (modern dance), to the questioning of the established parameters defining the danceable (contemporary reflexive dance). *The choreographic' delineates precisely the writing space in which movements and non-movements are simultaneously fixed and rationalized, meticulously recorded and efficiently ordered.* Within the process of choreographing, both operations condition each other. Each temporary or definitive inscription of a movement or a pose asks for a premeditated choice: the act's contingency elicits the mode of goal-rational thinking, obliging one to take into consideration and explicate the general purpose of the dance. And the already solidified, noted or recorded elements function as secure steppingstones for new selective fixations according to an already given, if minimal or vague, rationalizing logic. This double economy of writing dance comes down to a deliberate 'making scarce' or an intended poverty. Out of the countless movement possibilities available, only those actions are selected that fit the specific choreographic writing machine one is simultaneously constructing and employing. 'The choreographic' thus supplements both the medium of dance and ongoing definitions of the danceable with a peculiar practice of appropriating, archiving and assembling movements and poses, one that is profoundly marked by the modern process of rationalization and its concomitant logic of efficiency. Within choreographed dance 'the choreographic' even functions as an essential supplement that tends to continuously take over the dance's identity.

There is yet another defining feature of 'the choreographic' (and again more generally of 'the writable'). For to produce

written signs comes down to the creation of marks, whatever their character, that are in principle repeatable, and this also in the absence of the subject-writer or author. This legitimates the notion of a 'writing in general' that includes the oral use of language or fleeting gestures and other ephemeral movements. Indeed, a written sign, whatever its nature and however unique, is a mark that is structurally characterized by the possibility of being used again, of being reiterable in principle. 'This power, this being able, this possibility is always inscribed, hence necessarily inscribed as possibility in the functioning or the functional nature of the mark. ... Inasmuch as it is essential and structural, this possibility is always at work marking all the facts, all the events, even those that appear to disguise it. Just as iterability, which is not iteration, can be recognized even in a mark that in fact seems to have occurred only once. I say seems, because this one time is itself divided or multiplied in advance by its structure of repeatability', argues Jacques Derrida in *Limited Inc.* 'The choreographic' again and again opens up a writing space that positions ephemeral 'movement events' as re-citable, or as actions – including the action of not-acting – that can principally be made anew in an undefined time still to come. This peculiar type of blank space allows concrete operations of fixing and rationalizing because it records whatever kind of observed action as being a priori repeatable. In sum, *'the choreographic' explicitly re-articulates the medium of dance according to the principle of iterability that defines 'writing in general'.*

Embodying Structure

Minimal dance shows a close affinity with the wave of structuralism that dominated Continental philosophy and the human sciences during the 1960s. Both privilege *langue* (or language as a structured system of differences) over *parole* (or the individual speech act) and operate with the notion of an underlying structure made up of limited possibilities that conditions 'the sayable' (or the danceable). Anthropologist Claude Lévi-Strauss, the founding father of structuralism, thus repeatedly succeeded in reducing a vast corpus of various myths into a series of ordered transformations of a restricted number of narrative elements. Every existing singular myth may therefore in principle be treated as a particular version of a virtual foundational structure. In a comparable fashion, a minimalist choreography consists of a seemingly endless number of permutations of one or a couple of elementary movement sequences. *Minimal dance deliberately commits itself to the structural logic of the slightly altered serial copy that tends to outdo the original status of the initial phrase.* Through its rehearsal in a vast series of only minimal variations that are all presented as equivalent possibilities, the initial sequence of movements is indeed transformed into a possible yet unnecessary or contingent starting point – into yet another version of one of the many versions that it elicited. The basic phrase evidently grounds the choreographic composition from the point of view of its production, yet the repetitive nature of that very assemblage of movements retroactively deconstructs this 'working consensus'. A minimal dance work actually functions as a mirror hall: it is an accumulation of somewhat distorted reflections that subverts the founding nature of the echoed original. Not that the dance therefore necessarily enters the logic of the simulacrum, or the copy without an original (which for instance defines the realm of the digitally reproducible). Rather, a minimalist choreography, such as the duet to *Piano Phase,* oscillates between the persistent affirmation of the two basic phrases presented at the beginning and the undoing of their master status through the restless production of equivalent versions.

Structuralism became famous – some will say infamous – thanks to its joyful proclamation of 'the death of man'. The slogan targeted modern humanism and its concomitant anthropocentrism, which positions man (indeed *man*) as the indisputable master over nature and firmly locates the production of meaning, whatever its particular form, in individual self-consciousness. According to the humanist master narrative, the use of signs such as words is synonymous with their intentional appropriation by human subjects: 'to say something' equals 'wanting to say something'. On the contrary, Lévi-Strauss, Jacques Lacan or Michel Foucault lionized the anonymity of language, the unconsciousness, and historically shifting discursive formations or 'epistemes'. They hailed the decentring of the subject in the direction of a nameless '*ça parle*', an impersonal 'being spoken' and 'being thought' that the imaginary identification with the reigning ideology of humanism can only hardly conceal. 'It is no longer possible to think in our day other than in the void left by man's disappearance. For this void does not create a deficiency; it does not constitute a lacunae that must be filled in. It is nothing more and nothing less than the unfolding of a space in which it is once more possible to think', Foucault writes toward the end of *The Order of Things*, originally published in 1966.

Structuralism's positive valuation of anonymity not only followed from particular theoretical considerations but was also inspired, in the early writings of Michel Foucault or Roland Barthes for example, by a comparable tendency within the arts. Already during the 1950s, the *nouveau roman*, the *nouvelle vague* in French cinema or – on the other side of the Atlantic – the work of Merce Cunningham testified to an objectifying stance that privileged *an ethos of the impersonal* within the medium of literature, cinema or dance. In the following decade structuralism's fascination with the genuine power of anonymous structures had its aesthetic equal in the further spreading of the interest in the rhetorical force of radically self-decentred, zero-degree modes of producing art. Minimalism and Pop Art within the fine arts, and many dance works made within the context of Judson, exemplify this trend. Indeed, Judson generally privileged a neutral, task-oriented, and matter-of-fact or behaviourist presentation of often simple movements and poses above their expressive articulation. Lucinda Childs, who participated in the original Judson Dance Theater, pursued this objectivist mode of performing in her minimalist choreographies. Minimal dance not only became synonymous with a choreographic attitude that relied on the power of movement permutation or the sustained combination of sameness and difference. It also implied a thorough minimization of expressivity and a reduction of the dancer's subjectivity or bodily particularity, which accorded with both the anonymity of the urban grid fêted by architectural Modernism and with structuralism's preoccupation with the deeper logics conditioning the surfaces of an only apparently individually controlled speech, thought or action. At the same time, both currents and even more so the neutral execution-style in performing, showed a strong affinity with the modern logic of bureaucratization and its emphasis on the un-impassionate, efficient and rule-following factory or office worker. The matter-of-fact performing style of Cunningham, Judson or Childs indeed fits the clichés of the organizational man who continually conceals his private concerns behind an ever-unmoved social face, expressing personal non-involvement.

'The personal disappears into the general. The role of the artist's hand, a stamp of personal style or idiosyncrasy, fades. In the same way, the distinctive performance presence of the dancer is obliterated, blotted out by the workly concentration and withdrawn face', notes Sally Banes with regard to Yvonne Rainer's *Trio A* in a chapter aptly titled 'The Aesthetics of Denial'. The observation also fits the minimal dance of Lucinda Childs, yet is belied by Anne Teresa De Keersmaeker's *Fase,* which shatters the dominant image of that subgenre as cool and austere. *Fase* at once adopts and re-articulates the choreographic structuralism that characterizes Childs' work but does away with the ethos of the impersonal in the performing style by means of a twofold, contradictory representation of the dancing body. De Keersmaeker and De Mey first take a visible pleasure in the dancing: besides mental concentration, their facial expressions indicate genuine enjoyment in the physical reading of the rigorous choreographic score. In the duets this expressivity is more than once stressed by the exchange of furtive, often playful glances and brief smiles signifying pleasure. Yet this delight in the dancing gradually fades away as the score progresses and the performers' bodies become exhausted by the sheer repetition, in a highly rhythmic fashion, of the restricted movement vocabulary. 'Effort and fatigue become increasingly readable on the faces, counterbalanced by a strength of will that one gathers from the performer's lips. The resolution of this growing tension only finds its completion in the final part [of *Fase*], in which the dancers – who are continually exposed in profile in a dance that does not tolerate any formal variation – are even no longer able to keep up a steady emotional flow. The body is here near to transparency. ... The body, more than the forms by which it makes itself visible, blends with the tonic states and the emotional states endured by the dancers', concludes Philippe Guisgand in his in-depth description of *Fase*. However, he overlooks something quite crucial: the fatigue is partly emphasized and accentuated, not just acted out or passively presented but also actively represented – in other words, slightly theatricalized through the wilful insistence on the individual speech act against the structuring choreographic *langue*.

Exhibiting both pleasure and exhaustion would become a defining feature in the work of De Keersmaeker. Allowing this corporeal expressivity clearly goes against the dominant trend in minimal dance, ballet, or the modernist tradition of Cunningham, to conceal the joy or the effort of dancing. Besides the face, it includes being audibly out of breath or visibly sweating heavily. These exposed states predominantly concern the dancing body, not the psychological interior or individual personality of the performers. Exterior signs of physical pleasure or fatigue allude to the overall corporeal affectivity that the dancing induces in the dancer's body. The net effect of permitting the frequently somewhat theatricalized production of these indexical signs in *Fase*, and in subsequent productions directed by De Keersmaeker, is a peculiar mix of choreographic structuralism grafted onto the general principles underlying the musical score, and a genuine performative expressivity that produces a bodily narrativity showing the gradual shift from corporeal pleasure to physical exhaustion. Implied is a particular form of body humanism that actually redefines the relationship between performance and choreography, the physical reading of a 'dance text' and that score's status as an autonomous scriptural artefact. On the one hand, Rosas' performing style frames the dancer as an at once necessary and vulnerable medium, a highly trained but nevertheless finite human body whose capacity to dance in a skilful way offers profound joy, yet is also bound to certain unsurpassable limits. In this way, an imaginary space is opened up that partly bridges the gap separating the dancers from the audience. The spectator is first tempted to identify with the apparent pleasure of the performers, then invited to empathize with their visible fatigue. On the other hand, the expressivity of the body highlights the difference between performance and choreography, the now-time of reciting a 'dance text' and that score's disembodied and disciplining, idealist nature. What thus comes to the fore is a particular way of enacting the structural logic of a highly rationalized choreography, one that performs the 'dance text' with a critical distance towards the text's injunction to interpret it as close to the letter as possible.

In the deliberately created hiatus between performance and choreography, the disciplining effect of the Platonic ideal of a perfect embodiment of the latter that constantly haunts the former, is weakened. The fissure critically shows the profound difference between body-dependent performance and the 'ideality' of the choreography informing this very activity. What is at stake here is not the culturally established semantic opposition between body and mind, or matter and spirit, but rather the distinction between bodily immanence and transcendence. Immanence makes transcendence impure, all existing world religions teach us, and this also holds within the realm of choreographed dance: *the immanent body of performance unavoidably taints the transcendent or Platonic body presupposed by 'written dance' or choreography.* With a performing style, dance makers decide either for transcendence or immanence: they either go for the impossible to perform, only evocable purity of a perfect embodiment of the choreography; or they side, like De Keersmaeker, with the impurity of performing, or an enactment that critically exposes the presupposed exactness or self-contained character of the letter of the 'dance text'. The produced impurity may suggest the existence of another, natural kind of purity within the dancer's body, yet precisely this evident connotation is bracketed in Rosas' performances by the dancers' regularly observable emphatic breathing seconding their unintended sweating. In De Keersmaeker's work, the immanent body is not synonymous with naturalness but rather involves an at once controlled and uncontrolled mode of expressivity deconstructing choreography's implied transcendence. Involuntarily produced and theatrically manipulated signs of corporeal realness loop onto each other in the performative undoing of choreography's 'ideality', thus thwarting the suggestion – which was constitutive for modern dance – of a pure bodily presence.

Choreographing the Ordinary

Loud metronomic ticks fill the theatre space. They hint at the passing of time that irrevocably marks every performance and anticipate the predominantly rhythmically structured dance performance about to happen. The dancers enter the stage: first one, then a duo, and then another. They line up and stand still with their backs to the spectators. The metronome beat comes to a halt but the four dancers stay still – till they suddenly fall in unison to the floor and lie down with their faces in the direction of the audience. This is the opening scene of *Rosas danst Rosas* ('Rosas dances Rosas'), the work that consolidated Anne Teresa De Keersmaeker's international reputation as a promising young choreographer. The performance premiered on the 6th of May 1983 in the Théâtre de la Balsamine in Brussels and signalled the official inauguration of the Rosas company. For the original series of showings De Keersmaeker and De Mey were joined by Fumiyo Ikeda and Adriana Borriello. The choreography has meanwhile become a repertory piece that still tours, put on again with various casts. *Rosas danst Rosas* was made in close collaboration with the musicians Thierry De Mey and Peter Vermeersch, who composed a strongly percussive score in the tradition of musical minimalism. The performance consists of four sections plus a short coda and continues the combination, already known from *Fase*, of a quasi-mathematical, highly repetitive choreographic structure with a genuine performative expressivity. *Rosas danst Rosas* shows the dancing bodies lying on the floor (the first section), sitting on a chair (the second part), or moving upright (the third and fourth section). The situations of sleep during night, early morning mood, afternoon beach pleasure, and the squandering of physical energy during a night out loosely inspire the dance's four-part structure. Whereas the first two sections clearly hint at everyday movements and gestures, the third and fourth contain more abstract movements that appear to be appropriations from the vocabulary previously used in *Fase*. Indeed, it would later become a defining gesture in De Keersmaker's choreographic career to retake and rework an already employed basic phrase in view of yet to be explored possibilities.

The long opening section, which is somewhat reminiscent of Trisha Brown's *Group Primary Accumulation* (1973), begins on the floor and develops in silence. Through a combination of rolling movements and intermediate steps, the four dancers lying on the stage build up a diagonal movement from upstage right to front stage left, accompanied by the bodily sounds of breathing, rolling and of arms tapping against the floor. The basic phrase is repeated several times and primarily contains movements that remind the spectator of someone making involuntary gestures during her sleep or being awakened by a disturbing sound. The body is slightly raised or turns around, the right hand goes through the hair, the head is lifted and supported by a forearm or, on the contrary, rested upon an elbow... These simple, repeatedly performed movements are shown in near darkness — only a small stroke of ground light illuminates the dancers — and in a contrasting mode: slowness and precision are alternated with a more up-beat tempo and vigorous execution bordering on vehemence. The second section of *Rosas danst Rosas* takes place in small rows of diagonally positioned chairs. The movements consist of quick and energetic gestures responding to the percussive music with its metallic sounding beats. Once again there is a basic phrase, composed of small movement units, that is variously retaken but regularly interrupted by a recurrent sequence in which the dancers — seated with legs crossed, heads resting on the palms of their right hands and their other forearms hanging across their bodies – let the supporting forearm slowly drop, so that the head and upper body fall forward. The units in the basic phrase include friendly nodding to one another, quickly bending forwards with arms falling circularly, rapidly standing up and falling back into the chair, fiercely stretching the arms away from the body with closed fists, running the hands through the hair, or touching a breast. Like in the first section, the movements allude to mundane life, yet they are transformed into general choreographic signs devoid of any direct functionality. How to understand this oscillation between referentiality and abstraction, between being grounded in everyday life and being inscribed in a dance score marked by the play of sameness and difference?

Judson already widened the notion of the danceable by including quotidian movement in a theatre context. Exceptionally, this also involved the framing of genuine everyday actions as dance, witness Lucinda Child's *Street Dance*. In order to stress the ordinariness of the appropriated movements such as walking, sitting or eating a pear (Steve Paxton's *Proxy*), the activities were put on stage in a task-like or objectifying way that resembled their mindless execution in daily life. The theatrical 'as if' clause, or the willing suspension of disbelief, was thus given a specific twist already associated by Denis Diderot with the notions of absorption and the fourth wall. Judson performers did not deliberately stage an action for a witnessing audience whose presence is theatrically taken into account, but acted as if the public was absent by simulating being totally absorbed by the tasks at hand. In doing so, they primarily exhibited or displayed, rather than staged, mundane actions. This mode of representation indeed had a direct affinity with dominant practices within the fine arts. The stage was treated as an exhibition space in which the appropriated pedestrian movements were neutrally exposed, in order to be looked at in a focused way. The matter-of-fact performing style evidently added to this resemblance with the practice of displaying artefacts known from art galleries or museums. Judson's option for the literal staging of ordinary actions also committed itself to a mimetic logic of quotation that signified a clear refusal to rework the cited 'objects' according to whatever existing definition of the danceable. The quoted movements were shown 'uncooked', devoid of any pretension to make them more interesting or meaningful than they were in daily life. Indeed, it was with an overt polemical intent that Yvonne Rainer voiced a critical stance toward the idea of dance involving an enhancing or beautifying intervention from the side of the dance maker, in her short 1965 manifesto '"No" to Spectacle...': 'No to spectacle/ no to virtuosity/ no to transformations and magic and make-belief/ no to the glamour and transcendency of the star image/ no to involvement of performer or spectator/ no to style/ no to camp/ no to seduction of spectator by the wiles of the performer/ no to eccentricity/ no to moving or being moved.'

The first two sections of *Rosas danst Rosas* are partly in line with Rainer's incisive manifesto insofar as they shun away from illusion and make-belief, not in the least because the choreography's unfolding confronts the spectator with visible signs of physical exhaustion. Yet there is also an undeniable connotation of 'danciness' since the quoted everyday actions are rhythmically serialized and vastly formalized. The cited gestures are not matter-of-factly exhibited or displayed but clearly choreographed according to a scriptural logic that transforms them into abstract signs or repeatable marks. As such, the movements still retain a recognizable referential quality, yet they are first and foremost transformed into 'de-semanticized' signifiers that primarily function as formal elements within composed patterns and sequences. This redefinition literally amounts to *the making scriptural of ordinary movements within the space of 'the choreographic'*, which alters the nature of the represented everyday actions. They are now no longer bodily tics, involuntary gestures or intentional actions firmly located within an individual body or subject but rather anonymous signs prescriptively re-enacted by the dancing bodies.

The movements inscribed in the choreographic text of *Rosas danst Rosas* may originally stem from gestures rooted in the daily lives of the dancers themselves. This is how the performance's title can literally be read, particularly with regard to the first two sections and the original cast that partly inspired De Keersmaeker's choreographic writing (or *écriture*, an expression she clearly favours in interviews). Indeed, the phrase 'Rosas danst Rosas' seems to suggest that the four dancers perform movements drawn from their own experiences. Yet at the same time the title emphasizes that this possible autobiographical layer is *danced* and the possible input of personal gestures will therefore be shown in a transformed way, one that is deeply marked by the scriptural nature of choreography. The fact that this 'dance text' also follows the logic of repetition and difference that characterizes minimal dance, profoundly corrodes, and even tends to deconstruct, the representational value of the cited ordinary actions. Through their repeated enactment, the movements are transformed into choreographic signs gaining in connotative value ('this is dance') and gradually losing in denotative or referential value ('these dance movements refer to daily actions'). Or as art theorist Hal Foster, writing on the status of repetition in 1960s Minimalism, perceptively notes: 'Abstraction tends only to sublate representation, to preserve it in cancellation, whereas repetition ... tends to subvert representation, to undercut its referential logic.' However, the re-iteration of the representing signs does not completely do away with external references. Thus in the first and second sections of *Rosas danst Rosas*, the movements keep on alluding, with an albeit gradually weakening denotative force, to the everyday world outside the theatre. The signs never change into empty signifiers but retain, particularly from the point of view of the 'ideality' of 'the choreographic' or the idea of 'pure movement', traces of impurity. In sum, the dance in *Rosas danst Rosas* is betwixt-and-between: the movements continually open up a twilight zone in which they hover between form and content, materiality and meaning, the self-referentiality of the 'dance text' and its external referents.

Differential Dance

Rhythmic percussive sounds fill the theatre hall when the stage light goes on again; sound and lighting both indicate the start of the third part of *Rosas danst Rosas*. The chairs used in the previous section re-appear, now lined up against the back wall of the stage. One dancer sits on a chair to the far right and observes how the three other performers, forming a straight line accentuated by the light corridor, resume dancing. They sway the right arm forward with a clenched fist, making a semi-circular turn toward the stage's back wall while the swinging right arm also describes a half circle. The dancers then turn forward again and repeat the semi-circular turn, turn forward again and sway the right arm forward twice. Afterwards, they reiterate the semi-circular and the forward turn, and then rapidly bend their bodies to the ground with both arms firmly outstretched toward the dance floor. Throughout the third section of *Rosas danst Rosas*, this phrase is repeated and varied via the addition of gestures such as crossing the arms, throwing the head back, a couple of quick sideward steps, simulating the beginning of a fall, shaking the head rapidly, or running both hands through the hair.

At the beginning of the fourth section, all four dancers again form a straight line upstage and face the audience, their position accentuated by a corridor of light. Standing with legs set apart, the right arm swings out in a circular pathway from left to right, and, with a quick shift of the weight, is forcefully stopped to the front. This short phrase is repeated while, one by one, the dancers move front stage, clasping their arms and throwing their heads back with a slightly provocative air of 'here we are!' They line up at the proscenium, turn their backs to the audience, and start to dance in an allegro tempo. Circles and straight lines are alternated, while the basic phrase is at once reiterated and transformed through the addition of movement units such as swaying the right forearm with a clenched fist, nodding with complicity to one another, clasping the arms to the body while throwing the upper body and head backward and then bowing forward, or running the hand through the hair (indeed the most recurrent gesture in *Rosas danst Rosas*). These units gradually take over the initial phrase, which fades out and is transformed into a recent past that certain movements occasionally hint at in the mode of an imperfect recollection or a disappearing remembrance.

In unfolding the play between sameness and difference, the third part of *Rosas danst Rosas* opts for the first and the fourth for the second. The dancers often act in unison in both sections but even so, all possible variations of the number four are tested. For example, three dancers make the same movement while the fourth counters it; or they follow a course two by two, or one plus two plus one, and so on. The overall effect gives the impression of witnessing a dance work that sticks to a rigorous logic of permutation and partly hollows it out by the restless production of accumulations and genuine differences. The fourth section of *Rosas danst Rosas* in particular reframes the established idea of minimal dance and gradually subverts the spectator's expectation, raised by the previous sections, that repetition will always dominate. By continually injecting new movement units and their subsequent variations, the dance itself thwarts the choreography's anticipated identity. In this way, minimal dance is re-articulated as a predominantly *differential dance* that simultaneously affirms and deconstructs the underlying reiterative principle.

Rosas danst Rosas is a 'gridded' choreography that undermines minimal dance's presumed nature first and foremost

through the observable differences in the dancer's individual performing. Again and again the similar looks dissimilar because the
four dancers – and this regardless of the particular casts that have
performed it – embody identical movements with visibly divergent
accents that are sometimes slightly theatricalized. 'The dancers
seem alternately lost, nonchalant, determined, alarmed, provocative, suspicious, annoyed; every new movement, every declination
of the phrase, becomes the pretext for the disclosure of a new state
of being of the interpreters', observes Philippe Guisgand in his
analysis of *Rosas danst Rosas*. The performers are indeed allowed
to be genuine individual interpreters who continually particularize
the 'dance text', thus incessantly undermining the homogenizing
character and 'ideality' of the choreography through its polyphonic actualization. Sometimes the differences in dancing even seem
to be enacting a score that from the outset was written with the
intention that it be performed by heterogeneous bodily voices.

The dancers not only embody the written choreography
with an always particular emphasis but they appropriate it as
well with a 'bodily mind' and self-concentration that oscillates
between performing for oneself and the awareness of dancing
before an audience. The pure 'ideality' of the score is in this
way again rendered impure via the mimesis of its very logic in
the act of performing. For it is precisely the play of sameness
and difference structuring the choreography that is reiterated
through the performing of the varied readings of the 'dance text'.
Consequently, quasi-personae, or singular characters, emerge
who are not primarily expressing the dancers' personalities but
rather their 'dancing identities'. These peculiar self-portraits can
be seen as constantly moving pictures of the performers' divergent modes of 'being a dancer', which are linked to partly spontaneous, partly deliberately staged bodily differences. In this way,
expressivity is thoroughly displaced. In *Rosas danst Rosas*, this
notion no longer refers to a psychological state of being but points
to the at once individually controlled and unintended phrasing of
prescribed movements. *Through the agency of singularly enacting
the 'dance text', the dancers appear as both subjected to the choreography and as being autonomous bodily subjects.* The performers
indeed at once conform to and slightly deviate, in an always individual way, from the underlying score, which is thus repositioned as
both constraining and enabling their capacities. Or to paraphrase
Michel de Certeau again, whose view on the modern scriptural

economy informs the notion of 'the choreographic' deployed here: 'written dance' implies the existence of a strategic space for the production of compelling marks, yet the dancers are allowed to manoeuvre tactically with these injunctions. This would again become a defining feature of Rosas' performing style. The singular cultivation of the hiatus between choreography and performance remains to this day a hallmark of 'Rosas "dancing" Rosas' – that is to say of the dancers who are members of the Rosas company performing a 'dance text' associated with the name 'Rosas' and its director, Anne Teresa De Keersmaeker.

'Being a Woman'
In affinity with structuralism within the human sciences, as well as the modernist logic of bureaucratization, the various forms of minimalist art tended to do away with individual agency and to lionize the anonymity of chance methods (Cunningham and Judson), of rigid compositional principles and procedures (minimal music and also partly minimal dance, à la Childs), or of simple objects and modules produced in a factory-like way (Minimalism in sculpture and the fine arts). The corresponding neutral performing style subscribed to the evaluative premise 'that action, or what one does, is more interesting and important than the exhibition of character and attitude'; and therefore 'that action can best be focused on through the submerging of the personality: so ideally one is not even oneself, one is a neutral "doer"' (dixit Yvonne Rainer, describing the dominant practice of Judson in her self-contextualization of *Trio A*). What was thus deliberately negated was the speech act's double pragmatic locus: an always particular situation of sign use, and an always singular body mediating langue or another structured sign repertory. This enunciating body is never a pure medium but, on the contrary, is unavoidably marked by historically and culturally variable modes of 'being a woman' or 'being a man' (and also of course by skin colour, by age, not to mention by class differences, which structure one's corporeal *hexis* or overall way of physically behaving). The dominant gender script in contemporary society is intrinsically interwoven with a heterosexual norm that positions the female body as a visual object of pleasure for the male gaze. The ethos of the impersonal that characterized the performing style of Cunningham, Judson or Childs implied a neutral stance toward this gendered nature of the human body. However, 'pure dance' (Cunningham

or Childs) or 'pure movement' (Judson) vainly tries to negate what can never be undone but only performatively re-articulated: the gendered body of the dancer and its unavoidable positioning by the existing heterosexual regime.

Rosas danst Rosas restores the dancer's performing agency, thus foregrounding the speech act and its embodied nature. Moreover, the work emphasizes in various ways the gendered corporeality of the four female performers and their body's inscription, through the very act of performing, in the hegemonic gender discourse. Notwithstanding De Keersmaeker's consistent cautiousness regarding feminism in public interviews, *Rosas danst Rosas* does indeed at once affirm and question the 'being' implied by 'being a female dancing body' (this peculiar criticality informs all the works De Keersmaeker subsequently made until *Toccata*, a choreography on the music of J.S. Bach from 1993, that signalled in her choreographic trajectory a temporary return to the heritage of classical ballet). Some of the everyday signs or gestures that are quoted and choreographically transcribed in the different sections of *Rosas danst Rosas*, definitely connote a young femininity. The dancers' clothing, both simple and strongly marked, and the constantly re-occurring movement of running the hands through the hair, constitute prime examples. There are still other movements indicating femininity, such as touching one's breast, the gendered way of nodding to each other in the second section, or the spreading of the legs and the swaying of the hips in the fourth part. The actions are thoroughly choreographed and therefore possess the abstract, highly formalized quality of anonymous signs that the 'dance text' imposes on the four dancing bodies, with the explicit injunction of reiterating them again and again. Yet these very gestures or poses also act outside the theatre as at once impersonal and imperative elements that are — or rather: that have to be — constantly re-performed.

The average female body choreographed by the dominant gender script actively rehearses the many corporeal acts that signify femininity. Together with their socially hegemonic status, this repetition creates the impression that the gestures express a deeper female identity, one that does not seem to be the result of the constructive gendering of the body but points to a transhistorical essence. 'In other words, acts, gestures and desires produce the effect of an internal core of substance, but produce this *on the surface* of the body', Judith Butler argues in *Gender*

Trouble. 'Such acts, gestures, enactments, generally construed, are *performative* in the sense that the essence or identity that they otherwise purport to express are *fabrications* manufactured and sustained through corporeal signs and other discursive means.' The gendered body is indeed a performative product that consists of various corporeal acts or signs stating 'I am a woman' (or 'I am a man'), borrowed from the dominant heterosexual gender regime. The corresponding gestures and other bodily signifiers are literally quotes that are incessantly re-cited through their reiterated performing, which induces the idea of a fixed feminine (or masculine) identity. This very same logic of repeated re-quotation structures the choreography in *Rosas danst Rosas.* The four female dancers regularly reiterate quoted everyday signs that also function as continually re-performed citations in the mundane enactment of the female gender script. They mimic both these signs and the performative logic ensuring the production of a seemingly stable and natural female essence. The minimalist identity of *Rosas danst Rosas* therefore clearly exceeds the purely aesthetic. In this work, *the performative and recitative status of embodying gender in daily life is in part choreographically re-performed within the context of a performance,* allowing the spectator to observe the at once 'minimalist' and highly effective logic sustaining the social fiction of 'being a woman'.

Yet something has been left out: perhaps the most remarkable action in the third part of *Rosas danst Rosas* remains unmentioned here. The gesture in question is rehearsed in the short coda that closes the performance during which time three of the four dancers visibly recover from the exhausting choreography of the fourth section. The remaining dancer reveals with one hand one of her shoulders, then both, by removing slightly her T-shirt; the straps of her bra appear, but in a next action the shoulders are again covered and the T-shirt is buttoned up again. During the third part, the four dancers repeatedly make this gesture. The act is mostly done alone, in marked isolation from the group with whom the performer doing the act of baring the shoulder exchanges divergent sorts of glances. Every now and then two of the dancers each move to one side of the stage in order to exhibit the shoulder one or two times, occasionally also running a hand through the hair. The four dancers execute the action in a notably different way. Whereas a first one looks rather diffident, and timidly turns away the gaze, a second one performs the gesture in an at once openly seductive and ironic mode; while a third enacts it matter-of-factly, as if she is deliberately avoiding any sign of emotional involvement. A series of quasi-sculptural scenes thus develops in contrapuntal interaction with the dancing, in which obviously theatricalized differences in performing an analogous matrix of micro-movements deconstruct that very configuration's gridded character. Depending on how one or both shoulders are bared, the gesture either hints at the idea of personal vulnerability or seems to embody the notion of playfully going along with the dominant gender script. Nevertheless, in both instances the underlying structural positioning of women within the field of the male gaze is affirmed.

'The determining male gaze projects its fantasy onto the female figure, which is styled accordingly', writes Laura Mulvey in her classic essay on 'Visual Pleasure and Narrative Cinema'. 'In their traditional exhibitionist role, women are simultaneously looked at and displayed, with their appearance coded for strong visual and erotic impact so that they can be said to connote *to-be-looked-at-ness*.' Through the simple gesture of baring one or both shoulders, *Rosas danst Rosas* self-reflexively indicates that a dance performance is effectively a spectacle, or a scopic happening made to be seen, that is fundamentally marked by a general (the public's gaze) as well as a gendered (the male gaze), visual power relationship. The at once vulnerable and ironic mode of performing critically mimics and thus undermines the female subordination to a masculinized visual field implied by the very act of looking at a woman dancing. Either the gesture is carried out summarily as a compulsory performance, or with a sense of unwillingness; or it is executed with an ironic seduction that simultaneously signals a subjection to the domination of the male gaze and the desire to shift the power balance, to take the lead in a situation where one is actually led. This kind of mimicry fits Luce Irigaray's contention that 'to play with mimesis is thus, for a women, to try to recover the place of her exploitation by discourse, without allowing herself to be simply reduced to it. It means to resubmit herself ... to ideas about herself that are elaborated in/by a masculine logic, but so as to make visible, by an effect of playful repetition, what was supposed to remain invisible.' In *Rosas danst Rosas,* the reiteration of the outward behaviour that produces 'the being' of 'being a woman' is indeed simultaneously exposed and subverted, thus momentarily producing the state of 'being a woman'.

Second Movement: *Rain*, or Re-Defining the Medium of Dance

Phrasing Movements, Virtualizing a Phrase

'I hope it's not going to rain tomorrow.' This simple sentence, from the short story 'Rain' by the New Zealand writer Kirsty Gunn, is spoken at the end of *In Real Time*. Created in 2000, this improvisation-based performance brought together thirteen Rosas dancers and choreographer Anne Teresa De Keersmaeker, the four principal actors of the Flemish theatre collective Stan, the musicians from the fusion jazz band Aka Moon, and the Dutch theatre director and writer Gerardjan Rijnders. One year later, on the 10th of January 2001, *Rain* premiered at La Monnaie/De Munt in Brussels and turned out to be the meticulously choreographed answer to the multi-medial *In Real Time*. The switch is striking and may at first sight surprise, yet within her artistic trajectory De Keersmaeker frequently alternates between performances possessing a marked theatricality and works that are often categorized as 'pure dance'. The choreography for *Rain* was made in collaboration with ten dancers and is set to Steve Reich's *Music for 18 Musicians* (1976). Two different rhythms interact in the music: the regular rhythmic pulse of the pianos and percussion instruments, heard throughout the piece, and the much more extended rhythm of human respiration animating the female voices and the clarinets that resembles the ebb and flow of waves. The choreography in *Rain* sometimes accords with the music but predominantly develops contrapuntal patterns and accumulations. However, the 'dance text' also mirrors the slow surging of the voices and the wind instruments through the continual change between moments of articulate dancing and calmer ones in which some of the performers or the whole group refrain from making movements connoting 'danciness'. Tranquillity does not necessarily mean stillness: the phases of quietness usually consist of an informal stepping, often done by all dancers forming a circle or a straight line. The circular walking is reflected in what is probably the dominating movement theme in *Rain* from a spectator's point of view: all dancers running in a circular pattern, one after another or overtaking each other in constantly shifting and spiralling configurations.

The scenography of *Rain* by Jan Versweyveld, a regular collaborator of De Keersmaeker, also foregrounds the circle motive. On stage the dance space is demarcated by a high cylinder of gleaming ropes, open at the proscenium, with one sole rope hanging in the middle. Except for a couple of transparent chairs — the chair is without doubt the prop par excellence in Rosas works — the space is initially empty, yet the floor is heavily marked by varying lengths of adhesive tape in different colours that assist the dancers throughout the choreography in finding their positions. The performance commences with the ten performers calmly walking on stage one after the other. They start running around the cylinder while a huge spotlight is turned in the opposite direction and they subsequently slow down their action, and finally unite centre-stage. The running is briefly resumed, comes to a short halt, and continues anew. At the next brief pause, Fumiyo Ikeda starts dancing the basic phrase, which was already used in *In Real Time*. Standing centre-stage with her back to the audience, Ikeda first slightly twists her torso to the left, turns with her hands above her head, rotates, shakes her head and bends both knees with a somewhat shaking torso. Up again, she sways her right arm forward and rotates a couple of times with both arms alternately swaying or held close to her body and periodically twisting her leg. She bows, turns, and stretches her right arm two times angularly while the left one is in a semi-circular, quasi-solemn position known from ballet. After hitting her stomach with both fists, she falls forward on the dance floor and lies there for a second with her right arm stretched out above her head. Up again, she jumps backwards and then bends forward with her right leg stretched behind her torso and her left arm on her curved left leg. Her right arm and hand extend past her face through the air; her entire body follows, falling forward and she comes to an upright position again. After a couple of rotations with waving arms and a nearly stumbling motion, the phrase comes to an end for a first time. Ikeda repeats this sequence two times with heavy declinations. The other performers meanwhile continue walking and running, or briefly stand still and contemplate Ikeda's dance.

The entire phrase is danced in a fleeting fashion and with an even energy distribution that smoothens over the brusque transitions between the various components, which markedly differ from each other in character and connotations. Whereas the arm positions sometimes refer to ballet, the sharp bending forward of the torso or the knocking of the stomach with both fists evoke a very different register than the precious grace of classical dance. The non-linear sequencing of the discrete movement units incessantly produces discontinuities which, when looked at in detail, give the impression of a line being crushed. It is as if the different actions resemble singular words that are contingently arranged into a sentence, one after another and without any copula or syntax. In principle, this would result in a disjointed phrase with much unlikely juxtaposition creating the overall image of a distorted body. However, the divergent movements and poses are continually phrased in such a way that one runs into the next with hardly any friction. This is once again a defining hallmark of Rosas performances: within one sequence, heterogeneity (the singular movement cells) and homogeneity (their general articulation) seamlessly go together. The combination comes down to a genuine dialectical logic: *through phrasing, essentially juxtaposed actions are sublated into a fluid series of movements.* The phrasing acts as a general connector that supplements the absence of copulas joining the disconnected elements within the phrase itself: it smoothly couples what is in fact uncoupled, or makes continuous what looks in principle discontinuous. Through a controlled breathing and energy distribution, the dancing body takes over the role of the human voice in the speech act or, rather, in the realm of song. Phrasing a series of actions into a consistent sequence with a specific internal quality, such as fluidity or evenness, does indeed come down *to the use of the body as a uniting singing voice* in relation to the different corporeal gestures or actions. Both the movements and their phrasing are done by one and the same body, yet it seems as if two different kinds of corporeality are involved: a body that visibly acts in space, and a more hidden one that bestows 'from inside', through a differential play with musculature and energy flows, an articulated homogeneity on the essentially disconnected actions. In De Keersmaeker's performances, the phrasing also frequently follows a semi-narrative pattern: the beginning of a movement sequence is accentuated, at times so forcefully that the start looks quasi-explosive, after which the tone switches to a more controlled and predominantly even register.

With regular ebbs and flows, *Rain* unfolds the basic phrase in endless variation. Towards the middle of the choreography, in a section during which the stage is bathed in blue light, a scintillating dance develops. Solos and duets transform the dance space in a continually shifting constellation of mini-stages defined by the individual dancers' momentary positions and movements. The performers disappear behind the curtain of cords, enter again and shortly move in unison before breaking up anew into various solos and short duets emerging out of spatial encounters between the dancing bodies. Now and then, the whirling is interrupted by a brief gathering of all performers during which the group eventually lifts one dancer in the air or starts to run again in a circle. Gradually, the dance slows down and finally fades out, with the dancers walking quietly and maintaining a straight line while continually shifting positions. Further on in the piece two lines of dancers walk back and forth between the upstage and the proscenium, with the performers exchanging glances and visibly showing their fatigue through, for instance, gasping breaths. Throughout the performance, the dancers' style of performing and expressivity switches between a strong concentration during the more complex sections and rather informal behaviour, involving much mutual non-verbal communication, in the calmer parts. Two scenes stand out because of their markedly dramatic nature. In the first one, Taka Shamoto is pushed in the back a couple of times and seems temporarily excluded by the group. The other scene, situated towards the end of the performance, shows Cynthia Loemij and Igor Shyshko in a duet that is heavily emotionally charged: their slightly violent dance indirectly evokes a heterosexual couple vacillating between attraction and repulsion, eroticism and quarrelling.

The choreography in *Rain* endlessly rewrites the basic dance sentence, which is reversed and mirrored, multiplied and divided, rhythmically inflected and spatially twisted. The variations and permutations are so numerous, and more than once so drastic, that the starting phrase becomes unrecognizable and the actual movements often surprise. The play of sameness and difference known from De Keersmaeker's early choreographies tends mainly to follow a differential logic that is predominantly informed by the possibility of altering the units of the basic phrase through various operations 'upon' and 'with' that sequence. The final choreography therefore no longer resembles a classical fugue but looks like a fractured fractal. The identity of the original movement sequence opens towards a first horizon populated by the many different possible identities that it could also take and which the final choreography has selectively realized. This logic of continually redefining the basic phrase involves a general ontology of the virtual that relates the actually existing to the potential differences it contains as a proverbial subtext. The possibilities are not passively waiting in order to be realized but, on the contrary, are actively constructed and renewed with every permutation of the complete phrase or of its constituent components. They are at once absent and present: the movement possibilities exist virtually and thus only with the eventuality of being explored, actualized, and changed.

In line with this ontology, in *Rain* and other works, De Keersmaeker basically deals with 'the choreographic' as a writing space in which the initial phrase can be written differently, can even be overwritten, because it contains innumerable variations that are archived in that very sequence as a potential yet to be articulated. In short, *a dance phrase's identity is not a given but a continual becoming other through the selective actualization of some of the possibilities it virtually comprises.* This stance regarding 'the choreographic' repositions its underlying rationalizing or calculating logic in the direction of the meticulous exploration of the 'also possible' movements in every unit making up an initial phrase. It is a way of writing dance that decidedly breaks with the avant-garde idea — which still haunts artistic practice — of the successful art work being a genuine transgression, an absolute renewal or tabula rasa. De Keersmaeker's cautious way of choreographing is rather based on the intuition that every living reality instantiates the difference between 'that which it is' and 'that which it could become given what it is'. Such a being has a split identity since it is both determined and an open horizon of 'possible possibilities'. In sum, a living being, whatever its nature, is at once an actually defined being and an undefined virtual multiplicity. A phrase or series of movements can also be treated as a mode of being accommodating a virtual space made up of innumerable differences potentially altering that sequence's character. This makes it unnecessary to invent a new movement vocabulary or novel phrase at the start of each new piece. Originality is rather a by-product, a quality that one was not particularly after but that emerges as a non-intended side effect during the process of exploring the virtual nature of a pre-existing series of actions.

Intermezzo: The Temporalities of Dance
Seen from the angle of the modern concept of time, which sharply distinguishes between past, present and future, cancelling out the

possibility of a recurrent or cyclic time for instance, every dance work – in fact every instance of live performance – consists of movements made in the present tense that appear and disappear. A performance is composed of transitory now-moments or temporal events that are continually re-framed by actions that come and go during the entire duration of a dance work. Whatever their nature, the various actions operate as temporal self-markers: they (re-)present the fleeting presence of present movements or poses. This passing character of the events making up a performance may be regarded as constitutive of the modernity of theatre dance. 'Modernity is the transient, the fleeting, the contingent', Charles Baudelaire famously stipulated in his 1863 essay 'The Painter of Modern Life', adding that 'it is one half of art, the other being the eternal and the immovable.' Baudelaire actually speaks here of the watercolours and paintings of the now forgotten artist Constantin Guys. In Baudelaire's view, Guys succeeded in rendering the ephemeral quality of Parisian street scenes or fashionable female dresses in such a way that their elusiveness is at once represented and transcended, directly hinted at but simultaneously overcome in an image with classical status. Referring to only the first part of Baudelaire's definition, dance scholar Gabriele Brandstetter highlights the modernity of dance, particularly as developed by Isadora Duncan, Ruth Saint Denis and other pioneers of modern dance. By foregrounding the passing and the contingent, 'not only are the criteria for a definition of the modern outlined, but these features characterize the art of dance as well: the transitory or fleeting are basic features of dance as a prominent form of performance among the performing arts; and the feature of contingency becomes, *after* the break with the balletic aesthetic paradigm, a specific criterion of free dance, namely in the foregrounded meaning of chance, improvisation, and the presentation of the moving image as a "spontaneous" affective expression.' Yet what about the other half of Baudelaire's characterization of modern art? Is dance perhaps truly modern yet not a genuine modern art form because it never results in a however 'eternal' or 'immovable' representation of the passing of time and its contingent content?

Countless are the lamentations that deplore the difficulty, even the sheer impossibility, of fixing or marking, through a notational system, the elusiveness of dance. Within the ballet tradition and beyond, it has often been said how frustrating it is that the event-quality of movements or poses transgresses 'the choreographic'. The constituent components of a dance score may be written and yet, as a primarily temporal art, dance continually erases itself in a way that is impossible to record or archive. Movement is 'being on the move', and this ontology can never be fully inscribed or translated into the space of 'the choreographic'. Dance's transitory presence resists every mode of transparent representation, even exceeds visibility, and is therefore condemned to be forgotten. 'What tests both vision and inscription to their limits is presence: presence unfolding as a mode of being whose temporality escapes scopic control, presence as haunted by invisibility, presence as sentencing to absence', André Lepecki writes of the still widely established view that dance unavoidably cancels itself out in a present that cannot be made present again in another medium. 'Mostly, movement disappears, it marks the passing of time. Movement is both sign and symptom that all presence is haunted by disappearance and absence.' *Dance is thus framed as continually vanishing, as an allegory of mourning that in a Baroque-like fashion signals the inevitable corruption of life by death.* There exists however another reading of the volatile character of dance. This counter-interpretation was also co-constitutive for modern dance and can still be heard very often among dancers.

Isadora Duncan or Martha Graham conceived their dancing not in relation to the idea of Death but as a joyous affirmation of Life. In this view, dance is a vital force grounded in human nature that exposes the richness or potentiality of life such that movement's temporal disappearance is surpassed. Dance is thus discursively positioned as a continual being present that effectively implies, like Baudelaire's definition of the art work capturing modernity, a however small flicker of eternity – an instant being lifted out of present time into an eternal now in which bodily movement reconnects with human nature. It is probably not accidental that this alternative framing of 'being on the move' is predominantly voiced by performers and exists as an established self-representation within the dance community. The spectator witnesses the appearance and disappearance, the simultaneous life and death of movements or poses; and meanwhile the dancer may experience the trance of being at once present and absent in the now, of both being immanent to linear time and transcending its continual ticking away. The two testimonies are of course imaginary constructs or identifications. The spectator and the dancer observe the same events via a different mirror, but neither reflection represents the essential nature of dance. How one deals with the temporal character of dance depends on how one frames 'the transient, the fleeting, the contingent'. One either sticks to the ontology implied by the linear conception of time or one experiences the now-event as both an ephemeral now and a temporal fold in this present that constitutes a streak of eternity. Are these however the only two existing alternatives? Can the temporality of dance or performance not be thought differently?

'Performance's only life is in the present. Performance cannot be saved, recorded, documented, or otherwise participate in the circulation of representations of representations: once it does so, it becomes something other than performance', asserts Peggy Phelan in the opening lines of her often quoted – and also repeatedly criticized – essay 'The Ontology of Performance'. Yet how absolute or integral is performance's presentness? In a dance work, movements or stillness do not only repeatedly appear and disappear in a present resisting representation, but also constantly refer to each other blindly or reflexively, through their implicit entwining or through repeated motions that make an explicit link with a previous dance action. The performed actions effectively condense into a long series and the consecutive elements of such an unfolding sequence entertain relations of difference. Every choreographer knows this of course. Within the space of 'the choreographic', he or she in fact tries to tame and rationalize the play of differences between the various temporal elements. The dance maker is indeed familiar with the general phenomenon of self-reference, or elements referring to other elements that are at once similar (they are for instance all dance components) and dissimilar (the particular gestures or poses differ).

Theatre dance is temporalized self-referentiality: each movement is the temporal other of one or more actions already performed or yet to be performed, to which that movement refers. The self-referential relationships between temporally different dance elements are constitutive of the presentness of every particular action. A dance event happens now (and here), and this present only exists because it differs from both a before and an after. This twofold differential relationship genuinely defines the action's actuality and is included in its temporal identity through the references to past and future movements or poses. In sum, *within a self-referential series of dance events, the presentness of every event instantiates the unity of the difference between before and after.* An action's actuality always condenses a non-actuality, made up of selective traces of the past and anticipations of the future. 'This interweaving results in each "element" ... being constituted on the basis of the trace within it of the other elements of the chain or system', notes Jacques Derrida. 'Nothing, neither among the elements nor within the system, is anywhere ever simply present or absent. There are only, everywhere, differences and traces of traces.' Self-referential relations to other movements and non-movements reposition every singular dance element as a condensation of temporal traces that is itself a trace. The element's presentness is internally split up since it is unavoidably marked by the difference between the temporal retention and protention conditioning its very actuality. The now-time of a singular event therefore does not resemble an absolute or self-contained point in time but on the contrary enacts – with an expression coined by Niklas Luhmann – 'the simultaneous of the non-simultaneous'. Yet this paradoxical temporality evidently does not exist as such but is completely conditioned by the activity of one or more *observers* operating with the distinction between 'before' and 'after'. The spectator(s), choreographer or performer(s) witnessing the movements and stillness indeed actively create the strange loop between past, present and future with more or less self-reflexivity. Actions just happen: they are temporally blind operations – and it is an observer who puts these events in an order that frames them as subsequent actions in time. We may intuitively, without further notice or reflection, apply the scheme of 'before' and 'after' that is implied by the observation of an action realized in the present – but the action itself knows nothing of all this: it happens, period.

To an observer, every danced action's singularity appears as an instantiation of an at once temporal and informational difference. Both are intrinsically interwoven in the spectator's gaze (including the gaze of a choreographer creating a dance work). An actual movement or stillness comes and goes in a continuously updated present or 'now' because it temporally differs from particular past actions and an imminent one; moreover, it contains the information that it has a different shape or 'content' – or not: a simple action is simply repeated in an identical fashion. A previous movement or pose is then reflexively self-referenced or quoted so that no new informational value emerges but rather an already existing one is confirmed. Yet even this literal repetition also creates a temporal difference that positions the action as genuinely different. All this has considerable consequences for every dance element's identity: the eventual meaning of a performed gesture or pose also depends on its differential relationships with past and yet-to-happen events. The sense or significance of an individual dance element thus remains always open. *The position within and contribution to the overall dance work of a particular movement or pose is constantly deferred* and incessantly marked by the possibility of a future redefinition – until the moment the dance definitively comes to a standstill and the choreography comes to an end. A pose, for instance, may be slightly repeated, then varied in a later section and acquire another significance than it had in the moment of its first occurrence. Only after the work is completely performed, the minimal or vast re-articulation of a dance action at a later moment in time stops being an ever present possibility; and only retrospectively, 'after the end' and 'after the facts', a stabilizing reading of all presented movements and non-movements making up a dance work becomes feasible. During the performance, every actual action is on the contrary co-defined by an open future announcing actions yet to come that may retroactively interfere with the identity of the presently performed one. What one momentarily sees is indeed a fleeting action – but it changes into a temporarily fixed one once the flow of movements comes to a halt.

Performing the Unity of Dance and Non-Dance

Like every choreography, *Rain* enacts a definition of the danceable, or movements and poses that may be legitimately taken up in and shown during a dance work. Through 'the choreographic' they are transformed into formal elements or marks that can be combined into ever new sequences, which are then put into longer series and simultaneously distributed over the stage space. Insofar as the actions have a corporeal nature, an always particular body image emerges, one that articulates the legitimate dancing body. Thus a defining trait of the vocabulary demonstrated in *Rain* and all other performances of De Keersmaeker is the multiple ways in which the dancers' arms are used: they draw all kinds of circular, straight or broken lines in an ever-changing fashion. Continually shifting, they are swayed away from the body in all possible directions, curved, angular or broken at the elbow and wrist, and then for a brief moment brought back again close to the body before moving once again. This consequent choreography of one or both arms goes together with a versatile articulation of the hands.

Short moments in which they seem to draw a figure in a way reminiscent of Eastern dance cultures are alternated with the hands being opened or closed, moving to the left or right... during slow or rapid, wave-like or angular movements of the arms. Hands and arms thus both appear as the basic elements defining the dancing body. Yet together with the face, these very same parts of the body also play a prime role in communication outside the realm of theatre. De Keersmaeker's 'written dance' indeed commits itself primarily to the corporeal parts that reveal in daily life *the body as a gesturing entity* that constantly accompanies verbal speech with shifting movements of the arms and hands, underlining or belying what is being said. At the same time, Rosas performances again and again transform this gesturing body into a genuine dancing one through movements that look artificial and made-up, that partially quote or hint at the basic positions of classical ballet, or resemble involuntary tics and other actions that are non-functional and devoid of expressivity.

The ballet tradition and the kind of 'pure dance' produced within the space of the danceable delineated by Merce Cunningham exposes the legitimate dancing body as predominantly moving upright, in extension, and also as skilful, elegant, graceful. The floor is therefore only used as the secure foundation for formalized steps and stretched pointes or as a springboard for masculine jumps — in a word: as allowing footwork. On the contrary, De Keersmaeker's choreographies use the floor both as a magnet or attractor and as a surface that can support various parts of the body in creating movements. *Rain* shows a striking variety of modes of falling and making corporeal contact with the dance floor. Hands, elbows, shoulders, the back, knees, the hip or the stomach all serve as possible points of contact with the ground, and also act as points of support for the moving body. They mediate between the floor and the weight of the body, thus taking over the function usually associated with the feet. The dancers not only do handstands with one or both arms, but also perform shoulder stands, back stands, hip stands... This sometimes brings the dance in the vicinity of popular genres such as hip hop, breakdance or capoeira, and now and then also of gymnastics. Also, the dance floor is used for sliding and doing all kinds of rolls including somersaults, or for brief choreographies with arms and legs while lying down. Jumps are anything but absent, yet they avoid the ballet register. The entire body is swayed in the air in an angular, slightly bent or oblique position; or the dancers jump with a straight torso and both arms swayed out while the legs define circular, balloon-like figures, or, by contrast, move in rapid succession. A similar variation characterizes the lifting of one dancer by another. The choreography in *Rain* mostly rehearses the dominant gender division within theatre dance, with a male performer lifting a female one, but the lifts never resemble the graceful handling of the female body known from ballet.

Together with the regular bending of the knees with closed or opened legs, the semi-spastic curving of the entire body and other distorting movements, *Rain* considerably re-frames the legitimate dancing body. Like most of De Keersmaeker's choreographies, this one operates with a rather inclusive notion of the danceable. De Keersmaeker's work is definitely post-ballet, yet it retains from the classical tradition the rhythmic pacing of movements or standstills and their formalization into repeatable marks within the space of 'the choreographic'. At the same time, the dancing body as represented in *Rain* — and again in many other works of Rosas — both includes and clearly exceeds the human body's quotidian repertory of gestures. *Rain* in fact exposes and foregrounds this difference through the conspicuous contrast between the repeated informal running, walking or standing still of the dancers and the various movements or poses they otherwise perform. The opening scene therefore has an emblematic value: while her co-performers predominantly engage in pedestrian movement, Fumiyo Ikeda dances the elaborated basic phrase three times. The dissimilarity between her controlled phrasing of a distinctly constructed series of divergent gestures or poses and the informal behaviour of the group corresponds with the difference between markedly danced movements and basic everyday activity. Ikeda's actions presuppose 'the choreographic' and a highly trained body; by contrast, the group's activity establishes a link with the mundane body of the average spectator. The relationship is certainly indirect and theatricalized. The dancers' dresses are hardly quotidian, and their paced collective walking, articulated running, or meditated stillness have a composed character that transcends 'the democratic body' within the work of Judson, for instance. Nevertheless, whereas Ikeda's movements situate the performance within a particular artistic tradition and genre, the group's actions at least hint at the performance's grounding within daily life.

Anne Teresa De Keersmaeker's dance work repeatedly exposes the double gesture of at once affirming the autonomy of choreographed dance and relating it to its supposed negation or 'outside', consisting of the generic human potential to move and not-move. The gesture seems to involve a genuine paradox since it looks both exclusive and inclusive, simultaneously delineates a particular space of the danceable and de-defines that very same territory. A structural difference is constructed but also deconstructed – as if one hand wants to outdo the distinction drawn by the other one. De Keersmaeker's work thus positions itself in a marked way within the field of contemporary dance (at least as it was tentatively conceptualized in the previous chapter). Her choreographies reflexively interiorize the binary opposition between dance and non-dance within the context of performances that clearly enact the maker's commitment to the value of 'written dance' while simultaneously showing its 'other side'. In this way, the basic distinction or code currently framing potential dance works is underlined, even performatively enacted. Yet in De Keersmaeker's choreographic work this difference does not change into a 'differend', or an irresolvable conflict, because in the final instance *the realm of corporeal daily life action or 'non-dance' is represented as the condition of possibility of 'written dance'*. The opposition between dance and a certain idea of non-dance is in this way not sublated or reconciled on a higher level, quite the contrary. Rather, a strange paradox emerges in that De Keersmaeker's oeuvre seems to exemplify the idea that a work of dance can be the unity of the difference between dance and non-dance. This implies a choreographic practice that is both resolutely contemporary and consistently does away with the notion of 'pure dance' by showing the general dependency of dance's medium on the universal human capacity to move or not-move.

The split identity of *Rain* and other choreographies by De Keersmaeker spills over to the dancing bodies performing the work. They embody the difference between choreographed dance and its quotidian other, since they enact both complex and simple actions. The dancing body is thus reframed as being at once highly skilled and ordinary. Through the controlled performance of elaborated movements and poses it distinguishes itself from the average spectator's body, yet in the many moments of simple walking and running, however theatricalized, the dancing body also communalizes with the viewing one. This body is evidently not just a sheer corporeal reality of well-trained flesh and bones.

Dancing in the Rosas style requires, among other things, a particular kind of concentration and a self-consciously controlled distribution of physical and mental energy. The dancing body is indeed a dancing subject, represented in *Rain* as a divided self. The Rosas dancer never merely states 'I dance', with the 'I' referring to a genuinely individualized capability, since there are also the movements or poses that activate the body as the locus of a generic human capacity to move or not-move, which is impersonal. 'I dance' therefore implies 'one dances', or rather: 'one just moves or stands still'. *The dancing subject in a Rosas choreography is precisely this nexus of 'I' and 'one', individuality and anonymity.* This mixed existence is of course anything but exceptional, since it also characterizes the activity of the speaking subject that singularizes with every new sentence a shared linguistic capacity. The split subjectivity of the dancing self presented in *Rain* exposes this general fission of subjectivity, or the fact that 'the subject consists of the permanent interweaving of pre-individual and individual characteristics; the subject is this interweaving. ... The subject is ... composite: "I", but also "one", unrepeatable uniqueness, but also anonymous universality", dixit Italian philosopher Paolo Virno.

Dance's Potentiality

A dance is not but continually *becomes:* movement comes after pose comes after movement... — with each new action entertaining self-referential relations with those already performed that inevitably cross out the possibility of a pure 'being present' and fundamentally subvert the dance element's self-identity. Simultaneously an internal time (and space) unfolds, a 'time in time' (and a 'space in space'), a *durée* that, in a choreographed dance performance, is actively composed through the temporally differentiated enactment of the 'dance text'. '[The] dance after all is merely a form of time, the creation of a kind of time, or of a very distinct and singular species of time', emphasizes Paul Valéry in his famous 1936 essay 'Philosophy of the Dance', adding that 'this person who is dancing encloses herself as it were in a time she engenders, a time consisting entirely of immediate energy, of nothing that can last.' This is the always particular own-time or internal time of a performance that elicits spectator experiences such as 'the dance goes fast' or 'the movement flow oscillates between restless activity and quietness' (as is the case in *Rain*). Common wisdom asserts that dance is a time-based art, yet choreography does not just make use of the medium of time in general but rather plays out, in a controlled way, the constructed own-time against linear time. 'Written dance' rationalizes the internal time that every performance creates in the course of its duration within the overall medium of linear time. *Choreographed dance is indeed the art of the orderly temporalizing of time, or marking time with time, through the premeditated re-introduction of time in time and the concomitant production of an own-time.*

The self-produced temporality connects the different elements defining a choreography over time: it assembles the various movements and poses that presently come and go into a distinctive trans-present. The constructed time zone defines the dance's temporal plane of consistency, which functions as the genuine equivalent of a musical refrain. The plane may look consonant or dissonant, predominantly harmonious or, on the contrary, capricious, fragmentary, bordering on falling apart. Whatever its nature, the own-time informing the linear now-time is first and foremost marked by the articulated use of rhythm plus the many melodies it contains in the form of longer phrases. Each choreography stands out because of its particular rhythms and singular melodies. Whereas the movement rhythms act as recurrent temporal motifs, the melodies or phrases create bodily landscapes, momentarily stretching out time. Both dimensions of a dance's own-time territorialize its individual elements through the location of the different actions within a common temporal plane beyond their divided actuality or presentness. This surface of course also acts as a spatial territory, since the self-referentially connected actions produce at once an own-time and an own-space, or a mobile 'movement architecture' specific to the dance work. The own-time reintroduces time in (linear) time; the own-space marks the space of the stage through the ever shifting construction of a spatial plane of consistency made up of self-produced lines, circles and spirals, curves and bends. A choreographic refrain is, in sum, a space-time consolidation of succession and coexistence and choreography may be defined as 'the ability to organize time and space with bodies pertaining, for instance, to sound'. The stipulation stems from an interview with Anne Teresa De Keersmaeker, in which she also says: 'Arrange time differently when you walk and you have dance.'

During a dance's becoming, a virtual subtext develops which does not consist of actually performed actions but comprises

movements or gestures that could have been momentarily produced in light of what actually took place. Each action indeed
opens up a potential or horizon of other dance possibilities that
also look plausible within the performance's context. Every present movement thus appears as a contingent selection, a principally groundless transition from 'what could happen' to 'what
actually happens' that endangers the action's persuasiveness.
A spectator may notice this threatening contingency and effectively observe that another movement was possible than the one
presently made. The outward shape of a just performed gesture for
instance surprises one: 'it was too discontinuous and does not accord well with the previous movements.' The observation not only
implies the existence of an expectation that anticipates a series of
actions, however cohesive and articulate. The surprised spectator
also perceives the dance's constructed character, or the fact that
at each moment a different action could have been enacted. The
alternatives continue to exist as a virtual potential that accompanies every moment as an at once absent and present reality. The
becoming of the dance is therefore a double happening, one that
takes place in present time and one that is located in a virtual time
and space. Continuously made selections, commonly attributed
to the choreographer, connect the dance's actuality and virtuality. A successful choreography transforms the observation of the
selections' contingency and manages to create the net impression
in the eye of a beholder that the witnessed movements and their
current entanglement are credible in light of their virtual coun-
terparts. Or as Niklas Luhmann aptly remarks in *Art as a Social
System:* '[Art works] must persist against the challenge that they
could be different. They convince by evoking alternative possibilities while neutralizing any preference for the forms not chosen.'

Every dance action allows the observer to see the difference between that which it is and the proverbial cloud made up of
equally possible actions: *dance's presentness is an event that instantiates, within the medium of movement and non-movement, the unity
of the difference between actuality and potentiality, 'what is' and
'what could be'.* The virtual potential does not consist of specific
actions but is doubly structured. It comprises, on the one hand,
danceable possibilities that are rather probable, given all previously performed movements and non-movements. These past actions are more or less recorded and remembered by an observer
witnessing the dance work or its coming into being, such as an

average spectator or a choreographer during a rehearsal process. The memorized movements and poses co-define in every present moment of a dance performance what may follow next. They delineate a horizon of actually danceable possibilities, or a genuine potential in which the dance's past structures its own future through a present virtuality. On the other hand, the immediate future of the choreography is articulated by the movement or pose enacted 'now, here', which also opens up a virtual space of alternatives or differences and reconfigures the overall potential. A next movement or stillness selectively realizes this potential, which acts as its condition of possibility. A present movement therefore does not just come and go: an actual action not only 'is' or 'was' but also selectively actualizes a 'may be', an at once temporalized and future-oriented potential conditioned by the performance's past. This structured horizon of possibilities is continuously re-performed and altered. What happens 'now, here' does not only erase itself according to the mode of 'it is happening and thus will have happened' since it also grounds itself through its momentary potential, renewing that which may happen. The time of the dance is perhaps not (only) allegorizing death but rather symbolizes the minimal hope or expectation that something may happen...

Exit: Undoing Modernism, Sending Off 'Pure Dance'
The expression has already been deconstructed several times — and yet: the dance work of Anne Teresa De Keersmaeker and Rosas continues to be associated with the notion of 'pure dance'. Among dance audiences, programmers and dance artists, the idea of 'pure dance' vaguely connotes choreographed dance that primarily foregrounds the formal qualities of movements and poses performed by skilful, mostly young dancers. It implies that the dance is usually set to a musical score; verbal text or video-images are in principle absent or their possible use only emphasizes the assumed purity of the dance. The common notion of 'pure dance' also highlights the self-referential entwinement of movements at the expense of narration and the representation of emotions. Not that the genre always has an austere character and is predominantly danced in an impassionate way, but any bodily expressivity looks — as in the work of De Keersmaeker — overall restrained and moderate. In sum, according to the prevailing view 'pure dance' emphasizes, on the one hand, the trained capacity of human bodies to perform articulated, complex movements and poses, and on

the other, illustrates a dance maker's ability to order consecutive corporeal actions within the realm of 'the choreographic', mostly in relation to music.

Although the expression is usually employed in a rather unreflexive way, the idea of 'pure dance' can be given a more conceptual twist by linking it to the broader notion of modernism. This is effectively done in American dance studies, less so in European scholarship. The arch-doyen and most staunch defender of the idea of artistic modernism was undoubtedly the American art critic Clement Greenberg. In his view, the modernist tendency within the arts signals the sustained search for the medial essence underlying a particular artistic practice. Art first became modern with the advent of Western modernity, or the emergence of a society in which the various arts developed at an uneven pace into autonomous social spheres that are in principle, yet not at every historical moment, also de facto autonomous, free from political, religious or other external interferences. Modern art, Greenberg argues, transformed into modernist art through the intensification of the self-critical trend within every aesthetic genre to strip away those features that are not exclusive to it. The canonical story of modernism is therefore one of reduction or 'less is more', because it allows an artistic practice to concentrate on its defining medium. 'The task of self-criticism became to eliminate from the specific effects of each art any and every effect that might conceivably be borrowed from or by the medium of any other art', Greenberg asserts in his classic essay 'Modernist Painting' (1961). 'Thus would each art be rendered "pure", and in its "purity" find the guarantee of its standards of quality as well as of its independence.' This idea of modernism actually translates the notion of subjectivity into the realm of the arts. To be an autonomous subject means to be self-foundational, or to find the basis for personal opinions, individual intentions or wilful actions solely in one's self. In an analogous way, an art practice acquires a modernist identity insofar as it radically affirms its medial autonomy as its only foundation. In painting, modernism first resulted in non-narrative abstraction with Cubism, yet from American Abstract Expressionism or so-called Colour Field Painting onwards — which Greenberg clearly wanted to legitimate with his writings — the flatness of the painted surface became the presupposed medial essence of painting. Modernist painting was 'pure painting', and 'pure painting' was visible paint-on-canvas. And nothing more, stated the reigning American orthodoxy installed by Greenberg around the beginning of the 1960s. Did there also exist a modernist practice within dance around that time?

The abstract ballets of George Balanchine may be invoked as strongly exemplifying Greenberg's idea of modernism, since their author was the first to take up the 'tension between weight and weightlessness ... as the concealed essence of the ballet art, and especially as the essence of the phenomenon of grace', states the American philosopher David Michael Levin in the opening lines of his seminal 1973 article on 'Balanchine's Formalism'. Or one can point out that 'by using movement that is unequivocally dancerly to the naked eye, Cunningham tends to show us the quiddity of pure dance'; and one may strengthen this argument by adding that 'Cunningham's refusal to integrate the dance seamlessly with the music is another symptom of his modernist commitments.' This idea is put forward by the American dance scholars Sally Banes and Noël Carroll writing in 2006 on 'Cunningham, Balanchine, and Postmodern Dance'. Other possible candidates are Vaslav Nijinsky's at the time revolutionary choreography on *Le Sacre du Printemps* or even the overtly narrative and expressive approach of Martha Graham, which is commonly regarded as a prime instance of modern dance. Like in the other arts, dance's modernism is indeed not one but many things since it does not involve an abstract, let alone transhistorical medial essence of choreographed dance. During the twentieth century, the notion of 'pure dance' was shaped in relation to divergent dance mediums in the socio-cultural sense, so with respect to quite varied definitions of the danceable, which unavoidably resulted in multiple modernisms. Whereas Nijinsky and Balanchine choreographed within the ballet tradition, Graham thought she had discovered dance's essence in a purified kind of physical expressivity. And Cunningham is yet another story, one that starts after modern dance — hence the often repeated notion that he is the father of postmodern dance — but that is marked as well by the selective appropriation of several parameters of classical ballet. In sum, 'pure dance' or the choreographic endeavour that brings the quest for the medial essence of dance once and for all to an end, simply does not exist. *Every form of danced modernism or 'pure dance' is made impure by the necessary presupposition of cultural conventions with respect to what constitutes dance's prime medium.* A similar opinion was actually already put forward in the 1960s by another strong voice in the once vivid debate on modernism à la Greenberg within the fine arts. In 'Art and Objecthood', his fierce attack on Minimalism published in 1967, Michael Fried acknowledges that 'the essence of painting is not something irreducible. Rather, the task of the modernist painter is to discover those conventions that, at a given moment, *alone* are capable of establishing his work's identity as painting.' Yet historicizing modernism, and thus contaminating the idea of artistic self-foundation with a firm dose of external contingency, is perhaps not the most decisive gesture subverting the notion of 'pure dance'.

'When you're a performing artist, the idea of an audience counts anyway. In that case, the individuality of your art involves a kind of surplus that can only exist in a confrontation, a sharing with the audience. Perhaps this goes for all the arts, but the issue is the most immediate when you're performing live. You're physically on stage and being looked at', De Keersmaeker once said in an interview. Rosas works foreground in various ways that the performing of choreographed dance takes place before a witnessing public. Therefore the dancers are allowed to slightly theatricalize their dancing identities, or to perform actions that explicitly address the audience's gaze, witness *Rosas danst Rosas* and many subsequent works. Even in *Rain* and other choreographies that come closest to the common notion of 'pure dance', the performing style regularly accentuates the dance's public character. They also contain several actions that self-reflexively take into account the audience's existence. For example, the dancers walk in a straight line to the proscenium and overtly face the public: they look back, answering the spectator's gaze. Or the visual relationship between the stage and the theatre hall is symbolically doubled on stage, through situations where some dancers stop to look while one or more co-performers continue dancing. Moreover, the staging of De Keersmaeker's choreographies is in general oriented towards the audience. Frontally performed movements do not dominate but the overall spatial plane of consistency, or the mobile architecture erected within the choreographies' own-space, often supposes a visual field that is at least partly structured by the logic of perspective.

Rosas performances underline that a dancer's main mode of 'public being' is that of being watched. Within the general context of dance performed in a theatre, the dancers move and stand still in an articulated way before an audience made up mostly of strangers. Their individual actions are looked at and examined: they incessantly perform within an anonymous scopic field. Even if the dance visibly avoids the register of the spectacular, the performance remains in the literal sense of the word a spectacle: a series of actions that is deliberately staged in order to be seen. Notwithstanding its often taken for granted existence, the audience's presence principally deconstructs the idea of 'pure dance' or 'pure movement'. For *in theatre dance, 'pure dance' is unavoidably rendered impure by the fact of its being watched.* Spectators may have the idea that they are enjoying a splendid moment of 'pure dance' – yet their very presence transforms the contemplated actions into something else: the being-looked-at intrinsically negates the supposedly pure essence of the dance. Movements and non-movements indeed no longer solely actualize the medium of dance, since they are thoroughly remediated within the medium of 'the visual'. However, theatre dance nearly always self-reflexively anticipates this remediation in the choreographic score and, particularly, the performing style. The dance may look cool or exuberant, moderate or withdrawn... Whatever its defining quality, the performance takes into account the presence of the audience. The rather implicit or more explicit incorporation of the audience's anonymous gaze may even supplement the medium of dance with the medium of 'the visual' in such a profound way that 'the visual' turns out to be as essential as the dance's medial essence.

The live situation is constitutive for the life of theatre dance. For it is the spectators who observe with more or less perspicacity the non-realized possibilities that populate the virtual space unfolded during a performance. They perceive plausible links or, alternatively, discern unconvincing gaps between successive movements by relating actual events to plausible alternatives, 'that which is' to 'that which could have been'. During a performance this virtual space of danceable possibilities is an at once present and absent reality whose genuine existence depends on the observer. In the end, an ontology of the virtual does not exist in the strict sense, and nor does a split mode of being marked by the division between actuality and potentiality. There is just *virtuology, or the virtual possibility of a virtual observer perceiving a virtual space of possibilities in actual actions* of any nature. And it is also the spectator who continually distinguishes 'before' from 'after', thus noticing self-referentially linked movements or non-movements and presently performed actions. The viewer's presence makes the dance present: *no presence without co-presence* since an event only becomes present when witnessed. The spectator watches the dance — and the dance watches the spectator, a Lacanian psychoanalyst would add. Between the observer and the observed something takes place: a particular relation is established and reproduced that allows the observation of presently happening dance actions, for instance. Presentness is therefore both a temporal and a relational category. 'Presence refers to the kinetic structure through which that which is present germinates as something that enters in a space of encounter. Presence is movement in the sense of a drama of arrival, creation and reception. ... Presence is only given where there is human existence, and existence is only given where there is human coming-into-the-world', as the German philosopher Peter Sloterdijk notes in his book *Eurotaoismus*. The coming-into-the-world of dance is its being watched, which is probably the proper meaning of 'sharing with the audience' (De Keersmaeker).

Sources

Re-Viewing *Fase*
The description of *Fase* is partly
based on a video registration of one
of the performances at deSingel in
Antwerp in June 1997, danced by
Anne Teresa De Keersmaeker and
Michèle Anne De Mey. I moreover relied on personal recollections of two
performances by this original cast in
1982 (Stuk, Leuven) and June 1997
(deSingel, Antwerp), as well as two
performances in Brussels by De
Keersmaeker and Tale Dolven
in March 2007 at the Rosas
Performance Space and in March
2011 at the Kaaitheater, respectively.
The presented analysis retakes, at
times verbatim, some of the insights
already put forward in Marianne Van
Kerkhoven and Rudi Laermans, *Anne
Teresa De Keersmaeker*. Brussels:
Flemish Theatre Institute, 1998,
pp. 9-10. A more detailed examination of the score by De Keersmaeker
herself, complemented with her
comments on the work's genesis and
visual demonstrations of its constituent elements on the accompanying
DVD, can be found in Anne Teresa
De Keersmaeker and Bojana Cvejić,
*A Choreographer's Score. Fase, Rosas
danst Rosas, Eleana's Aria, Bartok*.
Brussels: Mercatorfonds, 2012. Steve
Reich's cited essay 'Notes on Music
and Dance' is reprinted in Roger
Copeland and Marshall Cohen
(eds.), *What is Dance? Readings in
Theory and Criticism*. Oxford: Oxford
University Press, 1983, pp. 336-338
(pp. 336-337).

Minimal Dance and/as Repetition
A synthetic overview of 'the minimal-
ist moment' in dance is still lacking.
For a perceptive discussion of 1960s
Minimalism in the fine arts, see the
chapter 'The Crux of Minimalism'
in Hal Foster, *The Return of the
Real. The Avant-Garde at the End
of the Century*. Cambridge (MA):
MIT Press, 1996, pp. 35-70. Yvonne
Rainer's essay 'A Quasi Survey of
Some "Minimalist" Tendencies in
the Quantitatively Minimal Dance
Activity Midst the Plethora, or an
Analysis of *Trio A*' can be consulted
in the anthology edited by Roger
Copeland and Marshall Cohen, *What
is Dance?*, pp. 325-332 (p. 331).

**Intermezzo: Defining
'the Choreographic'**
Michel de Certeau unfolds his
stimulating view on the modern
scriptural economy in *The Practice
of Everyday Life*. Berkeley (CA):
University of California Press, 1988,
pp. 131-153 (p. 134; italics in the
original). William Forsythe's statement on the virtual nature of ballet
is borrowed from Gerald Siegmund,
*Abwesenheit. Eine performative
Ästhetik des Tanzes. William Forsythe,
Jérôme Bel, Xavier Le Roy, Meg Stuart*.
Bielefeld: transcript Verlag, 2006,
p. 255. Jacques Derrida's definition
of iterability as the structural possibility to repeat every kind of mark
stems from *Limited Inc*. Evanston
(IL): Northwestern University Press,
1988, p. 47.

Embodying Structure
Claude Lévi-Strauss summarizes his
approach of myths in 'The Structural
Analysis of Myth', included in Claude
Lévi-Strauss, *Structural Anthropology*.
New York (NY): Basic Books, 1974,
pp. 206-232. Michel Foucault, *The
Order of Things*. New York (NY):
Vintage, 1970, is quoted page
342. In his two-volume *History of
Structuralism* (Minneapolis (MN):
University of Minnesota Press, 1998),
François Dosse offers an extensive
contextualization of 'the moment of
French structuralism'. Sally Banes'
characterization of Yvonne Rainer's
Trio A can be found in her book
*Terpsichore in Sneakers. Post-Modern
Dance*. Middletown (CT): Wesleyan
University Press, 1987, p. 50.
Reference is also made to Philippe
Guisgand's detailed description of
Fase in his study *Les fils d'un entrelacs
sans fin. La danse dans l'oeuvre d'Anne
Teresa De Keersmaeker*. Villeneuve
d'Ascq: Presses universitaires du
Septentrion, 2007, p. 31.

Choreographing the Ordinary
The analysis of *Rosas danst Rosas* in
this paragraph and the next is based
on personal memories of the following showings: the performance with
the original cast, consisting of Anne
Teresa De Keersmaeker, Adriana
Borriello, Michèle Anne De Mey
and Fumiyo Ikeda, during the first
Klapstuk dance festival in Leuven,
October 1983; two performances

in Warsaw in October 1995 danced by Cynthia Loemij, Sarah Ludi, Anne Mousselet and Samantha Van Wissen; the performance at the Brussels Kaaitheater in February 2009 with De Keersmaeker, Cynthia Loemij, Sarah Ludi and Samantha van Wissen; and the showing at, again, the Kaaitheater in March 2011 with Sandra Ortega Bejarano, Tale Dolven, Elizaveta Penkóva and Sue-Yeon Youn. I also relied on a video registration of a performance in June 1995 in the Kaaitheater (same cast as the one in Warsaw), the extensive analysis of *Rosas danst Rosas* in Philippe Guisgand, *Les fils d'un entrelacs sans fin,* pp. 32–41, and the short characterization in Marianne Van Kerkhoven and Rudi Laermans, *Anne Teresa De Keersmaker,* pp. 10–12 (which is retaken verbatim a couple of times). De Keersmaeker herself gives an elaborate presentation and visual demonstration of the choreography's components and overall logic in Anne Teresa De Keersmaeker and Bojana Cvejić, *A Choreographer's Score. Fase, Rosas danst Rosas, Eleana's Aria, Bartok.*

Denis Diderot's distinction between theatricality and absorption is discussed at length in Michael Fried, *Absorption and Theatricality. Painting and the Beholder in the Age of Diderot.* Chicago (IL): University of Chicago Press, 1970. Yvonne Rainer's '"No" to Spectacle...' is reprinted in Alexandra Carter (ed.), *The Routledge Dance Studies Reader.* London: Routledge, 1998, p. 35. Hal Foster underlines repetition's subversive nature regarding representation in the already mentioned essay 'The Crux of Minimalism', p. 63. The hinted at distinction between strategy (the space of 'the choreographic') and tactics (the personal appropriation by the performers of the produced choreographic marks) stems from Michel de Certeau, *The Practice of Everyday Life.*

Differential Dance
Reference is made to Philippe Guisgand, *Les fils d'un entrelacs sans fin,* p. 41.

'Being a Woman'
The following publications are quoted: Yvonne Rainer,

'A Quasi-Survey...', p. 328; Judith Butler, *Gender Trouble. Feminism and the Subversion of Identity.* London: Routledge, 1999, p. 173 (italics in the original); Laura Mulvey, 'Visual Pleasure and Narrative Cinema', in Philip Rosen (ed.), *Narrative, Apparatus, Ideology. A Film Theory Reader.* New York (NY): Columbia University Press, 1986, pp. 198–209 (p. 203; italics in the original); and Luce Irigaray, *This Sex Which Is Not One.* Ithaca (NY): Cornell University Press, 1985, p. 76.

Phrasing Movements, Virtualizing a Phrase
The analysis of *Rain* in this paragraph and a next one is informed by recollections of one of the performances during the premiere series at La Monnaie/De Munt in Brussels in January 2001 and a video registration of one of the showings at the Rotterdam Schouwburg in May 2001. In both performances the original cast was involved: Martha Coronado, Igor Shyshko, Alix Eynaudi, Fumiyo Ikeda, Cynthia Loemij, Ursula Robb, Taka Shamoto, Clinton Stringer, Rosalba Torres, and Jakub Truszkowski. I also attended the re-staging of *Rain* by the Paris Opera Ballet in May 2011, which is documented in the 2012 film of the same name, produced by Savage Film (Brussels) and directed by Olivia Rochette and Gerard-Jan Claes (with the participation of Anne Teresa De Keersmaeker). An in-depth examination of the score by De Keersmaeker herself can be found in Anne Teresa De Keersmaeker and Bojana Cvejić, *A Choreographer's Score. Drumming & Rain.* Brussels: Mercatorfonds, 2014. For a more detailed discussion of the association between phrasing and singing, inspired by recent works of De Keersmaeker, see Rudi Laermans, 'Intimating Intimacy: Movement's Singing, Singing's Movement', in Ilse Den Hond (ed.), *Hear My Voice. Three Essays on 'Keeping Still', 'The Song' and '3Abschied'.* Brussels: Rosas, 2011, pp. 15–36. The 'ontology of the virtual' presented at the end of the paragraph is primarily inspired by Niklas Luhmann's approach of the distinction between actuality and potentiality as developed in *Social Systems.* Stanford (CA):

Stanford University Press, 1995 and other writings such as *Art as a Social System*. Stanford (CA): Stanford University Press, 2000 and *Theory of Society. Volume 1*. Stanford (CA): Stanford University Press, 2013. Luhmann's view is loosely combined with the overall divergent Deleuzian framing of the difference between the actual and the virtual; see for instance Gilles Deleuze's short essay 'Immanence: A Life' in Gilles Deleuze, *Pure Immanence. Essays on a Life*. New York (NY): Zone Books, 2002, pp. 25–34 and several of the essays in Brian Massumi, *Parables for the Virtual. Movement, Affect, Sensation*. Durham (NC): Duke University Press, 2002.

Intermezzo: The Temporalities of Dance
References are made to Charles Baudelaire, 'The Painter of Modern Life', in Charles Baudelaire, *Selected Writings on Art and Literature*. London: Penguin, 1992, pp. 390–436 (p. 403); Gabriele Brandstetter, *Tanz-Lektüren: Körperbilder und Raumfiguren der Avantgarde*. Frankfurt am Main: Fischer, 1995, p. 36 (italics in the original); André Lepecki, 'Inscribing Dance', in André Lepecki (ed.), *Of the Presence of the Body. Essays on Dance and Performance Theory*. Middletown (CT): Wesleyan University Press, 2004, pp. 124–139 (p. 128); Peggy Phelan, 'The Ontology of Performance: Representation without Reproduction', in Peggy Phelan, *Unmarked. The Politics of Performance*. London: Routledge, 2006, pp. 146–166 (p. 146); Jacques Derrida, 'Semiology and Grammatology: Interview with Julia Kristeva', in Jacques Derrida, *Positions*. Chicago (IL): University of Chicago Press, 1981, pp. 16–36 (p. 26); and Niklas Luhmann, 'Gleichzeitigkeit und Synchronisation', in Niklas Luhmann, *Soziologische Aufklärung 5. Konstruktivistische Perspektiven*. Opladen: Westdeutscher Verlag, 1990, pp. 95–130 (p. 100). The approach presented at the end of the paragraph is inspired by other writings of Niklas Luhmann as well, such as the aforementioned *Social Systems,* and by Armin Nassehi,

Die Zeit der Gesellschaft. Auf dem Weg zu einer soziologischen Theorie der Zeit. Wiesbaden: Verlag für Sozialwissenschaften, 2008. For a more straightforward 'Luhmannian' view on the temporality of dance, see Rudi Laermans, 'Choreographing the Temporality of Movement (or, the present crossing out of presence)', in Gurur Ertem and Noémie Solomon (eds.), *Dance on Time*. Istanbul: Bimeras Publications, 2010, pp. 10–17.

Performing the Unity of Dance and Non-Dance
The use of the expression 'democratic body' in relation to the work of Judson implicitly refers to Sally Banes, *Democracy's Body. Judson Dance Theater, 1962–1964*. Durham (NC): Duke University Press, 1993. Paolo Virno's quoted characterization of the subject as a mixture of individuality and anonymity stems from his book *A Grammar of the Multitude. For an Analysis of Contemporary Forms of Life*. Los Angeles (CA): Semiotext(e), 2004, p. 78 (italics in the original).

Dance's Potentiality
This paragraph is predominantly inspired by Niklas Luhmann, *Art as A Social System*, which is also cited toward the end p. 92. The Valéry quote can be found in Paul Valéry, 'Philosophy of the Dance', in Roger Copeland and Marshall Cohen (eds.), *What is Dance?*, pp. 55–65 (p. 59). The notion of plane of consistency and its further framing in terms of rhythms and melodies is loosely borrowed from Gilles Deleuze and Félix Guattari, *A Thousand Plateaus. Capitalism and Schizophrenia*. London: Continuum, 2003 (particularly the chapter 'On the Refrain', pp. 310–350). For the quotes from Anne Teresa De Keersmaeker on choreography and dance, see Rudi Laermans, 'Sharing Experience. An Interview with Anne Teresa De Keersmaeker', in Pascal Gielen and Paul De Bruyne (eds.), *Being an Artist in Post-Fordist Times*. Rotterdam: NAi Publishers, 2009, pp. 81–96 (pp. 88–89 and p. 94).

Exit: Undoing Modernism, Sending Off 'Pure Dance'
The following publications are quoted: Clement Greenberg, 'Modernist Paining', in Francis Frascina and

Jonathan Harris (eds.), *Art in Modern Culture. An Anthology of Critical Texts*. London: Phaidon Press, 1992, pp. 308–314 (p. 309); David Michael Levin, 'Balanchine's Formalism', in Roger Copeland and Marshall Cohen (eds.), *What is Dance?*, pp. 123–144 (p. 123); Sally Banes and Noël Carroll, 'Cunningham, Balanchine, and Postmodern Dance', in *Dance Chronicle*, 29 (1), 2006, pp. 49–68 (p. 58 and p. 59); Michael Fried, 'Art and Objecthood', in Michael Fried, *Art and Objecthood. Essays and Reviews*. Chicago (IL): University of Chicago Press, 1998, pp. 148–172 (p. 169; italics in the original); Rudi Laermans, 'Sharing Experience', p. 84; and Peter Sloterdijk, *Eurotaoismus. Zur Kritik der politische Kinetik*. Frankfurt am Main: Suhrkamp, 1996, p. 149.

Re/Presenting the Body
Glosses on the Work of Meg Stuart & Damaged Goods

First Movement: *Disfigure Study* and *No Longer Readymade*, or Gesturing the Body

Studying the Body

Meg Stuart made her debut as a choreographer in October 1991 with *Disfigure Study*, originally danced by herself, Carlota Lagido and Francisco Camacho to music composed and performed live by the New York based musician Hahn Rowe. The work has meanwhile been staged with different casts; in 2002, Rowe also created a new, electronic-based score that greatly differs from the original one, which was dominated by rhythmic guitar chords. During the fifth edition of the Klapstuk festival in Leuven, the performance's premiere immediately caused a stir among the audience. The opening act already promised another kind of dance, one that rather drastically reframed the human body's capacity to act as a medium of movements and non-movements. As the theatre hall darkens, a pair of lower legs and feet appear in a spotlight centre stage. The feet caress each other and the lower legs. Suddenly, a head appears, kisses the feet and disappears again. A moment later the improbable kiss is repeated and the head starts to nuzzle and fondle the feet. Only the head is visible, the other body parts stay in the dark. Both feet and lower legs mostly resist the caressing; sometimes the limbs embrace the head in a way that resembles a stranglehold, at other times the head is supported in a pieta-like position. It looks overall as if head and limbs have emancipated themselves from their bodies and dialogue with each other as little quasi-subjects. 'Thought Object', the first longer section of *Disfigure Study*, creates a similar situation. A left arm and hand crawl over a back, while the rest of the body once again remains invisible. Suddenly the body turns toward the public and a female face appears. It is a defining moment in the performance: first only an anonymous corporeality exists, then a singular human body with a recognizable face emerges. The scene continues for some time with the performer remaining in the same position while making all sorts of angular bending and twisting movements with arms and hands at an alternately slow and fast pace.

'Held', the second section, opens with a female dancer holding another one by the neck and head. The supporting body lays the passive one down on the floor and a series of manipulations follows: the inert body is put in a half upright position, turned around, dropped down, or dragged across the floor. At the end, both performers lie next to each other as if sleeping. Suddenly, the till then inactive body turns away from the manipulating one: a proverbial sign of life? Throughout the entire scene, motion is framed as moving a motionless corpse that is mere weight or pure matter, with the neck and head as the only contact points of the manipulations. The most human part of the body is again foregrounded, yet the face of the manipulated body remains impassive. Frozen into a meaningless grimace, the face resembles a death mask.

At the beginning of the third part of *Disfigure Study*, entitled 'Phebe Street', a male dancer performs a solo of arms and hands. Besides many other twisting movements, both limbs recurrently make curling gestures around the neck. After some time, two female dancers come into the picture. A small beam of light shows them lying on the floor upstage left, doing turns and other movements, partly in unison. The dance fades out and one of the women, her freedom of movement highly restricted, starts to creep towards the man. Once the female performer has reached the male one, the latter stands up. Calm and matter-of-factly, without any sign of recognition or aversion, he walks away and lies down elsewhere on the stage. The female dancer renews the creeping and he once more rises when she comes near him. The situation is repeated several times at a quickening pace and in a register that avoids the symbolic or the dramatic. The faces seem again frozen or mask-like, without a single sign of emotion: the outward body is exposed as a merely physical reality devoid of psychological depth or expressivity. This general impression is confirmed by *Disfigure Study*'s closing section, which begins with a solo by one of the female dancers. For some time, her right hand and fingers move in and around her mouth at a rapid pace until her sustaining right arm is violently swept backward and a choreography starts to develop that is dominated by swirling arm movements. In the second part, the male performer stands with his back to the spectators, the female dancer standing next to him, frontally facing the audience, deadpan. The man touches the woman's body with the fingers of his right hand, including her feet, in a sporadically violent way. The woman sometimes resists these actions but overall she undergoes them with an impassive body and look.

The word 'study' in the performance's title has a programmatic meaning and links *Disfigure Study* with a longstanding tradition within the visual arts. In drawing, painting and

sculpture it is indeed customary to make studies of the human body. *Disfigure Study* frequently hints at the gaze of the visual artist observing the human body with a distant and neutral, objectifying attitude. The performance recreates on stage the visual field that corresponds to the detailed looking of the cartoonist, painter or sculptor who is drawn to a hardly perceptible fold of skin or becomes intrigued by a model's somewhat uncommon posture. What makes this implied gaze most apparent is the predominant interest in the sheer physicality of the outward body. The body's corporeality changes into an autonomous medium of a physical expressivity that remains detached from any possible underlying inner states or psychological motives. In sum, the movements, poses and surfaces of the outer body only signify physical states in the studious looking of the visual artist. In *Disfigure Study* and later works, Meg Stuart both retakes and displaces this *aesthetic behaviourism or corporeal materialism* within the realm of the performing arts. It is indeed done in a disfiguring mode that shows strong affinities with a modern, resolutely post-academic tradition of visually rendering the body.

The academic or neo-classical regime stuck to a Platonic epistemology: the representation of the human body had to highlight a transhistorical, ideal bodily essence. Contingent deviations from this perfect contour had to be negated as much as possible in the actually drawn, painted or sculpted human being. Beauty and Truth were still considered to be one, yet the visually represented body also contained an edifying moral lesson: 'this is how one should look'. The classical ballet body enacts this very same association between aesthetics, ethics and metaphysics (in the literal sense: an ideal corporeal form at once informing and transcending observable physical reality). The erected, meticulously self-controlled body of the ballet dancer – which nowadays looks highly artificial – once performed the elite belief that the perceivable human corporeality is only the pale incarnation of an ideal body that art could at least make partly visible.

Like modern art, modern dance decidedly broke with the premises underlying the academic regime of representation. Whereas Isadora Duncan or Mary Wigman betted on the possibility of expressing human nature's vitality through a supposedly unrestrained motion, the fine arts opted for the truth-value of the often ugly, contorted or mutilated body. *Disfigure Study* transposes this modern visual tradition to the stage without the accompanying claim of representing the true nature of the body. Rather, human corporeality is rearranged according to a constructivist spirit that primarily perceives alternative movement possibilities. The painterly work of Francis Bacon, an influence acknowledged by Stuart herself, is an obvious counterpart in the visual arts. Although the bodies in Bacon's pictures look recognizable and supersede any connotation of 'dirty realism', they also appear as a strange kind of 'facialized' flesh. Bacon's bodies, twisting apart at right angles, at once stand out within twentieth-century art and are part of a broader historical configuration that comprises, for instance, the later work of Oskar Kokoschka or 'a certain Picasso'. With occasionally overt references to this tradition, *Disfigure Study* maintains a primarily visual logic of representing the body that painting and sculpture, and to a lesser extent also photography and film, have explored throughout the twentieth century. Yet what precisely comes to the fore in this re-visioning of human physicality within the medium of dance?

Constructivist Choreography

Bodies do matter in a twofold way within a society or culture. They literally matter: they materially enact and exemplify the hegemonic notion of the 'normal' human body. Therefore our corporeality, for instance, conforms to the idea of an integrated or unified organism that is controlled by invisible coordinating movements (taking place in the consciousness, as the modern notion of the subject contends; or solely in the brain, as contemporary neuropsychology suggests). Through the repeated materializing of a culture's ontology of the human body, the particular shape and posture of this symbolic figure becomes normalized, even naturalized. The socially sanctioned culturalized body is actually a performed normative construct but it does not appear that way because it continuously 'matters' in daily life, not to mention in the countless standardized images of female and male bodies appearing in the various mass media. Yet bodies also matter figuratively: they concern us, they are not a matter of indifference. Publicly observable bodies reassure insofar as they are easily legible and more or less fit the prevalent script. Normal bodies possess a familiar intelligibility and inspire confidence thanks to a physicality that behaves according to the dominant symbolic regime. Disfigured, queering or otherwise 'abnormal' bodies often elicit feelings of uneasiness, since they publicly question the supposedly natural identity of the human body as an integrated organism of this and not that sex. Such bodies materially deconstruct the premised ontology that informs the literal and figurative 'mattering' of the body. They are also frequently experienced as personally threatening: an illegible corporeality subverts our identification with an at once gendered and cohesive body image.

Whereas much theatre dance thoughtlessly enacts, even glorifies, the overriding symbolic body, Stuart takes up 'the choreographic' as a space in which the common corporeal script can be critically rewritten and overwritten. Her choreographies are made up of contorted and awkward gestures, out-of-joint positions and seemingly out-of-control movements – in sum: a broken or fragmented physicality that undoes the human body as an integrated whole. Not that Stuart celebrates the dismembered or imploded body in a fetishist mode. She rather focuses on the human body as having an only supposedly normal shape and unity, which can be both estranged and reconfigured, for instance by bestowing the limbs or arms with an autonomous life. In doing so, she exhibits the human body for further examination as a revisable cultural form and movement potential, all without any utopian or dystopian intent. *Disfigure Study* and later performances do not want to show 'the real, hidden side' of human corporeality nor do they exemplify alternative modes of being a body that critically unmask the hegemonic discourse in view of a liberated physicality. There is never a trace of obscenity, nor the kind of deliberately provocative logic that informed most performance art of the 1970s, as well as the ritual actions staged by the Viennese Actionists. In the same vein, hints of profanation of the body in the name of a more authentic representation of its presupposed realness are also missing. Rather, Stuart's work opens up another space of corporeality in which the living 'corpus' enters new states of reality.

Stuart's corporeal constructivism renews the notion of the danceable by *relocating the medium of dance from the body as an organism or structured totality to single corporeal zones or strata* that can be treated independently. This redefinition rests on the twofold operation of analysing – in the sense of dividing – and resynthesizing the human body within the space of 'the choreographic'. On the one hand, human corporeality is split up in isolated entities whose activity is no longer over-coded by the organism's assumingly normal kinetic organization. The separated components each possess a capacity to move that can be choreographically articulated by disregarding as much as physically possible the corporeal unity that supports the foregrounded limbs, torso, mouth... On the other hand, the individual body parts are made to move and are coupled with each other according to artificial logics that also negate the idea of the body as an integrated organism with a fixed contour. New assemblages may be constructed that magnify bodily connections partly known from everyday life, such as moving your hand across your mouth or the spiralling of a hand that repeatedly touches, rests on or caresses the hip.

The body exposed in Stuart's performances often looks self-alienated or in profound disagreement with itself, because the choreographed situations are frequently in tension with the habits of a more unified body. Again and again, the dancing body is put into a state of friction by performing movements that are difficult to execute. In each such moment, a physical paradox emerges and is visibly enacted: the choreographed actions are in principle performable but they go against the grain of the functionally organized body and the dancer's trained capacities. This body-in-conflict becomes the surface for a purely physical expressivity that is greatly fostered by the performer's effort to stick to the troubling action. One could also say that the dancing body temporarily 're-matters' its usual materialization. 'The bodies in my pieces are constantly negotiating their boundaries, often their centre has exploded — it's all over the place, shifting, transferring', said Stuart in a 2008 conversation with visual artist Catherine Sullivan. Indeed, during a Stuart performance, the performers bodies seem to be continuously on the move within a virtual space of physical possibilities situated beyond the prevailing symbolic organization of human corporeality. No new identity starts to dominate the dancers' motion, nor do their bodies ever come to themselves but incessantly go on incorporating different modes of corporeality. 'Being a body' thus changes into a ceaseless exploration of the virtual multiplicity of the corporeal: an ongoing 're-mattering' and 're-embodying', *the continuous production of yet another body within the material medium of one's own body.* Or as Gerald Siegmund perceptively remarks in his analysis of Stuart's work: 'Their [the dancers'] bodies stand in a difference to themselves because they only exist as differences.'

Although at first sight the movements and poses displayed in Stuart's performances look rather uncommon and even weird, many of them do actually connect with actions known from ordinary life. Thus the dancing body that moves in a restrained or muzzled way has a well-known everyday equivalent. Crawling across the floor, moving one's legs with one's hands, carefully shuffling through the house — this is the behaviour of the handicapped, chronically ill, and other kinetically disturbed bodies. Stuart generalizes their uncommon ways of moving within the context of a choreographic stance that does not feel obliged by the prevalent norm in theatre dance to present the human body as highly agile and hyper-movable. The scenic emancipation of limbs has a real-world counterpart also. Autonomously moving body parts evoke the functioning of corporeal tics in the broad sense: the usually unconscious reflex actions of feet or legs, the pointless fiddling of hands and fingers with one's hair or clothes, the uncontrolled fidgeting of a child on the edge of a chair... With a tic, part of the body moves independently from individual consciousness and established standards of behaviour. Just as with an uncontrolled burst of laughter, one or more limbs become mechanically autonomous and seem to find an obstinate pleasure in the repetitive release of motoric energy. Physical tics therefore recall what Sigmund Freud calls the libidinal, polymorphic perverse child's body that finds joy in the compulsive reproduction of identical movements and gestures that outsiders may find painful. Stuart isolates them as an aspect of the body that is usually experienced as either insignificant or irritating. Within the space of 'the choreographic', observed tics are worked over, stylized and formalized into repeatable marks; taken together, they act as the basic layer of Stuart's movement vocabulary.

The constructivist dance maker à la Stuart is a particular kind of ethnographer who does fieldwork in movement research without the purpose of producing a scholarly treatise. The choreographer-turned-fieldworker primarily focuses on the mechanics of everyday gestures that are either deemed meaningless and annoying or confront the normally functioning body with its finiteness. On the one hand, the crippled or kinetically handicapped body presents us with a differently organized corporeality that points to the ever present possibility of suddenly losing one's freedom of motion via a car accident, a viral disease, a misstep while chopping wood... By staging bodies with a constricted or disorganized movement capacity, Stuart creates uncanny images that confront the audience with an at once known and repressed bodily virtuality, a diminished or reconfigured motion potential that is invested with negative feelings and arouses the unconscious fear of bodily disintegration. On the other hand, tics are often located within the realm of the overlooked. Bodies constantly make uncontrolled gestures in interpersonal communication, but unless they are emphatic, such movements do not come to the fore. The actions remain within the margins of one's visual field and are perceived without really being taken into account. Tics illustrate that our conscious looking is structured by a culturally coded visual attention that incessantly reproduces an 'optical unconscious' (dixit Walter Benjamin). In illuminating these at once seen and overlooked movements, Stuart not only directs the audience's gaze to the fringes of the civilized or self-controlled body. The highlighting of a kinetic impulsivity that apparently resists a culture's taming of the body also shows the psychic significance of seemingly insignificant movements of the arms, the hands, the feet... The exterior human body is exposed as being vastly involved in an interior, highly private enjoyment of an overall unconscious nature. Tics indeed defy the difference between inside and outside, the private and the public body: they show — in Lacanian parlance — the body in a state of 'extimacy' that undoes the distinction between the exteriority of the outer body and psychic intimate pleasures.

Dance/Image/Montage

The performances of Meg Stuart and her company Damaged Goods, officially established in 1994, display a fundamental shift in the operation of 'writing dance'. Besides the distinctive signature of her movement vocabulary, the early choreographies stand out for their almost sculptural feel. The simple act of moving forward or the enactment of otherwise uncomplicated movements of arms and hands is slowed down almost to the point of stillness, becoming momentarily transfixed before being re-animated by a sudden rapid movement. The actions acquire a plastic quality: 'writing dance' is partly reframed as the art of sculpting the body within the medium of time. However, a particular visual effect is added through the well-considered use of music and light. Singular parts of the body are highlighted, as for instance in the first two scenes of *Disfigure Study*; in other scenes the restrained use of light creates a dusky chiaroscuro-atmosphere. The dimmed lighting reinforces the image-like quality of the performed actions and results in the emergence of genuine *tableaux vivants*. Through the singular combination of sound, light and movement, the materiality of the performing bodies seems to disappear even in the very moment of their visual appearance. The produced images frame the bodies on stage to such an extent that at times they effectively look flat, two-dimensional, incorporeal. Yet what is an image?

The visual relationship that links the viewer to the viewed — in the performing arts: the audience to the stage — defines the general medium of 'the visual'. Actualized in always particular visual fields, this potential allows the controlled production of images, or the act of 'imaging': the bringing together of a disparate collection of sensations into a visual plane of consistency. The generated unity may look internally harmonious or, on the contrary, show fractures and folds. Whatever its nature, an image aggregates heterogeneous impressions into a plane that holds. It is also a temporal object since the occurrence of the variously assembled sensations takes at least a minimum amount of time. And an image may spontaneously emerge within one's visual field or be a deliberate creation, a thoroughly composed visual artefact. Such are the images that Stuart presents in her work, including her most recent performances. They actually involve a double operation: the visual appearance of movements or poses is rendered autonomous through the careful timing of their enactment; and simultaneously the appearances are forged together into meticulously ordered blocs of sensations with a certain degree of internal consistency. Images that are overly readable or lacking readability are avoided, but the performances of Damaged Goods usually also stay away from that artistically over-coded centre where actions visibly hint at 'deeper truths'. The images created are at once relatively legible and enigmatic: their possible meanings hover between the evident and the elliptical, the univocal and its pulverization. One sees, for instance, an arm and a hand slowly moving across a back. The scene as such is immediately recognizable, yet after a while a rather strange image emerges in which the limbs first seem to draw invisible figures, then acquire an uncanny 'faciality': it looks as if the limbs gaze back.

Within the space of 'the choreographic', movements and poses are by definition treated as scriptural marks that can intentionally be repeated and strategically assembled into phrases. But for Stuart, the created phrases also have to be convincing as living images. *Movement sequences define moving images and vice versa*: this could be a general motto of Stuart's choreographies.

The dictum implies a thorough redefinition of the theatre dispositive as a specific regime of representation. A long historical tradition associates the performing arts with the notions of spectacle and spectatorship. The Latin *spectare* means 'to view' or 'to watch': a *spectaculum* is a show, a series of events that is intended to be seen and anticipates the future presence of a gazing audience. Stuart rearticulates the theatrical spectacle in line with the predominance of moving images within 'the society of the spectacle' (Guy Debord). More than once, it looks as if the performing bodies are acting in a strongly delayed or a vastly sped-up movie, which they actually construct themselves through the particular pace of their movements and poses. The underlying choreographic stance reaffirms within the theatre a basic lesson of modern film practice: successive images are persuasive primarily through their linkage within a self-referentially produced plane of consistent motions. Cinema is the art of sequencing moving images, hence the expression 'a movie'; in combination with light and sound, choreographed movements can acquire a cinematographic quality through a particular timing or slicing of the performed actions. A sequence of mainly slow movements develops into a first image, which is then punctuated by a rapid action, resulting in a short-lived flashing image; and subsequently a third image starts to unfold through a slightly different mode of slowness. In this way, the locus of movement is constantly doubled: *movement is simultaneously happening within and in between the composed body images.*

Since Sergei Eisenstein, and other cinematographers who have insisted on a constructivist approach, we know that the essence of film is montage. Stuart's choreographies subscribe to this idea. Her 'pictures in motion' usually consist of long lasting singular body images that are combined into autonomous scenes, which then act as the building blocks of the separate sections that make up a total performance. With the notable exception of *Do Animals Cry* (2009) and partly also *Maybe Forever* (2007), Stuart's montages do not contain well-defined characters, a clear narrative context, or an evolving plot line. The conventional dramaturgy known from theatre, movies or television is absent: bodily movements appear and disappear without a psychological or narrative motivation. Moreover, scenes and sections are juxtaposed according to a logic of montage that partly takes into account the atmospheric resonances between the assembled actions. Indeed, it is mostly a general mood that unites the different fragments. The overall plane of consistency within a singular performance therefore resembles a connecting tone or implicit melody. The transversal atmosphere is never unambiguous and always difficult to pin down in words. The images in *Disfigure Study* and subsequent works of the 1990s connote social alienation and human desolation, though this general impression is partially undone by the predominantly neutral, unemotional performing style. Through the 'moody' collage of such ambiguous body images, brought together into a multi-layered whole, Damaged Goods' performances at once invite and resist interpretation. The various open fragments remain without subtitles − as if they are allegoric images still searching for an appropriate category, a fitting concept or illuminating commentary. In the end, the individual spectator is let down, left behind with a dozen hieroglyphs (the various scenes) and a difficult to decipher rebus (the overall performance). Each audience member is given the personal freedom to translate the observed atmospheric consistency in the montage into a coherent set of significations, yet without the possibility of a definitive reading that brings together all elements into a meaningful totality.

The prototypical Damaged Goods scene appeals to the spectator's imagination and personal experience through the creation of an excess of interpretative possibilities. Norbert Servos' observations on the work of Pina Bausch also hold for Meg Stuart's performances: 'The pieces are not "complete". They are not self-sustaining works of art because, in order to develop completely, they require an active onlooker. The key lies with the audience, who are asked to question their interest and their own everyday experiences. They should, and indeed must be collated with, and related to the events occurring on the stage. They should, and indeed, must, be collated against the happenings on the stage and related to them. A "sense connection" can be made only when the corporeality (the physical awareness portrayed) on the stage relates to the physical experience of the onlooker.' Like those of Bausch, Stuart's choreographies count on the spectator as an active and unifying reader who frames the observed actions on the basis of personal memories, bodily traces of pain or enjoyment and their unconscious remnants, imaginary identifications, rejections, et cetera. The audience is a co-author, the performance a genuine instance of what Roland Barthes calls the 'writerly text', or the kind of text that positions the reader as an active re-writer.

The ever-deferred completion of the 'dance text' in the act of its reception involves *the spectator as a virtual co-choreographer whose co-presence during a performance supplements the choreographer's absent presence.* The individual spectator is expected to include his own body as a necessary resonance chamber, without the guarantee that every scene will effectively start to produce singular effects within one's own embodied audio-visual archive.

Re-Viewing *No Longer Readymade*

Darkness, loud percussive piano hammering, stage right a young man dressed in a white shirt and black trousers suddenly appears in a spotlight. He shakes his head from left to right at a fast pace. Both arms are lifted one after the other in the direction of his restlessly moving head; three fingers are lifted, then the palm of the hand is turned inwards and a thumb appears, followed by two stretched fingers. He raises and lowers his arms repeatedly while his fingers continue to make counting movements near his face that alternate one, two, three — as if the moving head has to read the indicated numbers. After a while, his upper body also starts to move contortedly while his arms begin to gesture out of joint, but both hands regularly reiterate the counting actions. A next moving image shows the performer now and then standing still with a feverishly vibrating body, his mouth gasping for air before he resumes his frenetic activity. The basic gesture of the moving head is of course highly recognizable, yet through its vast acceleration another body within the medium of the dancing body is produced, one that incessantly differentiates itself from the supporting organism. Toward the end of the act, the exhausted arms go from position to position, till the dance fades out with performer Benoît Lachambre still shaking his head. This is the end of the remarkable opening sequence of *No Longer Readymade*, Meg Stuart's second full-evening's choreography, again set to music composed by Hahn Rowe. It premiered on the 12th of August 1993 at Theater am Halleschen Ufer in Berlin.

When the stage is lit anew, only a female waist and someone's back are visible. They stand close to each other and resemble the kind of decapitated sculptured torsos exhibited in museums of ancient art. Both waist and back are covered with all sorts of small artefacts that are attached with cheap tape. The objects recall personal memorabilia: a pebble, a perished flower, some photographs. The audience gets the time to contemplate the artefacts in silence before the two performers – Sarah Baud and David Hernandez – cautiously start to cover them by slowly putting on the shirts that were taken off until just above the shoulders. A mirrored unison of the arms and hands gradually unfolds. The hands entwine behind the performers' backs or on their necks, the right hand caresses their head and then moves further over the front of their body, a hand is placed on the chin. The actions develop at a slow pace that is now and then interrupted by a rapid, short and angular movement. The performers share the stage but their dance is anything but a duet, since they continually negate each other: they definitely move alone and are completely absorbed in their own actions. In combination with a slightly bent, upward-turned head, the enacted gestures are frequently reminiscent of poses known from classical painting and sculpture that are here brought to life or set in motion.

After a while, two other dancers become visible. Meg Stuart is calmly sitting on the floor upstage left, watching the actions of Sarah Baud and David Hernandez, with Benoît Lachambre standing behind her. A new scene starts to develop when Baud steps towards Hernandez and makes embracing movements without touching his body. At first he holds off the gesture, then gives in according to the same uncanny logic of hugging without physical contact (this action would re-occur in *Maybe Forever*, the duet that Meg Stuart and Philipp Gehmacher created together in 2007). While this failed encounter is repeated, Lachambre commences to kick Stuart's body forward, with his hands seemingly tied behind his back. Her movements are primarily framed by his seemingly violent kicks, yet Stuart also continually makes short leaps that sometimes go in the direction of Lachambre, whose body she vainly tries to embrace. There is no trace of emotional depth: the performers' faces do not display any sign of personal involvement.

The act ends with Stuart hugging Lachambre centre stage while the other two performers disappear. He slowly hands over his jacket, which he was wearing all the while backwards, to Stuart. She puts it on – the jacket is much too large for her – and starts to rummage the content of the jacket's pockets. They are stuffed with the kind of things that a hurried traveller distractedly hides away: various coins, a toothbrush, airplane and train tickets, a page torn from a newspaper, an unopened letter. The diversity and quantity of the artefacts suggest a nomadic life of constant travelling of the kind that is actually rather common within the internationalized world of contemporary dance. Stuart first attentively inspects every object as if she is looking for something particular. After a while, her pace quickens and she begins to rummage frantically in both pockets, things falling onto the floor, until the space around her feet is covered with objects. During the whole scene, Sarah Baud is visible upstage left. Like Stuart, she does not make steps and only moves the upper parts of her body. Baud performs slightly contorted movements with her head and shoulders, arms and hands. These sometimes look sculptural but at other times have an everyday character: touching her head with her hand, putting her forefinger in front of both lips or her hands in front of her face, or drawing out her upper body. The rhythm of Baud's movements is paced by the tempo of Stuart's actions. Baud also moves at an increasing speed, yet in marked contrast with Stuart's frontal position and gaze, Baud's body and face remain turned away from the audience.

Once the jacket's pockets have been emptied, Stuart takes off the garment. David Hernandez reappears on stage: he stands behind Stuart and gives her a hanger on which she hangs the coat. Hesitatingly, she takes of her dress with an ever more embarrassed face, her gaze directed at the audience. Hernandez passes her a second hanger for the dress; Stuart then takes over both hangers and puts one on each of her stretched arms. While standing in this position with a face that expressively underlines her uncomfortable posture, a fanfare tune sets in. At the same moment, a pink spotlight is directed at Stuart's body and the house lights are switched on. On stage, the three other performers line up behind Stuart, watching her with a neutral face. Stuart's facial movements reflect this being exposed in a ludicrous pose to the gaze of the audience as well as that of her co-performers. Signs of embarrassment change into signs of being ashamed, but there is simultaneously the connotation that the performer's uneasy situation is a shared one. In the final sequence Stuart takes off her dancing boots, places each of her two hands in one of the boots, and then covers her face with crossed forearms: she breaks the uneasiness of standing in an awkward position in front of an audience by hiding her face.

No Longer Readymade continues with a scene in which Stuart simulates being tickled through twisted bodily moves and sharp laughs. Her movements are in sync with those of David Hernandez, who stoops next to her and caresses a female dress lying on the ground with his head. He seems to indirectly cause her actions, mediated by the dress, a symbol of the skin one normally touches when tickling a body. In the subsequent movement sequence, Stuart moves her body on the floor with a visibly limited movement capacity. Her hands grasp again and again the parts of her body that have to be shifted in order to move further forward. The motion looks at once mechanical and functional, but the body itself resembles a disorganized corporeal mass lacking any immanent kinetic integration. After Stuart's solo has come to an end, the movement register appears at first glance to become decidedly more 'dancy'. Lying on the floor, the four dancers move in unison, their arms alternating between fast and slow movements; they erect the upper part of their bodies and sweep violently with both arms, make turns and shift their bodies forward by stretching both arms. The dancers start to move at an increased pace: they raise their bodies half or fully and subsequently fall with full weight back onto the floor, arms flailing. While his co-performers repeat this action, Benoît Lachambre stands up and begins to shuffle across the stage with his upper body slightly bent forward and his right hand covering his face — as if he does not want to see the dance. Among the now frenetically moving bodies of Baud, Hernandez and Stuart, he walks step by step in the direction of the proscenium. When he has almost arrived there, Lachambre suddenly turns around and the music comes to a halt; in the next moment, after an interruptive blackout, he holds the exhausted Hernandez in his arms. He then slowly carries the completely impassive Hernandez across the stage in various positions, now and then carefully depositing the body on the floor. During the action, Lachambre's lips mimic silent speech. The complete act suggests that he is a ministering angel, or at least someone who is affectively taking care of a gravely wounded or deceased body. The next scene returns to a movement motif from the opening sequence: Hernandez first touches his own body with a continuously trembling right arm and hand, before his entire body begins to shake. In the short closing act the two women bare their shoulders and also part of their upper bodies in unison, by removing their shirts. In the light of the overall choreography, these simple gestures appear as a contrapuntal movement that suddenly tips the performance into another register — as if the final scene wants to suggest that another kind of dance could have been possible.

Minimizing Meaning, or Radicalizing Dance Theatre

The keen dramaturgical use of lighting, music and sound, the gradual development of movement scenes into audio-visual *tableaux vivants* that frequently verge on the border of the cinematographic, the non-hierarchical juxtaposition of singular scenes or images, the concomitant preference for an associative rather than a narrative or linear dramaturgy: are we not in the realm of dance theatre instead of theatre dance? Do Stuart's performances perhaps rehearse and displace the recent tradition associated with the names of Pina Bausch, Susanne Linke or Reinhild Hoffmann? There is yet another link: the already hinted at play with the difference between bodily actions and their established cultural or symbolic meanings, the materiality of human corporeality and its continuous encoding or transformation into a readable 'text'. In everyday life and social interaction, physical movements or postures act as signifiers that convey one or more messages. Non-verbal communication is often vague and imprecise, yet this does not diminish the importance of the body's incessant metamorphosis into a discursive reality according to specific cultural conventions. Within daily public life, a human body indeed unremittingly chats and babbles: it functions as a complex medium of communication, a scripted producer of signs. Walking towards somebody, waving a hand, touching another body roughly, or keeping to oneself while remaining in close proximity to a group: these merely physical actions carry signification within our culture. They are not just bodily motions but genuine representations of individual intentions, emotions and other inner states.

German *Tanztheater* has vastly explored the difference between bodily behaviour and body symbolism, 'form' and 'content'. It excels in the articulation of the ever-present tension between the material and the textual body – or rather: between our culture's definition of 'corporeality as such' and the many codes that make this supposedly neutral physicality meaningful. Situations are constructed that foreground the observable physicality of the exposed actions and simultaneously allude to their meaning outside of the theatre context. The stage dialogues with the surrounding culture through the sustained creation of alternately small and marked fissures between bodily gestures or poses and their common significations. Women staggering in high heels, men making broad arm gestures, or women and men touching, kissing or hitting each other in a slightly overdone way are 'typical Bausch scenes' which the average spectator quasi-automatically interprets in the light of her cultural stock-in-trade. The exhibited corporeal actions look at once strange and recognizable: their somewhat twisted physicality does not thwart their overall legibility. Choreography à la Bausch is precisely the art of playing in a sometimes critical, often ironical mode with the difference between bodily signifiers and their established significations.

In her early choreographies, Meg Stuart strikingly intensifies the tension between human physicality and its cultural scripting. Matter and meaning appear as two separate planes that are juxtaposed to and coupled with the difference between stage and audience. On stage, the enacted movements and poses remain devoid of meaning and tend to become pure signifiers. The neutral, inexpressive performing style primarily sticks to the physicality of twisted arm movements or the laborious manoeuvring of a confined body on the floor. The same zero-degree state of meaning gives the bodily interactions between the performers an uncanny character. With a deadpan face, a male performer for instance paws a female body whose visage also shows no sign of personal involvement (the final scene of *Disfigure Study*). Or a man kicks forward a woman who vainly tries to embrace his body: a potentially dramatic scene, yet the performers only seem to execute 'pure movements' (a notable sequence in *No Longer Readymade*). In sum, actions are continually made abstract by annulling their signification in everyday culture. However, in the communication between stage and auditorium, the scraped-off meanings resurface: the spectator links the movements to familiar cultural scripts. Within the onlooker's culturalized gaze, the staged bodily actions unavoidably transform into significant, often dramatic gestures. In a word, the minimization of meaning on stage finds its elicited counterpart in the maximization of signification by the audience: *the choreographic action of 'de-representation' is crossed out by the spectator's act of 're-representation'.*

The onlooker's interpretative work is of course expected and therefore part and parcel of the overall choreography. In the early performances of Damaged Goods, the dancers and the spectators therefore occupy complementary roles within an overall dramaturgy. The total choreography indeed comprises both the 'dance text' enacted by the performers and its anticipated reading according to prevalent cultural scripts by the audience. This role distribution can already be found in German dance theatre but is vastly reinforced in works such as *Disfigure Study* or *No Longer*

Readymade. A double displacement is actually involved. On the one hand, bodily actions are stripped of even the slightest hint of a personal expressivity and consistently made anonymous. In contrast with *Tanztheater*, the performers do not acquire through their acts a semi-identity or the status of quasi-characters with a vague but nevertheless distinctive personality that gradually starts to shimmer through during the performance. Also in Stuart's later work, the exposed theatricality differs from the one characterizing the work of Bausch, Linke or Hoffmann. The dancers do not unfold an individual acting line over time that bit-by-bit suggests the existence of an inner unity, a however weak subjectivity that informs their way of behaving (*Do Animals Cry* is again a notable exception). Overall, the dancing body appears as the impersonal medium of a constantly re-articulated generic physicality that refrains from becoming personal. On the other hand, the neutral performing style known from Merce Cunningham and Judson also acquires a different value in Stuart's early work (in most post-2000 performances this neutrality is supplemented by a marked play with 'faciality', or the performer's making all kind of facial gestures). No longer does the modernist quest for 'pure dance' (Cunningham) or 'pure movement' (Judson) motivate the choreography but rather the possibility to structure the difference between the production of zero-degree motions and their anticipated reception. All in all, a particular 'as if'-clause frames Stuart's early performances, which also seals an implicit pact with the spectator: 'we pretend the actions shown are meaningless because you will make them meaningful.' This peculiar *politics of spectatorship* supplements the 'written body text' with an implied readership, one that commits itself to the hegemonic cultural representations of normal bodily behaviour in the very moment of their subversive 'de-representation' on stage.

Intermezzo: Theatricality and the Gazing Other

The most fundamental link between a staged performance, whatever its exact nature, and social life outside the theatre probably lies within the reflexive loop between doing and being watched that defines theatricality. Indeed, the theatre dispositive first and foremost isolates, exposes and magnifies a more general human mode of behaving in the co-presence of others. One observes that one is being observed or finds oneself in a situation in which this is an ever-present possibility; and one reflexively takes into account this being (potentially) watched in the way one acts. Movements, attitudes or words are no longer just made or uttered, let alone spontaneously enacted, but are consciously stylized in view of certain desired effects such as a credible self-image or looking normal and inaccessible (a common pose in public urban life). One's outward form and eventually also one's speech thus acquires a composed and fabricated character that may be more or less observable, depending on whether the actor behaves inept or convincingly. In sum, *acting in a theatrical mode is reacting reflexively within an audio-visual relationship by incorporating the situation of being observed into one's actions.* The opposite mode, as Denis Diderot has already argued in his analyses of eighteenth-century academic painting and sculpture, is absorption or being so wrapped up in an activity that one negates – or actively 'forgets' – the looks of others. This way of behaving may also be simulated in such a plausible manner that the feigned absorption smoothly persuades the viewer. Theatricality and absorption are indeed frequently fused within visual representations, performance and ordinary life. An observed state of somebody being engrossed by the action at hand is often also a reflexive response to a particular or general gaze, witness the convention of the fourth wall in theatre or the composed attitude of busyness that bureaucrats quasi-automatically adopt in the presence of clients or superiors.

It is rather obvious that the audience's co-presence defines the situation of performance and co-conditions both the presence of the performers on stage and the acts they effectively execute (indeed a point already made in the closing paragraph of the previous chapter: 'pure dance' is made impure by the spectator's gaze). 'The autopoietic feedback loop, consisting of the mutual interaction between actors and spectators, brings forth the performance', according to the German theatre scholar Erika Fischer-Lichte. 'The notion of the artist as an autonomous subject creating an autonomous work of art, which each recipient may interpret differently but cannot change in its materiality, evidently no longer applies here, even if the majority of audiences still fails to acknowledge it.' There are various modes of directing – the word 'choreographing' applies here too – the relationship between staged movements and their viewing. The physical being-on-stage can articulate the being-watched in highly different ways that vary from hamming it up, to a restrained self-conscious theatricality, to the neutral, matter-of-fact style of 'just doing movements'.

All these modes take into account the existence of an anonymous gaze or collective attention that is more than just the simple sum of its individual parts. The individual attention of every single member of the audience evidently contributes to the emergence of a collective gaze (and also of a collective ear when music or text is used during the performance). Individual perceptions make up that gaze, yet their mutual couplings generate an autonomous surplus effect that resembles the productivity of interaction effects in complex systems or the semantic and rhetorical autonomy of a plain phrase in relation to the words that are its constituent elements. The relative independence of the audience's collective gaze is confirmed by its rather stunning capacity to transform some simple steps on a stage into meaningful movements, for instance, or to change a relatively long-lasting silence of the performers into a seemingly profound statement. The momentary collective attention that corresponds with the audience's gaze may also greatly influence individual perception. The temporal functioning and actual impact of this social reality is vastly conditioned by the general behaviour of the viewing public. For neither individual concentration nor the emergence of a focused collective attention is possible without the silence and diligent behaviour of those attending a performance. In the final instance, modern performance and most of its supposedly postmodern avatars vastly depend on the generally taken for granted existence of a civilized spectator's body whose self-control is sublimated into a predominantly disembodied watching or disinterested pleasure, one that Immanuel Kant already considered as constituting the core of aesthetic involvement.

The collective gaze conditioning a performance is a relatively autonomous social medium that is fundamental to every sort of live performing art. Performers often associate this medial reality with a strange kind of black hole one is dancing or acting for. Yet the hole is not a passive opening or fold in which the performance continually disappears but *an actively gazing anonymous Other without a face*. 'One is looking', and this impersonal 'one' is simultaneously an uncontrollable multitude and a panoptic, disciplining Master Eye that gratuitously gives or refuses the aggregated public attention that the performance actually needs in order to exist in a genuine manner. The gazing Other is anything but neutral, since its functioning creates a visual power relationship. The looking is profoundly marked by the dominant heterosexual gender script and vastly structured by the standardized expectations regarding the noteworthiness of public events that contemporary mass media have instilled on the overall regime of attention giving. These conditioning features are at work each time the collective gaze operates during a performance with an often unconscious effectiveness. Within the context of a dance work, actions and stillness are therefore also transformed into something other than just 'pure movements': they become communicative acts. *To perform is unavoidably 'to be in communication'*, even if the dancer unwillingly forgets or deliberately negates this mode of existing. For communication is not only generated through the intentional sending of a message but occurs in the very act of observing whatever kind of event as a contingent utterance containing possible information.

Gesturing Im/Potentiality

Performances of Damaged Goods frequently contain scenes that, through a marked theatricality, emphasize the situation of being on stage and being watched. The immanent visual field that at once connects and separates the stage from the audience is exposed in a self-reflexive way through, for instance, slowed down, long-lasting movements with a sculptural quality or, by contrast, rapid gestures and swift movements. The performing style often simulates absorption: the dancers seem to be completely wrapped up in their actions and notably negate the audience's presence. Through their actions they enact the basic fictitious assumption defining fourth-wall acting: 'we do *as if* nobody is watching' (*No One Is Watching* is actually the title of the full-evening's performance that Meg Stuart created in 1995). In other scenes, the dancers move emphatically within, or even toward, the public's gaze and make all sorts of facial gestures. They perform actions that, like Benoît Lachambre's explosive head movements and shaking body in the opening sequence of *No Longer Readymade,* are not exactly 'dancy' but equally uncommon in both theatre dance and *Tanztheater*. The actions are neither polished or stylized to the point of being highly formalized, nor do they look provocatively wild and spontaneous. Within the context of choreographed dance, both the unusualness and peculiar energetic tension of the performed movements foreground their constructed or fabricated character. The actions reflexively indicate that they are conceived and performed 'now, here' in relation to the theatre dispositive.

Their slightly exaggerated or extremely overdone nature visibly takes into account that the stage delineates a symbolic space where human bodies appear in order to be watched, inspected, valuated. Theatricality is thus affirmed through a peculiar movement vocabulary and performing style, one that subverts the average spectator's expectation that choreographed dance consists of gracefully enacted movements.

Meg Stuart's remarkable solo in *No Longer Readymade* goes one step further and plays out theatricality against itself, which results in a live deconstruction of the theatre dispositive. 'I am tried and tested in front of the audience, who now share in my discomfort of seeing me so exposed, so unprepared for my obligation to entertain, awe and move them. I fail their test. I ask for help. They fail me. I stand there humiliated, letting time pass, waiting and looking for the next place', writes Stuart in one of the short notes on her solo. The act indeed self-reflexively engages with the visual power relationship between performer and public. The corresponding imbalance is not debunked in a straightforward manner, quite the contrary. At the start of the solo, the house lights are switched on again, nullifying the eventuality of the voyeuristic pleasure that the situation of looking at somebody — literally: some body — in the dark may offer. A principal material condition of the visual inequality marking the relationship between stage and audience is thereby made ineffective. Whereas normally only the performer is situated within the regime of the scopic, the public is now inscribed within a disciplining field of visibility as well. The audience's looking becomes observable, not only for the performers but for the spectators themselves as well. Stuart directly addresses this watching: she looks straight back with a face that gradually expresses an increasing embarrassment provoked by the uneasy situation that has been created. This not only obliterates the visual discrepancy between performer and audience, but the anonymously gazing Other is thoroughly redefined as well. For the gazing Other starts gazing at itself: the collective act of looking self-reflexively loops back upon itself, producing a rather uncanny effect.

Stuart's embarrassment expresses, before the eyes of the witnessing audience, that audience's very own visual harassment. The act of being exposed to the audience's gaze is publicly exposed, yet the spectators are also greatly implied in the performed failure. The awkward and overall painful scene that Stuart builds up evolves over time into a general fiasco in which the performer and the audience have a shared responsibility. Stuart's discomfiture does indeed have a double meaning. Her uneasiness signifies at once the shortcomings of the individual performer and the audience's own failure in the simple act of watching that is its very *raison d'être*. The audience perceives the growing embarrassment over its own failing, continually mirrored in the dancer's increasing shame. The solo installs a somewhat strange feedback loop between performer and spectators that simultaneously creates a situation in which this uncanny interaction effect starts to become observable. In sum, the failing co-presence of performer and audience is represented in the action of the representing agent, which is rather rare during a theatre or dance performance. In this way, a communication comes into existence that symbolizes the sheer absence of a genuine communicative relationship between the dancer and those watching her. This metacommunication does not bridge the gap separating the two sides that are involved in the action, quite the contrary. The reflexive exposure of being exposed in a situation of communicative failure rather foregrounds *the imaginary character of every seemingly transparent communication between performer(s) and audience.*

Stuart's solo enacts three failures: the performance goes wrong, the audience is exposed, and subsequently the relation between the dancer and the audience breaks down while the communication actually continues and therefore shifts into 'something like: "communication... without communication"' (Jean-François Lyotard). A failure points to a temporary incapacity, or the momentary non-realization of a potential. The audience could have come to the assistance of the performance – but it did not: the audience stuck to the passive role of spectator. And Stuart could have enacted a scene that highlighted her personal talents – but she preferred to deny the prevalent script of skilfulness and trained virtuosity. 'I was trying to *not* perform, ... I wanted to perform my inability', she states in 'What are you looking at?', one of the rare lectures she has ever given. The failure of the audience and of the dancer, as well as the resulting breakdown of the relationship, indicate that a virtual possibility did not occur. A realizable potential was not actualized during Stuart's solo, yet this incapacity is not external but immanent to the capacity to help, to dance, to relate. It is precisely this constitutive relationship between inability and ability that is enacted in Stuart's solo: it is a true gesture.

Failure and embarrassment are hardly exceptional topics in the performances of Damaged Goods. The performers' bodies are repeatedly put into difficult situations, such as moving with a seemingly crippled body or a restrained kinetic capacity that simultaneously shows incapacity. Over the years, Meg Stuart has broadened the procedure of confronting her (co-)performers during the rehearsal process and the final work with hard to execute and therefore also symbolically painful tasks. Physical paradoxes have been supplemented with performative situations that appeal to a dancer's 'psychological' weaknesses. The basic figure that continues to inform Stuart's work is the dialectical relationship between the possibility to do something and the negation of this potential in the act of failing, which may be more or less observable for the witnessing spectator. 'There is nothing I like more than to see someone on stage attempting an impossible task, not arriving, making a second futile but braver attempt, and then eventually giving up the task', says Stuart in her conversation with visual artist Catherine Sullivan, adding: 'I only realized two years ago that my dancers had been performing a perverse form of slapstick all these years.' Confronting the performers' bodies again and again with the eventuality of failing may look dehumanizing. Yet impotentiality, and therefore also erring, is constitutive for every human potentiality, including the individual power to move in a self-controlled, ordered way. Human motion potential per definition includes its literal negation, the capacity to not-move or to stand still (this observation already informed the definition of dance's medium put forward in the first chapter). It also comprises the eventuality of unsuccessful movements or poses, which do not fully realize the intended action or the activated possibility for movement. A failure crosses out a capacity during its affirmation — and this self-subverting action, not the perfect or virtuoso act, is 'human all too human'. The action thus changes into a particular kind of movement since *the failed actualization of a potential within the very moment of its realization is the defining trait of every genuine gesture.*

Every human being is a potentially qualified speaker, yet in our speech we always signify the impossibility of fully mastering this medium, through for instance a lapse, or an inadvertent cry, such as 'euh' or 'um'. Even skilful orators may suddenly stutter, before going on to complete the sophisticated sentence they had just begun to utter and which the stammering momentarily interrupts. These often unnoticed or politely disregarded utterances occur when a speaker is not able to figure something out in language. They signify a temporary inability to speak, briefly positioning the otherwise capable speaking subject as a non-subject, as an individual who fails in language because language is failing them. The failing subject is always located at the intersection of potentiality and impotentiality, and this position actually defines human subjectivity as such. Linguistic gestures do not point to a temporary shortcoming that may be overcome in the future but expose the speaking subject as a truly weak one that never acquires complete control over its being-in-language. The speaking subject usually thinks that he or she masters language and can easily put it to use with a self-consciously determined will — until a micro-logical silence or a short 'euh' signals once again that their speaking capacity escapes them for a short while. The brief interruption shows that language is not only a means to an end, such as articulated thinking or communication, but a material medium that surpasses human control.

'The gesture is the exhibition of a mediality: it is the process of making a means visible as such. It allows the emergence of the being-in-a-medium of human beings and thus it opens the ethical dimension for them', Giorgio Agamben asserts in his seminal essay 'Notes on Gesture'. To be human is to be multi-medial, to live in — rather than with — many mediums that all define a virtual potential or genuine capacity. Through the failing use of a medium, gestures display that very medium's existence as a never completely controllable potential — as one that makes human life possible but is impossible to fully rationalize according to the logic of means and ends. Although we often experience a medium such as language as a disposable object that can be manipulated at will, it actually constitutes a milieu in which we live. The same holds for the human body and its capacity to move and to not-move. The moving potential allows its instrumental use by consciously willing subjects, but the ability also regularly fails us. The disfigured or uncanny moving body that Meg Stuart frequently stages in her performances is first and foremost a failing body making gestural movements. Through a coagulated or fragmented movement capacity, Stuart's 'gesturing dance' foregrounds the body as pure means, a mere potential or medium. 'If dance is gesture, it is so, rather, because it is nothing more than the endurance and the exhibition of the media character of corporal movements',

Agamben notes in a sentence that could act as a general motto for Stuart's work.

Second Movement: *Highway 101*, or Deconstructing Liveness

Liveness and/or 'the Political'

In July 2000, the capital of Austria temporarily functioned as an imaginary stopping place on a fictitious Highway 101, the famous north-south freeway on the West Coast of the United States. Vienna, or rather a particular venue in the city, was momentarily remapped within the context of a series of site-specific projects that Meg Stuart initiated in the millennium year under the general heading of *Highway 101*. The Vienna stop was the second performance after the inaugurating one at the Kaaitheater studios in Brussels, March 2000. Four more editions would follow, respectively in Paris (2000, Centre Georges Pompidou), again Brussels (2000, La Raffinerie), Rotterdam (2001, TENT), and Zurich (2001, Schiffbau). 'We set up our virtual ghost ride in five places, guided each time by the architecture of the buildings. We talked about accumulating memories, desire and disappearance. Visual artists and composers joined us en route. The performers were asked to collect a private archive of material, which they re-experienced and recycled in new settings. The audience was asked to see the choreography from video screens, surveillance cameras, glass rooms, narrow hallways, sofas and parking lots', Stuart recalls in the essay 'In Pieces'. This is what the project became in the end: a travelling package of possible ideas and virtual intentions that were site-specifically translated and given a definitive shape in close dialogue with varying artistic collaborators. The actual starting point looked different. Stuart thought of developing 101 simple tasks that could be freely combined and performed in different contexts. These potential dances would be defined in an open way and grant the performers the opportunity to improvise or to appropriate the guiding instructions.

Besides Stuart, the permanent artistic core that animated *Highway 101* throughout 2000 and 2001 was comprised of dramaturge and set designer Stefan Pucher, video artist Jorge León, and the performers Simone Aughterlony, Heine Avdal, Nuno Bizarro, Varinia Canto Vila, Ugo Dehaes, Davis Freeman, Eric Grondin, Rachid Ouramdane and Yukiko Shinozaki. Each episode steered the public through the different spaces of the location in which

the successive actions were set. It was as if the audience received a guided tour of an art exhibition solely made up of live installations and videos, without the accompanying commentary. Reframing the notion of an engaging spectatorship, which already informed Stuart's choreographies of the 1990s, the spectators had to walk, to choose their own point of view, to negotiate possible angles with co-spectators. Indeed, like every site-specific project, *Highway 101* re-articulated the standard theatre situation with its clear separation between stage and auditorium. The distance between performers and public was no longer symbolized by the visible gap between proscenium and the first row of audience seats. This spatial relationship changed into an object of experimentation: a social choreography that directly involved the spectators' bodies and subjectivities became possible. What did that at once fixed and open 'dance text' look like in Vienna?

Whereas the other stops of *Highway 101* were accommodated in a central art venue, the Viennese episode takes place in an old workshop called the Emballagenhallen ('packing halls'). The building is situated at the outskirts of the city and will soon be demolished, which offers Stuart and set designer Pucher a considerable freedom in the styling of the different subspaces. The Vienna edition starts outside and continues with the public entering the building through a large gate. The audience comes into the space that the performers refer to as 'the lounge': blue carpet on the floor, scattered seats and sofas, some small tables and upright lamps, a couple of fridges filled with drinks (the big room transforms into a foyer and party-space after each performance). The back of 'the lounge' consists of a wall with two big openings at the left and the right that suggests the existence of a long corridor behind the concrete façade. The performers run back and forth in the tunnel-like space, to the melodic electronic soundscape of the Viennese duo General Magic, while gesturing with arms and hands. After awhile, they start to deviate from their straight lines, running into 'the lounge', and mixing with the audience. A performer jumps up and down on a sofa, another shows an ankle or a physical wound to a spectator, and a third dancer stands very close to a viewer or lies down on the ground next to a seated person. The overall action of erasing the difference between performance and audience space is of course anything but original. Nevertheless, the actual events in 'the lounge' still elicit embarrassment: the dancers cross a symbolic line and come too close, in the experience of most spectators. Therefore people blush when a dancer shows up near them or try to negate his or her presence. A basic pact between performers and public is indeed broken, yet the more general ideology of liveness that vastly legitimates the performing arts is deconstructed as well.

The idea of liveness suggests that the singularity of a dance or theatre performance resides in the performers' being present and acting 'now, here' in a direct relationship with the audience. Walter Benjamin therefore opposes the aura of the theatre actor to the artistic performance before a film camera. 'For aura is tied to [the actor's] presence; there can be no replica of it. The aura that, on the stage, emanates from Macbeth, cannot be separated for the spectators from that of the actor. However, the singularity of the shot in the studio is that the camera is substituted for the public. Consequently, the aura that envelops the actor vanishes, and with it the aura of the figure he portrays', Benjamin asserts in his famous essay 'The Work of Art in the Age of Mechanical Reproduction'. Yet within the theatre dispositive, the aura surrounding the performers or the impersonated personae is tied to their distant presentness. Their being on stage goes together with an aloofness in their being watched that actually counters the metaphysics of presence underpinning the ideology of liveness. Its effectiveness presupposes the standard theatre situation, which is literally spectacular and transforms every audience member into an almighty gazing subject that enjoys the observed actions from a safe zone. Performers and spectators are co-present but the latter remain physically absent in the visual relationship with the stage: this is the defining condition for the emergence of an auratic presence, or 'the unique phenomenon of a distance, however close it may be' (Benjamin).

The direct togetherness of performers and audience in 'the lounge' paradoxically deconstructs the dancer's eventual aura through the creation of a situation of *hyper-presentness or hyper-liveness*. The ideology of liveness is indeed literalized by visibly implicating the spectator's bodily co-presence. A liminal situation arises, which, like transition rituals, brings forth a state of being betwixt-and-between. The prevalent norms scripting the theatre dispositive no longer apply but new standards are not on hand. The average spectator feels therefore somewhat threatened and slightly lost. They suddenly have to improvise at the risk of not coming to terms with the unexpected hyper-liveness. There is the gaze of the other audience members as well: one may lose face. The spectators who become unwillingly involved in a dancer's action momentarily change into a performing subject, exposed individuals who have to invent 'now, here' their new role and fitting actions. Most spectators gesture their incapacity to act as audience members temporarily turned into performers. Their theatricality fails because they have not mastered the ability to improvise or to compose a convincing posture in response to their suddenly being put on the spot. Their uneasy movements and awkward poses are simultaneously noticed and excused, for the constructed scene of togetherness also brings forth a passive form of *communitas*, an unspoken solidarity grounded in the audience's shared experience of vulnerability. The audience is no longer a contingent multitude of individuals but transforms into a 'weak we' through being actual or virtual exposed to the gaze of the others in a situation of non-mastered theatricality. This latent commonality actually points to the origins of all political action: the public constitution of a group of people sharing a public concern, a common cause that makes common. During 'the lounge' scene, the Vienna audience acts as a proto-political public.

At the end of 'the lounge' part, the spectators are invited to enter through the left opening of the wall, the corridor functioning as the main performance space. They bump into a new, this time human wall: all the performers standing in line. The situation resembles that of a public demonstration, with the dancers in the role of the barring police force and the public placed in the position of a group of protesters. Silence and discomfort spread among the audience. How near could one approach the performers? How physically close dare you go? How may I (the spectator) relate to them (the performers, and partly also the co-spectators)? After a while, the dancers slowly begin to step backwards, simultaneously making beckoning hand and facial movements that indicate 'follow us'. Each time some audience members answer this invitation, the performers move a few paces forwards before receding again. Now and then a dancer lies down on the floor, or a couple of performers start pulling and pushing. The actions simulate possible happenings during a demonstration: the performers switch roles and partly take up the imaginary position conferred to the public. When about two-thirds of the tunnel trajectory is crossed, the lights are dimmed and a video projection starts on the rear wall. A still image of a large group of people slowly comes to life. A double movement unfolds since not only does the visual representation of the depicted people change but the overall image itself alters as well. While the filmed collective very slowly shifts to the bottom of the frame, the image becomes increasingly abstract. At the end, all that can be seen is merely a meaningless whole of countless coloured spots.

The video registration was made during one of the Viennese demonstrations in the spring of 2000 against the new Austrian government coalition between the Christian democrats and the populist right-wing FPÖ (Freedom Party of Austria) that was then still captained by the charismatic politician Jörg Haider. The tunnel scene continually hints at this social situation of a political rally, yet the gradually pulverizing video image also symbolizes the real vanishing point of the audience's actual togetherness. The present spectators form a proto-political public that contemplates a representation of effective political engagement, an image of a temporary community publicly expressing a common concern. Both the audience's commonality and the depicted demonstrators' concerted actions testify to a 'weak we', but a crucial difference evidently plays: the audience behaves outside the realm of the political. Although the spectators share a situation of personal uneasiness, this collective discomfort does not become a common cause that is openly discussed or negotiated. A personal problem does not translate into a public issue but remains unspoken − 'since this is just art'. In short, a potential political commonality is brought to the fore in a situation that crosses out this very possibility. Through this specific act of representing 'the political' within the realm of 'the artistic', the first appears as a de-activated potential that cannot be (made) present 'now, here'.

'What binds the spectators together is no more than an irreversible relation at the very centre which maintains their isolation. The spectacle reunites the separate, but reunites it as separate', arch-Situationist Guy Debord writes in *The Society of the Spectacle,* published one year before the legendary events of May 1968. The combination of communicative separateness and a common sensory focus creates a 'being in failing unity' that defines the functioning of the mass media as well as that of live performance. By undoing the difference between stage and auditorium, this paradoxical sociality is highlighted but the

communicative separation between performers and audience, or among the individual spectators, is not really overcome. When a performance moreover confronts the implied public with an image of a politicized commonality, the actual isolation experienced is even more magnified. Or does the interplay between a proto-political audience and the representation of a demonstrating mass perhaps hint at a possibility yet to realize within the performing arts – to a political commonality yet to invent, a togetherness and interactivity yet to discover and perform? The alternative hypothesis stresses the commonality that effectively binds the spectators during a performance in their being together apart. For the audience members both actively share and individually practice the human potential to sensorially perceive, affectively experience and make sense of the observed actions. 'This shared power of the equality of intelligence links individuals, makes them exchange their intellectual adventures, insofar as it keeps them separate from one another, equally capable of using the power everyone has to plot their own part. What our performances ... verify is not our participation in a power embodied in the community. It is the capacity of anonymous people, the capacity that makes everyone equal to everyone else. This capacity is exercised by an unpredictable interplay of associations and dissociations', as the French philosopher Jacques Rancière argues in his essay 'The Emancipated Spectator'. He may be right, but his observation leaves one crucial question unanswered: what would a future political commonality truly based on the always singularized practicing of generic capacities look like? Or is this in principle possible politics a utopian horizon, one that is time and again announced as an untenable promise in the emergence of a shared cause producing commonality? Perhaps both 'the lounge' and the tunnel scene in the Vienna stop of *Highway 101* hint at a *'gesturing politics' in which a constitutive dimension of the political is represented as an ever receding potential, an impotentiality of genuinely being together that grounds togetherness.*

Performing Postmodern Subjectivity

The Vienna edition actually starts before the audience enters 'the lounge': the dispersed public is being directed to a large outside window, through which it can look at a blue-toned video image of Simone Aughterlony projected on the back wall of the space. The image shows her sitting laidback in a worn-out sofa with a bottle of beer in her right hand. Aughterlony starts to talk about her own life, or so it seems: maybe she just invents a fictive autobiography before the camera? Who is indeed the actual subject of the fragmentary life story she recounts: the performing subject herself, a performed personae, or perhaps both in alternating positions? Aughterlony's words, transmitted via small speakers placed outside the building, are also slightly out of sync with the movements of her lips in the image. The minimal differences strengthen the artificial, cut-up character of the video recording and simultaneously emphasize the doubtful nature of the represented confessional speech.

The opening section has a live double within the performance. After the tunnel scene, the audience enters the space adjacent to 'the lounge' in which the initial video projection was shown. Meg Stuart awaits them on the same brown couch Aughterlony had been sitting on. She also starts to talk in an autobiographical mode in an at once nonchalant and slightly ironic way, but *I'm All Yours* — as the solo was named afterwards — is even more cut up and disintegrated than Aughterlony's performance before the video camera. The range of professed self-observations goes from 'This shirt is second-hand' to 'I was only raped once'. Mundane statements, dramatic confessions and casual self-commentary alternate in rapid succession, intermingling diverse speech genres, ranging from informal quotidian talk to psychobabble. What is foregrounded here is the contrived nature of seemingly personal speech within the mass media. The centrifugal utterances of both Aughterlony and Stuart do indeed conform to a standardized model of self-presentation known from media conversations and talk shows.

Aughterlony's and Stuart's solos are based on video interviews that were directed by Jorge León. He asked the performers questions that addressed very different imaginary characters: a warrior, a prostitute in Israel, a rock star, a sad old man. Whereas the session with Aughterlony was edited into a video with the questions erased, the interview with Stuart resulted in a live version that altered with each performance. Stuart uses the generated stock of answers as a potential that can be freely played with. The lines may be broken up, combined in whatever order, used as a stepping-stone for newly improvised utterances. 'I applied the same technique I use when working with physical states to language. My body is often at war with itself. It is becoming and it is unbecoming someone or something', says Stuart of *I'm All Yours*. A particular way of dealing with 'the choreographic' is transposed to a different kind of 'corpus'. Speech is treated as if it were a body: the individual sentences are like limbs that can be split off from the initial context and be rendered autonomous. The double operation of analysing and re-synthesizing, which already framed the choreography of the body in *Disfigure Study*, changes into a general procedure for the ordered transformation of all sorts of materials. Yet the fragmented, scattered speech in Stuart's solo does not result in linguistic waste or an artificial construct that no longer makes sense. Like the disfigured body in her early works, Stuart's seemingly directionless flow of autobiographical utterances is anchored in everyday life. The solo magnifies an ordinary mode of self-presentation, a subjectivity that fits the condition of post-modernity.

We are constantly being exposed through the omnipresence of all sorts of recording devices. The most obvious examples are the banal security camera in a street or a parking lot and the digital camera in whatever social situation. Camera-mediated images played a prominent role in every issue of *Highway 101*. Their artistic use doubled the normalcy of being watched in daily life and hinted at a continuity between the theatre dispositive and its outside that went beyond theatricality. The gaze of co-present others that one reflexively takes into account in theatricalized behaviour and communication is supplemented in ordinary life these days by a gazing anonymous Other, an unknown spectator whose scrutinizing eyes differ from the mechanical camera eye that mediates between 'me' and 'her', 'him' or 'them'. Mass media and internet, particularly digital social networks such as Facebook, have coupled the experience of continuously being exposed to a faceless Other to the desire to be intimate and to communicate private truths. The intertwinement of personal pleasure and public confession of course already existed before the arrival of technologically mediated communication. Modernity is 'a singularly confessing society', Michel Foucault notes in the first volume of *The History of Sexuality*: 'The confession has spread its effects far and wide. It plays a part in justice, medicine, education, family relationships, and love relations, in the most ordinary affairs of everyday live, and in the most solemn rites; one confesses one's crimes, one's sins, one's thoughts and desires, one's illnesses and troubles; one goes about telling, with the greatest precision, whatever is most difficult to tell. One confesses in public and private, to one's parents, one's educators, one's doctors, to those one loves... Western man has become a confessing animal.' These incisive lines were published in 1976, at a moment when feminists and homosexual or lesbian activists still advocated the strategies of 'speaking out' and 'coming out'. 'The personal is political', states a famous feminist saying, yet meanwhile willed self-exposure has become a mass product made for and by the masses. Within traditional mass media communication, public confession was a privilege of the famous; with the breakthrough of populist neo-television and digital social networks, the lust for intimate communication with an anonymous Other has changed into a common practice. Actions, intentions, thoughts, desires or preferences now have a double life. They exist before and after their publication – and for a growing number of people only publicly communicated private facts are real facts.

The solos of Simone Aughterlony and Meg Stuart enlarge the postmodern mode of subjectivity that shimmers through in the countless personal messages roaming around in digital space. The modern subject's centre of gravity lies within itself: it is a consistent ego made up of a reflective self-consciousness (Descartes' famous *cogito ergo sum*) and an autonomous will that private law sanctifies in the idea of the freely contracting individual. This subject's self-image primarily hinges on the symbolic recognition by a handful of significant others, such as one's partner, children, friends, or direct colleagues. The scattered self-presentation that Aughterlony and Stuart stage no longer points to such a coherent self whose relatively fixed identity is socially supported through the sustained interaction with others. The postmodern subject evoked here addresses an anonymous Other, an empty void that never speaks back and whose desired recognition must therefore be fantasized, even hallucinated. In its inevitably failing attempts to make contact with this imaginary One, the self behaves hyperkinetically and desperately tries out all sorts of communicative keys, out of the hope of being noticed and receiving some sign of positive feedback. Its fragmentary speech moreover reflects the absence of a firm identity that remains stable over a longer period of time. The new hyper-flexible self misses character and is a container of divergent scripts of behaviour and communication that are partly contingently, partly strategically deployed, according to the situation at hand. This is indeed the most striking feature of the subjectivity performed by Aughterlony and Stuart: *the postmodern speaking subject lacks personal substance and resembles an externally programmed linguistic machine* that erratically plunders the Great Book of Clichés in Confessional Self-Presentation. The magnified postmodern self continually shifts the register and smoothly jumps from banal observations to sexual confessions, but only rarely does it say something that sounds unexpected or truly individual. The stereotypical ego-talk can go on endlessly and produces a linguistic diarrhoea dominated by the fear to fall silent and to be confronted with one's very emptiness. For no genuine identity underlies this hysterical self-presentation: self-expression has imploded into a constantly revisited self-fashioning. The prototypical contemporary self has no psychological depth and is a pure surface of communicative appearances that are inconsistently re-performed. The question regarding the veracity of the fragmented autobiographical speech of Aughterlony and Stuart is therefore pointless. They just perform the performative nature of the postmodern subject: they stage the staging of the self that puts on mask after communicative mask at an accelerating pace.

Intermezzo: Liveness as Re/Presentation

Antonin Artaud derided traditional theatre practice for its 'logocentrism' or predominant textual orientation. The Word reigns, and therefore also representation. A given text is staged or 'brought to life' — yet the actors are not exactly living human beings, but puppets on a textual string. Countless are the attempts to realize Artaud's plea to do away with the double in theatre and to turn the stage from a representational dispositive into a site of pure presence. Artaud's 'theatre of cruelty' does indeed not aim at violent spectacles but envisages a multi-sensorial reality in which liveness approaches the presentness of Life. 'We must believe in a sense of life renewed by theatre, a sense of life in which man fearlessly makes himself master of what does not yet exist, and brings it into being. ... [W]hen we speak of "life", it must be understood we are not referring to life as we know it from its surface of fact, but to that fragile, fluctuating centre which forms never reach', Artaud writes at the end of the essay 'The Theatre and Culture' that prefaces *The Theatre and its Double*. With different accents, the founders of modern dance, such as Isadora Duncan, pursued the same ideal of a vital performing art that grounded the modern theatre tradition of 'de-representation'. Through assumingly natural movements originating in an ever present, transhistorical potential to move without artifice, dance could become a grandiose hymn to the irrepressible forces of Life. This new kind of dance would not be about Life but express it directly, without any symbolic mediation or narrative alibi. In reality, Duncan's performances and those of other advocates of modern dance, staged a particular idea of Life that was greatly informed by primitivism and its phantasm of the noble savage.

Socio-cultural representations of Life frame every attempt at 'de-representation', yet the dream that the stage can be transformed into a space only animated by Life itself keeps on fascinating both artists and theorists (and probably also an important part of the voyeuristic public). One of the more recent versions opposes the doubling within theatre to the notion of performance. Whereas theatre has a representational nature, performance is put on par with the mere presence of 'action taking place'. The non-theatrical performer is no longer an impersonator and functions as 'the point of passage for energy flows – gestural, vocal, libidinal, etc. – that traverse him without ever standing still in a fixed meaning or representation', the Canadian theorist Josette Féral writes in her seminal 1982 essay 'Performance and Theatricality: The Subject Demystified'. Féral refers to the practices of conceptual artists such as Vito Acconci or Elizabeth Chitty and the work of Robert Wilson, Richard Foreman and Jerzy Grotowski. She could as well have mentioned Judson's quest for 'pure movement' and many other examples of contemporary dance. Theatre of cruelty, modern dance, performance, pure movement: whatever the name, an important current within the performing arts seems mesmerized by the possibility of a mute stage presence that communicates nothing, symbolizes nothing, represents nothing. The reverse side of this genuine nothingness is the plenitude of Being as such, or so the project of 'de-representation' suggests. Making Being present is not necessarily a superhuman act. The historical avant-garde already equated the unmediated expression of Life with capturing the all but heroic enigmas of everyday life: quotidian gestures, ugly bodily postures, simple street noises, et cetera.

The various attempts to change the stage into a place of pure presence all reach out for an impossible limit of 'de-presentation' within the context of a dispositive inescapably marked by 'being in representation'. Jacques Derrida's characterization of the split

nature of presence is all the more true for any kind of stage presence: 'Presence, in order to be presence and self-presence, has always already begun to represent itself, has always already been penetrated.' Stage presence inevitably transforms into the representation of presence or a *represented presence* through the co-presence of a witnessing observer – of a spectator, a gazing audience, an anonymous Other. During a performance, actions are therefore not just taking place but indicate or signify their occurrence in a situation of co-presence. They happen 'now, here', and they reflexively represent this presence through a particular mode of theatricality. The performer's bodily presence is at once excluded and included in its public representation, which crosses out the possibility of pure action that so many theatre or dance makers have been after. The doubling can be enacted in several ways: the various modes of theatricality go together with divergent possibilities of representing presence. Or as theorist Cormac Power notes: 'presence is a function of theatrical signification' and must be approached 'in terms of how it is constructed/manipulated/played with in performance.' Presence is indeed performed within a theatre context, resulting in a performative presence that inevitably subverts that which it performs.

The operation of doubling or representing does not nullify the signified presence since the performers are spatially co-present in every moment that their 'being on stage' enters into representation. The performed presence is therefore at once metonymic and metaphorical. There exists a relation of contiguity between stage presence and its staged representation (metonymy), and yet it simultaneously looks as if the performers and their actions are 'just present' (metaphor). Precisely this paradoxical knot or strange loop defines live performance: *liveness is re/presentation, or the performed unity of the difference between presence and representation in a situation of co-presence.* The slash dividing 're' from 'presentation' points to a difference that can in principle be articulated in the direction of one of the two poles making up the distinction. Liveness is therefore haunted by both 'de-representation' and 'over-representation' – the possibility of mere presence cancelling out representation or the possibility of pure spectacle annihilating presence. Thus in theatre dance, such as the work of Judson, the moving body may try to thwart its inevitable 'being in representation' during a public performance: through the deliberate negation of the co-presence of the public, the physicality of movements or poses is stressed at the expense of their eventual denotations and connotations. The performer's body hints at its present being/being present, yet it simultaneously encounters an unsurpassable limit since it cannot 'de-represent' itself in such a way that it is only this body in relationship with itself. Or the alternative route is taken: by highlighting representation and making the spectacle hyper-spectacular, using all disposable means – sound, lighting, video images – the 'presences' on stage disappear in a dazzling surface of mere appearances. There is once again a residue, or a stumbling block, consisting of the mere materiality of the representing subjects and objects that resists all attempts at its complete neutralization. This non-erasable physicality confirms the status of the stage as the present locus of enunciation, as a 'now, here' that acts as the sender of the enacted representations making up a performance.

The theatre dispositive allows a twofold self-deconstruction, but the underlying split unity of re/presentation can never be completely undone: neither presence nor representation is destructible by its other. But then why does an important current within modern and postmodern theatre or dance consistently opt for the practice of 'de-representation'? How to explain the widespread aversion to 'being in representation', or the ever recurrent fascination with the impossible to realize possibility of staging an undivided presence or pure Being that remains uncontaminated by its being watched? What kind of unconscious drive animates the desire to literalize liveness in the direction of Life? What may latently be at stake in the puritanical belief in, what is often called, in a tellingly moralistic vocabulary, 'authenticity'? Why has the stage become one of the privileged places where a doubtful metaphysics of presence is enacted again and again? Why deny the obvious and try to subtract representation from 'being in representation'? Is it because live art can be a heaven in a heartless world, a heterotopic practice pointing to the utopia of a transparent and unmediated communication that overcomes the difference symbolized by the hyphen in the word 'co-presence'?

Subverting Re/Presentation

Technologically produced or reproduced images may highlight the inevitable 'being in representation' of the body within the theatre dispositive. 'In a dance performance, the multiplication of body images by video recordings, film pictures or computer animation makes clear that the body is always already a doubled one that presents itself to the gaze at the border of the symbolic and the imaginary. ... The body is never entirely with itself. It is always already a looked at body image that is supported by a symbolic structure such as the one of theatre', emphasizes Gerald Siegmund in his study *Abwesenheit*. Technological media moreover function as autonomous prostheses of the human body and its perceptive capacities. Marshall McLuhan therefore speaks of 'extensions of man' – dixit the subtitle of his classic *Understanding Media* – but camera or computer images also allow the creation of visual fields that profoundly differ from the human eye's perceptive capacity. In the same vein, microphones and other technological devices can transform the acoustic spectrum associated with the human voice. Take, for example, the studied interplay between camera angle and close-up in a banal movie: an ordinary face signalling doubt changes into an intriguing spectacle. The face becomes hyper-expressive, even enigmatic through all sorts of small movements and details of the skin minutely registered by the zooming in of the camera. Another 'faciality' emerges, which looks at once fragmentary and microscopic, artificial and hyperrealist from the point of view of human perceptivity. The filmed face is no longer just a visage but an anonymous landscape packed with fascinating details. Dimples, lines, shadows: it is all there, but hyper-sensual and much more intimate than in ordinary life.

'Evidently a different nature opens itself to the camera than opens to the naked eye. ... [The] camera intervenes with the resources of its lowerings and liftings, its interruptions and isolations, its extensions and accelerations, its enlargements and reductions. The camera introduces us to unconscious optics as does psychoanalysis to unconscious impulses', Walter Benjamin already observed in the 1930s, long before the digitalization of the image took off. Camera-generated images confront the perceptivity of the human eye with both its physical limits and cultural conditioning. They offer the viewer a mediated looking at the overlooked and have simultaneously reframed the common visualization of the various body parts and corporeal actions as well as the general impression of a human's physical appearance. Whereas the close-up technique produces a post-human visual intimacy, the possibility to slow down a camera recording reveals entirely unknown qualities in familiar movements such as using a knife and fork during a meal or walking down a staircase. And notions such as 'glamour' and 'the photogenic' indicate that the appreciation of the outer body has been profoundly altered by the constant exposure to the culture of the camera and its specific articulation in mass media communication. Not that reality as perceived by the human eye has fully imploded, as Jean Baudrillard has repeatedly suggested, into the hyper-reality of synthetic simulations. We rather constantly switch between two different modes of perception. The direct sensory contact with the world is constantly alternated and combined with the audio-visual perception of various sorts of technologically mediated representations, ranging from digital photographs to television images and the information on computer screens. Notwithstanding the various speculative reports on its waning presence within post-modernity, the human body still operates as a prime locus of perception and memory in our so called post-human times.

In the *Highway 101* project, the video camera regularly destabilizes the spectator's confidence in the directness of their vision. Thus 'the lounge' section in the Vienna edition does not only consist of the real time-actions of the performers. The dancers intermingle with the audience and simultaneously keep using the long corridor as their main performing habitat. It is a strange kind of stage, since only the two openings in the wall separating 'the lounge' from the tunnel-like space allow an immediate viewing of the performers' actions. Yet their running and gesturing in the tunnel is also registered by two video cameras hanging on the same level at the corridor's left and right hand side. Both camera recordings are projected in real time next to each other in 'the lounge', rendering an unobservable presentness observable. The symmetrical positioning of the cameras results in two images that mirror each other. Whereas in the first image the dancers run away from a sidewall, the second shows them running toward one. Now and then a performer stops before a camera, looks into it, and starts making rapid facial gestures. The spectator sees an improvised dance of the face, a continually re-articulated 'faciality' whose details would remain invisible in a live situation not mediated by the enlarged image produced by a focusing camera eye. Overall, the staged situation highlights the difference between presentness and representation, which is constitutive of the split nature of liveness.

Once the dancers begin to blend with the audience, the live registration of the actions in the tunnel is mixed with previously made recordings. A performer is thus physically present in 'the lounge', but the projected images sometimes show him or her still running up and down the corridor. Although the spectator quickly understands the technological artificiality of the situation, the doubling results in a confusing, uncanny loop between direct vision and the re-visioning of already looked at images. One sees a dancer 'now, here' among the audience, and one contemplates at the same moment a visual reminiscence of a just seen image of that very same performer engaged in another kind of action in a different space. Present observation becomes haunted by past observations: the spectator's possible forgetting is short-circuited through the re-screening of a real time image seen just minutes ago. The juxtaposition of direct perception and previously perceived representations creates a ghost-like, slightly hallucinatory visual experience that destabilizes the 'now, here' framing liveness. 'In this ingenious piling up of images, different levels of reality become blurred and at least one grand narrative that has clung to dance since modernism perishes, namely the notion of transience, of here-and-nowness, of livelier than live, or whatever "real" that may be ascribed to performance. At most we can distinguish degrees of visuality', concludes the Flemish dance critic Jeroen Peeters in his in-depth review of the *Highway 101* project.

Sound Magic, or the Closure of Representation

Montage or editing is the defining activity in the managing of technologically produced or reproduced representations. Manipulating sounds or images according to a constructivist logic was once a consuming operation that has since been greatly simplified with the breakthrough of 'the digital' as a unifying super-medium. The cheaply available computer-based technology has indeed changed montage from a predominantly aesthetic principle into a common activity. Processing information equals editing texts, sounds or images with the help of sometimes sophisticated software. Meg Stuart integrated montage as a prime compositional device in her practice of 'writing dance' right from the beginning. Already in *Disfigure Study*, both the conspicuous exposure of isolated body parts and the juxtaposition of individual 'dance sentences' into larger sections testify to a choreographic stance that fuses the logic of montage known from film editing with an awry view of the human body. In nearly every scene, subsequent choreographies exemplify Stuart's more specific commitment to the twofold epistemology of fracturing and re-synthesizing, which Cubism and Constructivism already introduced within the fine arts and cinema during the first quarter of the twentieth century. With greater or lesser emphasis, all sections in the Vienna edition of *Highway 101* also assume this particular mode of montage but one longer scene stands out. It is known as 'The House' and comes directly after Stuart's confession solo.

Leaving the room in which Stuart has just performed, the spectators enter a vast space. They are asked to stay behind a white line, about twenty metres from one of the walls of the space. A central stair, a couple of doors to the right of the stair, and some smaller and larger glassless windows indicate the existence of several rooms behind the wall; to the left of the stair, a significant part of the wall has been removed, creating an open space. To the electronic music of Viennese sound artist Peter Rehberg (aka Pita), the dancers perform all sorts of actions, often quotidian in nature, that are usually repeated over a considerable length of time. Walking and running, sitting and falling are alternated with frenetically jumping up and down or even, in the case of one male performer, simulating making love. The movement phrases as well as the performers' body images are frequently cut up. Thus two dancers each repeatedly walk from right to left behind one of the glassless windows. Yet they never visibly reverse the trajectory: stepping from left to right seems to have been eliminated. Or two performers use an intermediate floor in order to create an artificially composed body: the first dancer's upper body runs over into the second one's lower body. 'The House' contains several such scenes recalling video editing or film montage. Yet now and then the dancers also leave their 'house' and move or gesture, sometimes in a spastic way, in the open space separating the audience from the wall. This does not bring them closer to the public because Pita's soundtrack acts as an impenetrable fourth wall of a peculiar kind.

The musical score, *Untitled 3* from Pita's 1999 album *Get Out,* is an eleven-minute, slowly mutating composition starting very noisily and gradually developing into a short melodic line that is continuously repeated in different registers. Sound layers are added and varied with each new loop, resulting in a baroque collage that combines a blasting bass motif with shrill, high frequency tones. During 'The House' scene this composition is played very loud, which reinforces the overall acoustic impact of the music on the spectator's sensory experience of the observed actions. With increasing effect, the sound envelops the performers, their motions and the setting. After a while the performance is so cocooned by the music that the live movements no longer seem to take place in the physical space shared with the audience. A primarily optical, two-dimensional representational plane emerges that apparently reduces the performer's bodies to dematerialized shadow figures of themselves and gives the spectator the impression of witnessing a film or video screening. The perceived flatness is of course an audio-visual artefact, yet realizing this does not diminish the striking metamorphosing impact of the loud soundtrack at all. It is as if one contemplates an externalized hallucination, a spectral reality in which the physical world has imploded without leaving many traces of substantiality. The phantasm-like character of 'The House' is intensified towards the end of the scene. From their proverbial dwelling, the performers start to throw used radios, computers, toasters, et cetera in the direction of the audience. Amidst the piling up electronic waste, Yukiko Shinozaki frantically moves with a smile on her face.

'The House' still stands out within the oeuvre of Meg Stuart & Damaged Goods as an example of radical montage and of remediating dance towards 'the cinematographic'. The scene was retaken in the final edition of *Highway 101* in Zürich, which necessitated the complete rebuilding of the set in a very different type of space. For the scenography of *Visitors Only*, created in 2003, Stuart and set designer Anna Viebrock would also find inspiration in 'The House': the performance takes place in a labyrinth-like residence consisting of two floors and several rooms. Stuart also used variations on the basic principle underlying 'The House' scene in several of her evening-length works made after *Highway 101*. It actually comes down to a specific, inter-medial operation: *the medium of sound remediates the medium of dance*. The music 'infects' the dance and re-articulates the functioning of the theatrical dispositive, with the net effect that the tension between presence and representation is critically exposed. Indeed, 'The House' creates a split between the conscious knowledge that the performers are physically acting 'now, here' and the sensory perception of their existence within a two-dimensional visual field evoked by the pervasiveness of the music. The cognitively witnessed materiality of the dancers' bodies and the set disappears into a screen-like surface on which both turn up again as mere appearances lacking depth or substance. Spectacle reigns in this uncanny instance of 'over-representation' that does not rely on impressive manoeuvres, high-tech tricks or the dazzling of the senses through a bombardment of various stimuli. Presence is just thoroughly remediated and becomes immanently coupled to 'the cinematographic' through the complete 'soundscaping' of the dance. The identity of the theatre dispositive as a space dominated by the law of representation is thus magnified to such an extent that one has the impression of witnessing a stage hallucination. This experience is however immediately countered by the reminder that one remains together 'now, here' with the performers. The general effect of dematerialization indeed provokes an opposite effect: the 'over-representation' calls forth its negation in the spectators' consciousness. Their gazing oscillates between belief and disbelief in the produced visual surface. In this way, the paradoxical nature of liveness changes into a personal, even intimate experience. For it is now the spectators themselves who embody the unity of the difference between presence and representation: 'The House' makes one aware that the actual locus of liveness is not in the activity being observed, but rather in the audience's co-presence.

Through its continual exposure, liveness is impeded during 'The House' scene, while the 'being in representation', which defines the theatre dispositive, also acquires a different status. The imaginary flatness of the performer's bodies and actions actually simulates the contemporary identity of 'the visual', or its entwinement with the flatness of the screen. An almost pure filmic image emerges that only seems to refer to itself and no longer acts as a surface on which an external material reality enters into representation. Presence turns into absence through the deployed strategy of 'over-representation', which exaggerates to the extreme the stage's doubling nature. Representation is thus brought to a closure that does not end its performativity, quite to the contrary, but literally brings it to a conclusion in which representation loops back onto itself. This self-referential short circuit positions the theatre stage as a space of *playful* representation in which 'being in representation' crosses out 'pure being' – or 'pure movement' – without (a) drama or the doubling of a pre-given double. Or as Jacques Derrida states in the closing lines of his essay 'The Theatre of Cruelty and the Closure of Representation': 'To think the closure of representation is thus to think the cruel powers of death and play which permit presence to be born to itself, and pleasurably to consume itself through the representation in which it eludes itself in its deferral. To think the closure of representation is to think the tragic: not as the representation of fate, but as the fate of representation. Its gratuitous and baseless necessity. And it is to think why it is *fatal* that, in its closure, representation continues.'

Coda: 'Being Moved' and 'The Motioning'

'The House' lives on in several of Meg Stuart's post-*Highway 101* productions – as if this particular scene continues to haunt the work of Damaged Goods. Thus *Alibi* (2001), a performed meditation on the nature of human violence, ends with a striking choreography that is retaken in the opening section of *Visitors Only* (2003). Again enveloped by droning music, performed live by Paul Lemp and Bo Wiget, the dancers stand shaking their bodies over a long stretch of time. The stage transforms into an uncanny spectacle because the performers seem possessed by an invisible force that obliges them to endlessly repeat the same trembling motion. Indeed, the dancing bodies give the impression that their physicality is no longer controlled by an autonomous will and consciousness. In the void left after the undoing of the subject-form, surfaces a second, ghost-like body that incites its corporeal double to go on shaking regardless of the eventual pain or exhaustion it may feel. The scene is actually paradigmatic of the more general view on the body that Stuart started to develop during *Highway 101*. 'Often my performers are fighting invisible forces. They are haunted by something or someone. There are unresolved issues of manipulation and control in my work. Bodies are manipulated. The first statement I make when I teach a class is, "Your body is not yours."... Then, "Who owns your body?" Then, "Let's speak about possession. Let's see the body as a container, the body inhabiting other sources, being a filter." All these issues come right from the work', she says in the *Bomb*-interview with Catherine Sullivan.

The dancing body as a fragmented, multi-polar field of forces, differences or intensities: this quasi-Nietzschean view already informed Stuart's very first performances, witness the vast role that physical paradoxes and tics play in *Disfigure Study*. The approach definitely diverges from the primitivism that was constitutive for modern dance. For the kind of corporeal force field Stuart focuses on is not an always already given, transhistorical essence but is actively generated and meticulously explored through all sorts of improvisational tasks in the rehearsal process. Moreover, the physical states produced do not lead to a harmonious recon-ciliation of the dancing body with itself or an assumingly natu-ral mode of corporeality. The performer's body is rather put in a permanent situation of self-alienation and probable failing. It is also a state of excess – of potent forces or anonymous intensities exceeding, or at least being in friction with, the dancer's trained capacity to move with self-mastery. Continually risking her danc-ing self becomes the dancer's defining motto. The performer's body changes into an arena: intended motions incessantly meet resistance, opposing forces unrelentingly thwart a premeditated course of action. The dancer's prime task becomes to navigate these contrary material intensities, exerting a concentrated effort in order to achieve a desired effect.

The overall result of Stuart's approach is a distinctive body im-age in which multi-faceted traces indicate the existence of an invisible field of force structuring the potential to move or not to move. This re-framing of the legitimate dancing body evidently re-articulates the practice of choreography. By inventing various tasks, the dance maker not only searches for new movements or poses with outstand-ing aesthetic qualities that may end up in the final 'written text': the elementary materials *are* the induced bodily states, as well as the ob-servable physical marks they inscribe on the surface of the outer body. 'A state is activity plus intention, and the gap between what you pro-ject and what actually comes through is revealing', Stuart affirms in *Are we here yet?*, a publication documenting the creative processes that feed the work of Damaged Goods. 'It is a goal to show that process of questioning in movement, while completing tasks. Perhaps that process entails the first state: "I don't know who, where, what I am at this moment.".... The insistence and uncertainty are genuine, the confusion and questioning an integral part of it.'

Occasionally Stuart's work seems to endorse a certain still dominant idea of dance, particularly when the performers act in unison: moving in a way that is highly controlled and rhythmi-cally metered. However, mostly the choreography is related to invisible physical impulses to move, giving the notion of dance a definitive twist. The bodily states aroused during the rehearsal are not shown unprocessed but are continually worked over and patiently researched: carefree dancing is not exactly a defining feature of a Damaged Goods performance. Nevertheless, a distinct form of expressivity is retained throughout the performing because the underlying corporeal situation of friction and possible failure is continually reproduced live. Except for the overtly theatrical scenes, the staged actions appear to be born momentarily and seem to engage the performer's body to such an extent that the kind of mental reserve needed to take into account the audience's co-presence, becomes difficult to entertain. Stuart's work suggests that *performing dance is the concentrated expression of a choreographically framed 'being moved' by inner motion drives* (this stance even explicitly informs the 2011 production *Violet*). Such a primarily physical expressivity, which often resonates with body images familiar from everyday life or mass media communication, drastically reframes liveness. For although the enacted motions are scripted and rehearsed, it looks as if they are made 'now, here' out of an irrepressible impulse to move. In short, presentness is magnified in the represented presence of the body — but the impression of a pure performativity or of action momentarily taking place is also subverted by the signified invisible presence. The spectator is indeed confronted with a profound fissure, even an insurmountable lack in her field of vision since the inner corporeal force field sustaining the performed actions is at once absent and connoted in the created body image. The performed presence suggests that something peculiar and very intense is happening over there on the stage in the dancer's body, but what precisely is physically going on will be forever an enigma. The abyss of representation is foregrounded in the very moment bodily presence seems transparently represented: while the performer's body visibly communicates itself, the ultimate referent of the message remains obscure.

The observable remnants of inner corporeal impulses or intensities on the outer body act as an allegory of vital Life. Whereas a symbol suggests a flawless continuity between signifier, signified and referent, an allegory invokes an abstract Idea in order to highlight the unbridgeable gap between a representation and the represented state of affairs. The allegorical body staged in the performances of Damaged Goods thus enacts the Idea of Corporeal Vitality through repeated hints at a difficult to tame, plural movement capacity that structurally resists representation. The potential's autonomy in relation to its subjective steering is clearly stressed: physical forces of movement beyond the dancer's self-control literally animate her body like the well-known ghost-in-the-machine to which consciousness has repeatedly been linked in cognitive psychology and philosophy. Yet the enacted allegorical body first and foremost alludes to the potential to move and not-move that defines the medium of dance as such. The difference between actual and possible movements that every dance performance reproduces in each moment of its unfolding involves this capacity as well.

Like all public communication, theatre dance is a split event: the paradox of re/presentation is embedded in the divided reality of actuality and virtuality, realized and 'possible possibilities'. This was indeed one of the main issues in the discussion of *Rain* in the previous chapter. Given an observer, each movement or pose in the moment of being performed both involves and redefines a horizon of other actions that also look momentarily plausible. The implied virtuality is not just a transcendental condition of possibility that must be logically presupposed in the reconstruction of the act of spectatorship or, preceding it, the making of a dance work. The observer situates the virtual existence of other movements or poses in the dancers' bodily multiplicity, their presumed ability to move or to be moved differently. As an at once structured and open capacity, the dancing body is premised to form the material substrate of the alternative motion possibilities discerned 'now, here' during a performance. Like the physical forces structuring the allegorical body in Stuart's performances, this corporeal potentiality is the genuine blind spot within the spectator's field of vision. It remains forever a closed book, a virtual reality whose existence cannot be doubted but that the viewer is never able to perceive directly. From the spectator's point of view, *the movement potential embodied by the dancer(s) constitutes a performative absence grounding both the split nature of theatre dance (the actuality/virtuality difference) and of liveness (the presence/ representation difference).*

During a performance, a dancer's trained capacity to move and to not-move is selectively activated in line with the overall choreography and acts as the material yet unobservable source of all observable motions. Gerald Siegmund therefore speaks of 'the motioning' ('das Bewegende') when referring to the bodily reality at once supporting and accompanying all actions in theatre dance. 'The motioning is not invisible and therefore reducible to an abstract idea since it is tangibly corporeal. At the same time it is not visible because it ... makes up the absent in move-ment', he writes. 'It makes up the absent in movement because it is always that which is not danced but was nevertheless always possible. The motioning in the movement utters itself without be-ing a readable sign. The motioning in the movement is its illeg-ibility. It rather opens up spaces for potential bodies that do not exist yet or already no longer exist.' The dancing body is a split reality situated at the junction of movement and 'the motioning', actual actions and a virtual multiplicity of bodily differences pre-viously actualized or yet to actualize. 'The motioning' comprises a myriad of possible bodily states that may be physically realized or enacted. Given the inevitability of linear time, this excess of possibilities can only be explored selectively and successively, so through a continual re-affirmation of the dancing body's divided nature. The difference between performed and potential actions can never be directly represented, let alone bridged, and can only be hinted at via opaque surface traces that direct the spectator's gaze to an unreadable corporeality – to the all too mundane real-ity of flesh-and-bones that simultaneously embodies and differs from the potential it alludes to. At stake as well is an impossible identity limit for the dancers themselves. They can never dance what they are: the unity of the difference between actuality and virtuality forever eludes them.

Time and again, the dancing body singularizes its capacity to move and to not-move during training sessions and workshops, rehearsals and performances. Haunted by motion possibilities yet to explore, it experiences an endless metamorphosis without the prospect of a final arrival. There is no state of being wherein the moving body converges with itself, or discovers its proper exist-ence and becomes self-identical. The dancing body is destined to lead a nomadic life: it is *a becoming body* that enjoys countless eter-nal lives in the never accessible 'now, here' in which a movement at once appears and disappears ('now, here' is indeed nowhere). The incessantly singularized bodily motion potential – 'the motioning' – is the medium of dance made human, provided with a human face and bearing a proper name that inscribes the danc-ing body into the symbolic order of an always particular dance culture. As a purely virtual multiplicity, this medium is formless, mere chaotic Matter, unordered noise. No melody or, in another register, no calculus can grasp the hyper-complexity of a danc-ing body's unfathomable potentiality, which structurally resists representation and remains forever invisible in every one of its visible manifestations. 'The body of the dancer can take on, can take up, all forms. It is the possible', writes French philosopher Michel Serres in *Genèse*, his extended meditation on 'Being' as 'the noise of the world'. 'The body of the dancer is the body of the possible, it is blank, it does not exist ... It is Nobody. It is, literally, broken up. The foot can go in all possible directions; the leg, the arm, the hand, the torso can go in all possible directions. The body is shattered over all the directions of the space. ... Who am I, body that dances? A naked space. Not protected by a fortress of singularities. Without the support of qualities. A body without qualities.'

Sources

Studying the Body
The description of *Disfigure Study* is based on the video registration of a showing at the Berlin Volksbühne in December 2006, which was danced by Simone Aughterlony, Michael Rüegg and Sigal Zouk-Harder. I also relied on personal recollections of one of the premiere series performances in October 1991 at the Klapstuk festival in Leuven (cast: Francisco Camacho, Carlota Lagido and Meg Stuart) and of the first retake of *Disfigure Study* as shown in February 2002 in Leuven (cast: Simone Aughterlony, Joséphine Evrard and Michael Rüegg). The brief characterization of the academic regime of representation is inspired by Nathalie Heinich, *Du peintre à l'artiste. Artisans et académiciens à l'âge classique.* Paris: Minuit, 1993. Throughout this paragraph and the next ones making up the 'first movement' of this chapter, I now and then revisit ideas from the following essays that I previously published on Stuart's work: *Esbracejar/Physical Paradoxes: Vera Mantero/Meg Stuart.* Leuven: Klapstuk, 1993 (written together with Pieter T'Jonck); 'Dramatic Images of Society: Meg Stuart's Dance Theatre', in *Ballet International/Tanz Aktuell,* 2 (8/9), 1995, pp. 54–59; and 'In Media Res: A Walk Through the Work of Meg Stuart, in *A-Prior,* (6), Autumn/Winter 2001–2002, pp. 28–37.

Constructivist Choreography
The view on the human body presented at the outset is loosely inspired by Judith Butler, *Bodies that Matter: On the Discursive Limits of 'Sex'.* London: Routledge, 1993 and the chapter 'November 28, 1947: How Do You Make Yourself a Body Without Organs?' in Gilles Deleuze and Félix Guattari, *A Thousand Plateaus. Capitalism and Schizophrenia.* London: Continuum, 2003, pp. 149–166. The cited conversation between Catherine Sullivan and Meg Stuart appeared untitled in *Bomb,* (104), 2008, pp. 28–35 (p. 29). Gerald Siegmund analyses the dancers' bodies in Stuart's performances as only consisting of differences in *Abwesenheit. Eine performative Ästhetik des Tanzes. William Forsythe,*

Jérôme Bel, Xavier Le Roy, Meg Stuart. Bielefeld: transcript Verlag, 2006, p. 410. Sigmund Freud introduces the notion of polymorphous perversity in 'Infantile Sexuality', one of the constituent articles making up *Three Essays on the Theory of Sexuality.* New York (NY): Basic Books, 2000, pp. 39–72. 'Optical unconscious' is an expression used in passing by Walter Benjamin in his essay 'Little History of Photography', included in Walter Benjamin, *Selected Writings, Volume 2. Part 1, 1927–1930.* Cambridge (MA): Harvard University Press, 1999, pp. 507–530 (p. 512). The notion of 'extimacy' is put forward in Jacques Lacan, *The Ethics of Psychoanalysis (Seminar 1959–60).* London: Routledge, 1992.

Dance/Image/Montage
The proposed notion of imaging is loosely inspired by the closing chapter on art in Gilles Deleuze and Félix Guattari, *What is Philosophy?* London: Verso, 1994, pp. 163–200. Reference is also made to Guy Debord, *Society of the Spectacle.* Detroit (MI): Black & Red, 1983; Sergei Eisenstein, *Film Form. Essays in Film Theory.* Orlando (FL): Harcourt Brace & Company, 1997; Norbert Servos, 'Pina Bausch: Dance and Emancipation', in Alexandra Carter (ed.), *The Routledge Dance Studies Reader.* London: Routledge, 1999, pp. 36–45 (p. 38); and the difference between the 'readerly' and 'writerly text' as developed in Roland Barthes, *S/Z.* Oxford: Blackwell, 1990.

Re-Viewing *No Longer Readymade*
The description and further analysis of *No Longer Readymade* are primarily based on a video recording of the performance's premiere in August 1993 at Theater am Halleschen Ufer in Berlin (cast: Sarah Baud, David Hernandez, Benoît Lachambre and Meg Stuart). In addition, I relied on personal recollections of one of the showings, performed by the same cast, in October 1993 at the Klapstuk festival in Leuven.

Minimizing Meaning, or Radicalizing Dance Theatre
The global characterization of the tradition of German *Tanztheater*

is partly informed by Susanne Schlicher, *TanzTheater. Traditionen und Freiheiten: Pina Bausch, Gerhard Bohner, Reinhild Hoffmann, Hans Kresnik, Susanne Linke.* Reinbek: Rowohlt, 1987 and Royd Climenhaga, *Pina Bausch.* Abingdon: Routledge, 2009.

Intermezzo: Theatricality and the Gazing Other
The presented view on theatricality owes much to Elisabeth Burns, *Theatricality. A Study of Convention in the Theatre and in Social Life.* London: Harper, 1972 and Erving Goffman, *The Presentation of Self in Everyday Life.* London: Penguin Books, 1990. Michael Fried discusses Denis Diderot's art criticism at length in *Absorption and Theatricality. Painting and the Beholder in the Age of Diderot.* Chicago (IL): University of Chicago Press, 1970. Erika Fischer-Lichte's study *The Transformative Power of Performance: A New Aesthetics.* Abingdon: Routledge, 2008 is quoted p. 163. The thesis that an audience's collective attention acts as an autonomous medium is indebted to Niklas Luhmann's re-articulation of Fritz Heider's medium concept that grounds the communicative approach of art presented in Niklas Luhmann, *Art as a Social System.* Stanford (CA): Stanford University Press, 2000. For a further elaboration, see Rudi Laermans, 'The Politics of Collective Attention', in Sabine Gehm, Pirkko Husemann and Katharina von Wilcke (eds.), *Knowledge in Motion: Perspectives of Artistic and Scientific Research in Dance.* Bielefeld: transcript Verlag, 2007, pp. 235-241.

Gesturing Im/Potentiality
Meg Stuart's short notes on her solo in *No Longer Readymade,* of which one is quoted, were part of the official press dossier that was distributed during Klapstuk 1993. She further commented upon the solo in the lecture 'What are you looking at?', conceived together with Tim Etchells and delivered in September 2001 at Vooruit, Ghent. The complete text can be found in Jeroen Peeters (ed.), *Are we here yet? Damaged Goods/ Meg Stuart.* Dijon: les presses du réel, 2010, pp. 34-37 (p. 35; italics in the

original). Reference is also made to Jean-François Lyotard, 'Something like: "Communication ... without Communication"', in Jean-François Lyotard, *The Inhuman. Reflections on Time.* Stanford (CA): Stanford University Press, 1991, pp. 108-118; the already mentioned interview between Catherine Sullivan and Meg Stuart in *Bomb,* p. 34; and Giorgio Agamben, 'Notes on Gesture', in Giorgio Agamben, *Means without End. Notes on Politics.* Minneapolis (MN): University of Minnesota Press, 2000, pp. 49-60 (quoted twice, p. 58).

Liveness and/or 'the Political'
My reconstruction of the Vienna stop of *Highway 101* is based on personal recollections of a run-through and two actual showings, as well as my extensive review of the Vienna performance in 'Het lichaam als medium. Notities rondom de Weense stop van *Highway 101*' ('The body as medium. Notes on the Viennese stop of *Highway 101*'), in *Etcetera,* (73), 2000, pp. 66-72, and the in-depth analysis of the complete *Highway 101* cycle by Jeroen Peeters in 'Strategies of Adaption. Some Points of Entry and Exit Concerning Damaged Goods' *Highway 101*', in *A-Prior,* (6), Autumn/ Winter 2001-2002, pp. 68-81. Stuart's general characterization of *Highway 101* stems from Meg Stuart, 'In Pieces', in Jeroen Peeters (ed.), *Are we here yet?,* pp. 116-125 (pp. 120-121).

The invoked 'ideology of liveness' is critically discussed in Philip Auslander, *Liveness: Performance in a Mediatized Culture.* Abingdon: Routledge, 2008 (2nd edition). John Dewey's hinted at intuition that the gathering of a public around a common concern conditions political action has been revived by Bruno Latour; see, for instance, his essay 'From *Realpolitik* to *Dingpolitik,* or How to Make Things Public', in Bruno Latour and Peter Weibel (eds.), *Making Things Public. Atmospheres of Democracy.* Karlsruhe/Cambridge (MA): ZKM/ MIT Press, 2005, pp. 14-43. In addition, the following publications are quoted: Walter Benjamin, 'The Work of Art in the Age of Mechanical Reproduction', in Walter Benjamin, *Illuminations.* London/New York:

Pimlico/Random House, 1999, pp. 211–244 (p. 223 and p. 216); Guy Debord, *Society of the Spectacle*, paragraph 29 (not paginated); Jacques Rancière, 'The Emancipated Spectator', in Jacques Rancière, *The Emancipated Spectator*. London: Verso, 2009, pp. 1–24 (p. 17).

Performing Postmodern Subjectivity
Jorge León describes the making of the solos by Simone Aughterlony and Meg Stuart in a short interview fragment that is included in Jeroen Peeters (ed.), *Are we here yet?*, p. 194; the cited characterization by Stuart of her solo *I'm All Yours* can be found on the same page. Michel Foucault's *The History of Sexuality. Volume I: An Introduction*. New York (NY): Vintage Books, 1990 is quoted page 59. Kenneth J. Gergen's *The Saturated Self: Dilemmas of Identity in Contemporary Life*. New York (NY): Basic Books, 2000 inspired in part the short profile of the post-modern self.

Intermezzo: Liveness as Re/Presentation
Antonin Artaud's cited essay 'The Theater and Culture' opens his famous collection *The Theater and Its Double*. New York (NY): Grove Press, 1958, pp. 7–14 (p. 13). The definition of performance as 'action taking place' and the subsequent description of the non-impersonating performer stem from Josette Féral, 'Performance and Theatricality: The Subject Demystified', in *Modern Drama*, 25 (1), 1982, pp. 171–181 (pp. 173–174). Jacques Derrida deconstructs the possibility of pure presence in his quoted essay 'The Theatre of Cruelty and the Closure of Representation', which is included in Jacques Derrida, *Writing and Difference*. London: Routledge, 2009, pp. 292–316 (p. 314). Cormac Power offers an extensive review of the de-bates surrounding the notion of theat-rical presence in his study *Presence in Play. A Critique of Theories of Presence in the Theatre*. Amsterdam: Rodopi, 2008 (p. 198).

Subverting Re/Presentation
Reference is made to the following publications: Gerald Siegmund, *Abwesenheit*, pp. 202–203; Marshall

McLuhan, *Understanding Media: The Extensions of Man*. Cambridge (MA): MIT Press, 1994; Walter Benjamin, 'The Work of Art in the Age of Mechanical Reproduction', p. 230; Jean Baudrillard, *Selected Writings*. Cambridge: Polity Press, 2004; and Jeroen Peeters, 'Strategies of Adaption', p. 72.

Sound Magic, or the Closure of Representation
The idea that a medium taking over another one results in a thorough remediation of the latter, for instance when sound starts completely envel-oping a dance performance, is ex-plored at length by Jay David Bolter and Richard Grusin in *Remediation. Understanding New Media*. Cambridge (MA): MIT Press, 2000. Jacques Derrida's already mentioned essay 'The Theatre of Cruelty and the Closure of Representation' is quoted p. 316 (italics in the original).

Coda: 'Being Moved' and 'The Motioning'
Meg Stuart elucidates her view on the dancing body in the interview with Catherine Sullivan for *Bomb* (p. 32) and in the text 'Dancing States', in Jeroen Peeters (ed.), *Are we here yet?*, pp. 20–21 (p. 21). The latter book also contains a section, aptly titled 'Exercises' (pp. 154–165), in which Stuart provides many concrete examples of the kind of tasks she gives her dancers in view of inducing particular bodily states or physical force fields. My use of the notion of allegory is indebted to the two-part article of Craig Owens, 'The Allegorical Impulse: Toward a Theory of Postmodernism', in *October*, (12), Spring 1980, pp. 67–86 and *October*, (13), Summer 1980, pp. 58–80. Reference is also made to Gerald Siegmund, *Abwesenheit*, p. 103; Gilles Deleuze and Félix Guattari, *A Thousand Plateaus* (the notion of the nomadic or becoming body); and Michel Serres, *Genèse*. Paris: Grasset, 1982, p. 69 and pp. 73–74.

Dance Beyond 'the Human'
Thinking Through Recent Developments in Contemporary Dance

First Movement: Defining Reflexive Dance

Dance's Viewpoints

As the programme note succinctly but aptly puts it, *Vanity,* Vincent Dunoyer's 1999 creation, is indeed a triptych 'for a dancer, a percussionist, a video camera and a tape-delay system, on a music by James Tenney'. The show opens with a live performance of Tenney's 1971 composition *Koan,* ironically subtitled 'Having Never Written A Note For Percussion'. The score stipulates that a single note is to be played on an unspecified percussion instrument in the mode of a lasting swell that goes from soft to loud to soft again. Michael Weilacher executes the instruction on a gong, which results in a snowballing, then fading tremolo sound that is amplified and looped by sound technician Alexandre Fostier, who is also present on stage. At the end of his performance, the gong player bows and the surprised audience hesitantly applauds. A few minutes later it becomes clear that the sceptical applause has also been recorded: the manipulated loop of the clapping hands functions as the soundtrack for the second part, performed by Dunoyer himself. Partly inspired by old vanitas paintings, which explains the show's title, he makes contrived movements, first on the floor and later on in an upright position. The actions avoid the register of 'danciness', looking rather sportive or athletic. More than once, they resemble gymnastic exercises, since the almost naked Dunoyer — he wears only briefs — often stretches the muscles of his arms, chest or legs. At times, he moves as if on the verge of 'becoming (an) animal': 'cat', 'tiger' or 'panther' are evident connotations of his great physical agility. This striking corporeal flexibility, evoking a state of near-fluidity, was already the hallmark of Dunoyer's widely appreciated dance work with Rosas, the company he joined in 1990 and left six years later because he wanted to establish himself as an autonomous choreographer.

Dunoyer's movements constantly have a fixed point of orientation in the form of a small grey box that is apparently a mini-camera. The performer places the artefact before or beside his body, holds it in one or both hands, or rolls it up and down a rail at the edge of the proscenium in the final scene. With varying degrees of emphasis, all actions are literally performed for this miniature object. The box always mediates the relationship with the spectator, whose gaze hovers between the continuously displaced grey cube and Dunoyer's moving body. The closing section of *Vanity* suggests that the artefact is indeed a hand-held camera. For after Dunoyer has left the stage, the complete movement sequence is shown again, without sound, in black-and-white on the back wall of the stage, but now seen from the shifting point of view of the small manipulated box. However, barely noticeable micro-differences between the dancing in the live part and the screened images gradually start to cast doubt on the presumed relationship that connects both sections.

Is the video screening really a recording of the live performance? 'No', Dunoyer tells the curious spectator after the show. Whereas the replayed applause is effectively recorded live, the movements that are performed live try to re-enact as closely as possible a previously made video registration. In short, the part danced live anticipates the 'dead' images in *Vanity*'s closing section (and from an allegorical point of view also the spectator's recollections). The piece therefore reverses the assumingly normal relationship between presence and representation, or performance and its recording, distancing itself from the ideology of liveness still underpinning the dominant discourse on the performing arts. This deconstructive gesture is magnified by the live recording of the audience's applause and the projected images, which offer a much more intimate gaze on Dunoyer's moving body than even the best seated spectator could have enjoyed during the performer's presence on stage. The images indeed show parts of the mainly naked body in sometimes uncanny close-ups that are packed with anatomical details imperceptible to the human eye. It is ironically not the dancer's present corporeality but rather the pre-recorded replica that it tries to re-embody that comes skin-close to the viewers in their relationship to the stage.

Vanity raises yet another issue, one that questions the seemingly natural frontal mode of viewing that structures most dance work. Generally, the spectators have a broad, panoptic view: although this may actually be quite limited, they oversee the events on stage like true generals who seem visually in command. Yet something unavoidably escapes this master-eye or all-seeing subject because the viewers' scopic field is anything but congruent with the space at once inhabited and created by the dancing body. The spectators can discern the directions that the body and its various parts take: an arm goes up, then moves to the left, while the complete body is shifted to the right by taking an elastic leap. Through these self-referentially connected movements, the performer continually constructs an own-space within the territory of the stage. As long as it keeps on performing, the dancing body marks the surrounding space with actions, thus reintroducing choreographed space in objective space. A spatial plane of consistency emerges that is made up of self-produced curves, bends, diagonals, et cetera, and an often quite complex configuration of patterns drawn by a myriad of micro-movements. The dancing body is therefore *'a paradoxical body'*, concludes the Portuguese philosopher and dance theorist José Gil in his essay with the same title: 'This body is composed of special matter, which gives it the property of being *in* space and of *becoming* space.'

The direction of each performed movement implies a specific spatial point, a destination, as it were, that has to be reached and will be marked as a next coordinate within the own-space of the dance. In the second part of *Vanity*, this shifting target is continuously made visible through the positioning of the grey box. Depending on the action to be performed, Dunoyer places the small object facing himself head-on or off to the side, or holds it in one hand while moving. The video recording shows that the positioning is well-considered: repeatedly, the box is put at the coordinate towards which the dancing body will move, making the spectator aware of the spatial vanishing points of the enacted movements, which is no small matter. For although it is corporeally indicated, be it only in passing, we usually do not really notice the mobile point at which a movement will come to an end (except of course when a single gesture or a restricted series of actions is repeated several times). The dancing body visibly coordinates its movements on the basis of a volatile system of spatial points, yet this basic operation generally escapes the viewer's attention (Rudolf von Laban tried to encapsulate it within his so-called icosahedron, a model for all possible directions of human movement). And even spectators with a trained eye cannot take up the incessantly re-articulated vanishing point in the movements perceived as a genuine point of view. Knowledgeable viewers also witness the continual construction of an own-space from a fixed and distanced scopic position that prevents them from seeing the action happening from the spatial coordinates. This can only be done by a camera that moves along with the performed movements and is constantly placed on their spatial targets.

The closing section of *Vanity* thus for once makes visible *from within*, the own-space constructed by the movements that build it up in the own-time they simultaneously generate.

Choreography as 'Videography'

Vanity is a performed commentary on the practice of choreography in the age of digital video recording. Choreographing is much like an evolutionary process: it comes down to the variation, selection and retention of movements and non-movements, resulting in a 'written text' that is meticulously re-enacted during each performance. In principle, there is no definitive reading of the final text, no eternally identical execution of the choreographic score. Every performance, beginning with the premiere, varies the ideal or limit object that the choreography itself represents. The prescriptive 'dance text' is never perfectly realized but always haunts each of its enactments as a compelling injunction of literalness that the finite dancer's body cannot completely live up to. To perform a choreography is unavoidably to fail its 'ideality', to avow its at once transcendent character and transcendental nature (in the Kantian sense: the score as the dance's condition of possibility). During its enactment, the 'written text' is therefore both present and absent, however distorting its interpretation. The performance thus simulates that it is a truthful recital or a mere succession of quotes, dissimulating the constitutive absence of a genuine original or master-performance that is rehearsed again and again, because it can never truly realize the identity of the structuring score and its embodiment. This meanwhile established poststructuralist account of the relationship between choreography and performance, which vastly informed the interpretation of De Keersmaeker's early work as discussed in chapter two, is nevertheless somewhat unconvincing here. Something simple but important is missing.

If choreography equals writing (in Greek: *graphein*), then the video camera nowadays primarily acts as the scripting medium that, with considerable consequences, combines in one apparatus the blank page (the video cassette or, more contemporary, the hard disk) and the pencil (the camera lens). 'The choreographic', or the space wherein dance is written, thus tends to converge increasingly with 'the videographic'. Many, though not all, choreographers indeed rely on video recordings when fixing a series of movements or retaking a complete piece. Potential material is first generated and then further explored through task-guided improvisations

until the very moment when both a particular movement sequence and its singular execution acquire a prescriptive status. Video recording is nowadays the material condition of possibility for this transformation of the selected movements — including the idiosyncratic features of their contingent performance — into a binding 'written text'. Meg Stuart is just one of the many contemporary choreographers who openly admits to the structuring role that video has in her choreographic process: 'At one point I give up the responsibility for the material and throw it for the camera, and when a certain scene is where I want it to be, I'll have the dancers learn the material exactly from the tape, with every little mistake. This will take days. It's not about trying to improve the movement, but about accepting the version completely — that's where the rigor comes in.' The invoked 'rigor' is the disciplinary effect of choreography's scoring nature, which by definition implies restless mastering and mindless repetition in view of the formation of a stable corporeal memory. Yet the body that learns to mimic a series of video images also archives a singular performance of the score — or at least, it tries to do so. In sum, *choreography has to a great extent become 'videography', combining 'ideality' and actuality, a 'written text' and its contingent bodily interpretation.*

The entanglement of a choreography and its particular enactment within a video recording also guides the dancer who consults an available, more or less authorized documentation of a dance work when preparing to perform it anew. His or her embodiment of this 'written text' remains a singular approximation of an impossible to repeat series of archived traces. However, the implied text is again no longer only a transcendent ideal animating the dancer's body. It has a tangible material existence, which, in the form of video images, displaces and re-articulates the logic of presence and absence informing the relationship between performance and choreography. The dance critic or scholar who discusses this dialectical entwinement on the basis of particular showings usually also relies on video recordings, and in doing so rehearses the nowadays constitutive, even immanent relationship between 'choreo/videography'. These days, writers about dance are indeed more often than not re-writers who authoritatively refix what has already been fixed in another medium. They make explicit what the video recording does implicitly: canonizing a contingent performance into an exemplary instance of the underlying choreography.

In the age of 'videography', the image frequently precedes the live situation. Live performance is then reframed as a space of bodily re-mediation, even of corporeal resurrection. This is indeed the principal subtext of *Vanity*. The work enacts *the performative pressure of the 'dead' video image on the live dancing body* in a particular way: the dancing resembles the personal quest for a lost body. Viewed in retrospect, Dunoyer's agile body vainly tries to bring back a past body, consisting of the shapes and states his very own corporeality assumed in the moments that it had found itself before an actively recording camera. The performer's perceived corporeality is in the grip of a ghost, an actually unobservable double only made observable afterwards, which functions for the dancer as a transitory locus of imaginary identification. Bodily presence is thoroughly mediated by an objectified memory: the 'now, here' of liveness is haunted by the archived traces of a past forever gone — 'the live' transforms into a failing attempt to re-live. This is perhaps the actual vanity giving the performance its title: a dancing body desperately wanting to again become what it once was through the mimetic embodiment of a series of materialized mirror images.

Vanity can be regarded as a danced exposé of some of the key features of contemporary dance and choreography. The public performance of scored movement is indeed at once the performance's generating subject and addressed object. Various parameters are put into perspective: the conventional nature of public applause (why only clap at the very end of a performance and not after an accomplished task?), the present intertwinement of choreography and 'videography', or the active construction of a choreographed own-space. Did the spectator perhaps witness a danced treatise on theatre dance or, even more to the point, a specimen of so-called conceptual dance? This expression has gained some notoriety since the recent turn of the century. The category has the negative connotation of dry intellectualism, yet of greater importance is the explicit historical reference to the movement of Conceptual Art, which vastly shaped the history of the visual arts from the 1960s onward. Do works such as *Vanity* perhaps signal a belated attempt within contemporary dance to catch up with the evolution in the domains of sculpture and painting? Or are we rather seeing a however partial return of the past in a different context, a revival of a consequential self-reflexive stance already marking Judson after its blurred and overtly

relativist re-articulation within the partly politicized, partly popu-list wave of so-called postmodernist dance of the 1980s and the first half of the 1990s?

Intermezzo: Reconsidering Conceptual Art
This much is clear: Conceptual Art, or Conceptualism, was not one but several things. As early as the late 1960s, the notion point-ed to divergent attitudes within the visual arts. Artists' various uses of the new identity indicated varied strategies of differentiat-ing Conceptualism from Minimalism and Pop Art, the then reign-ing avant-gardes in the globally hegemonic field of American fine arts. Conceptual Art in the broadest and probably most evident meaning continues to refer to an idea-centred artistic practice. 'When an artist uses a conceptual form of art, it means that all of the planning and decisions are made beforehand and the ex-ecution is a perfunctory affair. The idea becomes a machine that makes the art', Sol LeWitt writes in his seminal 1967 essay 'Para-graphs on Conceptual Art'. The informing concept need not be a theoretically articulated notion: a general or abstract idea will do. Whether it is simple or complex, rooted in intuition or informed by more elaborated considerations, the underlying notion visibly structures the art work. Nevertheless, a small or big leap usually separates the initial idea from its material realization and distin-guishes Conceptual Art from mere rational or conclusive think-ing. Whatever the singular relationship between the concept and the artefact produced, the art work does not treat the spectator to 'an emotional kick' but offers a 'mentally interesting' experience, as LeWitt notes. Conceptual Art is indeed mostly emotionally neutral and predominantly addresses – in common metaphysical parlance – the mind instead of the body.

A more distinct stance says that Conceptualism questions the notion of art as such. 'The "purest" definition of conceptual art would be that it is inquiry into the foundations of the con-cept "art", as it has come to mean', asserts Joseph Kosuth in 'Art After Philosophy', another defining statement on Conceptualism, originally published in 1969. Such an explicitly self-referential and deconstructive artistic practice can materialize into palpable arte-facts that present the spectator with an actual viewing experience. This is however not a necessity according to Kosuth: 'Objects are conceptually irrelevant to the condition of art.' Like Kosuth, Lawrence Weiner or the Art & Language collective therefore furthered a linguistic Conceptualism consisting of written utterances that provoke with more or less directness the reader's preconceptions about art's nature. Weiner's practice of publicising statements on exterior walls or free posters involves yet another strand of Conceptual Art. Self-reflexivity is shifted herein from the singular work to the more general socio-cultural conditions of art's reception and its institutionalized links with society, such as the white cube and the museum, the art market and the mediating role of criticism. This way of doing Conceptual Art had well-known forerunners. As Marcel Duchamp's readymades aptly demonstrate, the historical avant-garde already subverted the autonomy of art and cut through its relations with liberal individualism (the artist as a singular author) and modern capitalism (the art work as a unique commodity). Artists such as Daniel Buren or Hans Haacke re-articulated this heritage through works that at once deconstructed the dominant definitions of art and politicized artistic practice. Both orientations only went hand in hand for a short while. During the early 1970s, an ever growing split emerged between the institutional critique of the art market and the museum à la Marcel Broodthaers, and the more activist stance of Martha Rosler, Alan Sekula or the various Latin-American offshoots of Conceptualism, exemplified by the work of, for instance, Hélio Oiticica or Cildo Meireles. It is again a legacy that keeps on informing contemporary art production. Like the reproach of intellectualism, the difference between critical practices primarily addressing the art world's internal functioning and an overtly politically engaged attitude has become vastly entrenched within the visual arts. A seemingly irresolvable 'differend' opposes the supporters of institutional critique and the advocates of an art that actively links up with feminism, the alter-globalization movement, or locally embedded forms of protest.

Conceptual Art profoundly contested the dominant belief in the originality or uniqueness of the art work, the authorial function of the artist, and the still influential remnants of the romantic culture of emotionalism (the idea that the art work must deeply affect and elicit an intimate experience). The self-critical wave that penetrated the field of the visual arts between the mid-1960s and the mid-1970s also tackled the ideology of the aesthetic, or the modern notion that art works mobilize the human sensory capacity in order to generate a communication potential superseding natural language or discourse. The radicalization of

Duchamp's famous invectives against 'retinal art', which inspired his invention of the readymade procedure, resulted in various sorts of de-materialized works. They subverted the logic of commodification and countered the dominant mode of presenting artistic artefacts in a white cube. Art works were made and shown in unusual environments – witness so-called Land Art – or reduced to an ephemeral happening or passing performance. Conceptual Art contested the critic's mediating role too. The practice initiated by the historical avant-garde and revived within Minimalism was magnified: artists self-explained their works and developed their own interpretations of the stakes of Conceptual Art. It all served to solidify the re-articulation of spectatorship set up by the historical avant-garde. The viewers had to read and to think hard if they wanted to keep up and understand. They moreover had to decide autonomously whether a potential candidate for (visual) art could pass the test. Duchamp already buried Beauty on the dunghill of art history and placed the act of naming or not-naming an artefact a work of art in the spectator's centre of attention. Conceptualism self-reflexively completed this tendency to do away with aesthetic judgment in the traditional sense. Art works were willingly conceived as possible artistic propositions – and it was up to the spectator to agree or disagree. Indeed, as I put forward as the central hypothesis of the first chapter when discussing the notion of contemporary dance, has this not become a defining feature of most contemporary art, in the temporal sense, after the eclipse of Conceptualism?

Conceptual Art as a distinct artistic movement was a rather short-lived affair, roughly spanning the decade between 1965 and 1975. These were also the years of sustained protest against the Vietnam War, youth revolt and counter culture, the second feminist wave and the public contestation of the heterosexual regime, the first eco-wave, and a renewed interest in the more unorthodox wings of Marxism. A New Left was born, based on an anti-authoritarian stance that was difficult to reconcile with the disciplinary nature of traditional left politics. Conceptual Art belonged to this broader configuration of contestation and revived the hope of French Surrealism or Russian Constructivism that the questioning of established art practices could be an integral part of a variegated protest movement. The promise did not last long. Already during the first half of the 1970s, artists such as Robert Smithson or Mel Ramsden, together with fellow travellers of Conceptual Art such as critic Lucy Lippard or curator Seth Siegelaub, emphasized the limited scope of critical art practices. Their socio-cultural impact remained confined to a small inner circle, the verdict read. The diagnosis was difficult to rebuke and stimulated many artists' radicalization in the direction of an openly politicized art activism. Conceptual Art moreover proved to be marketable and saleable, collectable and reconcilable with existing modes of mediating art. Around the mid-1970s, it was patently obvious that Conceptual Art had become a legitimate way of producing art and acted as a seedbed for alternative modes of commodification. Preparatory sketches and designs of art works, or signed photographs and authorized video-registrations of performances, opened up new niches within the expanding market for contemporary art. Both public museums and private collectors embraced these possibilities to appropriate the most recent history of art through novel kinds of artefacts. Even the more activist expressions of Conceptual Art, or at least their collectible traces, have meanwhile ended up being what they once vehemently contested to be: autonomous art works enjoyed within the social-political vacuum of the museum space.

Conceptualism continues to haunt contemporary art practices. Neo-Conceptual Art seems forever in fashion after the brief interlude of postmodern painting during the 1980s, or the self-reflexive staging of expressive painting as an imitative second-degree gesture. Damien Hirst, Tracey Emin or Liam Gillick – to mention just three obvious names – conspicuously reiterate a once epoch-making artistic attitude within a totally different context. The repetition alternately looks like a blunt market move (Hirst), an artistic act of despair (Emin), and a keen re-appropriation of former instances of institutional critique (Gillick). Yet Conceptualism primarily lives on through *conceptual art in the generic sense, or the double-sided artistic practice to start from researched ideas and to take self-reflexively into account the contingency of the categorical difference between art and non-art.* Generic conceptual art fuses the notions of an idea-based practice (LeWitt) with an investigative or deconstructive attitude (Kosuth), while leaving the question of the work's critical stance toward the institutional context open. Looking for 'a good idea' and refining it through research are in line with the currently dominant notion that an art work is a project, a future objective that has to be prepared, thought out, planned. There is a wider context to this reigning attitude. As sociologist Max Weber already asserted at the beginning of the twentieth century, modernity equals goal rationalization and therefore intellectualization, or the reflexive tuning of possible means in view of desired ends. The neoliberal refashioning of modernity's identity from the 1980s onward greatly furthered the institutionalization of this logic of instrumental rationality within the arts. Neoliberal governmentality induces the artist to behave like an individual entrepreneur who has to intervene within the art market with a distinctive, well-conceived product. This advances a project-oriented work ethic: the artist changes into a flexible self-manager who administers a public portfolio of ongoing and future artistic investments.

Contemporary artists work in the wake of Conceptual Art's meanwhile widely acknowledged completion of most of the historical avant-garde's missives (though not of its aim to re-integrate the liberating potentials of art into life). The embrace of Conceptualism by the institutional apparatus conditioning art's production and mediation did indeed have a genuinely transformative effect. The performative act of naming or not-naming something a work of art is a basic operation today in the various art worlds, frequently exposed by the artefacts themselves with more or less playfulness. Most aesthetic disputes therefore no longer involve matters of aesthetic appreciation ('is this beautiful or ugly?') or personal taste ('does one like it or not?') but predominantly centre on the cognitive or ontological question: 'is this art, or is it not-art?' In short, a minimal operation of classification replaces the connoisseur's act of evaluation. Helmut Schelsky's famous sociological question: 'Can continuous reflexion be institutionalized?', raised in his 1957 essay of the same title, thus received a straightforward affirmative answer within the sphere of contemporary art. Particularly the re-entry of non-artistic references within a context institutionally associated with art, such as the exhibition of only slightly altered daily objects or mass cultural images in a gallery, results in a principally endless oscillation of the exhibited artefacts between both art and non-art, which curators, spectators or critics have to bring to a halt. They resolve, in potentially opposing ways, whether an object or practice can effectively claim the name of art. Contemporary art therefore functions as a paradoxical social system that rather smoothly combines the negative value of non-art with the positive self-description stating 'it's all about art': the system's self-negation became integral to that very

Moving Together

202

system's core activity of mediating art works. This performative self-contradiction confirms the art world's societal autonomy. 'As a form of practicing autonomy, the self-negation of the system is only one operation among others, an attempt to press the system to its limits so as to include the excluded, or to surpass with its negativity everything that preceded it, or to allow every possible non-artistic reality to re-enter the realm of art', Niklas Luhmann observes, adding: 'Any attempt of this sort presupposes the autonomy of art and seeks to realize autonomy in a limiting case. This is true even when autonomy is practiced as a renunciation of autonomy.'

From Postmodern/ist to Conceptual Dance

The Judson Dance movement shared the main concerns defining the historical moment of Conceptualism. Judson works were often idea-based and firmly questioned existing notions of dance or choreography by incorporating everyday movements and rule-bound improvisation. Institutional critique was practiced overall without much discursive elaboration, yet actually went in many practical directions: collective authorship and the collaboration with non-professional performers, performances in public spaces, or the self-organization of 'concerts of dance'. Through self-management and the making of process-oriented works, Judson moreover subverted the commercial logic of the dance market. Notwithstanding these affinities with Conceptualism, the work of Judson has not been chiefly categorized or analysed as Conceptual Dance. Yvonne Rainer spoke of 'minimalist tendencies' in her famous 1968 essay on *Trio A*, but this association did not last long. Judson is now commonly regarded as the main historical seedbed of postmodern dance because the work of the movement's protagonists departed from the aesthetic standards and values set by the tradition of modern dance (exemplified by the oeuvres of Martha Graham, Doris Humphrey or José Limón and their followers). However, the same goes for Merce Cunningham's choreographies, which are also regularly interpreted as instances of modernism. Postmodern dance indeed does not by definition equal postmodern*ist* dance. Whereas the first notion has primarily a broad historical meaning, the latter term involves a conceptual distinction pointing to the modernist belief — discussed at the end of the second chapter — that dance's artistic autonomy resides in an unalienable medial essence made visible in 'pure dance'.

It is, in fact, still debatable whether most of the 1960s works of Yvonne Rainer, Steve Paxton, Lucinda Childs and other representatives of Judson effectively transgressed the framework of modernism or, on the contrary, stuck to the axioms that Clement Greenberg had already forcefully codified for the visual arts in the 1950s. Numerous were the meanwhile emblematic Judson performances that consisted of ordinary movements and poses enacted in a flat, neutral mode and without a supplementary context rendering them meaningful. They can be read as rather straightforward modernist propositions favouring the idea that dance's essence is 'pure movement and non-movement' of whatever sort. In the alternative interpretation, Judson's wilful incorporation of everyday actions testifies to the conviction 'that a dance can be composed of any kind of movements; that there is no perceptible property that marks a movement to be, by its intrinsic nature, dance; and that there is no visually discernible boundary between so-called dance movement and any other kind of movement, including the movements of daily life. Thus, postmodern dance not only rejects modern dance; it also rejects modernist dance of the sort that we have identified with some of Balanchine's work and most of Cunninghams', assert Sally Banes and Noël Carroll in relation to Judson. The modernist reading evidently assumes a medial identity of dance that the alternative view deliberately eschews: either the scholarly observer specifies dance's essence, or one refrains from doing so. Be that as it may, postmodern dance seems to differ from the 'anything goes' spirit of much presumably postmodernist dance. The kind of work produced during the 1980s and early 1990s in particular clearly goes beyond the de-definition of the notion of dance through the appropriation of movements lacking 'danciness'.

A definitive breakdown of the traditional distinction between high and low culture, resulting in artefacts deemed art that show a marked fascination for schlock and kitsch; a new depthlessness, celebrated by the logic of the simulacrum (the copy lacking an original), the hyper-real image without any anchorage in reality, and the new cult of pastiche or blank parody; a strong weakening of historicity and the concomitant transformation of the cultural past in an a-historical supermarket of stylistic features quotable at will; 'the waning of affect' in the advancing preference for 'intensities' or brief emotional kicks, which is in keeping with the societal hegemony of 'the spectacle': these are the dominant trends within postmodernist culture and art, argues Frederic Jameson in his seminal 1984 essay 'Postmodernism, or the Cultural Logic of Late Capitalism'. The characterization rather fits *postmodernist dance, or the endeavour to produce unmistakably 'impure dance'* through the joyful quotation of all sorts of popular music and culture, the multi-medial incorporation of text fragments and video images, and the ironic play with semi-characters, emotional theatricality and narrative non-linearity – all this with or without overtly political intentions. 'Impurity' also means diverse references to vernacular dance traditions or formerly illegitimate performing genres (such as comedy or Broadway dancing), as well as virtuoso eyewinks to the vocabulary of classical or romantic ballet in the pastiche mode. Although some of these features already co-defined German *Tanztheater* of the 1970s, they particularly came to the fore in the deliberately eclectic, sometimes spectacle-prone stance of 1980s dance makers such as Karol Armitage, Urban Bush Women, Jean-Claude Gallotta or Joseph Nadj. Within and outside the dance field, postmodernism has meanwhile become a thing of the past – or so it seems, judging from the gradual vanishing of the expression, even its transformation into an intellectual taboo-word, during the second half of the 1990s (*The Drama Review* already put the question 'what has become of postmodern dance?' to a distinguished panel of critics in 1992). Perhaps the militant phase of postmodernism, which roughly corresponds with the decade of the 1980s, was only the moment in which the contingent nature of dance was fêted with a formerly unseen exuberance? This may at least partly explain the growing popularity of the more neutral expression 'contemporary dance' during the 1990s. Like the notion of contemporary (fine) art, the idiom takes for granted the existence of a fragmented, plural field in which both the modernist quest for 'pure dance' and the postmodernist longing for 'impure dance' only make up particular niches. However, within the field of contemporary dance made in (Western) Europe, a new and already hinted at label recently re-shuffled the cards with which critics and theorists, and partly audience members also, play the game of naming and blaming.

Around the recent turn of the century, Western European dance commentators started to use the expression 'conceptual dance', first hesitantly, then in a more recurrent but still predominantly casual way. The list of dance makers commonly associated with the label is quite long: Jérôme Bel, Nada Gambier, Boris Charmatz, Eszter Salamon, Felix Ruckert, Antonia Baehr, Xavier Le Roy, Cuqui Jerez, Martin Nachbar, Ivana Müller, La Ribot, Ula Sickle, deufert&plischke, Juan Dominguez, Thomas Lehmen, Didi Dorvillier, the Kinkaleri and Superamas collectives, Andros Zins-Browne, Anne Juren, Philippe Quesne, VA Wölfl/Neuer Tanz, Isabelle Schad, Lilia Mestre, Mette Ingvartsen, Christian Rizzo, Vera Mantero, Mårten Spångberg. In marked contradistinction to the historical movement of Conceptual Art, the notion of conceptual dance is neither publicly defended and interpreted by individual artists, nor widely claimed by a self-conscious generation of dance makers who produce stylistically related works. The related dance practices can take so many different directions that every attempt to postulate a shared aesthetic is thwarted from the very outset. Besides, hardly any of the presumably involved artists have endorsed the notion of conceptual dance as a fitting self-descriptor or identity marker. In fact, dance makers rarely mention the term in writings or interviews at all. And the exceptions confirming this rule usually voice strong reservations or reject the label straightforwardly. 'I don't consider myself as a conceptual artist and I don't know of one choreographer who works in dance without a concept', thus Xavier Le Roy, often considered to be one of the leading proponents of conceptual dance, once asserted.

Indeed, no choreography or dance is without one or more general underlying concepts. Every dance culture condenses the general medium of dance into a handful of notions on the legitimately danceable; and each choreographic oeuvre expresses, with more or less internal consistency, particular 'dance ideas'. Thus the concepts directly informing Cunningham's work can be found in the disconnection between movement and music or sound, the redistribution of performing bodies in space according to other logics than that of classical perspective, and the use of chance procedures to further the desired production of inharmonious series or disjointed movements. Yet dance theoretician and dramaturge Bojana Cvejić also had a point when she stressed, during a public conversation with Xavier Le Roy, that 'from the 1990s on, concepts are being thematized and discussed for every choreographic work of the new practices'. The explicit framing of rehearsal processes and performances by means of abstract ideas or theory-informed thoughts was vastly stimulated by the growing preference among dance makers for project-based research. A project is per definition future oriented and has an open nature, which the notion of research still further expands in the direction of a deliberate uncertainty about possible outcomes. General ideas allow such a work process to be structured in a flexible way: they delineate a space of interest without fixating the possible. Conceptually substantiated self-descriptions were also encouraged by the institutionalization of the neoliberal logic of project funding within the field of contemporary dance (necessitating the writing of well-argued proposals), the spreading of the practice of working together with academically schooled dramaturges, and the increased share of theory courses within European dance education. There is the heritage of the postmodernist dance wave of the 1980s as well and its willingness to make dance 'impure' through the integration of language, video images, or cross-references to mass media formats and popular culture.

The postmodernist wave is over or, rather, has become widely assimilated within current performance practices. A new, 'open concept of choreography' (Cvejić) has become firmly entrenched within the world of contemporary dance. Choreographers no longer only order bodily movements and non-movements in view of a 'written text', since the process of composition nowadays often involves a vast array of materials. When the space of 'the choreographic' becomes populated by heterogeneous elements, varying from corporeal movements to video images as well as all sorts of sounds and divergent text genres, it is precisely one or more general notions that may guide the individual or collective dance maker when rationalizing the many possibilities generated during a work process. These end-framing ideas either (partly) differ from or overlap with the initially inspiring ideas and lead to the creation of a primarily conceptually articulated compositional consistency. Within this currently widespread practice, which much postmodernist dance already anticipated without foregrounding the implied concepts, *the choreographic' remains a writing space in which marks are fixed, yet they now also have a manifest ideational nature.* This allows for a more flexible relation between choreography and performance by using, for instance, task-based improvisation that expresses an underlying thought. However, does the increased reliance on structuring ideas in both the work process and the final choreography sufficiently justify the label 'conceptual dance'?

The Name of Reflexive Dance

Many contemporary European choreographers create performances that both visibly actualize thoughts and destabilize still reigning ideas on the nature of dance. Take for example Dunoyer's *Vanity*: the performance obviously deals with liveness and self-reflexively deconstructs that very notion's framing role for the audience witnessing the performance. The enacted movements lack a clear-cut immanent meaning since no underlying pattern weaves them together into a sustained emotional tone or a particular portrayal of masculinity. The work is first and foremost structured by two general thoughts, which assure its choreographic consistency too. Whereas the first idea states that the spectator's viewpoint is incompatible with the spatial points marked by the moving body, the second says that much live dance nowadays is rooted in video recordings made during the rehearsal process. The performance's main signification therefore coincides with a two-sided idea-based operation: the act of copying a pre-recorded video is put on stage, followed by the showing of the video itself — and that's about it. *Vanity* also raises questions about the exact status of the work and, more generally, the difference between dance and non-dance. Something — some thing, some artefact — is publicly presented as an instance of dance but subverts some of the associated connotations, for instance by opening with a gong concert. Is this actually a dance work? Like all Dunoyer's pieces, *Vanity* takes into account that the contemporariness of a potential dance performance is co-defined by the individual viewer's act of naming or not-naming it a work of dance. Yet in marked contrast with Conceptual Art and the practice of Judson, the open nature of this categorizing is just assumed, not focussed on or provocatively self-emphasized: *Vanity* presupposes as evident the contingent character of the label 'dance'.

Global — or at least worldwide hegemonic — contemporary (fine) art has profoundly assimilated the lessons of 1960s Conceptualism, which is why Marcel Duchamp became, in retrospect, the most emblematic artist of the twentieth century. Much of contemporary European dance also exemplifies the notion of *generic conceptual dance, which takes for granted the idea that a dance work enacts ideas that are simultaneously defying received ideas on dance.* Most instances of this practice actually display a conspicuous lack of interest in the name of dance and even more so in the name of art, a fact that many a choreographer regularly airs in interviews and other public statements. Nevertheless, with the notable exception of the format of the lecture-performance, concept-oriented dance works refrain from undoing 'the perceptual' in favour of 'the linguistic'. The (possible) dance work may look vastly de-defined but is not completely de-materialized by reducing dance to statements on dance. Questioning traditional expectations has taken the overall form of tangible performances that usually generate a broad pallet of audio-visual perceptions. Aestheticism is, however, clearly avoided. Many of the works associated with the label 'conceptual dance' show a clear preference for a sober presentation format and a task-oriented – but not necessarily flat or neutral – performance style. Every connotation of 'the spectacular' is excluded: no opulent lighting or flashy costumes, no decorative props or music, no suspense- or plot-oriented dramaturgy, and no virtuoso statements. These negations indeed quasi-automatically bring to mind Yvonne Rainer's famous 'No' manifesto.

And yet, the notion of generic conceptual dance will not suffice in order to grasp the many-faceted issues publicly put forward by so-called conceptual dance. Thus *Vanity* not just questions the ideational framing of dance and choreography but actually does this by addressing their current technical conditions of possibility, particularly video recording, and live performance's visibility. The work exemplifies the recent trend within European contemporary dance to focus on the many supplements that implicitly co-structure the appearance and disappearance of bodily movement (or dance's commonly assumed essence), such as stage lighting and sound, singular movement or training techniques, the observable marking of gestures or poses as mutually different, or on their inscription in broader societal discourses regulating gender and bodily norms. The latent constructive nature of all sorts of parameters informing the de facto use of the medium of dance is thus made manifest through various critical operations. 'Conceptual dance' therefore regularly goes beyond the double stake of generic conceptual dance. The alternative identity card, the use of the label 'reflexive dance', was already put on the table in the opening chapter and tries to do justice to this produced surplus.

Reflexive dance deconstructs, in the mode of generic conceptual dance, contemporary dance's material and discursive conditions of possibility through questioning performative gestures, simultaneously pointing out the impossibility of a pure presentness in live performance by selectively highlighting its manifold mediations. Most works commonly labelled 'conceptual dance' fit this definition, yet reflexive dance is less a genre and more a critical practice that may provisionally inform, even greatly permeate singular research processes or performances by dance makers who are usually not regarded as genuine conceptualists. Thus *Highway 101* (2000-2001) and other pieces of Meg Stuart, or Anne Teresa De Keersmaeker's *Keeping Still* (2007) and *3Abschied (*2010), made in collaboration with fine artists Ann Veronica Janssens and Jérôme Bel, respectively, stand out as examples of reflexive dance. Whatever the peculiarities and specific context, working in a reflexive mode always comes down to a particular kind of knowledge production about dance and choreography. The information is generated in mostly collaborative research processes whose variegated nature exceeds the essentialist premises of earlier forms of movement research. Each activity that may lead to the delineation of a framing problematic and the formulation of fitting ideas or concepts is equally valued. Studio-based research is therefore alternated with the reading of texts, dialogues with theorists and discussions with peers, or quasi-ethnographic fieldwork in a setting deemed relevant for one's project. In short, reflexive dance is a way of doing dance studies in other modes than the academic (which may partly explain why academic dance study has become greatly interested in this practice, at least in Europe).

Is reflexive dance perhaps a belated offspring of Judson? 'Everything can be dance today, including (and above all without a doubt) the more banal gesture or even the more absent and still one. This calling into question of the identity of the choreographic can be read as a determined return to the American postmodern dance of the 1960s and the 1970s', observes Frédéric Pouillaude in '*Scène* and Contemporaneity', his insightful essay on the main trends within the French contemporary dance world after the 1980s. In this respect, dance company Quatuor Albrecht Knust, which included Jérôme Bel, Boris Charmatz, Emmanuelle Huynh, Xavier Le Roy and Christophe Wavelet, is exemplary, performing in 1996 're-readings' of Steve Paxton's *Satisfying Lover* (1967) and Yvonne Rainer's *Continuous Process Altered Daily* (1970). Next to these re-enactments, Bel, Charmatz and Le Roy had occasional collaborations with Paxton and Rainer. Vincent Dunoyer also worked with Steve Paxton, who co-authored *Three Solos for Vincent* (1997); video material of that collaboration was included in Dunoyer's more recent *Encore* (2009), a performative looking back on his dancing career. However, reflexive dance is much more than a temporal rehearsal (first the 1960s, then the 1990s) and a spatial displacement (first the U.S, then Europe), since the delayed re-performance of some of the central stakes of Judson has a genuine performative effect on that movement's status. Indeed, its recent and current after-effects within European dance greatly transformed both Judson's historical significance and the understanding of its promises and potentials. Involved is 'a complex relation of anticipation and reconstruction', a logic of deferred action (Freud's notion of *'Nachträglichkeit'*) in which the Judson movement of the 1960s and the later trend toward reflexive dance 'are constituted in a similar way, as a continual process of protension and retention, a complex relay of anticipated futures and reconstructed pasts'. This kind of complex temporal loop 'throws over any simple scheme of before and after, cause and effect, origin and repetition', Hal Foster argues, against a purely historicist view of the relationship between fine art's historical avant-garde and the neo-avant-gardes of the 1950s and the 1960s. Rather then just rehearsing Judson, reflexive dance acts indeed on this past as much as it is acted on by it. The looping back first and foremost regards what Judson could have also been, the possibilities this movement virtually contained and whose actualizations were ever present eventualities. Or, to retake a notion already introduced in the first chapter: reflexive dance is a specific instance of the contemporary danceable, or present day dance haunted by the potentials suggested by the dance of the past.

The deferred action of Judson comes with an important difference. Not unlike the historical avant-garde, the Judson movement was situated at the fringes of the institutional apparatus ensuring the production and distribution of, in this case American, dance. Reflexive dance is a rather different story because, and in this it is comparable to the neo-avant-garde, it happened and continues to take place within the recently created institutional centre of contemporary dance made in Western Europe. During the 1980s, the latter underwent a marked transformation thanks to the boom of new festivals, the establishment of novel production facilities such as the Centres Chorégraphiques Nationaux in France or the so-called workspaces in Flanders, and the marked increase in the number of presentation platforms thanks to, for instance, the new arts centres in Germany and Belgium. During the same decade, international co-production networks became customary while the funding possibilities for contemporary dance increased (although quite unevenly within different countries or regions). The net outcome was – in the vocabulary of Pierre Bourdieu – the emergence of an autonomous, strongly internationalized field for contemporary dance in Europe in which cities such as Berlin, Brussels, Paris or Vienna nowadays act as condensers.

Around the mid-1990s, it became increasingly clear that the institutionalization of contemporary dance came at a price. Numerous were the lamentations, which have not exactly subsided, on the high level of production pressure, the manifest demand for relatively easy to sell works that could keep on engaging a new dance public, the constraint to deliver distinctive products to the market, and the implicit pressure on individual dance makers to stick to a particular style or aesthetic signature. In addition, the new artistic field functioned as a cultural market with a markedly uneven distribution of symbolic capital. Whereas some choreographers became instant stars and were widely solicited by trend-setting festivals and dance houses, most dance makers had to labour hard in precarious conditions for only a small amount of recognition (more on this context in the sixth chapter). The movement associated with the label 'conceptual dance' did not completely alter this picture but succeeded in putting into perspective the star system through a sustained practice of shifting collaborations on a project-by-project basis. This implied a clean break with the traditional company hierarchy and the labour division between the author-choreographer and the mainly executive dancers who have no decisive say in the generation of material or the final choreography. The stress on collaborative research, which will be addressed at length in the second part, also regularly goes against the grain of the market logic of commodification, since it frequently results either in open, process-oriented works or in rather fixed performances that enact an always particular history of dialogical questioning, so lacking the recognizable and repeatable stylistic stamp of an Author. Last but not least, their deconstructive and idea-oriented nature positions reflexive dance works of whatever kind as anything but spectacular, ready-to-consume shows. Which is not to say that they cannot be entertaining or humorous: reflexive dance has inherited from postmodernist choreography a preference for sometimes mild, often biting irony.

Second Movement: Generalizing Dance and Choreography

Performance's Contemporaneity

The year is 2006, the piece premiering bears the title *La Magnificenza*. The choreographer is Etienne Guilloteau, a native Frenchman who studied at P.A.R.T.S, the international Brussels based dance school started by Anne Teresa De Keersmaeker in 1995. He subsequently decided to stay in Brussels and to go for a combined career as an independent dance maker, theatre technician, and dancer-performer (he participated in several pieces directed by Flemish choreographer Marc Vanrunxt). Upon entering the theatre hall, the spectator sees performer Vincent Dunoyer standing stage right, calmly inspecting a long sleeved sweatshirt, which he holds before him with outstretched arms. His face shows no signs of involvement or curiosity. He is just looking at the ordinary shirt, his head now and then tilting slightly as if he wants to scrutinize a specific detail. After a short blackout, during which Dunoyer leaves the stage, first one, then more spotlights are switched on and off in silence. A choreography of light? Several minutes have passed before the second performer, Guilloteau himself, enters the stage from the left and lies down with his head in the direction of the audience. The play with the lighting is briefly resumed before he starts moving in a strikingly slow way. He turns his body while shifting his legs, gets up in a half-upright position, lies down again, squats on his haunches, stands, and walks a few steps. After lying down again, he engages in actions connoting 'danciness' such as elegantly swaying his arms while turning his upright body; yet, the sequence ends with an abrupt, anything but refined fall.

The stage is again empty in the next scene. The fourteen spotlights used during the performance are all turned on and a rectangle of big dots appears on the stage floor. *Room*, a piece for prepared piano by John Cage, meanwhile sounds, filling the theatre with a gamelan-like soundscape. The music's volume is turned down when technician Hans Meijer comes on stage, carrying a ladder. With a deadpan face, he begins to remove a first spotlight, then a second one. Dunoyer, who at the other end of the stage starts winding one of the black stage curtains into a roll, joins Meijer in this rather improbable scenic action. The sequence will be repeated several times during the performance, until the stage has been transformed into the very opposite of a play area or a space that may support diverse sorts of fictive actions. After Meijer has done his job, Dunoyer remains alone on stage. Accompanied by the sparse piano notes of Erik Satie's *Harmonies*, he takes a few steps, stops and attentively looks around, and walks again. This could be, say, Steve Paxton imitating everyday gestures in a 1960s Judson piece. When Dunoyer leaves, Guilloteau enters with big jumps and swinging arms. His giant steps, which are both non-ordinary and non-'dancy', gradually become more rhythmical and at the end even acquire an air of folk dance. The complete sequence unfolds without music: the harsh sound of Guilloteau's powerfully descending feet acts as the equivalent of live music. After a new round in the removing of a pair of spotlights and the wrapping of a couple of stage curtains, Dunoyer installs three tripod microphone stands. Satie's *Vexations* second his manifold manipulations: the tripods are laid on the floor and put on end again, are spread out over the stage and re-assembled, are bent in different directions.

According to a by now predictable pattern, Meijer again removes two spots while Dunoyer makes room for Guilloteau. With his back to the audience, Guilloteau first walks downstage right from the scene's end to the proscenium with rhythmically moving arms. The sequence announces a burst of physical energy: bowing his torso and swaying his arms forcefully, stepping with his head and torso thrown forwards... The idea of a restless physicality or 'brute force' is enacted with such an engagement that the distinction between a genuine bodily involvement and its mere representation blurs. The action ends with a clear counterpoint: the puffing Guilloteau walks toward the audience, slightly bent forwards. Dunoyer then again begins to wind some stage curtains in a roll until a gunshot is heard. The performer drops to the floor and starts making the sort of quasi-gymnastic movements known from *Vanity* in a conspicuously informal way. Cage's *Nowth Upon Nacht* accompanies his actions: a shrill, loud female voice utters a text by James Joyce in a hysterical staccato tempo. Another pattern is thus confirmed, one that emphasizes the overall differences in motion quality between the two performers. Whereas Dunoyer moves with a pliable body that connotes lightness and detailed self-control, an unpolished physicality and a seemingly uncontrolled energetic drift primarily mark Guilloteau's actions. In the next scene, the two performers for once share the stage. Dunoyer sits with his back to the audience while the piano tones of Cage's *Four Walls* are heard; he rises and stands still while Guilloteau comes on stage and begins to move his upper body with both arms raised in the air. His co-performer takes over the gestures for a brief moment and then returns to manipulating the microphone tripods while Guilloteau leaves. Dunoyer covers the tripods with a black blanket, disappears under it, and continues shuffling the tripods around until the complete 'installation' goes down. A difficult to misread image emerges: a dead body covered by a black blanket with uncanny, skeleton-like legs (the ends of the microphone stands stick out from under the blanket). At the very same moment, Meijer starts taking away the two remaining spotlights, with the last one being removed with full stage work light. *La Magnificenza* concludes rather surprisingly because the expected complete darkening of the stage does not actually happen. The proverbial moment of death announced by Meijer's interventions and Dunoyer's simulation remains in suspension as a virtual idea whose promised actualization strangely coincides with the performance's ending.

La Magnificenza self-reflexively plays with the difference between the stage as a neutral, unmarked space and the way it functions as a symbolically framed and made-up scene that allows artificial actions to take place with a certain plausibility. Guilloteau's choreography can indeed be read as an empirically demonstrated argument, stating that *scenography, or the use of the stage as a partly technical, partly rhetorical set-up to bestow actions with an always particular impression of presentness, is a constitutive feature of liveness.* For the spectator always witnesses occurrences that are strongly articulated by lighting, sound or silence, stage curtains, and whatever kinds of props. These scenographic parameters co-structure a performer's actions in an often self-evident way. Unnoticed and therefore all the more effective, they drastically mediate the dancer's presence and grant it a supplementary power that magnifies the spectator's experience of 'now, here'. *La Magnificenza* denaturalizes 'the scenographic' and concomitantly re-defines the live character of the bodily enacted events. Through its gradual removal, the work positions the lighting as the ultimate condition of possibility for every public performance – an obvious fact for sure, but also one that goes together with a thorough framing of the audience's looking that is often disregarded. There is also the striking alternation between the silent scenes and the sections in which music, mostly sparse piano notes, accompany the observed corporeal actions. The dissimilarity is so vast that the spectator's attention becomes quasi-automatically focussed on the differential effect of enveloping actions with or without sound. The individual performer's movements or poses are distinctively present when executed in silence or not — again something that is a matter of course, yet *La Magnificenza* highlights its genuine performative nature. The sensation of liveness also visibly varies with the absence or presence of props. Dunoyer's manipulations of the microphone tripods thus create an uncanny co-dancer, the missing partner that the lonely actions performed in the other scenes seem to long for.

Guilloteau stages a consequent exercise in 'de-scenography' that subverts the 'being in mediation' of the performer's body and its actions and inactions, making visible the very parameters conditioning both their 'being observable' and their 'being now, here'. The French choreographer Boris Charmatz, who authored several works that integrate a keen play with visual perception together with a well-thought out dramaturgy of sonority, lighting and props, puts it this way: 'The scenographic and dramaturgic context is not elaborated besides the dance. In this sense, it is not what is usually called a "context". The light and the music do not "colour" a dance that would go on existing by itself unaffected. The "context" is not around it, it is not an addition, even less a plumage for the movements. It modifies their meaning, it is inside them.' *La Magnificenza* is overall a spectacle that actively foregrounds the normally 'contextualizing' factors structuring the spectator's perceptions during a performance. Yet the piece also contains several scenes in which nothing particular seems to happen, witness for instance the opening section or the one in which Dunoyer's performing recalls Paxton-anno-Judson. Simple movements or poses are enacted in an apparently probing way; their possible significance is continually deferred, so that they remain in the end utterly pointless. This mode of performing directs attention to the decisive event in which an action publicly comes into being but is not yet symbolically or choreographically framed. No metaphysics of presence is implied, since *La Magnificenza* continually stresses the mediating role of scenography, thwarting every 'ontology of performance' that celebrates movement's ungraspable moment of 'being now, here'. Rendering a movement's becoming manifest is an act whose temporality involves rather a differential series of events condensing into *a duration-event, a happening self-reflexively marking itself as happening.* The duration-event is double-sided or internally split, as it is made up of both the performer's action and the audience's inaction, a movement being performed and simultaneously being watched. This mediated togetherness unavoidably bears the stamp of the impossible to cancel out contingency of the actually present Other signalling, through its anonymous gaze, the co-presence supporting the work's manifestation.

At the moments when *La Magnificenza* highlights the coming-into-presence of actions, the work joins one of the prime stakes of reflexive dance. For this dance genre, which is not one, recurrently focuses on the relational coupling of the staged movements or poses and the audience's gaze, or *the literal contemporaneity of 'those who do' and 'those who watch' conditioning performance's performativity* (indeed a point already raised at the end of the second chapter). Reflexive dance is therefore neither modern nor postmodern but 'contemporary, in an extra- or parahistorical sense', Frédéric Pouillaude concludes. He goes on to note that the new emphasis on the immanent relationship between performance and contemporaneity puts the deferred action of Judson within recent dance practice into perspective: 'Whereas postmodern dance was understood as the analytic questioning of an essence (What is dance?), operating by eidetic variation and testing the limits (How far can one go without ceasing to produce dance?), our mutation seems rather to shift the questioning to the essence of *performing* (To what extent is there an event when I do something – or not – in front of somebody who does not do anything?). It is only from this calling into question of performance itself that the medium "dance" is, in turn, re-questioned.' Testing the limits of performance's performativity equals the self-reflexive production of liminal duration-events that have a betwixt-and-between nature: action and inaction happen without 'really' something happening. Movements or poses are rarefied or diluted – yet they do happen: something like an event lacking eventness or a living death exhausting liveness. The prototypical reflexive dance work is a terminal dance living on as an all too real ghost of dance's traditionally presumed essence.

Intermezzo: Performing Ideas
According to G.W.F. Hegel, fine art acts 'as the first reconciling middle term between pure thought and what is merely external,

sensuous, and transient'. A successful art work's appearance points beyond itself and always gives us an idea through its sensually apprehended forms (for Hegel, the beauty of art therefore exceeds that of nature: it is spiritual). Yet in a time dominated by abstract reflection and general maxims, the days of fine art are over. 'Thought and reflection have spread their wings above fine art' to such an extent that 'art, considered in its highest vocation, is and remains for us a thing of the past. ... Art invites us to intellectual consideration, and that not for the purpose of creating art again, but for knowing philosophically what art is', Hegel says in the introduction to his 1820s lectures on aesthetics. Arthur Danto at once re-states and re-dates this both famous and infamous thesis in his influential 1984 essay on 'the end of art'. Not Conceptualism, as one would perhaps expect, but Andy Warhol's *Brillo Box* – the work that already figured prominently in Danto's epochal essay on 'The Artworld' (1964) – is the historical tipping point that erased the difference between art and philosophy by focussing on the distinction between art and non-art, a staple of real Brillo boxes containing soap powder and its silk-screened simulacrum in an art gallery. In Danto's reading, *Brillo Box* is intentionally made to reflect on this conceptual issue, which makes the work akin to the philosophy of art (Hegel would not agree: like religion, art in his view is only a phase the Spirit passes through in its dialectical unfolding in the direction of philosophy). 'The end of art' does not of course mean the literal death of art production. 'Art after the end of art' (Danto), or visual art's prosperous afterlife beyond the *Brillo Box*, has merely given up the historical quest informing 'the Age of Manifestos' for an essentialist delineation of art's nature. The difference between art and non-art has become an overall self-reflexively acknowledged matter of contingent framings: art can be anything artists and their various patrons say it is. 'How wonderful it would be to believe that the pluralistic art world of the historical present is a harbinger of political things to come!', Danto enthuses in *Art after the End of Art*. Some scepticism may be appropriate. The non-foundational heterogeneity of current artistic practices makes them contemporary, yet this situation does not always resemble a state of peaceful coexistence in the liberal mode of tolerance. Today's art fields sometimes rather fit Carl Schmitt's contested definition of the political, implicitly rehearsed in Pierre Bourdieu's sociology of the arts, as involving a near struggle of life and death between friends and enemies — between those granting the name of art to certain artefacts and those denying this appreciation.

To a large extent, 'art after the end of art' is synonymous with generic conceptual art. How to grasp its idea-based nature, when Hegel's view on beauty as harmoniously mediating between the sensuous and the mental or spiritual realm will not do? What does the operation of reflexivity come down to within a work questioning the constitutive parameters of (possible) live dance? Someone, who considers himself a choreographer, has a handful of intuitive thoughts, for instance about the formative role of scenography in the perception of liveness and the coming into being of an action on stage. After a laborious research process, Etienne Guilloteau presents a temporalized series of events in a theatre venue in Flanders, which the institutional actors directly concerned consensually frame as a work of dance. The artefact engages the spectator along several lines of inquiry. Some audience members muse over whether *La Magnificenza* is truly an instance of dance, others accept this definition without much after-thought but feel uncertain about the work's content. What does this choreography precisely aim to express? Which idea(s) does it want to make visible and audible through (in)actions and (non)-sounds, respectively? Perhaps the work wants to draw attention to a particular concept of staged movement ('there is a marked hesitation in the performing')? Or...?

In the obvious reading of all this, one or more thoughts — in the sense of mental constructs — frame both the production and reception of a choreography. The maker's ultimately guiding ideas are expressed in bodily movements and poses, which is not unlike a book articulating a series of concepts within the medium of language. The spectator's final thoughts only arrive after the completion of the piece and are elicited by innumerable sensory perceptions. In any case, the work does not faithfully mediate or neutrally transmit the choreographer's conceptions since these remain in his sealed-off consciousness. The spectators look, hear and have thoughts that do or do not correspond with the maker's views: they actively co-produce the performance by grasping it mentally. For the dance is a publicly observable artefact, offering perceptions and inducing emotional states that bring forth an autonomous quest for meaning, resulting in certain overall conceptions or a spectator's interpretation of the work (which may be altered by later discussions with co-viewers or the reading of a review). In short, the act of reception revolves around the question 'what is said here?' because the individual art work is an independent, compact communication using the human faculty of perception as its prime medium. 'Consciousness cannot communicate, communication cannot perceive', Niklas Luhmann notes. 'Art makes perception available for communication, and it does so outside the standardized form of a language (that, for its part, is perceptible). ... Art integrates perception and communication without merging or confusing their respective operations.' This observation is a variation on the original meaning of the Greek word *aesthesis,* which refers to sensuous experience, by inscribing it within the logic of communication and locating both perceptions and the ideas grafted onto them solely in an observer's consciousness.

The alternative view sticks to the art work and conceives it as a genuine medium of thought. 'Art thinks no less than philosophy, but it thinks through affects and percepts', Gilles Deleuze and Félix Guattari assert in *What is Philosophy?* Not that the ideas inspiring a dance work have the shape of quasi-Platonic essences that the spectator's mind's eye has to detect behind the visible or audible layer of sensory appearances. The expressed thoughts are materially enacted not through but literally *in* the temporal creation of a constantly re-articulated network of self-referentially enchained sensations, brought forth by perceived movements, images, sounds, et cetera. Immanence rules: the Platonic scheme of essence and appearance misses the point. The reflexive dance work is therefore anything but a univocal statement or clear-cut argument. It may only appear as such in retrospect, after it has ceased to be a perceptual and affective journey implying a big or small adventure of thought. Subtracting the perceptual does not show the work in a pure conceptual state but only results in its destruction: one is left behind with a handful of sometimes fairly simple ideas. They may only become operative thanks to the created network of heterogeneous materials used: *'dance ideas' are performed thoughts, with every idea being a multiplicity distributed over countless events and immanent to a great variety of percepts and affects.* Comparable to a book in which a thought takes on the form of an assemblage consisting of many phrases and words, a 'dance idea' only exists in the plural and is irreducible to the supposed oneness of a conceptual essence, spiritually inhabiting the mental space of consciousness. Most conceptual art in fact deconstructs this prevailing metaphysical image of thought inherited from Plato.

Idea-based dance turns thoughts into multidimensional conceptual personae that are part and parcel of the performance. Thus the notions of scenography and the duration-event acquire, in *La Magnifizenca*, the status of active forces that, not unlike actors in a theatre performance, overtly co-direct both the general course and the spectator's experience of the dance work. These conceptual personae have an anonymous nature and are not stand-ins for the individual thinking of the choreographer: no theatrical doubling or representation is implied. What Deleuze and Guattari observe about the philosopher and conceptual personae also goes for the relationship between enacted conceptions and a choreographer or a dancer in an instance of reflexive dance: 'I am no longer myself but thought's aptitude to finding itself and spreading across a plane that passes through me at several places. The conceptual persona has nothing to do with an abstract personification, a symbol or an allegory since it lives, it insists. The philosopher is the idiosyncrasy of his conceptual personae.' Consider the conceptual personae of a dance performance as the at once performed and performative thoughts that create *a conceptual plane of consistency differing from, but immanent to, the work's sensuous plane of consistency*. The conceptual plane consists of the dance idea's becoming, which is only halted at the end of the performance. Simultaneously realized in but nevertheless diverging from the performed, self-referentially coupled movements or non-movements and the manifold perceptions or affects they provoke, this virtual plane is continuously in a state of emerging or breaking through. Two compositional logics are implied: a two-dimensional choreography unfolds in the mode of a double, intertwined helix. Although the first are immanent to the second, the performed ideas and the enacted percepts or affects entertain shifting relationships. Sometimes concord and harmony reign, at other times the two planes of consistency each go their own way, undermine each other or even collide. While the conceptual plane cannot exist without its sensuous counterpart, it also functions as the latter's motivating force. Two planes intermingle and simultaneously produce de-territorializing flight lines, percepts and affects or ideas that seem to go nowhere when captivating the spectator's body. Most reflexive dance works indeed create a remainder not fitting the work's planes of consistency. Flying

percepts and affects or free-floating ideas resemble wandering no-
mads without a territory. They may temporarily destruct an art
work from within, or they can act as liberating counterpoints in
relation to the work's informing rhythms and melodies. An idea-
based dance work's compositional logic is the unity of the difference between its conceptual and sensuous plane of consistency,
and also between territorializing series of movements or poses
and de-territorializing flight lines. Composition contains its negation: the convincing contemporary art work, however defined,
survives the self-enacted tendencies towards de-composition and
pure fragmentation. *Paradoxology', or a tense dialectics without
reconciliation, is perhaps generic conceptual dance's non-thought
identity made thoughtful.*

Deconstructing Body Humanism
'Contemporary European dance ... challenges absolutely the very
"saleability" of the dance object by withdrawing quite often from it
what should be its distinctive (market) trait: dance', André Lepecki
affirms in his surveying essay 'Concept and Presence: The Contemporary European Dance Scene'. He therefore concludes that
'the end result looks more like a subtraction. And what is being
subtracted by the proposals from the European choreographers
... is the word "dance".' The deliberate production within reflexive practices of absences, or the leaving out of one or more ingredients traditionally associated with dance and choreography,
has met with quite some resistance among spectators and critics alike. The overall lament is that the deconstruction of dance
equals its destruction. The charge usually presupposes the existence of an immutable, transhistorical essence of dance. Michael
Kirby, who earlier on wrote an influential book on acting and
non-acting, distinguishes dance from non-dance by means of
three distinct parameters: regularity or rhythm, energy distribution, and the formalization of movement. Critics or spectators
who reject reflexive dance are usually less interested in a nuanced
set of criteria and do not regard the difference between dance
and non-dance in terms of a continuum allowing for positions in
between. The dividing line rather delineates being from non-being:
either something is a genuine instance of dance, or it is not at
all. Such an ontological and essentialist way of arguing oversteps
the evident observer-dependency and performative status of every
statement on dance. As was already argued at length in the opening

chapter, dance's contemporariness, which reflexive dance only aggravates, partly hinges on this contingency of the act of naming or not-naming an artefact a work of dance. A substantially realist stance denies both the implied act of categorization and its non-foundational nature through the projection of the particular qualities put forward in the act of observation into the actually observed artefact. The observers thus negate their agency and suggest they are not actively interpreting a publicly shown work but only determining an objective difference between dance and non-dance. The denial leads to a performative statement, which claims that it is not performative. This paradox is then usually further unfolded through the reiterative utterance of supplementing 'dance is...'-statements. The net outcome resembles a credo, an individual proclamation of faith in a particular dance culture or a singular definition of the legitimately danceable.

Reflexive dance is an instance of *post-foundational art* that swaps ontology for 'virtuology' and shows what dance may also be within the general medium of movement and non-movement. What could also be termed dance? What kind of performance may also live up to the name 'dance' thanks to an ideational framing yet to be formulated? Through a differential play with the material and discursive conditions of possibility informing performance, reflexive dance indeed researches dance's potential identities in the additive mode of 'also this'. This practice deploys subtractions in order to produce additions – or so it can at least be interpreted once one puts aside the imaginary logic of identification underlying realist first order-observation. The performed logic of the conjunctive ('also' = 'and, and, and') and the virtual ('may also be' = possible identities) actualizes dance's medium beyond its historical condensations in specific dance cultures, thus creating both a new dance culture – the one of reflexive dance – and a history yet to come. This future is actually *an endless becoming in which dance's identity is continually deferred through a conjunctive production of differences*, of yet again another proposal of what dance can be. It also implies a shift from the presumed disciplinary criteria of quality calibrated in the past, to the value of actual interest as framed by an always singular, individually bound acquaintance with past and present dance, as well as an implicit horizon of future dance. 'A work of art needs only to be interesting', Minimalist artist Donald Judd famously asserted in his 1965 essay 'Specific Objects'. The statement could be the fitting motto for the ethics of spectatorship implied by the deferred action of Judson in current reflexive dance — which one of course may refuse to endorse.

Most critical rejections of reflexive dance are embedded in the broader expectations regarding art as edifying the audience and offering emotionally interesting, intimate experiences. Within this modern humanist understanding, often associated with nineteenth-century bourgeois culture and the German notion of *Bildung*, art appears as a quasi-sacred realm in which the moral truth of core values such as freedom, justice or solidarity is affirmed by aesthetical means, for instance the dramatization of the difficulty of living up to these values in daily life. Through an elaborated use of sensory forms, the eternal conflict between 'the good' and 'the bad' — or 'the banal' — can be magnified within the medium of writing (the art of the novel), theatre (the genre of the tragedy) or music (the quasi-narrative structure of the symphony). Art's percepts are moreover premised to speak an emotional language that makes the reader, spectator or listener susceptible to the utopian prospect of a harmonious life — Stendhal's notorious *'promesse de bonheur'* — that every genuine art work supposedly articulates. These are indeed old-fashioned notions whose idealist nature and conservative implications Herbert Marcuse already spelled out in 1937 in this perceptive critique of 'the affirmative character of culture'. Yet the humanist past continues to haunt the post-humanist present. Flemish dance critic Pieter T'Jonck therefore contrasts the 'paranoid view' of reflexive dance, which enacts the suspicion that every impression of unmediated presentness is infected by a yet to discover instance of mediation, with the belief in dance's ability to express the human condition in an at once cognitively transparent and emotionally affecting mode. 'In the way new dance and performance are described, you can hear an ethical argument', T'Jonck observes. 'This broadly comes down to the opinion that the work is too intellectual and leaves no place for wonder, for emotion, in short for everything that makes us human. That is what art, however, should really do, without being vulgar.' The dance maker subscribing to the credo that art should express human truths — T'Jonck mentions Alain Platel — resembles a contemporary shaman who has the genius to communicate *la condition humaine* in an emotionally convincing aesthetic vocabulary. However idiosyncratic, if it is successful the work appeals to an assumingly universal humanness; concept-oriented artists are, on the contrary, often portrayed as alienating pedantics because they investigate blind spots, thereby creating — again in T'Jonck's words — 'no sweeping emotions, no sudden recognitions, but a more often than not rather dumb, uneasy sense of bewilderment'. Reflexive dance indeed contains the not always fulfilled promise of *a consequent de-humanization of the medium of dance*, a fundamental break with the body humanism still solidly informing the dominant discourse on dance and choreography.

Since the legendary days of Judson, the physical vocabulary deployed in choreographies has been vastly expanded. Movement possibilities that were once firmly rejected as abject or deemed unremarkable have since become genuine choreographic building blocks. Dance makers discovered — in the encapsulating expression of Sally Banes — 'democracy's body': dance's medium entered the era of 'the body in general'. All in all, body humanism was not contested but only rendered more inclusive, more open also to corporeal forms or actions that Western society stigmatizes or forecloses. In a word, dance became more human. With the body-centeredness of the reigning dance discourse corresponds a choreographic practice, or at least a self-understanding of making dance works, that necessarily doubles the dancing body in a presence that is simultaneously absent in the partly symbolically coded, partly imaginarily invested representation that the spectator enjoys. Precisely this split is the hallmark of the presumably 'pure dance' of, for instance, Balanchine or Cunningham and their many offspring. This choreographic tradition tries to reduce the dancing body to a tautological expression of itself, but to no avail. 'I dance that I dance', this body supposedly says — yet it is a statement, a representation in which the dancing body does not encounter itself but can at the most indicate its own absence. If the moving human body is regarded as dance's prime medium, the conceptualization of the dancing body tends to coincide more often than not with a limit exercise trying to encircle the real void — in Lacanian parlance: the void of the Real — in the proverbial slash distinguishing the real body from its symbolic and imaginary realness when dancing on stage. And not only is the real body, in the common-sense meaning, at once present and absent in a dance performance, but so is the body-as-medium. Like language or sound, this medium can only be alluded to: every movement or non-movement instantiates a non-representable potential, a virtual infinity of possibilities, only some of which are actualized during a performance (this was indeed the concluding thought of the previous chapter). Maybe the virtual materiality contained by an organized organism is the very same Body without Organs that Deleuze and Guattari have tried to theorize? Of still more importance is the question of how a particular strand of contemporary dance questions the central premise of the discourse that still predominantly mediates and interprets it. What does the notion of choreography perhaps refer to in performances that re-choreograph the hegemonic understanding of that very practice? In short, what does post-humanist dance and choreography look like?

Co-Writing Dance

fieldworks, formerly called deepblue — indeed twice spelled without capital letters and with 'deepblue' in one word — is a Brussels-based artistic collective initiated by dancer-choreographers Yukiko Shinozaki and Heine Avdal in collaboration with dramaturge and digital sound researcher Christoph De Boeck. Their 2003 production *closer* (again without a capital letter) is anything but a regular performance, since it undoes the virtual fourth wall, which in a traditional theatre setting divides the audience from the stage and the performers. Before entering the performance space, the spectators are asked to take off their shoes and are given headphones. They then step into a vast closed-off and only dimly lit room in which they can freely walk about or sit down. There is a small open area in front of a wall, but the space is dominated by a surrounding wood of bamboo rods; these are attached to the ceiling, do not reach the floor, and vary in length. While wandering through this dreamy landscape, which has everything of 'a world within the world' or a monadic island, digital clicks and cuts begin to sound in the spectator's headphones that sometimes condense into a massive wave of electronic sound. Both the colour and the intensity of the lighting regularly change, partly in relation to the sound dramaturgy. Now and then a video image is projected against the wall in the back, showing for instance the face of Yukiko Shinozaki. The total space is a multi-layered atmosphere, a moody environment lacking a clear signification but nevertheless populated by potential meanings and virtual expectations about possible happenings. Together with the bamboo rods, the interaction between the shifting sounds, the varying lighting and the projected images creates a qualitative own-space within the geometric setup, inducing a vague tension asking to be articulated by a supplement yet to come – by the actions of the two performers perhaps? In any case, they will intervene in an already marked atmosphere that they may take into account as a possible partner or as a limit meant to be surpassed.

Yukiko Shinozaki and Heine Avdal come and go, alone or together. They perform quite simple movements amidst the audience: crawling around on the floor, moving one or both hands, stretching out an arm or gesturing with both arms, standing upright and looking around with a neutral face. The dancing body – 'but is it dance?' – here mainly behaves as the corporeal double of the dispersed public body watching the performance. An average audience member in good physical shape could imitate most performed movements without much difficulty, yet they are not exactly common gestures or poses. The spectators rather witness actions or inactions they could also enact but would probably not dare to perform publicly. This suggests a twofold interpretation of the production's title, *closer*. The obvious reading focuses on the physical proximity of the two dancers to the public, as well as the soundscape heard through the headphones. However, Shinozaki and Avdal never directly touch an individual spectator. The individualized sound experience moreover separates the audience members from each other and from the performers, who do not wear headphones. A highly particular fourth wall therefore frames the actual live experience of *closer*, one that encloses each spectator in an isolating sonic capsule. By contrast, the title's more metaphorical interpretation concentrates on the dancers' non-virtuoso corporeal actions, which position them as intimate ghost bodies hosting the spectator's virtual performing body. The overall setting, however, transforms the spectators from passive on-lookers into partial performers. The public's observable looking, sitting and reacting is an integral part of the performance, since every audience member's mode of being present is a potential object to be watched and scrutinized. One does not just contemplate Shinozaki's simple arm gestures or Avdal's spastic floor movements, one also gazes at the surrounding spectators who are uncomfortably lying or sitting on the floor, who look absentminded, or who are immersed by the sound-waves distributed through the headphones. In short, each spectator's seeming passivity acquires an active, even performative quality because it can be looked at and inspected.

closer exemplifies the more general trend within reflexive dance to focus on the contemporaneity of performance by drastically redefining the usual role distribution between performers and audience. The piece functions as an installation, reframing liveness through the active deconstruction of the traditional difference between 'doing' and 'observing'. The inclusion of the spectator's co-presence also informs the performance's performativity: through its incorporation of the audience, *closer* considers the viewer's visual and physical experience of the work as a constitutive action in its own right. And however fleeting and contingent the actual mode of signalling their co-presence, the way the audience is marked by the created context makes them unmistakably part and parcel of the intended choreography. *closer* therefore exemplifies *an at once total and open notion of choreography* involving a fixed, heterogeneous frame of pre-set props, sounds, images, lighting rays or corporeal movements and poses that changes the individual spectators unpredictable 'readings' into co-defining choreographic elements. In short, including the audience results in an encompassing choreography that envelops each and everything present during the performance. This re-choreographing of 'the choreographic' comes without a totalizing move, a solid integration of all elements into an overarching whole. That is the work's openness: neither the spectator's performative co-presence nor the possible interactions between the dancers and the audience is fixed. Whatever happens, happens — but choreographically appropriated and emphasized.

Yet is 'the choreographic' not synonymous with writing? *closer*'s deliberate porosity with regard to the audience pushes the idea of choreography to that paradoxical limit where the very act of the spectator's contingent co-writing of the performance continually alters the enacted 'dance text'. What has been written previously is visibly overwritten by its many readers: the performance extends reflexive dance's focus on contemporaneity to the realm of 'the choreographic'. Roland Barthes' idea of the 'writerly text' positioning the reader as an active re-writer here becomes literally embodied by performatively including the spectator's co-presence. Every audience member is no longer a virtual but an actual co-choreographer, and also a co-performer who keeps on motivating the other viewer's acts of looking. The contingent public reactions are genuine choreographic marks: they at once purportedly co-structure the performance's composition, and they can in principle be repeated or reiterated. In fact, during showings of *closer*, the audience members were seen to rehearse modes of co-presence and responses to actively being watched. The public's overwriting of the prime 'written text' is indeed strongly influenced by the dominant cultural standards codifying shyness, indifference, coolness, et cetera. The interaction between the context created by the initial 'dance text' and the iterative nature of the many standardized signs visibly indicating the spectators' co-presence transforms these very symbols into choreographic marks. Or in Jacques Derrida's words, already quoted when 'the choreographic' was defined: 'Inasmuch as it is essential and structural, this possibility [to iterate] is always at work marking all the facts, all the events, even those that appear to disguise it. Just as iterability, which is not iteration, can be recognized even in a mark that in fact seems to have occurred only once. I say seems, because this one time is itself divided or multiplied in advance by its structure of repeatability.'

'Dance (or Choreography) in General'

The expression 'contemporary dance' nowadays points to an unstable, constantly redefined experimental zone in which artists from various backgrounds cooperate and combine, in a seemingly boundless way, text, physical movement, video technology, lighting, high and low musical genres, and so forth. Since the middle of the 1990s, contemporary dance has indeed become performing art's prime laboratory and vastly contributed to the striking broadening of performance's performativity beyond body humanism. To name just two examples: the first part of Romeo Castelluci's *M.#10 Marseille* (2004) stages a series of living pictures, à la Mark Rothko's famous monochromes, with no perceivable human body on stage; and the Belgian Kris Verdonck, who has a background in architecture and visual arts, creates installation-type works showing the mechanic movements of an engine (tellingly named *Dancer #1* [2003] and *Dancer #2* [2009]), as well as producing full evening's works such as *I/II/III/IIII* (2007) or *End* (2008), consisting of the actions of non-human machines and of human movements directed by technical artefacts. Like *closer*, these and several other recent works, such as Eszter Salamon's *Tales of the Bodiless* (2011) or Mette Ingvartsen's *The Artificial Nature Project* (2012), reflect an inclusive approach to dance and choreography open to the possible performativity of non-human elements. Sound, video imagery, light or specific elements of the set are no longer only used to support a choreography, but are explored as movement sources in their own right, even as performers, thereby supplementing the human body as the presupposed prime medium of dance. The trend has a transversal character and clearly exceeds the varied practices of so-called conceptual dance makers, witness for instance Meg Stuart's *Highway 101* discussed in the previous chapter, Anne Teresa De Keermaeker's *Keeping Still* and several works by William Forsythe. How to make sense of this post-humanist conjuncture?

Thierry de Duve has coined the notion of 'art in general' in his in-depth discussion of the Duchamp-effect within the visual arts. 'I propose to use the term *art in general*, or *art in the generic sense of the word*, to refer to the *a priori* possibility that anything can be art. ... *Art in general* is the name, one might say, for the new deal that has become established in the "post-Duchamp" era. It replaces the old generic term "fine arts", which relates to the situation before Duchamp', De Duve contends. The current situation in the performing arts tends towards a *performance art in general* that goes on hybridizing the once evident borders between the established genres beyond the postmodernist legacy, while simultaneously exploring alternative modes of performativity in various media. What singles out particular instances of contemporary dance and choreography within this new field is their firm focus on the public performativity of divergent kinds of movements or poses. Thus *closer* does not only create a symmetrical relationship between the performer's actions and the bodily presence of the spectators. The changing light waves, broken by the bamboo rods, or the technologically mediated sound waves are also rigorously treated from a dramaturgical point of view. Both are taken up and framed as movements in their own right: they are indeed choreographed.

'Dance in general' re-articulates dance's medium — or the unity of the difference between movement and non-movement — *through a consistently symmetrical, non-hierarchical handling of the motion potentials of the human body and those of non-human materialities.* Putting human and non-human capacities to move or to not-move on par implies that the second no longer serves the first, nor are they dramaturgically related to a totalizing meta-narrative integrating all elements of the stage or performance space. Instead, sound, imagery or light are deployed as virtual potentials to produce a variety

of always specific actions that instantiate the medium of dance beyond its human-centred understanding. Sound waves or light rays no longer just emphasize bodily actions, adding or subtracting possible meanings, but interact with them as movements displaying their own characteristic physicality. The distinguishing aspect of a 'dance performance in general', admittedly a somewhat awkward expression, is therefore the way it deals with its non-human components. Video technology, microphones, electronic soundscapes or elaborated light designs have all become quite ordinary within contemporary dance. The non-human material aspects usually sustain, frame or highlight the performance of human bodies: their possible agency is limited to 'the scenographic'. The medium of the human body then still provides the primary locus and focus of the choreography, even while it may be fragmented by video projections, de-familiarized by an uncanny soundscape, or set to work in a conceptual mode. In marked contrast, a 'dance performance in general' treats the performative qualities and potentialities of human as well as non-human actions as equal. In addition to (human) bodily movements, the lighting, sounds, props and video-images become active, deliberately deployed agents — components that do something 'now, here'. These non-human elements take on the shape of quasi-bodies that are able to make physical movements, which evidently differ from human corporeal gestures, yet converge with the latter in their dramaturgically valued capacity to act on other material movements and on the bodies of the witnessing viewers too.

The art of composing 'dance in general', so *'choreography in general', comes down to the making and modulation of assemblages*, the explorative associating and final coupling of materially heterogeneous kinds of actions and inactions. Every assemblage, as Gilles Deleuze and Félix Guattari argue in *A Thousand Plateaus,* extracts a territory from one or more milieus but is simultaneously carried away by various lines of deterritorialization. This is an assemblage's vertical axis, which shows an irresolvable tension between processes of consolidation and destabilization. On its horizontal axis, 'an assemblage comprises two segments, one of content, the other of expression. On the one hand, it is a *machinic assemblage of bodies*, of actions and passions, an intermingling of bodies reacting to one another; on the other hand, it is a *collective assemblage of enunciations*, of acts and statements, of incorporeal transformations attributed to bodies', Deleuze and Guattari write.

Consider once again *closer*. The wood of the bamboo rods territorializes the assemblage, adding to the creation of a stable own-space. The sound waves distributed via the headphones also often assume this role, yet they regularly go their own way: sonic flight lines temporarily opening the performance's territory onto an undefined elsewhere. The bamboo rods simultaneously belong to the work's machinic assemblage of human and non-human bodies. This segment of content moreover contains all other material components, including the public's corporeally experienced affects induced by the perceived interactions between a sound wave, a living image and a series of performed movements. When the latter actions first start murmuring, then signifying, an incoherent chain of enunciations occurs: a segment of expression hesitantly emerges, wavering between territorialization and the counter-becoming actively undoing this tendency.

The heterogeneous elements making up an assemblage are not constituted by the continually shifting relations they entertain with each other. Notwithstanding its particular agency within a singular network of entities, a sound, image or prop remains materially independent and may therefore be put to work in another assemblage. Within the new constellation, the transposed element will act differently because it interacts with other parts. The intrinsic features defining a given component must be distinguished from its abilities to interact with other entities, Manuel De Landa rightly stresses: 'While its properties are given and may be enumerated as a closed list, its capacities are not given — they may go unexercised if no entity suitable for interaction is around — and form a potentially open list, since there is no way to tell in advance in what way a given entity may affect or be affected by innumerable other entities.' Both dance's potentiality and 'the choreographic' is therefore profoundly redefined in many current practices since 'choreography in general' explores, within an always singular assemblage, the potentials to interact that go along with particular human and non-human elements. Through specific couplings, the associated entities acquire a defining agency when put into motion. The assembled performers, whatever their nature, are indeed truly relational entities. Or as Bruno Latour, one of the founders of Actor-Network Theory (ANT) asserts: 'An actor is what is *made* to act by many others.' The hyphenated expression 'actor-network' precisely tries to designate this paradoxical state of affairs. One always has to move from the actors to the network they form with other actors within an assemblage because their actual performativity depends on the peculiar configuration they support. Yet the performed action or inaction is also constantly overtaken by other network components, which use, for instance, a movement or stillness as an input for their own activity. The overall performativity of a 'dance performance in general' therefore consists of countless mutual translations or modifications of the entities' singular doings. A combined surplus-effect arises from the many interactions, or the networked actors constant overtaking of each other's actions: *an assemblage is a continually changing force field producing an emergent total performativity.*

Choreography's Governmentality

The assemblage defining a 'dance performance in general' usually contains rapidly altering associations between light rays with a variable luminosity, all sorts of sonorities and silences, (human) bodily movements and pauses, refracting or re-synthesizing images, various kinds of objects and the underlying operations of technical artefacts such as microphones, computers or video projectors. The constituting dance elements are actualized possibilities of action and non-action, or *singularities generated within different material potentials that have an event-quality.* A gesturing arm or a series of sound particles exists as a singularity precisely because they are non-representable instantiations out of a virtual range of possibilities. Whereas a particularity exemplifies a general category ('this is an apple'), a singularity defies categorization: it forms a temporal and spatial *becoming.* The corresponding line or movement makes up a 'haecceity' or 'thisness' marking abstract time and space through its current coming into being; and it is also an *intensity* since the line or movement acts as a force that affects other singularities but is simultaneously affected by them (and partly derives from this being affected its own capacity to affect). A sound wave, for instance, interferes with an image or a movement and is at once capturing that visual representation or bodily gesture and captured by it. During a 'dance performance in general', such singularities unremittingly interact, thus creating a total performativity that the spectator usually experiences and speaks of in atmospheric terms ('dark', 'uncanny', 'bright'). Whatever their nature, the singularities' existence presupposes the virtual being of an underlying potential, which is actualized by every intensity with a variable force or energy. The act of singularization is not a non-representable event justifying an ontology of performance, but rather asks for a 'virtuology' that takes seriously performativity's already signalled becoming or duration-eventness.

Every choreographic assemblage constructs a complex force field that has to be modulated or governed from the point of view of its possible internal consistency − or, a tenable distribution of the different forces and their many intersections. The verb 'governing' is indeed appropriate here. In fact, choreography always necessitates the exercise of power in a Foucaultian sense: not only a forbidding of statements or a repression of movements but first and foremost a strategic acting on possible actions and their mutual coupling into a composed series of events. 'A "conduct of conducts" and a management of possibilities': this is what the exercise of power generally comes down to, according to Michel Foucault. The governing can be the single or collective responsibility of those human beings involved. Be that as it may, when making a 'dance performance in general', the exercise of constraining and enabling power is by definition confronted with divergent actions stemming from non-human performers who have their own characteristics and must therefore be addressed in specific ways, and do not always do what they are told. Sound waves, images or props, not to speak of their sustaining technologies, have the capacity to counter-act and to subvert − to produce deterritorializations, undesired flight lines, or simply an outright strike. A video projector momentarily refuses to work − and the technician begins to grunt against the poor machine; a computer acts differently than was expected on the basis of the given commands − and the woman at the screen asks the artefact why it disobeys. Posthumanist practices indeed tend to revive the anthropomorphic outlook commonly associated with pre-modern times.

'Choreography in general' is the art of constructing a multi-medial performance machine consisting of mutually interacting forces that affect each other within the composed plane of consistency. Some intensities possess a bodily or material character, others such as light or sound or spoken words have a disembodied nature (at least to a human observer: physics tells another story). The final work resembles a tamed multitude, with the regulated force field pointing to a genuine form of sociality: a heterogeneous common inhabited by both human and non-human movements acting as singularities. The created common is the principal locus of the performance's total performativity. Trying to dissect this emergent effect or to attribute it to one or more particular performers would be a vain attempt. 'The sound did it all', says a spectator for instance upon leaving *closer*. It may be wiser to ascribe the work's performativity to the continually changing assemblage of the soundscape with other dance elements. For *closer*'s prime medium, even its main performer, is the non-hierarchical performative network this live-installation consistently instantiates. This performer has neither a name nor a face: *'it' performs*.

The rapid breakthrough of the computer as the new material super-medium remediating text, sound or image in meaningless zeros and ones has undoubtedly furthered the transformation of the art of scenography into 'choreography in general'. Theoretical and aesthetic post-humanism both rely and focus on the consequences of digitalization: they use this trend as both a resource and a topic. 'Dance in general' therefore asks for a new kind of criticism, one that complements the still dominant text-oriented hermeneutical or interpretative paradigm concentrating on possible meanings. The poststructuralist master-story regarding the constantly deferred meeting of the signifier with the signified no longer suffices. For the crucial question when observing a 'dance performance in general' is not only 'what does it mean?' but 'how does it work?' What logics or rationalities regulate the governing of the observed configuration of singularities? Precisely because it is choreographed, the witnessed assemblage is – in the words of Nikolas Rose – 'an intelligible field with specifiable limits and particular characteristics, and whose component parts are attractions and coexistences'. The intelligibility of a particular specimen of 'choreography in general' refers to the discovery of, and the experimentation with, one or more rationalities that imply deliberately, even tactically selected means-ends relations and a general thoughtfulness. Both the ideas informing a 'dance work in general' and the management of the corresponding assemblage take the form of operative logics regulating the interactions among the constituting elements. They may be translated into technical procedures, rules of action, or norms governing the actualization of the deployed potentials to move and to not-move. Dance criticism should perhaps focus more on *chore-ography's governmentality, or the way a dance work fuses, through particular rationalities, various 'mentalities' or 'dance ideas' with singular logics of directing heterogeneous dance elements.* The same holds for the practice and theoretical understanding of dance dramaturgy, which is to a great extent just another word for governing, detecting and solidifying connections between various elements according to an always particular rationality.

The possible relations among the assembled material and immaterial actions and inactions are usually not only tried out and tested in view of the creation of both a perceptual and conceptual plane of consistency. The expected co-presence of the spectator, or the sustained moment of dance's contemporaneity, is usually a concern as well. How to organize this co-presence, or how to make it governable? How to manage the performance machine under construction in relation to the audience's presumed capacities to be affected? 'Choreography in general' is indeed also the art of capturing and modulating the audience's sensory attention. In the French language, the verb *'capter'* possesses a double meaning: 'to catch' (to collect, to intercept, to absorb) and 'to take by stratagem'. Choreographing the public's attention is a matter of creating spatial condensates, conspicuously playing with, for instance, a strange grey box (Dunoyer's *Vanity*), first drawing the spectators into and then keeping them immersed in a massive soundscape by means of a well thought-out dramaturgy, or firmly directing the viewer's gaze through the lighting (the last two strategies are regularly deployed in Meg Stuart's performances). This is a tactic game with by definition uncertain outcomes and the ever-present temptation to fall back, with or without irony, on the recipes of 'the spectacular' or of mainstream cultural production, including news shows. Despite this, numerous are the examples of performances in which the unfolded strategies to capture the spectator's sensory attention display an ingeniousness that predominantly draws on the effectiveness of rather weak means, such as a dislocating repetition of movements. Or the work's underlying functioning as a capturing machine is made observable by fully involving the spectators' bodies and modes of attention in the created assemblage (witness again fieldworks' *closer*). Whatever the stratagem used, an uneven power balance is involved: no choreography without a deciding instance, an individual or collective 'writer' to whom the dance work will be attributed. Even in post-humanist times, we continue to need names and subjects that can be held responsible. The operative fiction called 'author' remains powerful despite its many deconstructions.

Coda: Dance's Medium, Choreography's Nature

A final thought that may put into perspective some of the assertions made in this chapter and the previous ones. The observations assembled under the heading 'dance/choreography in general' partly overlap with the tendencies already mapped in 1999 by German theatre theorist Hans-Thies Lehmann in his search for the prime features of what he calls post-dramatic theatre. However, whereas Lehmann emphasizes the specifics of the post-dramatic vis-à-vis dramatic theatre and its conflict-driven, textual cosmos, the expression 'dance/ choreography in general' attempts to suggest an inclusive conceptual gesture that both generalizes, re-articulates and de-humanizes notions of dance and choreography, and, by implication, of performance and performativity. It goes beyond more established notions such as multimedia performance or post-dramatic theatre. The concept itself is inspired by Thierry de Duve's characterization of the field of the fine arts 'after Duchamp' as an 'art in general', in which (at least in principle) everything seems possible because of the lack of genuine technical standards and aesthetic norms. The appropriation of De Duve's concept awards the term 'in general' a somewhat more particular content, assuming a generic definition of dance's medium as the unity of the difference between movement and non-movement. This, in the end, may imply a trace of essentialism that should be principally resisted. The same holds for the proposed notion of 'the choreographic', which deliberately rehearses the traditional associations with writing and composition.

Within contemporary dance, movement and non-movement have become de-humanized and de-embodied (though not really de-materialized in the strict physical sense). The consistently applied definition of dance's medium can cover this change because it remains silent on the exact nature of the elements making up the corresponding potential. Involved is an abstract idea, tailored out of the necessity to delineate in an at once clear and open mode the subject under discussion. Nevertheless, both this approach of dance and the conceptualization of 'the choreographic' in terms of a writing-in-general, or the production of iterable marks regarding actions and inactions, decisively anchor the constructed epistemological objects in a specific medium. Besides a trace of essentialism, this may signal a minimalized modernist leaning that does not seem up to date with the attitudes explicitly informing current 'post-postmodernist dance'. Yet the crux of both essentialism and modernism is precisely their fixing, even immortalization, of contingent socio-cultural conventions on the nature of the elements making up a medium. Theorizing can counter-act this tendency through an at once professed and self-reflexively corrected inclination towards an *empirical formalism* informed by the pasts, presents and probable futures of the discussed subject(s).

Is a post-medial dance thinkable, one no longer rooted in the difference between movement and non-movement enacted in whatever more specific material medium or substrate? Post-Cunningham dance has stretched the legitimately danceable in marked leaps, provisionally ending in the inclusion of the potentials of non-human materialities to move or to not-move. This has strikingly re-framed dance's assumed medium but not truly superseded it. In the same vein, 'the choreographic' has been pushed to that limit where a 'written dance text' can contain self-reflexively framed ideas and may also be actively overwritten by a performance's contemporaneity or the contingent modes indicating the public's co-presence. The change, again, rather confirms choreography's immanent connection to the acts of writing and composing. For the moment, an abstract medial approach still offers the possibility to describe and analyse contemporary dance's current stakes. This proverbial proof of eating the pudding should do — but indeed only for the moment: until dance de- and re-mediates into a becoming an other whose face may strike us as monstrous. Until the historical tipping point of Judson stops producing after-effects and we truly enter the era of post-Judson: *until the name 'theatre dance' becomes obsolete.*

Sources

Dance's Viewpoints

The presentation of *Vanity* is based on personal recollections of the performance in the Brussels Kaaitheater (November 2000) and the Tanzquartier Wien (November 2001). I furthermore relied on the work's interpretation in Gerald Siegmund, *Abwesenheit. Ein performative Ästhetik des Tanzes. William Forsythe, Jérôme Bel, Xavier Le Roy, Meg Stuart.* Bielefeld: transcript Verlag, 2006, pp. 207–210 and Rudi Laermans, 'The Spatial Vanishing Point of the Dancing Body', in Hugo Haeghens (ed.), *Media Mediations. On Vincent Dunoyer and Others.* Maasmechelen: Cultureel Centrum Maasmechelen, 2003, pp. 76–81 (partly retaken verbatim). The José Gil-citation stems from his article 'Paradoxical Body', in *The Drama Review,* 50 (4), 2006, pp. 21–35 (p. 28; italics in the original).

Choreography as 'Videography'

Meg Stuart stresses the defining role of video for contemporary choreography in the untitled conversation she has with fine artist Catherine Sullivan in *Bomb,* (104), 2008, pp. 28–35 (p. 33).

Intermezzo: Reconsidering Conceptual Art

The discussion of Conceptualism is primarily informed by Alexander Alberro and Blake Stimson (eds.), *Conceptual Art. A Critical Anthology.* Cambridge (MA): MIT Press, 2000. Particularly inspiring were the editors' double preface (pp. xiv–xxxviii) and the reconsiderations of Conceptual Art, reprinted in the book's closing section, by Jeff Wall ('Dan Graham's Kammerspiel', pp. 502–513), Benjamin H. Buchloh ('Conceptual Art 1962–1969. From the Aesthetic of Administration to the Critique of Institutions', pp. 514–537) and Mari Carmen Ramírez ('Blueprint Circuits. Conceptual Art and Politics in Latin America', pp. 550–563). This anthology also contains the quoted publications of Sol LeWitt, 'Paragraphs on Conceptual Art', pp. 12–16 (p. 12) and Joseph Kosuth, 'Art After Philosophy', pp. 158–177 (pp. 171–172). For defining statements on institutional critique, see Alexander Alberro and Blake Stimson (eds.), *Institutional Critique. An Anthology of Artists' Writings.* Cambridge (MA): MIT Press, 2009.

Max Weber summarizes his view on the intertwinement of modernity and instrumental rationalization in 'Science as a Vocation', included in Hans H. Gert and C. Wright Mills (eds.), *From Max Weber. Essays in Sociology.* London: Routledge, 1982, pp. 129–156. For a brief sketch of contemporary neoliberal governmentality, inspired by the pioneering work of Michel Foucault on this issue, see Rudi Laermans, 'The Condition of Neoliberalism', in *A-Prior,* (19), 2009, pp. 6–17. Reference is moreover made to Helmut Schelsky, 'Ist die Dauerreflexion institutionalisierbar?', in Helmut Schelsky, *Auf der Suche nach Wirklichkeit. Gesammelte Aufsätze zur Soziologie der Bundesrepublik.* München: Wilhelm Fink, 1979, pp. 268–297 and Niklas Luhmann, *Art as a Social System.* Stanford (CA): Stanford University Press, 2000, which is quoted pp. 193–194.

From Postmodern/ist Dance to Conceptual Dance

Yvonne Rainer explicitly relates *Trio A* to Minimalism in the fine arts in the essay 'A Quasi Survey of Some "Minimalist" Tendencies in the Quantitatively Minimal Dance Activity Midst the Plethora, or an Analysis of *Trio A*', which is reprinted in the anthology edited by Roger Copeland and Marshall Cohen (eds.), *What is Dance? Readings in Theory and Criticism.* Oxford: Oxford University Press, 1983, pp. 325–332. Sally Banes first interpreted the work of Rainer and Judson in a truly modernist, Greenbergian mode in the 'Introduction to the Wesleyan Paperback Edition' of her overview study *Terpsichore in Sneakers: Post-Modern Dance.* Middletown (CT): Wesleyan University Press, 1987, pp. xiii–xxxix. A quite different reading is proposed in Sally Banes and Noël Carroll, 'Cunningham, Balanchine, and Postmodern Dance', in *Dance Chronicle,* 29 (1), 2006, pp. 49–68 (p. 60). Frederic Jameson's epochal essay 'Postmodernism, or the Logic of Late Capitalism' first appeared in *New Left Review,* (146),

1984, pp. 53–92 (he extended his original argument in his 1991 book of the same title) and should be read in combination with Hal Foster, *Recodings: Art, Spectacle, Cultural Politics*. Seattle (WA): Bay Press, 1985. For further theoretical considerations on postmodernism and dance, see for instance Ann Daly a.o., 'What Has Become of Postmodern Dance?', in *The Drama Review*, 36 (1), 1992, pp. 48–69 and Nick Kaye, *Postmodernism and Performance*. London: Macmillan, 1994. We still lack a synthetic overview of the kind of postmodern/ist dance that was performed on both American and West European stages during the 1980s and the first half of the 1990s (and which would include, for Flanders, the names of Jan Fabre, Wim Vandekeybus or Marc Vanrunxt). Building stones for such a future history may be found in, for instance, Martha Bremser (ed.), *Fifty Contemporary Choreographers*. London: Routledge, 1999.

Gerald Siegmund discusses the notion of conceptual dance in 'Konzept ohne Tanz? Nachdenken über Choreographie und Körper', in Reto Clavadetscher and Claudia Rosiny (eds.), *Zeitgenössischer Tanz. Körper – Konzepte – Kulturen: Eine Bestandsaufnahme*. Bielefeld: transcript Verlag, 2007, pp. 44–59. Xavier Le Roy's 2004 quote on the same subject is mentioned in André Lepecki, *Exhausting Dance. Performance and the Politics of Movement*. London: Routledge, 2006, p. 135 (note 2). Bojana Cvejić presents the pros and cons of the expression 'conceptual dance' in Xavier Le Roy, Bojana Cvejić and Gerald Siegmund, 'To end with judgment by way of clarification...', in Martina Hochmuth, Krassimira Kruschkova and Georg Schöllhammer (eds.), *It takes place when it doesn't. On dance and performance since 1989*. Frankfurt am Main: Revolver, 2006, pp. 49–56 (two times quoted p. 52).

The Name of Reflexive Dance
Yvonne Rainer's manifesto '"No" to Spectacle...' is reprinted in Alexandra Carter (ed.), *The Routledge Dance Studies Reader*. London: Routledge, 1998, p. 35. Frédéric Pouillaude's perceptive essay on the main trends within contemporary dance, originally published in French in 2004, was given a wider audience thanks to the English translation 'Scène and Contemporaneity' in *The Drama Review*, 51 (2), 2007, 124–135 (p. 132). Ramsay Burt briefly discusses 'Judson in Europe' in *Judson Dance Theater: Performative Traces*. Abingdon: Routledge, 2006, pp. 193–196. That such a belated reception must be grasped in terms of a deferred action is argued at length in 'Who's Afraid of the Neo-Avant-Garde?', the opening chapter of Hal Foster's *The Return of the Real. The Avant-Garde at the End of the Century*. Cambridge (MA): MIT Press, 1996, pp. 1–34 (p. 13 and p. 29). Pascal Gielen extensively analyses, partly inspired by Pierre Bourdieu's field model, the Flemish case of contemporary dance's institutionalization during the 1980s in the second part of his book *Kunst in netwerken: artistieke selecties in de hedendaagse dans en de beeldende kunst (Art within Networks. Artistic Selections in Contemporary Dance and the Fine Arts)*. Leuven: LannooCampus, 2003, pp. 23–98. A comparable but more succinct description of the genesis and overall structure of the field of 'new French dance' is offered by Sylvia Faure, 'Les structures du champ chorégraphique français', in *Actes de la recherche en sciences sociales*, (175), 2008, pp. 82–97.

Performance's Contemporaneity
The description of *La Magnificenza* is based on the video recording of the March 2007 performance at Buda Fresh festival, Kortrijk (with the original cast: Vincent Dunoyer, Etienne Guilloteau and Hans Meijer) and recollections of the work's re-performance in Cultureel Centrum Berchem, with Noé Soulier replacing Vincent Dunoyer, during the January 2009 edition of the Amperdans festival. Boris Charmatz underscores the importance of scenography in Boris Charmatz and Isabelle Launay, *Entretenir: A propos d'une danse contemporaine*. Dijon: les presses du réel, 2003, p. 158. Frédéric Pouillaude's already mentioned essay 'Scène and Contemporaneity' is quoted p. 134 and p. 132 respectively (italics in the original). For a broader contextualization of the cited argument, see Frédéric Pouillaude, *Le Désœuvrement chorégraphique. Etude sur la notion d'œuvre en danse*. Paris: Vrin, 2009.

Intermezzo: Performing Ideas
G.W.F Hegel's 'Introduction to Aesthetics' is quoted from the extract, containing the first three chapters, in David E. Cooper (ed.), *Aesthetics. The Classic Readings*. Oxford: Blackwell, 1997, pp. 137-149 (p. 144 and pp. 146-147). Arthur Danto's 1984 article 'The End of Art' can be found in his essay collection *The Philosophical Disenfranchisement of Art*. New York (NY): Columbia University Press, 1986, pp. 81-115. Danto restates his views in *After the End of Art. Contemporary Art and the Pale of History*. Princeton (NJ): Princeton University Press, 1997, particularly in the second chapter, 'Three Decades after the End of Art', pp. 21-40 (p. 37). That the political is based on the difference between friend and enemy, who must eventually be eliminated, is the main contention of Carl Schmitt's (in)famous text *The Concept of the Political*. Chicago (IL): Chicago University Press, 2007. The following works are quoted also: Niklas Luhmann, *Art as a Social System*, pp. 47-48; Gilles Deleuze and Félix Guattari, *What is Philosophy?* London: Verso, 1994, p. 66; and Gilles Deleuze and Félix Guattari, *Qu'est que la philosophie?* Paris: Minuit, 1991, p. 62 (the middle sentence in the quote is missing in the English translation, *What is Philosophy?*, p. 64).

Deconstructing Body Humanism
André Lepecki's essay 'Concept and Presence: The Contemporary European Dance Scene' is included in Alexandra Carter (ed.), *Rethinking Dance History*. London: Routledge, 2004, pp. 170-181 (p. 173 and p. 180). How Michael Kirby tries to delineate dance from non-dance can be read in his essay 'Danse et Non-Danse. Trois Continuums Analytiques', in Odette Aslan (ed.), *Le corps en jeu*. Paris: CNRS, 1993, pp. 18-28. That 'a work of art needs only to be interesting' is asserted by Donald Judd at the end of the essay 'Specific Objects' (1965), republished in his *Complete Writings*. New York (NY) and Halifax: The Press of the Nova Scotia School of Art and Design, 1975, pp. 181-189 (p. 189). Why the traditional bourgeois-humanist understanding of the sphere of the arts tends to a quasi-religious and conservative outlook is explained at length by Herbert Marcuse in his 1937 essay 'The Affirmative Character of Culture', reprinted in Herbert Marcuse, *Negations. Essays in Critical Theory*. Boston: Beacon Press, 1968, pp. 88-133.

Pieter T'Jonck contrasted the humanist view on art with the 'paranoid view' of reflexive dance in his introduction to a panel discussion, organized in October 2004, regarding the sometimes fierce debate that followed the 11th edition of the Leuven-based dance festival Klapstuk, which was curated by Jérôme Bel. The original Dutch version of his text, 'Dans en paranoia. Aantekeningen bij Klapstuk #11 (en #10) ('Dance and Paranoia. Notes on Klapstuk #11 [and #10])', was published in *Etcetera*, (95), 2005, pp. 49-52. The non-paginated and rather imperfect English translation, entitled 'Klapstuk #11 bis: introduction', can be consulted on the website of Sarma (www.sarma.be), a Brussels-based organization that among other things aims to digitally archive and open up the work of dance critics. The notion of 'democracy's body', mentioned in passing, is borrowed from Sally Banes, *Democracy's Body: Judson Dance Theater, 1962-1964*. Durham (NC): Duke University Press, 1993. 'Body without organs' is an expression coined by Antonin Artaud, which Gilles Deleuze and Félix Guattari conceptually upgrade in 'November 28 1947. How Do You Make Yourself a Body Without Organs?', the sixth plateau of *A Thousand Plateaus. Capitalism and Schizophrenia*. London: Continuum, 2003, pp. 149-166.

Co-Writing Dance
The discussion of *closer* partly relies on the memory traces this work produced during the performance I attended in June 2004 in the city theatre of Kortrijk. I furthermore consulted a video recording of an unspecified performance. Roland Barthes develops the invoked notion of the 'writerly text' in *S/Z*. Oxford: Blackwell, 1990. The Derrida-quote stems from his essay *Limited Inc*. Evanston (IL): Northwestern University Press, 1988, p. 47.

'Dance (or Choreography) in General'

Like the next one, this paragraph retakes sometimes verbatim some of the ideas I already put forward in the essay "'Dance in general", or choreographing the public, making assemblages', in *Performance Research. A Journal of Performing Arts*, 13 (1), 2008, pp. 7-14. The principal argument owes much to the work of Thierry de Duve, who analyses the Duchamp-effect and 'art in general' at length in *Kant after Duchamp*. Cambridge (MA): MIT Press, 1997. He gives a succinct presentation of some of this book's main ideas in 'The Post-Duchamp Deal. Remarks on a Few Specifications of the Word "Art"', in *A-Prior*, (6), Autumn/Winter 2001-2002, pp. 141-147 (pp. 142-143; italics in the original). Deleuze and Guattari recurrently put forward the notion of assemblage – it still remains to be seen if this translation truly covers the original French expression *'agencement'* – in *A Thousand Plateaus* (p. 88; italics in the original). Manuel De Landa slightly re-articulates the concept in *A New Philosophy of Society: Assemblage Theory and Social Complexity*. London: Continuum, 2006 (p. 10). There is also an affinity with the idea of 'actor-network', as is indicated by the title of Bruno Latour's authoritative presentation of ANT, *Reassembling the Social. An Introduction to Actor-Network-Theory*. Oxford: Oxford University Press, 2005 (p. 46; italics in the original).

Choreography's Governmentality

The notions of singularity, 'haecceity' or 'thisness' and intensity are borrowed from Deleuze's and Guattari's *A Thousand Plateaus*. Michel Foucault defines power as government or the 'conduct of conducts' in his 1982 essay 'The Subject and Power', reprinted in Michel Foucault, *Essential Works 3: Power*. London: Penguin, 2002, pp. 326-348 (p. 341). Nikolas Rose further explores Foucault's intuitions in *Powers of Freedom: Reframing Political Thought*. Cambridge: Cambridge University Press, 1999 (p. 33). André Lepecki discusses 'choreography as apparatus of capture' in his essay with the same title, published in *The Drama Review*, 51 (2), 2007, pp. 119-123.

Coda: Dance's Medium, Choreography's Nature

Hans-Thies Lehmann extensively presents post-dramatic theatre in his epochal study *Postdramatisches Theater*. Frankfurt am Main: Verlag der Autoren, 1999. Some of the substantial arguments and case studies supporting this specific perspective are, unfortunately, absent from the abridged English translation *Postdramatic Theatre*. Abingdon: Routledge, 2006.

Part 2

Making Contemporary Dance

Making and
Valuating Art
On the Social
Nature of
Autonomous Art
Worlds

First Movement: Deconstructing Art's Singularities

Framing Art's Autonomy

It is a truism that Western art became increasingly autonomous from the mid-eighteenth century onwards. Romanticism and the humanist notion of *Bildung*, or the idea that a regular participation in the various arts makes for more complete human beings, were at once active cultural motors and passive semantic expressions of this structural tendency. Impressionism rounded off the process of autonomization within the sphere of the fine arts; Isadora Duncan did the same for modern dance and the medium of movement and non-movement at the beginning of the twentieth century. Autonomous art does not serve political interests or religious causes, at least not in a direct or propagandistic way, and is no longer practiced within the restrictive frame of academism and its morally backed imperative to stick to detailed rules of representation and veracity. Through divergent acts of negation, the historical avant-garde actually ratified art's new societal status as an independent socio-cultural realm with characteristic social institutions and positions, a particular mode of communication and a specific economy of worth. Futurism, Dadaism and Surrealism all wanted to fuse art and daily life, which only proved possible thanks to the then recently completed autonomy of art. During the 1960s and 1970s, the neo-avant-garde explicitly confirmed this verdict by critically focusing on the museum and the white cube gallery, the traditional theatre house setting and its marked split between stage and public, and other basic institutions co-securing art's autonomy. These were also the years that Conceptualism, discussed in the previous chapter, revisited the historical avant-garde's deconstruction of the prevailing frames of meaning or traditional expectations pertaining to art that were still in force. Some artists, such as Joseph Beuys, even profoundly put into question the notion of the artist as a specific social role. 'Every human being is an artist', Beuys (in)famously proclaimed. This provocative statement could only be authoritatively made by a consecrated artist, which again corroborates the observation that art's autonomy is generally questioned on the basis of that very socio-cultural independence.

Autonomy does not imply isolation, quite the contrary. Art's current position has indeed a paradoxical nature: *art's societal independence is possible thanks to many indirect interdependencies.*

Today's autonomy of the arts, or of a particular art world, is made possible and sustained by the many relations of structural coupling to, for instance, the realms of higher education (read: the input of art schools), politics (governmental funding or subsidizing) or the economy (art markets). Also, there is a general dependency on existing social inequalities, since the public participation in the arts mirrors current class differences to a great extent. The arts partly owe their autonomy to a system of stratification in which a considerable number of the members of the upper social strata are willing to support expressions of 'high culture' for reasons of status or distinction (this elite support is actually waning due to the re-composition of the bourgeoisie and the institutionalization of creative niches within mass culture, witness so-called alternative pop or rock music). Besides, art's societal status is firmly backed by the predominant cultural notion of individual freedom that underlies the common idea of artists as people who are able to affirm their subjective capacities in a genuine way. The list of manifest and latent dependencies may be extended, but that would not radically alter the overall picture: art's autonomy is relative and socio-culturally conditioned. Nevertheless, the structural couplings between the different art spheres and education, politics, the economy or the prevailing class system, do not directly determine the production and mediation, let alone the valuation of singular art works. Contemporary art fields delineate independent arenas wherein the central performative act of naming or not-naming something an art work, and subsequently calling someone a true artist, is not causally steered by the dominant teachings at art schools, the contingent outcomes of arts funding, or the whimsicalities of the art market.

A particular mode of aesthetic communication singles out the art sphere from the point of view of the social production and reception of meaning. During the second half of the eighteenth century, Alexander Baumgarten and Immanuel Kant – in his trail-blazing *Critique of Judgment* (1790) – took up the original signification of the Greek word *aesthesis* (which points to the act of perceiving, feeling or sensing) in view of a new discipline that would concentrate on both sensory experience, in particular of art works or 'beauty', and its usually laborious translation into words or language (in Kant's approach, this comes down to the formulation of judgments). Given the prevailing cultural framing of art, *autonomous art objects actually address the difference between sensual perception and communication.* They seize the eye and/or the ear by means of the materiality of words, colours, sounds, images or movements, and in so doing they communicate meaningful information. Soaps and Hollywood movies or straightforward dance tunes and enchanting advertisements function in a comparable way, yet try to simulate the possibility of the de facto impossible unity of the conscious processing of sensory experiences and the also conscious apprehension of the information conveyed. Whereas direct involvement or immediate fascination typifies entertainment, aesthetic communication in the artistic mode tends rather to irritate both perception and understanding. The difference between sensuous apprehension and the act of communication is magnified through the continual offering of percepts that may not be immediately grasped: some movements are made on stage and accurately witnessed, but what do they 'really mean'? A fissure or eventually even a gap is produced, and it will be recurrently recreated through various actions or inactions during an average contemporary dance performance. This also holds for novels or poetry, since modern literature uses language in such a way that the reader observes the difference between the conscious associations that the words evoke and their possible significations in the context of a story or a poem. In short, transference of meaning is interrupted or deferred through the very same perceptions that sustain the ongoing process of communication. Or, as the German sociologist Dirk Baecker trenchantly states, art 'establishes that perceptible meaning which finds its meaning rather in the perceptibility than in meaning itself'.

The autonomization of artistic communication came at the price of a growing commodification: no autonomous art without art markets, at least not within the context of modern capitalism. Even if they can rely on direct or indirect government funding, independently operating artists must find buyers for their produced artefacts within today's globalized distribution networks. Yet although the offered artefacts are always also commodities, an outright commercial attitude is as a rule frowned upon. With the possible exception of the speculative segment at the higher end of the market for contemporary fine art, most art worlds still show a marked repudiation of the economic rationality characterizing the more mundane realms of buying and selling. An art field typically affirms its autonomy by taking its distance from the expectations and behaviours dominating established economic practices. Not only are commercial interests in the narrow sense banned to the social unconsciousness (from where they more often than not continue to haunt the involved agents). 'The challenge which economies based on disavowal of the "economic" presents to all forms of economism lies precisely in the fact that they function, and can function, in practice – and not merely in the agents' representations – only by virtue of a constant, collective repression of narrowly "economic" interest and of the real nature of the practices revealed by "economic" analysis', Pierre Bourdieu asserts in his epochal essay 'The production of belief'.

Art worlds exemplify the double negation of both the underlying material or financial economy and the specific symbolic economy regulating all autonomous fields of cultural production and mediation. Economy means scarcity, and what is certainly not abundant in an art world is *symbolic capital*, or the public recognition an artist or art mediator receives from already consecrated peers or others – read: from important critics, established curators, 'serious' collectors, and the like – who have the legitimate power to ascribe value. Contemporary society shows striking inequalities in the overall distribution of economic and educational capital. The same holds for art worlds, in which the uneven distribution of symbolic capital differentiates a relatively small core of widely consecrated artists from a more densely populated second circle made up of those who still have a relatively fair chance to get some international attention; in its fringes survive the countless local artists who go on producing artefacts that are not held in much esteem, out of the mostly vain hope of being discovered at some point in the future. Accumulating symbolic capital, which can over time be converted into economic capital, is one of the prime imperatives – but certainly not the only proverbial motor, as Bourdieu suggests – animating the many actions within an art field. Again, this implicit quasi-law is mostly practiced in the mode of disavowal or denial. Whatever position one takes up, one has to act in a visibly disinterested way. On the social stage, artists, gallery owners or curators neither attach great importance to economic gains nor make much ado of secured symbolic profits. The famous motto 'art for art's sake' encapsulates it all: the dictum at once glorifies the autonomy of art and effectively sanctions the public behaviour of all those working within an art world.

The Regime of Singularity

Each autonomous artistic field also functions as a cultural community that subscribes to specific definitions, norms and presuppositions, not the least with regard to the distinction between art and non-art. Without this mostly implicit fund of collective beliefs and rules, internal cooperation goes awry and cannot be properly conducted. Yet there is also a transversally shared conviction saying that art works are singular products made by singular individuals. Innovative art works and their makers are therefore usually held in much higher esteem than the artistic hangers-on who just follow the latest trend or fashion. Whatever their more particular outlooks, modern and contemporary art worlds enact, through a plethora of activities, this highly specific mode of appreciation and justification. *Autonomous art equals the value regime of singularity*, concludes the French sociologist of art Nathalie Heinich: it stands for 'a system of appreciation, based on an ethics of rarity, which tends to privilege the subject, the particular, the individual, the personal, the private; it opposes itself diametrically to the "regime of community", based on an ethics of conformity, which tends to privilege the social, the general, the collective, the impersonal, the public.'

In conspicuous contrast with academism, the standard of singularity operates in anything but a uniform or homogeneous way: comparable to a meta-norm, this general axiological principle is differently interpreted within various art worlds. A particular art world may, or may not, take into account a minimum of craftsmanship as an aesthetic necessity when assessing a work's peculiarity. Likewise, it may or may not take into account the rarity of a self-reflexive stance towards the history of the artistic discipline involved, the originality of an overtly political attitude, or the individual way in which one or more existing definitions of art are joyfully transgressed. Within an aesthetic genre, such as sculpture or dance, the daily application of the common rule of singularity is indeed notably plural, yet this diversity is also accompanied by a profound inequality in the overall legitimacy of the invoked qualities. Not that generic conceptual art, discussed in the previous chapter, has become the binding *doxa* in all artistic fields, but it certainly possesses a considerable symbolic weight in many aesthetic genres nowadays. Nevertheless, both the heterogeneity and the differences in authority marking the arts' regime of originality and individuality come with a widely established consensus regarding its cornerstones. The value of singularity has meanwhile been condensed into exemplary historical figures (such as Vincent van Gogh or Pablo Picasso) and canonical artefacts (such as Marcel Duchamp's *Fountain*) that tower above the ongoing disputes about the assumed merits of this or that artist or art work. They in fact function as difficult to contest models because they supposedly illustrate what the notions of artist and art work actually imply according to the existent consensus: to be, respectively, a free creator or author-subject and an ever enigmatic object or self-contained monadic world.

A particular stance, magnified in the tradition of Romanticism, indeed informs the view on art works within the regime of singularity: the individual art object is positioned as both original and unique, and therefore regarded as truly authentic. This lends an artefact the enchanting kind of appeal that Walter Benjamin famously associated with the concept of 'aura' in his essay 'The Work of Art in the Age of Mechanical Reproduction'. The auratic art work is at once close and at an unbridgeable distance. Spatial and perceptual intimacy merges with a semiotic or communicative aloofness: the material artefact is 'now, here', but as a genuine work of art it simultaneously inhabits a strange, impossible to locate elsewhere. For the observed painting or sculpture visibly transcends its materiality or 'objecthood': it opens up a vast realm of possible significations that seem at once evident and opaque. The successful art work precisely enthrals because it speaks for itself but also remains a profound enigma, a hieratic hieroglyph that may perhaps never be fully deciphered. Both dimensions making up 'the aesthetic' momentarily diverge, so that the spectator feels simultaneously included (sensually) and excluded (communicatively): the admired painting is a visually apprehended bundle of lines and colours with recognizable figures or shapes, yet this materiality partly disappears in the work's appearance as an autonomous reality of signification. Or one sees bodies moving and posing on stage, and their physical presentness only renders the representational value of the observable actions ever more mysterious. In short, the authentic art work is conjecturally experienced as a puzzle — and the visible indications regarding its possible solution only add to the riddle. It speaks in tongues and addresses the appropriate senses in a bewitching language whose singularity is experienced as an unfathomable code, impossible to break. Only an irreparable fissure seems to link the observed material signifiers to the suggested immaterial signifieds or meanings. The gap evidently merely exists in the eye of the beholder who interprets the artefact according to the interiorized imperatives of the hegemonic regime of singularity. In the final instance, it is all a question of *a socially shared belief in originality or particularity that is collectively misrecognized and essentialized* (and also a question, as every sociologist will add, of a minimum amount of cultural capital at the root of this belief).

'Works of art are received and valued on different planes. Two polar types stand out: with one, the accent is on the cult value; with the other, on the exhibition value of the work. Artistic production begins with ceremonial objects destined to serve in a cult', Benjamin observes. He prophesizes that in 'the age of mechanical reproduction' − read: of movies and mass circulating photography, since the essay was written in the mid-1930s − the traditional cult value, even the charismatic aura of the art work, is doomed to fade away. For the exhibition value, or the sheer fact that a photograph is widely published in a weekly magazine or a daily newspaper, and thus made easily available, will outstrip the desire to be spatially close to a unique artefact. Yet the opposite diagnosis possesses perhaps a larger grain of truth: the culture of the readily accessible copy greatly favours the cult of the difficult to witness reproduced original. Art's regime of singularity seems indeed rather strengthened by the worldwide availability of reproductions in whatever form. The live show outdoes its video registration, however accurate, and the innumerable copies of the *Mona Lisa* only add to the specific aura of Da Vinci's *La Giaconda* in the Louvre. The ideology of liveness, still dominating the performing arts, is actually just a particular instance of the central idea accompanying the regime of singularity − that only the direct and unmediated, corporeal experience of the unique art work's presence can do justice to its authenticity. The spectator must be face to face or in a relation of intimacy in order to grasp the ultimately ungraspable nature of the art work's grandeur, stipulates the reigning credo. In sum, the ethics of singularity goes hand in hand with a metaphysics of presence that magnifies the spectator's physical co-presence. The crowds still drawn with each new edition of the Venice Biennale or the restaging of a renowned choreography, illustrate that this 'presentism' is not exactly on the wane.

All this may sound quite clichéd or worn out, legitimating the critical notion — made famous by literary critic Terry Eagleton — of 'the ideology of the aesthetic'. Nevertheless, art's regime of singularity still vastly informs today's discourse on art, and does so often even when it opts for a counter-intuitive interpretation or a deconstructive reading that goes against the grain. Every unique art work's particular formal or communicative qualities are, in the last instance, assumed to be ineffable or beyond words. They may only be experienced through a multi-faceted act of individual witnessing that even the best personal photograph can never reproduce. Granted the evident differences between attending a live dance performance and the viewing of a video recording, the ethics of rarity and originality singles out the sheer power of the unique art object to overwhelm or to take possession of one's body and mind when experienced in vivo. The never fully understood aesthetic otherness of a successful painting or a dazzling dance performance is considered to be the genuine effect of the work's direct agency, which every reproduction necessarily lacks. The artefact deemed art is indeed usually treated as an object that acts as a subject and possesses qualities commonly ascribed to human persons. Art works seduce and convince, come near and run away, speak and remain silent; they also amaze, enchant, compel, delight, entrap, et cetera. In sum, *the successful singular art object is construed as a quasi-subject that captivates the spectator.* The agency attributed to the art work resembles that of an adored beloved one — hence the expression 'the love of art'— or the influence exercised by a magician or a worshipped religious object. Within the modern secular world, unique art works act as religious icons such as a Holy Mary painting or sculpture in traditional Catholicism: they possess an uncanny, difficult to assess, absorbent power. The similarity between religious artefacts and art objects evidently conceals a crucial difference. Whereas the fabricated representation of the Holy Mary acts as a token for a strongly codified and socially sanctioned belief system, the unique art work's magic spell is a singular experience testifying to the artefact's particular agency or aura. Nevertheless, in both instances a cult or performative conviction is involved that grants an object the active power to make an autonomous human subject completely passive, even quasi-masochistically submissive. Fetishism or reification is the established conceptual name for this paradoxical fact.

The Art Work as Fetish

While ransacking the coast of Guinea, the Portuguese colonizers stumbled over amulets of the Holy Mary and saints worshipped by the indigenous population. Interrogated by the white invaders, who were after all very Catholic, the locals responded that they had indeed fabricated the objects in question but that this did not at all prevent them from idolizing the artefacts. The Portuguese were baffled and introduced the expression *feitiço* in order to frame this strange state of affairs. The adjective stems from *feito*, the past participle of the verb referring to making, forming or configuring; yet the word also connotes artificiality or being fabricated as well as enchantment or fascination. These different meanings all fit the patently ethnocentric notion of the idolized object. The venerated fetish is a human creation that bewitches and may also be used to cast a spell on an enemy. At least from a secular viewpoint, its efficacy rests on an act of human projection: within the context of a particular belief system, the object is actively bestowed with its supposed power to mediate between the profane and the sacred world. However, the artefact can only be operative if the collective human action sustaining it remains hidden. The disavowal is crucial to the object's impact and transforms it into a reified one, an autonomous thing (in Latin: *res*) with a seemingly independent efficacy that in reality fully depends on the misrecognized human act of projection. In sum, to worship a fetish is a performative act whose success paradoxically hinges on the straightforward denial of the act's performativity.

Together with Sigmund Freud, who coined the notion of sexual fetishism, Karl Marx has given the expression 'fetishism' its letters of conceptual nobility. 'The mysterious character of the commodity-form consists ... simply in the fact that the commodity reflects the social characteristics of men's own labour as objective characteristics of the products of labour themselves, as the socio-cultural properties of these things', Marx writes in the famous chapter on 'the fetishism of the commodity and its secret' in the first volume of *Capital*. 'In order, therefore, to find an analogy we must take flight into the misty realm of religion. There the products of the human brain appear as autonomous figures endowed with a life of their own, which enter into relations both with each other and with the human race. So it is in the world of commodities with the products of men's hands. I call this the fetishism which attaches itself to the products of labour as soon as they are produced as commodities, and is therefore inseparable from the production of commodities.' Commodity fetishism equals the forgetting within the act of consumption – in Marx' terms: in the sphere of circulation – of the social labour that lends every priced object a particular exchange value. With the negation of the work necessary to produce the commodity, the social relation of exploitation characterizing the manufacturing of goods within capitalism also disappears. The oversight happens in a quasi-natural way because commodities effectively turn up as autonomous goods on markets. In a mundane shop window or supermarket, the merchandise is just there, as if the appealing clothes or enchanting fashionables have fallen from heaven and are only waiting to be gazed at and bought. Their exchange value seems to translate their intrinsic properties: the price-tag assumingly expresses the observable value of the sensible object itself, rather than the likely underpaid hours of labour it embodies and to which it actually owns its particular qualities.

'All reification is a forgetting', Max Horkheimer and Theodor W. Adorno assert in *Dialectic of Enlightenment*, their bleak diagnosis of modernity as the ever increasing domination of a calculative, purely instrumental rationality. Commodity fetishism forgets the labour accumulated in most priced objects (handmade goods testifying of craftsmanship may nowadays be a noteworthy exception). The same holds for *artistic fetishism, or the negation of the labour presupposed by the hailed singularity of the art work and its concomitant transformation in a reified artefact that speaks for itself of itself through itself.* As with every commodity, the average work of fine art anticipates its effects, seemingly waiting, within the aggrandizing atmosphere of the white gallery cube or museum, the minimum of attention in order to be able to convince, capture or astonish. There are usually also no visible traces of hard work, which is all the more striking in the performing arts. Beads of sweat notwithstanding, theatre and dance performers commonly show no visible signs on stage hinting at the often exhausting physical and mental labour the act of performing usually requires. The actors act as if they are only enacting a god given inspiration, and the dancers dance as if they are only expressing a natural talent. This is to a great extent still the overall rule, yet of course there are also many exceptions. The examples of art works that subvert artistic fetishism – or at least try to do so – range from so-called process art, in which the end product is not the principal focus, to performances à la Judson, which through a task-oriented approach to 'being on stage' underline the labour necessary to bring forth a work of art, to the kind of performing style à la Rosas — discussed in the second chapter — that deliberately makes visible traces of the dancer's physical exhaustion.

Notwithstanding the various attempts to counter artistic fetishism, the average spectator probably still enjoys a theatre or dance spectacle as a monadic time-object whose singular value is first and foremost ascribed to observable qualities that are reified. Movements were man- and woman-made, but what is actually admired and discussed afterwards are primarily their meanings as such, cut off from the stage labour to which they own their very existence. Hermeneutics and 'textualism', or the common equation of a performance with its observed significations, rest indeed on a rather blatant reification; the same is actually true for the sensualist reduction of the art work to a medium of percepts and affects. A double forgetting informs this all too mundane fetishism (which was indeed rehearsed more than once in the previous chapters). The first negation gives artistic fetishism a specific twist within the realm of the performing arts. When admiring a choreography or the dramatization of a theatre text, even the rather enlightened spectator with a keen eye for the performer's actions and singularity tends to forget the huge amount of preparatory labour presupposed by the actual performance. One is taken in by what happens 'now, here', thus negating all the countless hours of rehearsal and, in particular, the never ending process of permanent training and maintenance of skills. The second forgetting penetrates all artistic fetishism: the captivated spectators overlook the performative nature of their own looking. They very much misrecognize that the appreciated singularity of an art work partly relies on their active framing of the esteemed object as an autonomous artefact having the agency to turn one upside down or on the contrary to annoy ad nauseam.

Art works are constructions that exist thanks to the active forgetting of the necessary acts of fabrication. Since the legendary days of the historical avant-garde, both this artistic fetishism and the underlying regime of singularity have been recurrently contested. 'The Dadaists attached much less importance to the sales value of their work than to its uselessness for contemplative immersion', Benjamin observes. 'What they intended and achieved was a relentless destruction of the aura of their creations, which they branded as reproductions with the very means of production.' At first sight, Duchamp's emblematic *Fountain* is indeed anything but an auratic object with unique qualities and an enigmatic, ever receding signification. In addition, the endless repetition of the Duchampian gesture of defining mundane objects as potential art works has meanwhile turned the artefact's shock value into a mere cliché. Yet the innumerable imitations also added to the historical aura nowadays surrounding *Fountain* and many other artefacts made by the consecrated masterminds of the historical avant-garde. Moreover, the Duchamp-case exemplifies the partial displacement of aura within contemporary art from the singular art work in the direction of its charismatic maker. Even when the presented object's near material nothingness is recognized, the boldness implied in exhibiting it or in the assumed originality of the supporting idea might be greatly applauded and subsequently ascribed to the unfathomable brilliance of the artist. We know by now the outcome of this shift in the location of artistic aura, particularly within the fine arts. Today even the most casual mark or thumbnail sketch can be exhibited and sold when stemming from an at once consecrated and intriguing artist. Some artists have become fetishes in their own right (though the notion of the shaman may be more appropriate).

The Artist as Author-Subject

The value register of the regime of singularity positions the artist as someone with a special gift. However, not every talented artist succeeds in making works that possess real singularity. One may be an outstanding painter from a technical point of view, but if one's works do not testify to a personal vision and touch, they will usually not be held in high esteem. In a word, a good painter is not by definition a good artist. The ethics of singularity indeed greatly outdoes formerly dominant categories such as craftsmanship or the capacity to comply with the rules of good taste, which was once highly regarded within the academic regime. It furthermore introduces a neat division within every art world — to paraphrase art sociologist Howard Becker — between its core members and support personnel. Thus, the choreographer and to a certain extent the soloists too are the core members in the ballet world, whereas corps de ballet-dancers, technicians and administrators function as support personnel. The former are considered to be genuine artists with particular talents; the latter may perform their jobs more than satisfactorily, yet they are replaceable. And when it comes to the difference between the dance maker and the soloists, the activities of the first are commonly valued much higher than the virtuosity of even the most outstanding ballet dancer. For the dancer only 'passively' performs the score actively written by the choreographer: the first executes, the second creates. Whereas the dancer's singularity is subjected to the enacted text, the choreographer is considered to be its free author-subject.

'The coming into being of the notion of "author"', writes Michel Foucault in the opening lines of his famous essay 'What is an Author?', 'constitutes the privileged moment of individualization in the history of ideas, knowledge, literature, and the sciences. Even today, when we reconstruct the history of a concept, literary genre, or school of philosophy, such categories seem relatively weak, secondary, and superimposed scansions in comparison with the solid and fundamental unit of the author and the work.' By the end of the 1960s, post-structuralism firmly announced 'the death of the author' (Roland Barthes), yet to a great extent this was clearly a case of wishful thinking. For the individualizing view of art still vastly underpins disciplines such as aesthetics or literary science and most social communication on art. Critics may fiercely debate the value of a particular work of fine art and regular theatregoers can overtly question the artistic merits of the most recent production of a well-reputed theatre group — but critics usually attribute the painting to the woman who signed it, and theatregoers will hold the director of the play responsible for its overall quality. Likewise the arts pages of newspapers and magazines proudly offer exclusive interviews with the conductor of a symphonic orchestra, the organizer of an exhibition, or the writer of a novel because the interviewee is assumingly the principal author. Within the arts sphere, there is clearly a rationale to this widespread appeal of 'the author-function' (Foucault), or the attribution of singular works to an individual.

Even if they have a figurative or realist nature, or on the contrary look utterly minimal, art objects are notoriously multi-interpretable (artistic fetishism of course greatly contributes to this interpretative polyphony). The prototypical aesthetic artefact is — in the well-known characterization of Umberto Eco — 'an open work' whose presumed enigmatic character elicits a plethora of often contradictory readings. For the detached spectator, the work has no fixed signification but delineates a complex horizon of virtual messages that every single interpretation can only reduce at the foreseeable risk of being disputed. The prime function of the author notion resides in its capacity to 'de-potentialize' this semantic potentiality – to halt the endless play of possible readings, to arrest the ever deferred possibility of a final meaning. The author is seen as the one possessing the ultimate signification of the work because he or she is its supposed origin and therefore its genuine ground of existence as a meaningful or communicative artefact. 'The Author, when we believe in him, is always conceived as the past of his own book: book and author stand automatically on a single line divided into a before and an after. The Author is thought to nourish the book, which is to say that he exists before it, thinks, suffers, lives for it, is in the same relation of antecedence to his work as a father to his child', Barthes remarks on the literary writer in 'The Death of the Author'. The capital letters are intended to highlight the God-like character of the novelist and every other kind of artist-creator. According to the modern notion of authorship, which law has solidified into a difficult to oppose juridical fact, making an art work effectively implies the sort of world-making power traditionally associated with gods. The fictive character of the fabricated universe does not undermine the primary relationship of individual mastery and personal expressivity that links the creator to his or her creation, quite the contrary. Thanks to Carl Schmitt, the expression 'political theology' has gained some currency; perhaps we should also speak of an *artistic theology*, forged by Romanticism, in which the artist appears as the secularized heir of a sacred deity?

The concept of the subject acts as the intermediary term between the traditional idea of a single, almighty God and the notion of the autonomous artist-creators who freely express themselves within the medium of language, sound or movement, thus bringing forth a world-within-the-world. The Latin word *'subiectum'* literally means 'lying beneath', hence the expression 'being subjected to power'. Yet that very same signification is also used in the active sense: the subject as the 'bearing surface' or sustaining ground of, for instance, a power relationship or a singular act of world-creation. Within the various monotheisms, God acts as the ultimate Subject to whose impenetrable Will all that exists is subjected without recourse. With his famous dictum *'Cogito ergo sum'* ('I think, therefore I am'), Descartes in every sense of the word displaced the subject. He opened up the tradition of modern-secular subjectivity by invoking the faculty of self-consciousness as the sole foundation for every individual act of thinking and, by implication, of reflexive decision-making and premeditated intentional action. Each person who is in the possession of this capacity is literally the subject of his or her own life stipulates the meanwhile mundane Cartesianism. *Being a subject equals self-foundation through self-consciousness and therefore autonomy*, but not every human being is automatically granted this quality. The capacity to maintain a reflexive relation with one's self or consciousness is denied to children and those who exhibit crazy or irrational behaviour; besides, it was also not assigned to adult women and the colonized by Western law and society for a long time.

The modern notion of authorship entrenches the liberal concept of the subject within the sphere of artistic and intellectual work. However, a shift is implied, again mainly due to Romanticism, since the artist-creator may behave as anything but a rational individual, frequently indulging in dreaming and delirious fantasizing, indecisiveness and erratic behaviour (all of which may add to their personal charisma or aura). Nevertheless, even the utterly eccentric, bordering on lunatic artists are considered to be the source of the produced art works. They only seem to confirm the primary lessons of psychoanalysis on the split subject, whose quotidian or watered-down versions have to a great extent become heavily mixed up with the Romantic view on personhood and its concomitant quest for authenticity. Freud's most essential teaching drawn from 'the dissection of the psychical personality' indeed asserts that the self-conscious ego is permanently seconded, not to say haunted, by an unconscious alter ego or 'bearing surface' – the notorious 'Id' – made up of morally reprehensible drives or tabooed desires. The apparently straightforward distinction between consciousness and unconsciousness, manifest and latent motivations is a widely shared way of making sense of personal life in general and artistic creation in particular. It remains to be seen if this cultural scheme suffices to grasp the divided nature of the subject affirming the social role of the artist (more on this topic in the next chapter).

The author-function nearly always comes with its unavoidable twin, the notion of oeuvre. The artist transforms into a genuine sustaining ground precisely through the systematic attribution of one or more identical intentions, be they conscious or unconscious, to a series of works. Authors produce various individual art objects, and taken together they make up an oeuvre, which is still considered to be the most important interpretative context for the understanding of particular poems or specific paintings ascribed to an individual artist. This brings the author-function full circle: tame the semantic differences between singular art works by presupposing an identical subject, uniting them in one oeuvre revealing an underlying consistent expressive intention (or assume the smallest possible number of such conscious or unconscious purposes if manifest breaks are observed). The couple of author and oeuvre is indeed, as Michel Foucault has pointed out in 'The Order of Discourse', just one instance of 'the will to know', which is unavoidably mixed with 'the will to power' − the desire to interrupt the flow of possible interpretations and to install a difficult to deny 'truth' grounded in the always complicated reality lying behind the name or signature holding together a series of art works. The net result is a totalizing act of symbolic power: *the interpretative potentiality of the individual work is partly made impotent through the modern author-oeuvre code.*

Artistic Heroes, or Practicing Individual Autonomy

'No artistic autonomy without a predominantly artistic intention of the maker', as the hegemonic view within art worlds stipulates. Mundane discussions on the autonomy of art indeed tend to focus on the underlying motives of artists' actions. In line with the regime of singularity and the dictum 'art for art's sake', it is rather imperatively expected that video makers, choreographers or composers manage the mix of freedom and dependency to which they are subjected in such a way that their degree of artistic independence increases. A particular value-rationality is involved: 'you consistently try to realize the ideal of artistic freedom, even if it obliges you to make sacrifices'. Although most art makers probably adhere to this norm, the regular members of an art world frequently indulge in gossip about artists supposedly making quick art for fast money. This informal murmuring reinforces the institutionalized standard of behaving disinterested and parasitizes on the logic of double disavowal that informs the overall functioning of autonomous fields of cultural production. The disapproved stance of 'selling out' is regarded as undermining the artistic status and qualities of an artefact because in such cases the work is predominantly conceived according to the economic logic prevailing in commercial cultural markets. In the social imaginary dominating art worlds, material gains and artistic honesty are even opposed to such an extent that financially successful artists are almost automatically suspected of having compromised their artistic interests in the process.

'Like the pursuit of scientific knowledge, or spiritual grace, or the love of family for that matter, the love of art has always been seen as expressing a fundamentally different, higher form of value. Genuine artists do not produce art simply in order to make money', anthropologist David Graeber observes in line with the reigning view, rightly adding: 'What's more, the market value of their work is dependent on the perception that it was produced in the pursuit of something other than market value. People argue endlessly about what that "something other" is — beauty, inspiration, virtuosity, aesthetic form — ... but all pretty much agree that, were an artist to be seen as simply in it for the money, his work would be worth less because of it.' Particularly art makers with an already solid career are routinely accused of only publicly paying lip service to the ideal of making art for art's sake while behaving in an opposite manner backstage. The basic accusation goes like this: 'you play a hidden and for that reason all the more strategic, even perverse game with your dependency on buyers and audiences in view of direct financial profits, which you actually value higher than artistic freedom'. Since individual intentions are not directly accessible, the various speculations about the secret motives of successful artists can proliferate endlessly and sometimes they feed straight into conspiracy thinking. In any case, most art lovers not only take pleasure in discussing the aesthetic merits of art works, they also greatly enjoy the many anecdotes that may prove or disprove the sincerity of an artist's intentions (sharing such information is a prime social ritual during the openings of exhibitions). Indeed, the average art world member expects artists' actions to be motivated by an unaffected love for art and eagerly helps in overseeing and sanctioning the desired purity. The tremendous amount of anything but neutral gossip probing the 'real motives' of a renowned painter is often symptomatic of the moral status surrounding the artist's expected embodiment of the ideal of autonomy. Effectively corresponding with the regime of singularity is a binding, socially shared morality the prime subject of which is the artist. Artists do not actually have to do that much to act as esteemed guardians of the quasi-sacred value of artistic independence. A sincere intention when making art will do — but again: that motive is not a transparent given.

Artists are admired, and sometimes even transformed into cultural heroes, when they give shape to a life of freedom through the creation of works that attest to a genuine aesthetic vision. Dismissing this moral stance as a dubious descendant of eighteenth-century Romanticism will not do. The imaginary of artistic autonomy is a social fact and has very real constraining effects: it vastly influences the public reputation of art makers and may even result in a widespread denial that someone is still 'a real artist'. Something culturally more profound is therefore at stake here. The artistic freedom as practiced by artists is monitored so intensely precisely because of the more general appreciation of individual autonomy or subjectivity within modernity. In the modern-liberal social imaginary, leading a free life is a many-sided albeit central value, probably even the core element. Personal freedom is nearly unanimously hailed and legally backed by the constitutional right to express oneself in the public realm. In ways that have remained rather underexposed in the historiography of art, the autonomous expression of artists through art works is intimately tied up with this political notion of freedom of speech. Although the link mostly only catches public attention when artistic expression is officially censored, there is a principal elective affinity between the ideas of political and artistic freedom. Both are only meaningful when exercised in public, and both contain an appeal to an effective practice of individual autonomy. Every real affirmation of artistic independence may even be regarded as an implicit confirmation of the modern-liberal political order and its stress on the freedom of speech as the basis for a democratic plurality of opinions.

Modern philosophy has intellectually cemented the ideal of individual autonomy with the already discussed concept of the subject. Personal freedom can be exercised in a selfish way, but that is definitely not the ethically or culturally legitimate form. The normative view of the autonomous self actually comes in two main versions. The first centres on the possibility of making independent moral judgments and of living the life of a genuine ethnical subject that commits itself to reasonable moral standards (such as Kant's famous imperative to act according to maxims that can be universalized). A paradox is indeed involved here: in freely restricting oneself in a morally sensible way, one effectively practices the ideal of personal liberty. The second version links individual autonomy to the capacity to express one's self in a truly free mode. Expressive individualism, which will be further discussed at the end of the next chapter, puts a high premium on the capacity to publicly externalize or objectify one's ideas, emotions or other inner states in artefacts or a general way of life. The more one is able to do so in an original or innovative way, the more one behaves as a free individual. Both the ideals of moral and of expressive autonomy act as simultaneously diffuse and hegemonic normative forces in our society, but they do not do so to the same extent. For within our late, hyper- or postmodern times, expressive individualism has by far outstripped its moral counterpart. To put it bluntly: late-modern individuals prefer self-expression by means of various sorts of lifestyle goods to the self-chosen restraints of ethical subjectivity.

The cultural value of expressive autonomy has become institutionalized within the sphere of the arts. The link between expressive individualism and aesthetic communication was forged by the Romantic Movement during the second half of the eighteenth century, which considerably accelerated the emancipation of the arts from religious, political or moral imperatives (that story is well-known and was already hinted at a couple of times). Artists have become normative models who give shape to personal ideas or affects. In this respect, the much debated difference between abstract and figurative art or between more conceptual and predominantly emotional forms of artistic expression is rather irrelevant. Whatever the particular niche they are working in, artists do what many others long for but are not capable of doing: to express an individual point of view or a personal emotional state in such an innovative way that the more common ways of speaking, visualizing or moving pale in comparison. Or rather, that is what they are expected to do according to the more general valuation of 'expressivism'. Precisely this broader cultural context explains in part why the ideal of artistic freedom and its enactment through an authentic desire to make art, is so scrutinized and moralized. At stake here is not just a remnant of romanticism or an ideological chimera that conceals economic and other dependencies or interests: *artists must behave autonomously because they represent a cultural ideal that is highly performative.*

The regular members of an art world may endlessly speculate on the real nature of a maker's dominant intentions, but in actuality they operate with a more practical definition of artistic freedom. Autonomy equals singularity, and singularity equals originality, which can be read as the differences among art works or the gap an artefact creates vis-à-vis current artistic fashions. Not every difference counts as a true one. A nineteenth-century academic painter would have been regarded as an artist with an individual signature if he or she — most often a 'he' — was able to follow the canonical rules of his art and simultaneously gave it a personal twist. Being innovative was indeed synonymous with the capacity to individualize collectively shared aesthetic standards of beauty without transgressing them. The academic notion of originality-as-variation still lives on within the spheres of mass culture. An original pop song does not transgress but particularizes the rules of a popular music genre; in the same way, a good thriller, be it a movie or a book, re-articulates established conventions without conspicuously breaking them. On the contrary, the notion of singularity currently informing the ideal of artistic autonomy praises the art producer who is inventive in an absolute sense and develops a previously non-existing aesthetic vocabulary. An autonomous art maker is therefore self-expressive in a non-imitative way: one is truly a free creator because one fabricates artefacts that markedly differ from the objects produced by other artists and do not conform to more general rules. Hence the paradox that a conformist contemporary artist must produce art works that do not conform to any existing aesthetic standard.

Yet what about postmodernist art and its lionizing of paraphrase and the quoting of past stylistic conventions or of pastiche and simulation? The concomitant works indeed copy previous artistic styles and appropriate existing mass cultural artefacts, yet they do so between quotation marks of a specific nature. For the artefact to be recognized as an autonomous postmodernist art work, the act of paraphrasing should be done differently, without visibly paraphrasing the features of the paraphrases of others. The trick is to quote or simulate in an original way, thus affirming one's individuality and freedom through an act that only apparently cancels out one's artistic sovereignty. The prime example is of course Andy Warhol, one of the doyens of postmodernist art. His famous silk-screens of popular icons all look imperfect because he did not bother to correct the possible slips of the screen or the uneven inking of the roller. The failings are Warhol's distinctive signature and attest to the autonomous decision not to act, which at least in principle can be linked to the maker's expressive intentions. Warhol's highly paradoxical mix of passive imitation and an equally passive inventiveness therefore fits the dominant equation of artistic autonomy with the production of an authentic difference through the exploration of new aesthetic possibilities. That the innovative quality of the created otherness and not the subject-matter or the demonstration of skills matters most, is perhaps one of the primary lessons of postmodernist art with regard to the ideal of artistic autonomy (a point already well made by Conceptualism). The various instances of postmodernist art – a label that nowadays does indeed sound out-dated – therefore only reproduce the modern, or perhaps rather: modernist, definitions of artistic originality and individual expressivity. The accompanying poststructuralist discourse may have declared 'the death of the author', but socially and culturally the artist-as-author who freely creates is anything but dead. *The art maker who willingly gives up authorship has to do so in an original way, as an author-subject confirming the denied regime of singularity.*

Second Movement: Reconsidering Art's Sociality

Against 'Sociologism'

A seemingly irresolvable dispute – a 'differend' – opposes large parts of the humanities to the social sciences when it comes to art. Many literary scholars, art historians or musicologists still tend to focus on the internal or formal qualities of poems, paintings or musical compositions, thereby assuming that art works are genuine autonomous aesthetic artefacts. On the contrary, sociologists and their allies within cultural studies or the new social history of art excel in a thorough de-centering of art-related practices and products. They explicitly want to deconstruct the dominant discourse on artistic autonomy by showing the many societal dependencies, which stand for as many influences or even determinants, in the processes of making, mediating and evaluating art works. The widely appreciated work of Pierre Bourdieu is a prime example of this tendency to debunk the secular myth inherent in the notion of the author-subject, exposing the idolized art work as a collective misrepresentation of the actual functioning of art worlds. Scholars who stick to the notion of autonomous art are therefore castigated for actively reproducing the ideological idea of 'art for art's sake' or 'the ideology of the aesthetic' through a highly contestable act of purification. Feminist art scholar Griselda Pollock, for example, blames conventional art history because it 'works to exclude from its fields of discourse history, class, ideology, to produce an ideological, "pure" space for something called "art", sealed off from and impenetrable to any attempt to locate art practice within a history of production and social relations.' Researchers committing themselves to a viewpoint highlighting collective determinants and mechanisms, willingly de-fetishize the work of art: from reified object, the aesthetic artefact turns into a strongly conditioned instance reproducing class-bound representations, the male gaze underlying the heterosexual regime, or the struggle for distinctiveness and symbolic capital within artistic fields. The sovereign author-subject undergoes the same fate and is transformed into a bundle of relations with peers, art dealers, critics, bourgeois patrons, et cetera. A non-unified, plural social subject or 'bearing surface' is concomitantly constructed, consisting of many forces acting upon each other through multiple relationships.

The decomposition of the singular art work and the individual artist into a causal network of various social factors markedly increases the number of relevant agents. Indeed, sociologists of art act as multipliers and 'socializers' in their quest for general models that explain away uniqueness, originality or rarity. The often joyfully enacted deconstruction of the dominant regime of singularity therefore more than once inclines to its critical destruction. Such a reductive stance bordering on cynicism rather testifies to a dogmatic 'sociologism' that contradicts a self-reflexive sociological outlook recognizing its specific presuppositions and immanent limits. Every consistent dilution of individuality into sociality also inevitably comes up against its self-produced restrictions. For there is nearly always an intriguing remnant, a series of blatant, literally idiotic facts whose stubborn resistance cannot be overcome. The invoked social contexts only enhance the annoying presence of these relics of a robust singularity, however minimal it may seem after the unfolded analysis aiming at its nullification. A famous painting is, for example, convincingly situated within a constraining assemblage of divergent factors and relationships — yet if one refuses to discuss compositional issues, why the conspicuous lines in the middle are coloured yellow will remain forever enigmatic. There is also something utterly paradoxical in the tendency to fully undo the aura of an aesthetic artefact. Existing definitions of grandiose art serve as the starting point that will be subsequently put into perspective, even vastly disputed. Nevertheless, the implied value judgment usually remains the basis for the whole undertaking and will greatly colour its public reception. So when Pierre Bourdieu reads Gustave Flaubert's famous novel *Sentimental Education* against the grain, his sociological analysis compels admiration — at least among fellow sociologists — precisely because of the work's high status. Deconsecrating consecrated art works or artists is, implicitly or explicitly, a parasitic act that secretly appropriates the aura it pretends to deconstruct.

The sociological or external view commits itself to the collective regime, highlighting anonymous and uniformly operating social factors, which indeed by definition clashes with the ethos of singularity that the internal approach subscribes to. General social mechanisms such as cultural conformism, competitive commodification or the blind reproduction of established gender stereotypes are critically played out against the common-sense ideas of subjectivity, originality and rarity. A strong claim to truth usually prevails, positioning 'externalist' interpretations of art quasi-automatically as instances of ideology critique that promise enlightenment. The metaphor of infra- and superstructure, known from Marxism, is given a broader sociological twist: social components, eventually including economic ones, determine the overall functioning of an art world, yet the hegemonic ideology of artistic autonomy and 'the aesthetic' profoundly conceals this allegedly true state of affairs. However, the reigning regime of singularity possesses a performativity that clearly exceeds the mere functionality of a necessary misconception. For this misrecognition of the social makes a particular cognition of art possible, especially of the immanent logics sustaining individual art works. Artistic fetishism effectively opens up a productive space of heterogeneous interpretations whose specific focus on the tandem of oeuvre and author yields an irreplaceable kind of knowledge that is anything but cancelled out by its overall framing as 'worn-out bourgeois formalism'. A consistent constructivist outlook countering every form of 'sociologism' seems therefore more appropriate. *With the regime of singularity and the collective regime indeed correspond two different 'regimes of truth', two interpretative perspectives with firm own-values and quasi-objects* that are routinely used to assess the claims pertaining to, for instance, an art work's supposed grounding in individual intentions or — in the 'externalist' approach — the law of symbolic capital accumulation assumingly motivating artists' actions.

Either one concentrates on the stylistic uniqueness of a series of art works and painstakingly tries to make plausible the fact that the peculiar vision they embody originates, for instance, in the artist's lifelong quest to express as directly as possible certain traumatic experiences. Or one describes that very same corpus of aesthetic artefacts as a successful move within an art world that strategically brought into play the art maker's biography and involved a plethora of other actors whose alternately equal and power-ridden cooperation conditioned the oeuvre's fame. Two completely different objects of knowledge are constructed, and two divergent 'regimes of truth' are invoked to argue one's case. Various research methodologies will be deployed in order to dig up empirical facts, even conclusive evidence, yet the body of presented data does not speak for itself: its relevance, plausibility and persuasiveness greatly depends on the overall perspective a study takes. The internal approach elucidates the blind spots of the external view, and vice versa – but adding the one to the other does not exhaust the possible truths regarding the series of works in question. Although such a pluralistic scholarship may be applauded, it merely juxtaposes two distinct epistemological objects that do not seamlessly fuse into a total picture. For that matter, politicizing the discussion is to no avail. Both the ethics of singularity and the regime of community, co-shaping the 'internalist' and the 'externalist' view respectively, are value-loaded and connote divergent political positions. Whereas the first usually leans towards a liberal point of view on the social, the second often explicitly commits itself to a leftist agenda of social equality and an ethics of communality. Granted that liberalism is hegemonic, siding with the collective regime and a predominantly social analysis of art seems to make good sense: it promises to enhance the chance of generating insights that at least de-familiarize an all too evident individualizing definition of art works and their makers. However, originality and estrangement are not only core values of the 'liberal' regime of singularity but can evidently also be practiced within its confines, so without recourse to social factors or a general sociological model.

Resituating 'the Singular' and 'the Collective'

There is some sociological irony implied in the often heated intellectual debates between 'internalists' and 'externalists', those praising the incomparable uniqueness of a work of art or an artist's vision and those consequently arguing from and for a social perspective. Even many sociologists tend to overlook that both viewpoints actually build on vocabularies or discursive repertoires that are constantly employed in the everyday interaction within art worlds. Speaking of 'the singular and the collective value regime', Pascal Gielen rightly stresses that 'it is important to realize that both of these regimes unambiguously form part of the art world. ... Yet, the two regimes constantly function in a state of tension within the same network.' Not that art makers, curators, gallery owners or fervent art lovers are quasi-schizophrenics who erratically switch between the fetishist attitude that naively puts art works or artists on a pedestal and a proto-sociological way of communicating that debases both. Involved here is rather a situationally embedded difference between *two action logics of justification and valuation: whereas the collective regime is routinely invoked when art is in the making and mediated, the regime of singularity prevails once the art work is finished and enters the public domain.* The Janus face of science that Bruno Latour portrays with much gusto in *Science in Action* indeed fits the functioning of autonomous art worlds. Scientists discuss their activities within a laboratory setting in a very different way than they present the discovered facts. Whereas the work of fact-finding is admittedly a multi-faceted active process involving external funding, trial-and-error procedures and various kinds of conversations with peers, the final result is put forth as an objective datum only passively mirroring some part of 'the world out there'. In a similar way, members of an art world use two distinct discursive registers to justify or valuate art-as-work and the art work, respectively.

Imagine that you have just attended the latest dance performance of a choreographer with whom you are slightly acquainted. You have mixed feelings about the show: most parts were interesting and aesthetically pleasing, some clearly missed structure, and overall the dancing lacked precision. After the show, you run into the choreographer, who is curious to hear your opinion. You diplomatically voice your critical thoughts, to which he or she smilingly replies: 'You're completely right; the piece is a bit sloppy. That's because I didn't have enough money to research the movement vocabulary and to pay the dancers. I had to cut down the planned rehearsal time. But that's life, no?' The likelihood that a choreographer offers such a justification straightforwardly referring to the collective register is rather small. An artist may perhaps acknowledge that a work's shortcomings are partly the outcome of the particular circumstances in which it was produced but will probably not invoke them as the overall rationale. He or she will speak about the work in aesthetic, conceptual, political or whatever terms, but will not defend it on primarily economical or practical grounds. Like the average spectator or the specialized critic, most artists stick to the notion that a finished, publicly shown art work stands on its own and should be discussed as an autonomous aesthetic reality. Nowadays, there are many discursive frames to valuate an art work's specificity, and of course also art as such (or more particularly dance), but it is commonly not done to interpret, let alone to appreciate it solely in reference to the social or material conditions of its making. The regime of singularity reigns, and with it comes the all too mundane talk of the artist's intentions. These may have been only partly given shape by the contingencies of the work's production context, which can be legitimately invoked to justify some of the visible flaws in the final product. In this way, elements of the collective regime such as the available funds or the cooperation with hired dancers can explain away deviations from the dominant expectations corresponding with the author-work code. Evidently, a minimum condition is required: the shortcomings may not be too numerous, for then the artefact will fail to define itself as a genuine work of art. A logic of exception is at work here, one that confirms the general appropriateness of the vocabulary of uniqueness, autonomous composition and expressive authorship, but selectively includes the opposite register in order to make sense of minor irregularities observed in the light of the regime of singularity.

That is not the whole story, though. Imagine a second situation: you come across the same choreographer while he or she is in the midst of preparations for a new piece. Not that many questions are needed to have them talking nineteen to the dozen on all kinds of practicalities: the writing of a dossier for government subsidies, the many meetings with potential co-producers, the organization of rehearsal time, the cooperation with the hired dancers, et cetera. That will not be all they have to say about the upcoming performance: they also refer to what it is about and discuss the initial aesthetic, conceptual or other motives for making the work. Nevertheless, there is a fair chance that a substantial part of the talk is devoted to mundane matters, in-cluding the selling of the new piece when it is near completion or the prospects of a good press. And yes, it will be readily admitted that, for instance, the available economic resources directly in-fluence the horizon of possibilities within which the future work is taking shape: 'I conceived the piece for six dancers but since I only have money for four, I've had to adapt my initial plans.' Or they spontaneously start complaining about the difficulties in working with a dancer from whom they expected a serious creative input. The social in all its complexity is invoked in order to explain the particularities of the work's making. In short, the collective regime does not function as an exceptional resource but as the principal register of talk and justification. The same holds for the curator discussing the organization of an upcoming exhibition or the artistic director of an arts centre explaining his personal choices for the next season. The vocabulary of singular-ity regularly crops up through the references to this 'great art work' or that 'brilliant artist', but they are greatly tempered by the many invocations of the public's taste, the relations of friend-ship and adversity with other agents in the field, or one's board of directors. The discourse that one hears within an art world on the making and mediation of art works indeed markedly differs from the one on artefacts recognized as genuine artistic objects. The former acknowledges the partial heteronomy of art-makers and mediators, or their dependency on various sorts of material constraints, of subsidies and market opportunities, of public suc-cess and critical recognition, and also of both cooperation and competition with direct peers. Everything that is denied having normative importance for a final art work's value or an exhibi-tion's critical success is put forward as a reasonable argument co-legitimating its actual production and mediation. In sum, art's autonomy has a discursive Janus face within independent art worlds, which one-sided generalizations of either the regime of singularity or the collective register cannot account for.

Art Worlds as Cooperative Networks
Art-in-the-making comes down to the creation and subsequent strengthening of an always particular assemblage made up of het-erogeneous subjects and objects linked to each other by divergent sorts of relations. For example, the production of a contempo-rary dance work usually involves a choreographer, one or more

dancers, technicians, and co-producers, books and bank accounts, computers and video equipment, lightning and props, and so on – to mention just the obvious. To choreograph actually implies the constant directing or governing of this often difficult to coordinate multitude, whose constituent members indeed do not always do what is expected of them. One may consistently describe the total assemblage as an actor-network configuration comprising human and non-human agents that possess diverse kinds of agency partly derived from their mutual relationships (this was indeed the perspective that informed the discussion of 'dance/choreography in general' in the previous chapter). Or one opts for the established humanistic view on the social and reduces the network to the collaborative activities bringing together human beings. Although there is much to say in favour of the first approach, it also seriously complicates every ethnographically informed analysis of a particular art work's production or a specific art world's functioning. For one thing, objects or technical artefacts do not usually speak for themselves but have to rely on human representatives in order to be heard at all. A symmetrical view on objects and subjects is therefore difficult to keep up: one stumbles over severe methodological problems. Howard Becker outlines in great detail the alternative, 'human all too human' route in his semi-classic study *Art Worlds*, probably also one of the most nuanced sociological portraits of the production and distribution of art ever written.

'Art worlds produce works and also give them aesthetic value', Becker asserts. The statement looks deceptively simple, but it conspicuously leaves out the individual artist as the *'subiectum'* or ultimate ground of art works. Not that Becker flatly denies the constitutive role of the author-subject within contemporary fields of cultural production, but he rather puts this social figure into perspective by consistently focusing on all the cooperative activities necessary to produce an artefact claiming aesthetic merit and, subsequently, to the potential collective substantiation of this pretension. Whereas some of these practices have a direct social nature, others involve a less visible concerted action or a mediated cooperation at a distance. Take, for instance, an orchestra director and a composer. Several fixed appointments with others, such as the orchestra's rehearsal schedules or the dates of the premiere and ensuing performances, very much bind conductors. Moreover, they must negotiate a productive working relationship with the orchestra during their meetings. They have to motivate the different instrumentalists, convince all musicians of the plausibility of the offered interpretation of the score, and bring all orchestra members into line in view of a successful performance. Conducting is thus an evident example of a truly social artistic practice that combines, with more or less tensions, power differences and the pleasures of making music together into a specific assemblage of joint action. However, the dominant individualizing view of art remains operative. With considerable social consequences, the conductor, who is esteemed as an authentic ('executive') artist, is differentiated from the musicians. And among the latter, the soloists are considered to be closer to the ideal type of the author-subject then the other instrumentalists. The already hinted at distinction between core members and support personnel indeed 'saves' the regime of singularity when artistic practices have an evidently social nature. Precisely because music performances are so visibly a matter of social cooperation and collective interdependency, the involved activities are strongly recoded on a hierarchical scale that goes from the least to the most artistic.

At first sight, the picture looks completely different when we turn to the solitary practice of composers who work on a score for orchestra in the splendid isolation of a room with a view. They only use some sheets of music paper and a pencil, or a computer and specialized software. Since they do not rely on a direct cooperation with others, they do not have to plan in great detail the activity of writing out the score. Nevertheless, the lonely composer evidently needs an orchestra — and all that this brings with it in terms of institutional mediation — in order to have the final composition performed. Perhaps he or she may also greatly benefit from the conversation with fellow composers in order to persevere when the writing process slows down. Yet probably even the most important relationships our composers maintain with peers have a rather hidden and indirect nature. And so the artists' rooms are filled with countless mental talks with numerous dead composers who co-define the musical traditions and general examples of good practice they are drawing upon (both are primarily acquired within the collective setting of a conservatoire). There are also the many indirect meetings, mediated by scores or other artefacts, with contemporaries also composing music for orchestra. Some act as direct competitors: the admired models one hopes to outdo; others are taken up as negative examples:

'how not to write with sounds on this theme!'; and still others linger in the background as instances of the kind of mediocre work one abhors. The music score therefore partly emerges out of an indirect polyphonic dialogue with many fellow artists. Its social character may become partly observable in specific stylistic features pointing to an affinity with the work of other composers. 'The style of a work of art allows us to recognize what it owes to other works of art and what it means for other, new works of art', Niklas Luhmann rightly emphasizes. 'Style corresponds to and contradicts the autonomy of the individual work of art. It respects it and despite this diverts surplus value. It leaves the uniqueness of the work of art untouched and yet establishes lines of connection to other works of art.'

What goes for the seemingly lonely practice of composing also holds for other artistic activities that at first sight possess a highly individualistic character, such as writing novels and poetry or creating visual art works in the monadic space of a studio. They draw inspiration from alternately admiring and highly critical meetings with peers; and for their public existence they depend on mediators, whether publishers or galleries, critics or museums. In addition, they rely on shared interpretative frames or forms of knowledge, often condensed into particular skills, which are passed on in art schools and are sustained, and perhaps contested or renewed, in informal conversations with other artists or critics. The frames function as backgrounds experienced as positive or negative influences and as traditions taken for granted, within which the activity of writing poetry or painting makes sense. At the same time, they facilitate direct cooperation since one can implicitly expect that the acquired knowledge is collectively shared within one's art world. *Every art work presupposes the joint action, however mediated, of several inhabitants of an art world; and each art world is a specific social network, consisting of all the people, their cooperative activities and the competences or conventions upon which they rely* — the just mentioned frames — and which are necessary to produce the artefacts which that world, and perhaps outsiders as well, considers to be art. Without this collective activity, presupposed standards and various kinds of knowledge or skills, which may of course be transgressed and re-articulated, neither art works nor artists can exist. 'Works of art, from this point of view, are not the products of individual makers, "artists", who possess a rare and special gift. They are, rather, joint products of all the people who cooperate via an art world's characteristic conventions to bring works like that into existence', Becker concludes. A slight trace of 'sociologism', which should be resisted, still colours this verdict: art works are not only fabricated by talented author-subjects but indeed always testify to a multi-faceted interaction with others.

No collaboration without communication, whatever its nature. Given the regime of singularity, it is common parlance that art works, particularly successful ones, communicate in a specific way. Yet every instance of aesthetic communication only exists thanks to innumerable previous communications between, for instance, a choreographer and the contracted performers or between the company manager and an individual member of the official commission deciding on the subsidies for dance. Also, aesthetic communication generates further communications, varying from outright verbal praise to critical reviews or a casual remark during a dinner conversation. In short, every art world is a volatile communicative system in which aesthetic communication is always embedded within a flow of other modes of uttering information that both enable and constrain the production, mediation and reception of the kind of artefacts called art works (as it was argued in the first chapter, it is precisely this naming, or not-naming, something an art work or somebody an artist that singles out contemporary art worlds). The countless communications constituting an art world are by definition fleeting events. From a social point of view, the words 'dance', 'music', 'painting' or 'video-making' indeed do not point to stable practices, let alone to fixed objects, but rather stand for communicative rhizomes that are in a constant state of flux and transformation. Friendly communication does not always dominate, quite the contrary. Artistic cooperation time and again encapsulates relationships marked by inequality and rivalry, not to mention the sometimes destructive effects of narcissism. Pierre Bourdieu is partly right in emphasizing the existence of at times fierce competition for symbolic capital or public recognition. An explicit proviso therefore seems appropriate: *cooperation in the neutral sense equals the unity of the difference between harmonious working-together and inharmonious competition.* Perhaps the neologism 'co-opetition' better fits the positively and negatively experienced realities of joint action within art worlds?

Analysing art worlds in terms of networks of cooperation touches a contemporary nerve. The generalization of what Luc

Boltanski and Eve Chiapello call 'the projective city', or the logic of working together alternately face-to-face and by means of digital technology with varying peers within the context of an always singular project, corresponds to a marked pressure to build up and sustain contacts with countless others. Project workers are social networkers: they have to maintain a broad portfolio of the most diverse and remote kinds of connections with an eye to possible projects. The network functions on the one hand as a potential of virtual resources that can be selectively activated when a project begins to take shape, and on the other, as a complex configuration in which one may be momentarily mobilized by others' activities. Networking as such is the principal practice structuring 'the projective city', which outdoes the traditional divisions between work and leisure, wage-earning and voluntary work. 'Activity aims to generate projects, or to achieve integration into projects initiated by others. But the project does not exist outside of the encounter', Boltanski and Chiapello observe. 'Hence the activity par excellence is integrating oneself into networks and exploring them, so as to put an end to isolation, and have opportunities for meeting people or associating with them.' Within the arts in general, but particularly within the world of contemporary dance, the current network ethic that comes with 'the projective city' goes hand in hand with a marked preference for artistic collaborations of the more equal and diverse kind. Projects not only bring together choreographers and dancers, but also take on board sound makers, visual artists, critics, producers, dramaturges or academics, in view of a productive cooperation. The de-definition of the genre within reflexive dance has without doubt greatly furthered this trend toward a revival of collaboration in modes sometimes reminiscent of the Judson collective. However, performer and dramaturge Myriam Van Imschoot rightly underscores that 'it does not explain why there exists so much emphasis, to the point of sheer over-determination and a compulsive repetition of the term. It seems as if collaboration functions as an uncritical marker or signifier, an honorific that must signal more than it actually performs.' Perhaps a closer, ethnographically inspired look at the practice of working together within contemporary dance and the underlying motives, hopes and desires of those directly involved, can help to clarify at least some of the stakes of the recent institutionalization of the ethos of collaboration within this artistic field. Such an undertaking may at the same time highlight the differences between collaboration in the neutral sociological sense and the experience as well as the ethics or politics of the regime of 'the collaboratory'.

Sources

Framing Art's Autonomy

Peter Bürger opens his *Theory of the Avant-Garde* (Minneapolis (MN): University of Minnesota Press, 1984) with a succinct but insightful sketch of the main phases in the autonomization of art and subsequently discusses the paradoxical position of the historical avant-garde. The notorious saying of neo-avant-gardist Joseph Beuys, that 'every human being is an artist', can be found in his 1973 text 'I am searching for field character', which is included in Carin Kuoni (ed.), *Joseph Beuys in America. Writings by and Interviews with the Artist*. New York (NY): Four Walls Eight Windows, 1993, pp. 21–24 (p. 22). That the socio-cultural independency of modern and contemporary art actually supposes many dependencies is one of the core ideas of Niklas Luhmann's *Art as a Social System*. Stanford (CA): Stanford University Press, 2000. The presented view on aesthetic communication also follows Luhmann's view as further unfolded in Dirk Baecker's essays 'Die Adresse der Kunst', published in Jürgen Fohrmann and Harro Müller (eds.), *Systemtheorie der Literatur*. München: Wilhelm Fink Verlag, 1986, pp. 82–105; and 'Etwas Theorie', included in Dirk Baecker, *Wozu Soziologie?* Berlin: Kulturverlag Kadmos, 2004, pp. 43–50 (p. 49). Pierre Bourdieu analyses the particularities of art markets in detail in his seminal article 'The production of belief: contribution to an economy of symbolic goods', in *Media, Culture and Society*, 2 (3), 1977, pp. 261–293 (p. 241).

The Regime of Singularity

Nathalie Heinich extensively discusses art's regime of singularity in *Ce que l'art fait à la sociologie*. Paris: Minuit, 1998 (p. 11) and *L'élite artiste. Excellence et singularité en régime démocratique*. Paris: Gallimard, 2005. Furthermore, this paragraph draws inspiration from Walter Benjamin's classic essay 'The Work of Art in the Age of Mechanical Reproduction', in Walter Benjamin, *Illuminations*. London/New York: Pimlico/Random House, 1999, pp. 211–244 (p. 218) and Terry Eagleton's study *The Ideology of the Aesthetic*. Oxford: Blackwell,

1990. The casually mentioned notion of 'objecthood' implicitly refers to Michael Fried's (in)famous attack on Minimalism, 'Art and Objecthood', originally published in 1967 and reprinted in Michael Fried, *Art and Objecthood. Essays and Reviews*. Chicago (IL): University of Chicago Press, 1998, pp. 148–172.

The Art Work as Fetish

The information on the origins of the word 'fetish' stems from the opening pages of Bruno Latour's *On the Modern Cult of the Factish Gods*. Durham (NC): Duke University Press, 2011. Pierre Bourdieu uses the notion of artistic fetishism several times, mostly in passing, in *The Rules of Art: Genesis and Structure of the Literary Field*. Stanford (CA): Stanford University Press, 1996. The following publications are also quoted: Karl Marx, *Capital. A Critique of Political Economy (Volume 1)*. Harmondsworth: Penguin, 1976, pp. 164–165; Max Horkheimer and Theodor W. Adorno, *Dialectic of Enlightenment*. New York (NY): Herder and Herder, 1972, p. 230; and Walter Benjamin, 'The Work of Art in the Age of Mechanical Reproduction', p. 231.

The Artist as Author-Subject

The distinction between core members and support personnel was coined and put to use by Howard Becker in *Art Worlds*. Berkeley (CA): University of California Press, 1982, pp. 77–92. Michel Foucault's 'What is an Author?' is reprinted in Michel Foucault, *Essential Works 2. Aesthetics*. London: Penguin, 2000, pp. 205–222 (p. 205). Roland Barthes' essay 'The Death of the Author' is included in Roland Barthes, *Image Music Text*. London: Fontana Press, 1977, pp. 142–148 (p. 145). For a more elaborate view on the notion of the subject, see for instance Vincent Descombes, *Le Complément du sujet. Enquête sur le fait d'agir soi-même*. Paris: Gallimard, 2004. Mentioned in passing are Umberto Eco, *The Open Work*. Cambridge (MA): Harvard University Press, 1989; Carl Schmitt, *Political Theology. Four Chapters on the Concept of Sovereignty*. Chicago (IL): University of Chicago Press, 2006; Sigmund Freund, 'The Dissection of the Psychical Personality', in Sigmund Freud, *New Introductory Lectures on Psycho-Analysis*. New York (NY): W.W. Norton & Company, 1989, pp. 71–100; and Michel Foucault, 'The Order of Discourse', in Robert Young (ed.), *Untying the Text. A Poststructuralist Reader*. London: Routledge, 1981, pp. 48–78.

Artistic Heroes, or Practicing Individual Autonomy

This paragraph partly retakes, sometimes verbatim, some of the main ideas developed in Rudi Laermans, 'Artistic Autonomy as Value and Practice', in Pascal Gielen and Paul De Bruyne (eds.), *Being an Artist in Post-Fordist Times*. Rotterdam: NAi Publishers, 2009, pp. 125–138. David Graeber's quoted observation on the necessarily non-economic character of artistic value, however defined, can be found in his 2008 essay 'The Sadness of Post-Workerism', pp. 11–12 (retrieved via the website of *The Commoner*: www.commoner. org.uk). That moral autonomy and expressive individualism are two very distinct articulations of the idea of individual subjectivity is argued at length by Charles Taylor in *Sources of the Self: The Making of the Modern Identity*. Cambridge (MA): Harvard University Press, 1992. Albert Boime discusses in *The Academy and French Painting in the 19th Century* (New Haven [CT]: Yale University Press, 1986) the notion of individuality underlying the academic regime, to which reference is also made in other paragraphs. The idea that contemporary art practice is marked by the paradox of a conformist non-conformism is borrowed from Nathalie Heinich, *Le triple jeu de l'art contemporain. Sociologie des arts plastiques*. Paris: Minuit, 1998. With regard to postmodernist art, Frederic Jameson's *Postmodernism: Or, the Cultural Logic of Late Capitalism* (London: Verso, 1992) remains one of the most authoritative sources.

Against 'Sociologism'

The difference between 'internalist' and 'externalist' approaches of art partly informs Vera Zollberg's *Constructing a Sociology of the Arts*. Cambridge: Cambridge University Press, 1990. The quote from Griselda Pollock stems from her 1980 article 'Artists, Mythologies and Media', which is cited by Janet Wolff in *Aesthetics and the Sociology of Art*. Ann Arbor (MI): University of Michigan Press, 1995, p. 16. Pierre Bourdieu analyses Gustave Flaubert's novel *Sentimental Education* in *The Rules of Art*, pp. 1–46. The constructivist idea that the regime of singularity and its collective counterpart form two 'regimes of truth' is inspired by Michel Foucault's already mentioned musings on 'The Order of Discourse' and his essay 'Truth and Power', which is included in Michel Foucault, *Essential Works 3. Power*. London: Penguin, 2000, pp. 111–134.

Resituating 'the Singular' and 'the Collective'

The proposed use of the difference between a regime of singularity and a collective regime clearly goes beyond Nathalie Heinich's original view in *Ce que l'art fait à la sociologie* (and this not only because the notion of 'collective regime' implies an explicit distance from the social homogeneity that the expression 'regime of community', favoured by Heinich, seems to imply). It is much indebted to the work of Pascal Gielen, in particular his empirical study *Kunst in netwerken. Artistieke selecties in de hedendaagse dans en de beeldende kunst (Art within Networks. Artistic Selections in Contemporary Dance and the Fine Arts)*. Leuven: LannooCampus, 2003. A summary of his view on the dialectics of 'the singular and the collective regime' can be found in his essay '"Deciding" on Art in Global Networks', in Pascal Gielen, *The Murmuring of the Artistic Multitude. Global Art, Memory and Post-Fordism*. Amsterdam: Valiz, 2009, pp. 153–190 (p. 159). The suggested argument partly departs from Gielen's approach because it aligns itself with Luc Boltanski's and Laurent Thévenot's view in *On Justification: Economies of Worth* (Princeton [NJ]: Princeton University Press, 2006) and, in particular, the consequent two-fold approach of 'science in the making' and 'made science' unfolded by Bruno Latour in *Science in Action. How to Follow Scientists and Engineers Through Society*. Cambridge (MA): Harvard University Press, 1988. The two evoked imaginary situations of

conversation with a choreographer
are vastly inspired by my personal
familiarity with the world of contemporary dance, which also informs
several other observations in
this chapter.

Art Worlds as Cooperative Networks
This paragraph partly relies, sometimes verbatim, on Rudi Laermans,
'Deconstructing Individual Authorship: Art Works as Collective Products of Art Worlds', in Bert Demarsin
a.o. (eds.), *Art & Law*. Bruges/Oxford:
Die Keure/Hart Publishing, 2008,
pp. 50–61. It opens with a brief reminder of the possibility of studying
art worlds in line with the general
approach advocated by Bruno
Latour in *Reassembling the Social. An
Introduction to Actor-Network-Theory*.
Oxford: Oxford University Press,
2005. The main sources of inspiration are Howard Becker's books *Art
World*s (p. 38 and p. 35) and *Propos
sur l'art*. Paris: L'Harmattan, 2000
(this French collection of translated
articles has no equivalent in English).
Reference is moreover made to
Niklas Luhmann, 'The Work of Art
and the Self-Reproduction of Art',
reprinted in Niklas Luhmann, *Essays
on Self-Reference*. New York (NY):
Columbia University Press, 1990,
pp. 191–214 (pp. 196–197); Luc
Boltanski and Eve Chiapello, *The
New Spirit of Capitalism*. London:
Verso, 2005 (p. 110; they also use, on
p. 132, the notion of 'co-opetition');
and Myriam Van Imschoot and
Xavier Le Roy, 'Letters in Collaboration', in *Maska*, (84–85), 2004,
pp. 61–69 (p. 62).

Co-Creating Contemporary Dance
Paradoxes of the Semi-Directive Mode of Participatory Collaboration

First Movement: Observing Heteronomous Autonomy

Dance Capital Brussels

The production, distribution and reception of contemporary dance are 'glocal' affairs: at once global and local, inter- or transnational and situated in particular regions, cities and venues. On the map of 'dance made in Europe', some cities clearly stand out because they show a higher concentration of activity and also function as obligatory points of passage when amassing peer recognition or critical esteem. Together with Berlin, Paris and Vienna, Brussels is one of these principal junctions in the European field of contemporary dance. Many factors help to explain the present position of Brussels, which is the official capital of both Belgium and Flanders (the city may claim the unofficial title of capital of the EU as well). Particularly, a calibrated and relatively generous funding via both long-term support and incidental project subsidies, especially from the side of the Flemish government, helps to sustain a layered network of large, medium-sized and small institutions catering to the dance community in Brussels and Flanders. Whereas Brussels art centres such as Kaaitheater or Beursschouwburg regularly show new dance works that they sometimes also co-produce, Workspace Brussels, and its equivalent structures in Flanders such as wpZimmer (Antwerp) or Buda (Kortrijk), promote contemporary dance through a combination of short-term residencies, technical assistance and other production facilities, international networking, and administrative follow-up. Structurally subsidized companies such as the Brussels-based Rosas or Ultima Vez (directed by Wim Vandekeybus) and various kinds of funded projects secure a steady flow of job opportunities for dancers, who can alternate the position of performer with that of creator through individual grants or government money for developing personal projects. The Belgian social security system is also rather kind to artists. After having worked a certain number of days, they may claim a special status that basically warrants long-lasting unemployment benefits during periods when they do not have work. In addition, Brussels is a relatively inexpensive capital city with convenient train and flight connections to other European capitals. Even the rents in the city centre, which is not exactly a glamorous spot, are low in comparison to Paris or London.

A decisive element in the hybrid network of ingredients that consolidated the renown of Brussels as a dance capital was the establishment by Anne Teresa De Keersmaeker of P.A.R.T.S. (Performing Arts Research and Training Studios), in 1995. The initiative's lasting success has much to do with the unique combination of De Keersmaeker's international artistic fame and an innovative curriculum that goes beyond passing on the Rosas aesthetic to future generations. Located outside the centre of Brussels on the same premises as the Rosas company, P.A.R.T.S. encourages a self-reflexive stance toward dance and choreography among its students. The institution's main educational purpose is to train 'thinking dancers', as the school's founding documents state. The ideal P.A.R.T.S. graduate combines artistic versatility — a feature befitting the conceptual de-definition of dance — with an inquisitive attitude that takes nothing for granted about the activity one actually engages in or prepares for. The simple but essentially unanswerable axiomatic question 'what can dance be today?' informs both this general objective and the curriculum's constant re-articulation. Not knowing what contemporary dance actually is but nevertheless offering supposedly helpful building stones for the active performing of its possible identity: this paradox forms the very heartbeat of the school's at once artistic and pedagogical project. A thorough training in traditional, modern and contemporary dance techniques is therefore complemented with extensive classes in theatre, music and theory. Students learn Rosas-repertoire, but they can also participate in workshops by high-profile choreographers who subscribe to dance aesthetics that differ from De Keersmaeker's own. Personal work is greatly encouraged, especially in later years, and may be rewarded with being selected for the international graduation tour that introduces every new P.A.R.T.S. generation to the public, through presentations at several European venues. Since 1998, the year the first class of students graduated, P.A.R.T.S. has nourished, with notable impact, the field of contemporary dance. After completing the school (or dropping out earlier on), many ex-students have settled in Brussels and used the city as their principal base for their work as dancers and/or choreographers. This dynamics continues to this day and helps explain the significant increase in both size and international character of the Brussels dance community from the end of the 1990s onward.

A local art world is both an assemblage of loosely coupled institutional arrangements and a visible social scene, a series of locales that function as established meetings points and nodes of information exchange. Anno 2014, members of the Brussels dance world predictably gather on the occasion of performances in Beursschouwburg or Kaaitheater. Particularly the showings in the smaller Kaaistudios, which regularly serves as the stage for cutting-edge work, tend to attract an audience made up of numerous peers and semi-peers, like dramaturges or critics. Those present are often personally acquainted with the choreographer or one of the dancers involved in the featured work and will stay to discuss it with them after the performance. When the theatre bar closes early, the talks may continue in one of the cafés in central Brussels patronized by the dance community. Since employed dancers have to be physically fit during the week, nightlife mainly unites scene members on weekends, particularly at private house parties. The various locales act as productive junctions of creative dialogue and enhance mutual solidarity. New dance works and on-going or planned projects are scrutinized at length with other scene members, who are also regularly invited to run-throughs when a work is nearing completion. In such informal conversations doubts can be voiced and personal opinions can be expressed without the public pressure to defend a specific poetics or a consistent view on contemporary dance. Notwithstanding the competition for social recognition or funding and the frequent gossip, even including the occasional slander of the not-too-kind variety, the Brussels dance scene is overall notably amicable and conflict-free: a friendly familiarity prevails. People effectively behave as if belonging to a community because they have the same artistic frame of reference, maintained by shared viewing experiences, and they regularly collaborate within the context of companies and projects. Also, the scene operates as a market for job opportunities and other resources. Choreographers sound out the personal interests and practical availability of potential dancers when preparing a new creation; or a dance maker and a performer may discover during an informal chat about a possible project that they might be helpful to one another, or even find out that their current artistic concerns go in the same direction. Everyone informs each other about their plans or activities in the near future, thus contributing to a virtual collective database on current trends, fashionable buzzwords and potential jobs. It all testifies to the scene's functioning – says Elisabeth Currid – as 'a social production system' characterized by the kind of 'hypersocialization' that fuses strategic individual networking and personal or artistic affinities into one immanent loop.

No official statistics are available on the actual size of the Brussels dance community. The number definitely goes into the hundreds, with the majority carrying a foreign identity card. Most members are dancers, yet a substantial part also regularly takes on the role of choreographer. Periods of working for a befriended dance maker are alternated with risky investments in one's broader artistic capacities. Much of the actual work may be done in a studio located in Brussels or Flanders. However, regardless of their origins or nationality, quite a few Brussels-based dance artists move back and forth between different places. Due to foreign co-productions and temporary residencies, they often rehearse an upcoming performance in various other locations across Europe. And upon completing the work, an international tour usually follows that may include countries further afield. Participation in projects or creations initiated abroad also obliges one to stay for longer periods of time in for instance Berlin or Vienna. A dense information flow, made up of e-mails and Facebook or Twitter messages, fosters this nomadism. As with other professional worlds, social networking among dance artists nowadays comprises both intensive face-to-face dialogue and extensive digital contacts of the more casual kind. 'The performing artist today inhabits and manoeuvres within a perfect hybrid between the old-fashioned and contemporary definitions, the analogue and digital representations of community', observes dancer-choreographer Eleanor Bauer, a native American who settled in Brussels after studying at P.A.R.T.S. 'For as dancers we have to be physically present in order to create and perform ... and on the other hand, the international scope of the professional networks we move within reflects the breadth and distance facilitated by and inherent in the contemporary definition of community.' Because of the frequent border crossings, the multi-territorial nature of the involved production or distribution circuits and its obviously hybrid make-up, the notion of a transnational community rather than an international one seems appropriate when defining the Brussels dance world. A substantial part actually consists of foreign dance artists who are only temporarily residing in Brussels for professional reasons. They may be regarded as artistic seasonal workers since both their personal mobility and their stay in the Belgian capital are primarily job-driven. Some become genuine migrants when they decide to settle in Brussels permanently; in most cases, this is not a preconceived notion but a possible scenario that only takes shape over time.

Intermezzo: Dance Artists' Precarity

Doing 'movement work' nowadays entails 'being on the move', and this not just spatially but socially as well: moving from one place to another frequently means entering different work contexts. Dance artists are indeed more often than not job hoppers. Their professional trajectories generally fit the idea of a borderless career, not structured by a long-lasting commitment to one employer. Only a tiny minority work for several years with the same company; most others combine successive short-term contracts or occasional grants with unemployment benefits and perhaps revenues from secondary jobs such as teaching or giving workshops. Since structural funding is limited, those taking up the position of choreographer usually also move from one temporary project to the next interim collaboration and are quite lucky if the nearly unavoidable in-between periods of inactivity are infrequent and short. In present conditions, this regime of flexible artistic accumulation necessarily implies social and economic vulnerability. The ideologically flavoured rhetoric regarding 'the new creative class' or the eulogies by policy makers on 'creative cities' tend to conceal the precarious status of artists and other freelance workers engaged in inventive activity. Being a member of the creative 'precariat' in fact equals a job flexibility that definitely goes beyond the already problematic economic insecurity that accompanies short-term contracts. Variable working hours, unregulated by union-backed frameworks, prevail in the world of contemporary dance. Under these unstable labour conditions, performers are expected to give the best of themselves in exchange for a rather meagre salary and uncertain symbolic returns. The real amount of work often exceeds the length of formal employment, the disparity being bridged by means of unemployment allowances or unpaid labour altogether. And there is the substantial share of non-remunerated or self-paid work that choreographers perform when preparing a new project dossier (which may not be successful) or that unemployed dancers have to accomplish in order to stay physically fit and remain employable (such as regularly attending dance classes or workshops). Still other disadvantages may add to the, on average, financially unrewarding careers of dance artists: a limited health insurance, no paid holiday leave, no extras or bonuses whatsoever, no protection against wrongful dismissal, and so on.

Although their professional nomadism seems at first sight imposed by funding modalities and a volatile job market, many 'dance workers' actually prefer shifting collaborations above a stable company contract. Indeed, as a rule they do not publicly complain about their precarity, although they may occasionally voice their concerns during informal conversations. In their experience, both the long working hours at a modest fee and the lack of job security are sufficiently balanced by the pleasure of regularly doing personally gratifying work in a relatively autonomous way. Notwithstanding the inherent stress, dance artists therefore tend to accept the steady erosion of the distinction between work and non-work and do not massively contest the blurring of the traditional line separating wage-earning and unpaid voluntary work, especially when a deadline is near. The economic or social cons of precarity weigh less then the valued pros, such as the possibility to negotiate individual artistic choices when engaging in collaborations or the chance to deepen one's personal capacities as a dancer or choreographer through successive projects. In short, *the external precarisation induced by the meanwhile institutionalized neoliberal or post-Fordist regime of flexible artistic accumulation is intrinsically interwoven with a partly voluntary self-precarisation, stemming from the desire to be a creative subject.* The literal meaning of the word 'subject', already foregrounded in the previous chapter, again applies here: one tries to ground one's labour in one's personal artistic competences and their momentary exploration or actualization. In fact, the corresponding subjectivity often hovers between the genuine subjectification of potentials on the one hand, and being strongly subjected to all sorts of pressures and risks on the other. Autonomy and heteronomy, free choices and economic or social constraints indeed condense into a difficult to untwine knot. 'Experiences of anxiety and loss of control, feelings of insecurity as well as the fear and the actual experience of failure, a drop in social status and poverty are linked with this state of self-precarisation', notes Isabell Lorey with regard to the 'virtuosos of freedom' populating the worlds of creative labour. 'It is for this reason too that "letting go" or other forms of dropping out of or shedding the hegemonic paradigm are difficult. You have to stay "on speed" or else you would be eliminated. You always feel threatened. There is no clear time for relaxation and recuperation. Then the desire to relax and "find oneself" becomes insatiable.'

Within art worlds, the current mode of self-precarisation actually reproduces the predominant idea that making art is first and foremost a personal yearning. Successful art, as the reigning cliché already discussed in the previous chapter stipulates, gives evidence of an epochal innovativeness originating in the kind of god-like creative autonomy suggested by the notion of the subject. However, the regime of singularity frames the artist's independence not as a contingent social role or a deliberately chosen profession but as pointing to a truly individual 'will to make art' that acts as an irresistible force. The modern notion of artistry indeed represents this intention as ultimately rooted in a compelling urge to create, a pressing desire — even a destiny — to be expressive beyond established artistic standards or common aesthetic norms. Producing art is placed outside the realm of society or culture and thoroughly naturalized, which brings the regime of singularity full circle and simultaneously transforms it into a particular myth of origins. Artistic subjectivity or authorship changes into a quasi-religious vocation that combines, in a nearly magical way, autonomous activity ('I am creative...') and aesthetic passivity ('...because I have to be'). 'To have a vocation ... means to feel that one has a *calling* to perform an activity, not out of a calculation of self-interests or the obedience to conventions or obligations but as a personal, interior desire to embrace a career for which one feels made, to which one feels predestined', Nathalie Heinich writes on 'the vocational regime'. Creating art is by this account less a matter of free choice and more an existential condition fitting the contingent cultural identity of the modern artist. 'I have to make art': this simple statement refers both to an explicit subjective state of being and an implicit subjection to the regime of singularity.

Speaking of the vocation and profession of politics — the German word *'Beruf'* has both meanings — Max Weber once famously remarked that 'Either one lives "for" politics or one lives "from" politics.' The distinction emphasizes the difference between a vocational stance and a primarily job-oriented attitude by giving it an economic twist. Either one mainly works in order to make a living, perhaps also to accumulate financial profits; or one's primary vocational motivation generates such an overwhelming intrinsic interest in an activity that one is rather uninterested in the material rewards it may bring. In other words, the immanent 'psychological' gains of doing what one existentially experiences as a calling vastly compensate all the possible disadvantages this may entail. The willingness to sacrifice actually functions as a difficult to doubt external sign of a vocation's authentic character. Though this idea may in principle hold for all those active within a creative profession, it still markedly stamps the discourse on the arts. And this to great effect: most painters and other visual artists, as well as countless dancers and choreographers, effectively endorse the notion of material asceticism, which the vocational regime contestably essentializes into an undisputable symbol of a true 'will to be creative'. 'Poverty becomes an elective identifying mark of the sacrifice one makes for art, thus appearing as an indication of a total engagement, a proof of the indomitable character of one's calling', sociologist Gérard Mauger rightly stresses in his discussion of 'the specific capital' defining artistic practices. The reasoning matches the more general norm co-structuring the overall functioning of art worlds: neither financial gain nor symbolic capital or public esteem are explicitly at stake when producing or distributing art. 'Art for art's sake' is, once again, the notorious motto that best sums up the conspicuous denial of the economic forces shaping the publicly observable behaviour within artistic fields. Yet how does all this inform the actual work relationships within the world of contemporary dance 'made in Brussels'?

Revisiting Rosas Anno 1995
The setting is Brussels in the summer of 1995. In one part of the vast, somewhat austere looking Rosas rehearsal space situated at the outskirts of the city — the other half is used for the rehearsals of retaken repertoire — some fifteen dancers informally gather around choreographer Anne Teresa De Keersmaeker and a sound system. Some of them have a score on their lap; others seem ready to take notes. Music resounds: the CD is stopped, played again, stopped... De Keersmaeker reads the score and points out specific passages; some dancers ask questions, but most of them just listen attentively — only one or two look slightly bored. The music is Arnold Schönberg's original version of *Verklärte Nacht* (1899), a string sextet in one movement composed in the tradition of late-Romanticism, based on the sexually charged poem of the same name by Richard Dehmel. There are two more persons present, both silently taking notes: De Keersmaeker's personal assistant (who is regularly instructed to write down this or that) and the sociologist (myself) who is allowed to witness the creation process for the new Rosas work. The rather brief choreography on

Verklärte Nacht will be part of a Schönberg evening, which will premiere in November 1995 in the Brussels opera house La Monnaie/
De Munt and also includes the staging of the one-act monodrama
Die Erwartung (1909) by Klaus Michael Grüber (the choreography
would subsequently be integrated into the 1996 dance work *Woud,
three movements to the music of Berg, Schönberg and Wagner*; in
2014, De Keersmaeker created a new trio version on Schönberg's
arrangement of *Verklärte Nacht* for string orchestra).

The sociologist turned ethnographer aims to do some
fieldwork on the making of dance and is therefore not primarily
interested in the final aesthetic outcome of the rehearsal process
or its subsequent life in the transnational field of contemporary
choreography. At stake is the possibility to counter artistic fetishism, discussed in the previous chapter, by opening the black box
named 'art work' through the personal observation and documentation of the preceding work, in the sense of labour or production.
No labour without always particular labour relations; no production without more or less equal forms of cooperation, particularly
when the involved work has a direct social nature. But what does
contemporary dance as a peculiar regime of co-creation actually amount to in an internationally renowned company? How
is movement material collectively generated, varied and selected
within such a context? What does it mean to choreograph not
only a series of movements to a musical score but also, as that very
activity's necessitating social condition of possibility, to direct a
diverse group of people coming from all over the globe, bringing with them different aesthetics or personal tastes, diverging
capacities, and an always singular life history or artistic motivation? In order to answer these and related questions, I observe and
take field notes, albeit not continuously (still other duties have to
be fulfilled as well), socialize with the dancers or the choreographer during breaks (it takes some time before they get used to
the presence of an outsider), and conduct a concluding in-depth
interview with all dancers in the months following the premiere of
Verklärte Nacht.

The gathered material is condensed here into an ideal-
typical representation of *the semi-directive mode of participative
collaboration*. The unfolded portrait is not exactly an empirical
generalization covering all sociologically relevant aspects of the
referred to rehearsal setting. In line with the notion's original
meaning as put forward by Max Weber, an ideal type accentuates

certain characteristics at the expense of others and is deliberately one-sided. Therefore the paradoxes underlying the semi-directive regime will be regularly foregrounded, even slightly exaggerated. Not that this work relationship is a mere sociological construction, quite the contrary. Whereas the making of ballet still tends to be highly directive, the semi-directive regime, which nowadays prevails within contemporary dance, clearly does not position the performers as mere passive executers of a 'dance text' that is preconceived, partially or entirely, by an author-choreographer before the start of the work process. Neither do the dancers act together in a social setting characterized by an outspoken hierarchy between both the choreographer and the performers and among the dancers themselves: within contemporary dance, the differentiation between principals, soloists and corps de ballet members simply does not apply. In a semi-directive work relationship, the dancers actively co-create the basic material through processes of improvisation or movement research that may be variably framed by the choreographer on the basis of leading ideas, concrete tasks, references to images, and so on. Although dance makers mostly act as an enabling coach, they remain in an authoritative position since they are the company's artistic director or have initiated a temporary project for which they hold the final aesthetic responsibility. This role is often openly affirmed once the creation process enters the end stage of making final decisions on the generated material and its choreographic articulation. The semi-directive mode of making dance together therefore hovers between the overtly hierarchical style known from ballet and the 'flat' collaboration typifying the functioning of genuine dance collectives. Participatory co-creation differs from an equal collaboration in which all those involved take up the positions of both dancer and choreographer, yet the first mode may approximate the second one more or less strongly.

A Rosas working day anno 1995 is relatively scheduled but often also quite varied at the beginning and in the middle of the process of creation. Between 9.30 in the morning and 6 or 7 in the evening, the dancers may switch between different sorts of activity: generating material and perhaps showing it to the choreographer and the group, learning already developed phrases from co-dancers, making structured variations on a movement sequence in order to deepen its potential (for instance by reversing the phrase or recounting the constituting elements in a different rhythm), exploring particular material under the direct guidance of De Keersmaeker, rehearsing or teaching an existing repertory piece, et cetera. The specific timing of a working day is collectively decided during the first group meeting with the choreographer around 11 a.m. following the, in principle, mandatory dance or tai chi class. Many dancers regularly skip a class or enter late – a tolerated 'misbehaviour' when it is not too frequent. For that matter, all dancers have a one-year contract. The general company manager negotiates the possible prolongation of the employment agreement in the light of De Keersmaeker's future plans and her personal opinion of a dancer's individual qualities.

During the first and most extensive work period, the active production of movement material through a mostly loosely structured research process is combined with further exploring that material. Although De Keersmaeker frequently gives them a specific task or feedback directing, the dancers experience this phase as highly creative and sometimes intensively challenging their personal capacities. They have the feeling of being genuine co-authors, a status the dancers see confirmed in the possibility to have a say and give personal comments, even to voice serious objections or strong counter-opinions (mostly in a diplomatic way: civility reigns). Quite diverse resources are tapped into in order to invent new material: film fragments, verbal sayings that are literally danced, ordinary gestures and poses, music (everything goes, from classical to pop kitsch), as well as personal memories. For example, one of the constituted phrases ending up in the final choreography is directly inspired by the act of ironing; yet another movement sequence that is subsequently elaborated has its roots in images of sculptures. In the course of their further articulation, both phrases are transformed to such an extent that their original sources are no longer observable. By and large, the various points of departure function as contingent, even relatively arbitrary occasions to initiate a series of movements whose visible physical qualities may be appreciated as having more or less artistic interest, or whose potentialities look greatly, a bit or not at all promising. The underlying motivation matters less than the perceptible exterior of actions and inactions, including the various connotations they suggest. In short, the signifier prevails over the original signified or referent. The evaluated secondary meanings can have a direct aesthetic content ('smooth', 'elegant', 'too awkward') or are briefly discussed by the dancers in more cultural terms: 'it is very feminine', 'that gesture looks powerful'. The small number of poses or movements developed according to a rather strict rationale of expressivity form a noteworthy exception. For instance, the making of a love duet insinuating mutual attraction and rejection – a central scene in *Verklärte Nacht* – asks for somewhat strongly coded actions that are immanently motivated by their overall meaning.

While generating or exploring material, the dancers do not work within a socially blank space: the choreographer's gaze – an expression that will be further elaborated in the next paragraph – indirectly informs their work. The performers frequently refer to 'Anne Teresa's taste', which they deliberately anticipate in their activity. From former choreographies of De Keersmaeker, and perhaps also from previous collaborations with her, the dancers have deduced a relatively stable and mutually shared idea about the kind of material she may be interested in. This particular translation of the notion of the legitimately danceable – or 'De Keersmaeker's dance culture' – very much guides them and reduces the space of possible poses and movements while doing research. Even in the absence of more specific tasks or sources of inspiration, the dancers' initial improvising is therefore always already structured. However, a straight reproduction of the assumed Rosas style is clearly avoided. The performers want to surprise and captivate the choreographer's gaze with original proposals, which also have a greater chance to end up in the final choreography. The net result is a clear paradox, an implicit injunction that resembles a double bind: *one has to produce dance material that simultaneously conforms to and deviates from a presumed poetics*, looks at once familiar and unfamiliar in the light of De Keersmaeker's presupposed aesthetic taste. Mostly the dancers deal with this ambiguity by going for an original variation, or material that gives a legitimate twist to the assumed Rosas style and will probably not be observed as an individual idiosyncrasy, let alone as a straightforward transgression. Given the general regime of singularity dominating the valuation of art, the operation has two latent implications. The dancers acknowledge the uniqueness of De Keersmaeker's choreographic signature, yet they simultaneously try to re-articulate its distinctive features through personal interpretations.

During the shorter second phase of the creation process, De Keersmaeker, without much individual consultation or collective deliberation, settles two issues. Which engendered

movements and poses will be presented in the definitive work? And who will actually perform the chosen material that makes up the final choreography? Many of the selected phrases are therefore first communalized: they are *de-authorized* and change from personal into collective dance material. With the notable exception of the one solo or duet that was already reserved for particular performers, all dancers indeed learn most of the selected movements and poses. This facilitates the exploration of potential unisons and allows a singular kind of body test: what material fits which dancer(s) most? The final corpus is then definitively edited and fixed, assigned to individual Rosas members, and further rehearsed. The dancers now change into predominantly passive performers who have to interpret the assigned actions as well as possible, though De Keersmaeker leaves ample room for personal appropriations (this is in line with the expressivity characterizing Rosas performances as discussed in the second chapter). As the date of the premiere approaches, work becomes mainly repetitive and, predictably, quite stressful. Overall, in this concluding stage the relationship with the choreographer tends to be more directive and hierarchical. Not that a plain command structure takes over: rather than involving a straight authoritarian-like relationship, the final work period contains several author-marked moments in which De Keersmaeker affirms and implements her personal artistic vision without much consultation. The basic idea informing this stance runs like this: 'It is my work since it is ascribed to *me*. Therefore *I*, and not somebody else, am responsible for its artistic quality, which *I* therefore have to watch over' (this is not a literal statement of De Keersmaeker, but a condensed summary of her view on artistic authorship as she explained it to me during an informal conversation in 1995).

The knowledge that the concluding rehearsal phase will inevitably come induces insecurity among the dancers during the first work period. For they individually generate and elaborate, with an often strong individual commitment, various material without knowing if it will end up in the performance. And even when some of the proposed movement sequences make it to the finish line, the dancers cannot be certain that they themselves will publicly perform the phrases they personally created or co-produced. Some dancers anticipate this eventual loss of authorship — 'ownership' may be the better word here — by initially not working at the top of their capacities. Only when they have a minimum guarantee about their material's final fate, do they really start to adapt or deepen it. However, De Keersmaeker herself also reflexively takes into account this self-produced uncertainty in view of a higher level of involvement or a more intense competition among the dancers. She may, for instance, suggest very indirectly, without even the slightest hint of making a binding promise (an enthusiastic 'that's interesting!' will do) that a phrase-in-the-making is a likely candidate for the definitive work. In that sense, the temporal insecurity on the final choreography partly allows the choreographer to manage the work relationships within the company. Since the dancers observe this regulating activity, a reflexively played tactical game of implicit manipulations and counter-manipulations unfolds in which the choreographer is often but not always the most successful agent (during informal conversations, both the dancers and De Keersmaeker repeatedly illustrate this logic with sometimes hilarious anecdotes: it is indeed a collectively known social game).

Evidently, a more strict artistic logic co-motivates the avoidance of early decisions: the choreographer reserves latitude. She avoids the path dependency of decision-making, or the simple fact that every definitive selection pre-structures possible future choices. Moreover, the deferment of hasty fixations within the realm of 'the choreographic' prevents a too rapid framing of the compositional potential of the created material. Nevertheless, this logic of aesthetic freedom goes remarkably well with the logic of social regulation. The affinity illustrates that 'the artistic' and 'the social' are not by definition two neatly distinguishable polar realities but may strongly intermingle in cooperative processes of making art together. One-sided 'aestheticist' or 'sociologistic' accounts usually overlook *the converging, in provisional non-decisions, of the preservation of a compositional decision potential with the capacity of governing artistic collaboration.* By postponing both choreographically and socially binding selections, the artistic director indeed at once retains an aesthetic manoeuvring space and keeps most dancers 'on their toes'. At the same time, the choreographer avoids that the company all too quickly splits into a motivated core group and a not so committed periphery of dancers who already know that they will have a mainly supporting role in the final performance (read: they will not dance solos, duets or trios and will only participate in group scenes).

The Choreographer's Gaze

The initial creation, further development and final refinement of material are not just a matter of moving and standing still. Rather, *making contemporary dance together involves a continuous loop between doing, watching and commenting.* For example, a Rosas performer first tries out a series of movements with a fellow-dancer and may receive immediate feedback from him or her in the process of phrase construction. Or they work together for some time, say an hour, and subsequently ask other available dancers to have a brief look and give personal comments. This *peer coaching*, as Helena Wulff calls it in her anthropological study of three ballet companies, is almost always remarkably short: the exchange of only a couple of allusive sentences will do most of the time. The offered comments are usually quite evaluative, ranging from the admiring 'that's really nice!' or the negative perception 'it looks a bit flat, no?' to a more precise brief observation such as 'the dynamic changes conspicuously when you raise your right arm in the middle of the phrase'. They are for the most part not really substantiated and are often received without much further discussion. Given their vagueness or poly-interpretability, this may seem somewhat surprising. Yet the dancers have a shared sensibility that is very much framed by their previous experience in the field of contemporary dance and the shared orientation to De Keersmaeker's presupposed aesthetic taste. A collective stock of expressions exists, whose meanings do not need further elucidation, such as 'flat', 'awkward' or the much-used notion that a movement sequence is 'interesting'. Moreover, the open or inconclusive nature of the received feedback is valued as such because the dancers are actually first and foremost looking for general lines of orientation that they can subsequently interpret, appropriate and individualize on the basis of self-observations. These may stem from mirror images, though Rosas dancers usually work without the mirror wall known from ballet practice and only sparsely make use of video recordings. For their self-observations, they primarily rely on internal body images that are sustained by a well-developed proprioceptive sense.

Peer coaching is now and then alternated and also regularly mixed with more direct commentary by De Keersmaeker. The mixed situation may emerge during the frequent moments that newly created movement material is presented to both the choreographer and the group. These moments provide room for collective reflection but are predominantly regarded as an opportunity for the choreographer to give feedback. Some dancers therefore experience the interim presentations as public examinations during which De Keersmaeker administers, as a rule without much emphasis, plusses and minuses by showing the extent of her personal interest in this or that proposed material. However, most performers do appreciate the feedback as such since it offers them at once workable and legitimate guidelines for the immediate future. Despite the possible relevance of other dancers' comments, the choreographer is indeed implicitly bestowed with an authoritative voice, which she only now and then overtly assumes. The overall setting actually confirms the discursive inequality of those present: De Keersmaeker sits on a chair in the middle of the space, frontally facing the proverbial stage, surrounded by the dancers sitting or lying on the floor. The choreographer's degree of interest is partly read from her comments. Sometimes De Keersmaeker formulates detailed suggestions, at other moments she limits herself to a couple of cryptic hints (which may afterwards become the object of a lengthy process of deciphering by the implied dancers), and a third time only a telling 'thank you!' resounds. Yet of equal, if not greater, importance is the mere length of De Keersmaeker's attention to this movement sequence or that phrase-in-the-making. Quantity is systematically translated into quality and coupled to the specific nature of the explicitly voiced feedback in order to assess the presumed amount of symbolic capital or recognition one momentarily enjoys in De Keersmaeker's 'masterful eye'. Comparable to an artistic field, the company indeed delineates a collective space in which the dancers, mostly implicitly, compete for the artistic esteem distributed by the choreographer. The general field rule, discussed in the previous chapter, that this should be done in the mode of negation or disavowal applies even more strictly within this smaller social arena. Dancers who overtly try to advance their symbolic position, for instance by constantly flattering the choreographer or soliciting a private meeting, threaten the minimum of solidarity without which collaboration and company life become difficult. One's artistic status, as indicated by De Keersmaeker's attention span, is commonly validated by most other dancers, which results in a latent hierarchy that is by and large only openly acknowledged during informal backstage conversation. Newcomers in particular have to go through an initial phase of relative status insecurity. Such dancers' symbolic capital, and concomitantly their social position in the company, may change quite drastically when De Keersmaeker takes them apart in order to refine the material they proposed.

All in all, *the relationship between choreographer and dancers resembles a specific artistic attention regime that is at once authorial and authorizing.* For the Rosas performers, getting (more) attention from De Keersmaeker acts as a crucial incentive and important reward for their work and incites them to persevere in the developed lines of action or research with an even greater personal engagement. To be noticed in a noteworthy way is moreover regarded as a genuine validation that they are true co-creators. Through the amount of attention dispensed, the choreographer eventually authorizes co-authorship – a state of affairs that implicitly confirms her position as Author on the basis of a quasi-magical logic of aura-contamination. At stake is a peculiar symbolic economy in the strict sense, so a rarefied artefact that is the subject of competition. Given the choreographer's limited time budget, the disposable volume of attention is by definition scarce, which helps to explain why the dancers consistently re-interpret its distributed quantity in qualitative terms. De Keersmaeker of course knows and observes that they actively vie, though in general not openly, for her attention. The net outcome is once again a reflexive tactical game between the two parties involved. For example, a negative remark by the choreographer may result in ostensible signs of disengagement, which the choreographer subsequently counters with a positive comment during a next public group showing. De Keersmaeker actually follows the general rule that in order to avoid social tensions, her attention must be distributed in a relatively equal extent among the various dancers and their materials. This general receipt knows two obvious exceptions. There is the couple of dancers who have been attributed a central role right from the beginning since they were asked to create a solo or a duet: they were, are and will be given a serious amount of attention. And there are the 'difficult cases', or the performers who the choreographer evaluates as only minimally engaged because of a 'bad work ethic': they receive little feedback. This last exception can in turn become the object of yet another uncommon line of action. When De Keersmaeker is convinced that a not so committed company member is really talented, she may try to enhance that dancer's personal motivation by promising her a more substantial role in a next production. Despite its rather ambiguous nature, a single statement such as 'perhaps we should work together a bit more closely in the near future' can give a Rosas dancer a significant boost and act over a longer period of time as a motivating force.

The choreographer's gaze functions as the structuring principle underlying the entire creation process. Some dancers regularly experience this gaze as strongly evaluating, and at times also as overtly controlling and greatly disciplining their activity. For it is the instance that approves or turns down, praises or blames, offers much or little personal recognition. Yet that very same gaze also represents a widely esteemed sensibility for perceiving artistic possibilities in the generated material, which the dancers themselves may not immediately identify. Precisely therefore De Keersmaeker can operate without much contestation as a validating authority and legitimate distributor of symbolic recognition. She descries in the performers' proposals virtual possibilities they tend to overlook: *the renowned choreographer acts as the consecrated second-order observer who knowledgably corrects the blind spots in the dancers' first-order observations of their materials' potentials.* In line with the overall structure of a creation process, a double potentiality is involved. During the first work period, De Keersmaeker's suggestions often point to the intrinsic aesthetic possibilities of a singular movement sequence or a particular duet. 'Make it more neutral', 'rework the phrase a bit in the middle by stressing the arm gestures': the dancers greatly appreciate such comments, and not only because they offer legitimate guidance coming from – to paraphrase Jacques Lacan's famous characterization of both the psychoanalyst and unconsciousness – 'the subject supposed to know'. The remarks are often also taken up in the mode of 'I did not see that myself', so not as schoolmasterly correcting but as truly improving the presented movement sequence. As the work process progresses, and especially once the first definitive selections are made, the choreographer's gaze gradually focuses more intensely on the still virtual total context of the performance yet to come. Can particular phrases be articulated in such a way that they fit each other because they may be relatively harmoniously combined or, by contrast, convincingly work as counterpoints? Their choreographic potential now comes to the fore: the looking at and scrutinizing of diverse kinds of actions corresponds with their possible inscription as 'movement sentences' within the space of 'the choreographic'. Various combinations of phrases and fragments are thus tried out in view of an artistically consistent 'dance text', or a movement composition that holds. Video recordings play an important role in this process because they allow the 'dance writer' to look back in time. The choreographer's consultation of the video archive may actually result in surprising moves, for instance when De Keersmaeker suddenly asks a dancer to re-perform a particular sequence that has not been deployed for a long time.

The final phase of selecting, editing and fixing all available material in a sense acts as the rehearsal process' moment of artistic truth. At the same time, this short but intense work period constitutes a social dénouement, a provisional end point in the labour relationship between dancers and choreographer. Indeed, De Keersmaeker autonomously decides, this time with publicly visible consequences, on the selection and performance of the final material. Losing the direct author- or ownership over one's material is a possible first symbolic blow. Although the dancer's creativity and efforts are artistically validated, passing on the movement sequence to another performer comes across as a direct affront. For the dancer is withheld the final reward: 'somebody else will receive applause for my material'. The second blow consists in the definitive removal of personal material in which the authors have invested many hours of hard work. Upon the first signs of approval they continued to elaborate the phrases — and suddenly these are deemed worthless and risk ending up on the dustbin of dance history. Both symbolic rejections are frequently experienced as personal and elicit a lot of behind-the-scenes commentary. The hurt may be so profound that a dancer starts contemplating the option of leaving the Rosas company. The choreographer can once again reflexively anticipate this state of affairs and try to forestall it. Material is therefore sometimes included in the final choreography in order to avoid an open conflict or to prevent a talented dancer from looking for another employer. The decision may come at a serious price when it results in a weaker passage or a dramaturgically not so persuasive scene in the final performance.

A more general issue is at stake here. Having one's self-generated material selected, as well as being allowed to publicly perform it, is the crucial sign of recognition that the dancer is the work's authentic co-author. In a company such as Rosas, perhaps even within the world of contemporary dance in general, this esteem seems to be valued significantly higher than merely being appreciated as a technically gifted performer. Nonetheless, choreographers give the desired credit first and foremost through the final choreography with which they simultaneously affirm their authorship. This structural ambiguity once again confirms the general observation that *the semi-directive work relationship rests on the paradox of a heteronomous autonomy* whose intensity overall accrues and becomes more visible in the moments that the choreographer gazes, speaks or selects. Within this production context, the dancer in general enjoys great artistic independence. He or she freely creates and explores movement material, alone or in tandem with fellow performers – yet it is primarily the choreographer who credits it as aesthetically interesting and decides on both the action's choreographic end value and the dancer's individual ability to perform it on stage.

'Being Hurt' and the Logic of Symbolic Exchange

Sociological research on artistic labour relationships is relatively rare. Scantier still are ethnographically informed insights on current work practices in the field of dance. In *Danser. Enquête dans les coulisses d'une vocation (Dancing. Survey in the Backstage of a Vocation)*, one of the few sociological studies on the world of, in this case French, contemporary dance – the results of which are generally in line with many observations presented in this and the next chapter – Pierre-Emmanuel Sorignet links the at once assessing and accrediting function of choreographers, above all consecrated ones, to a more general uncertainty. Many dancers experience 'a fragility in respect to their legitimacy to exist within this occupation', he observes, adding: 'This makes the choreographer the one who validates and certifies the dancer's belonging to the dance world.' Part of the symbolic aura surrounding a choreographer like De Keersmaeker effectively spills over in a near magical way to a performer through the act of finding her personal artistic proposals particularly noteworthy. The uncertainty that is temporarily remediated in this way, possibly with a longer-lasting impact, pertains to the actual nature of a dancer's capacities, or his or her individual ability to live up to technical standards and to be truly creative in developing or interpreting material. A performer's singularity is indeed not an established Fact, but only a possible state of affairs that needs an interpersonal confirmation by a 'subject supposed to know'. The heteronomous autonomy pervading participatory collaboration therefore primarily points to the social loop in which *dancers actualize their individual artistic potential in view of its validation as legitimately singular by a dance maker already validated as singular.* Notwithstanding the often striking socio-economic insecurity that marks artistic careers, a dancer's precariousness has predominantly to do with the socially bestowed, and for this very reason always uncertain, identity of being a singular artist. Performers may regard themselves as autonomous subjects, yet their artistic subjectivity greatly hinges on an external act of valuation that makes it vulnerable and which must be repeated over time in order to condense into the socially ascertained self-description 'I am a talented dancer'.

A particular ambivalence recurrently surfaced in the many loose talks and more formal interviews I had with the members of the Rosas company in the mid-1990s. These conversations were in several instances hesitant, vacillating between overt acknowledgement and profound doubt, which may have been partly motivated by the question: 'what am I prepared to say to an outsider?' The fragile, precarious dependency on a particular choreographer's gaze or words was alternatingly affirmed and contested, openly voiced – sometimes with much gratitude – or implicitly disputed and directly put into question on the grounds that one's real individual powers were not adequately noticed or sufficiently appreciated. It was not exactly a matter of receiving recognition or not, or of being 'in' or 'out' of grace. Rather, the observed ambivalence touched upon the difficult to express psychological hurt inflicted by dependency as such, and the social heteronomy prevailing over one's sense of artistic autonomy. The dancers regarded themselves as singular artists but conceded both the general necessity and personal desire for a genuine social validation by a renowned Other; and simultaneously, out of the longing to have one's artistic potentiality valued as an existing, unquestionable Fact, they doubted a singular choreographer's capacity to grant this worth. Heteronomous autonomy may be an existential condition defining the precariousness of human life as such. '[We] are, from the start, even prior to individuation itself ... given over to some set of primary others' and therefore share 'a common human vulnerability, one that emerges with life itself ... [and] precedes the formation of "I"', contends Judith Butler. Artistic work relationships highlight this social ontology precisely because they are individually experienced and interpreted in line with the reigning regime of singularity still greatly informing today's art worlds. Indeed, this regime regiments an artist's identity: it subjects their artistic subjectivity to 'the subject supposed to know'. However, I have heard Rosas dancers voicing still another hurt, one that is intimately linked to their dependency on the choreographer's gaze or recognition but simultaneously points to the underlying symbolic logic structuring the semi-directive mode of participatory collaboration.

In line with the logic of differentiation characterizing social modernity, artistic work relations associate in a peculiar way 'the economic' and 'the aesthetic', the contractual dimension framing the purchase of labour power on the one hand and the vocational regime still co-defining artistic practices on the other. Dancers who work for a company or in the context of a delimitated project in fact always have a double status. They are employees legally engaged by an employer according to a work contract, which mentions the agreed monthly salary and perhaps additional remunerations (such as per diems when touring) and which obliges the hiring party to contribute to premiums for health care or retirement. And they are also individual artists who will produce – in Marxian parlance – a difficult to quantify artistic surplus value through their collaboration with the choreographer and co-dancers. In the same vein, the choreographer occupies the opposite positions of both employer and artistic director. Yet everything contractual is usually delegated to and handled by the company's general director or the external management office taking care of a project's legal and financial aspects. The performer's and dance maker's twofold social status therefore corresponds with a structural split between 'the economic' and 'the artistic' that reproduces the general disavowal of the first term and the concomitant autonomization of the second one within modern art worlds. *Dancer and choreographer can have a purely artistic work relation because their day-to-day collaboration is organizationally purified from everything economic by transferring this 'impurity' to a purely managerial body.* The dance maker therefore does not address the dancers as employees but consistently approaches them in line with the prevailing image of the artist: the performer supposedly acts out of a personal vocation to dance, to create, to develop a singular artistic potential. The company member who does not live up to this commonplace is reproached for having a 'bad work ethic'. The negative valuation usually comes with the observation, which may be voiced openly, that 'one is not in a dance company like Rosas just to make a living'. In other words, the individual motivation regularly linked with the employee status is denied the dancers in their relationship with the choreographer. The 'dance worker' who is not really approached as a labourer therefore has to disregard the possible discrepancy between the market value of the co-produced artistic product and the contractually fixed remuneration. The reality of surplus value creation − or, also in Marxian terms: of labour exploitation − is rather crassly sealed off by this socially mandatory negation, which may be viewed as a somewhat particular instance of artistic fetishism and, more broadly, as a rather perverse ideological effect of the regime of singularity. Yet this is only half of the story, since the assumingly mere artistic liaison between performer and choreographer greatly resembles the moral economy of gift and counter-gift qualifying symbolic exchange relations.

The French anthropologist Marcel Mauss famously put forward the idea of the logic of the gift cycle in view of an encompassing conceptual model of the kind of general trade-off − he himself speaks of 'total prestations' − between clans or other groups in societies that do not have a separate economic system of contractually regulated transactions rooted in egotistic calculations. Symbolic or gift exchange essentially implies a threefold obligation: A has to give, B is expected to accept the 'present', and the receiver must complete the cycle with an appropriate counter-gift, since otherwise he would remain in debt. The actual effecting of the expected quid pro quo does not end the interaction but recreates the initial situation: the counter-gift functions as a gift necessitating yet another counter-gift. Within more or less durable relationships, the overall rule of reciprocity propelling symbolic exchange thus brings forth a vast dynamic, a continuous passing of diverse kinds of goods or services that may be mixed with the imperative to outdo each offering with a more expensive counter-gift (this is the well-known phenomenon of the potlatch). 'In all groups we see the archaic form of exchange in the gift and the return gift', Mauss writes. Symbolic exchange characterizes pre-modern societies but indeed lives on in modernity − or post-modernity − beyond the intimate ritual of offering presents and honouring, balancing or outbidding this act through counter-presents. Particularly *creative work relationships are co-structured by the moral gift economy informing the threefold symbolic commitment to give, to receive and to meet the accepted accomplishment.* So besides their physical or mental capacities, the Rosas performer offers an artistic potential that is actualized through the creation of singular material. The choreographer responds to the gift with a standardized counter-gift. De Keersmaeker donates individual attention or dispenses artistic recognition, yet above all she is both willing and able to challenge or deepen the dancer's potency through various tasks and distinct comments based on a personal artistic vision and a validated choreographic know-how. From her point of view, these acts also constitute her principal first gifts for which she expects an adequate professional engagement, physical skilfulness and a genuine co-creativity in return, as well as a broad trust in her artistic competences. If everything goes well, the cycle of gift and counter-gift results in a productive process in which both parties constantly stimulate each other. For instance, at the start of the creation process, the dancer may propose material that raises the choreographer's interest and elicits a more than average attention, encouraging feedback and directive comments, which allow the performer to enhance the phrase-in-the-making. The esteemed counter-gift is then quasi-automatically followed by a renewed gift from the dancer: she now comes up with an augmented or accentuated artistic potential. The choreographer subsequently challenges the appreciated capacities even harder, whereupon the dancer develops yet another creative move or presents a surprising re-interpretation of the given indications. And so on: within a proliferating semi-directive work relationship, the artistic powers of both dancer and choreographer regularly boost each other according to the logic of gift and counter-gift.

Reciprocity is not the same as generosity: artistic collaborations rest on shared expectations regarding legitimately exchangeable accomplishments. Anthropologist David Graeber therefore rightly distinguishes the 'open reciprocity' in 'a relation of permanent mutual commitment', such as a long-lasting intimate bond, from the 'closed reciprocity' within a well-delineated framework offering the possibility of 'a balancing of accounts'. Precisely the latter may not happen because the at once anticipated and regulated exchange is not realized. The choreographer, for instance, observes that a company member performs below par or proffers movements that do not exactly show much creativity. Or the dancer finds his or her individual ardour and capacities insufficiently valued during a creation process, or sees personal material not being used, or passed on to a co-performer in the final phase. The cycle of gift and counter-gift then stalls: the clear-cut logic of reciprocity becomes fuzzy. Whereas the choreographer can, as a rule, compensate a particular performer's shortcomings with a stronger personal investment in the activities of other collaborators, dancers have only two options. Either they successfully discuss the problematic situation with the artistic director or they temporarily disengage and then definitively leave the troupe upon the expiration of their contract. Like the offhand backstage complaints on 'a failing collaboration' or the lesser aired personal hurts provoked by a lack of attention or feedback, both possibilities point to the morally charged expectations that surround the giving and counter-giving that frames symbolic exchange. Motivated dancers with 'a good work ethic' propose material according to their abilities — and the choreographer is under the obligation to scrutinize the phrase-in-the-making with a minimum of interest and to answer this metaphorical present with at least one apposite remark. Not fulfilling this expectation often generates anger or frustration but may at times also result in profound self-doubts with regard to one's artistic capacities: 'if the Other refuses what she should give me in return, I am perhaps not worthy of the act.' It is all aggravated by the personal nature of both gifts and counter-gifts. 'The thing itself is a person or pertains to a person', notes Mauss of the objects exchanged among the Maori, adding: 'Hence it follows that to give something is to give a part of oneself.' The observation directly applies to the work relation uniting dancer and choreographer: they indeed trade in an artistic subjectivity.

Second Movement: Disentangling Dance Artists' Social Subjectivity

Talking Contemporary Dance

The quasi-natural fetishist stance still dominating the reception of aesthetic communication actively negates that every art work is a, however minimal, accumulation of previously performed work that conditions its existence. Witnessing the collaborative practice preceding the public presentation of, for instance, a dance performance breaks this spell. One might also opt for another mode of observation — a different research method — and primarily take stock through in-depth conversations with artists about their autobiographical experiences in making art together. This is an approach I in fact pursued. Between 2008 and 2011, I staged a series of open interviews with dance artists that addressed artistic collaboration and directly related issues at length (the average dialogue lasted three hours but with several interviewees I had two such conversations). The majority of these dancers belong to the transnational Brussels dance community; those who were not members of this art world at the time of the interview were either former members or continued to have strong professional links with it through active residencies in Flanders, the co-production of their work by, for instance, Kaaitheater or Beursschouwburg and regular showings in Brussels venues. Twenty of these recorded dialogues have guided me greatly in the attempt to further elucidate the general stakes, personal motivations and regulating expectations underlying the collaborative creation of contemporary dance.

The analysed conversational material is fairly gender-balanced (nine interviewees are male, eleven are female) and relatively evenly distributed when it comes to age or career span. Whereas some interlocutors were, at the time of the talk, professionally active from three to five years, others had eight to fifteen years of work experience; a few could look back on an even longer artistic trajectory. The transnational character of the Brussels dance community is reflected in the heterogeneity of the respondents' nationalities: two Belgians, one American and one South-American, and the others carrying an identity card issued in one of the many EU-countries. With the noteworthy exception of a couple of interviewees who limit performing to their own choreographies, most conversational partners also regularly switched between the status of choreographer and the role of performer in the work of others. Several were or are still active in an established company headed by a renowned artistic director, however temporary projects constituted the majority of the working contexts discussed or referred to. Some of the dance artists I spoke with had experience in collective-based work of the more democratic sort, marked by a truly shared decision-making and a continual blurring of the roles of choreographer and performer (and even of technician or dramaturge). Nevertheless, the already partly disentangled semi-directive mode of participative collaboration predominantly informed their discourse. There is, however, a notable variation in the actual work relationships discussed in the interview material. Co-creation in the semi-directive mode can be more or less hierarchical: it ranges from a rather staunch relational inequality between choreographer and dancer to an artistic cooperation gravitating towards social self-reflexivity through permanent consultations and collective deliberations. Multiple arrangements are possible in between these two poles, as the varied reports of my conversational partners demonstrate.

Cooperation also defines the open interview practice, which tries to retain as much as possible the condition of a collaborative dialogue among equals without denying the principal positional difference between an interviewer and a respondent. Not unlike a collective dance improvisation, the situation actually relies upon the possibility of a conversational dynamic in which the unexpected statements of the interlocutor inspire new questions or probing remarks that the interviewer could not have premeditated. The interview then changes into a focussed talk of the self-productive kind: the dialogue feeds itself and engenders communicative sparks or surprises. That many of my conversations did momentarily meet this ideal type may have to do with my extensive familiarity with the interviewees' artistic trajectories. This not only created a common ground, facilitating short-cut references to their personal work or to the projects they had been participating in. Also at stake was, once again, the logic of symbolic exchange: the personal time and attention I had already given to the interlocutors' artistic accomplishments, including informal chats after performances, acted as an implicit gift counter-balancing their donation of precious time and professional information, filtered by personal experiences. The reciprocity defining the symbolic cycle applied in still other respects to this particular interview process. First hand-information was traded off for scholarly attention and the, however minimal, feeling of personal recognition elicited by the observation that one's individual point of view or accounts were taken seriously.

In scrutinizing the recorded talks, I hear the interviewees predictably speak with different voices, regularly articulate distinct opinions and invoke a wide variety of past first-hand experiences. Often insightful and at times hilarious anecdotes illustrate more abstract arguments or lines of thought, which frequently end on a personal note. Nevertheless, in their reports and 'readings' of, more often than not, intricate and multi-layered individual experiences, my conversational partners simultaneously deploy a shared vocabulary of motives, voice collective expectations or aspirations and make use of established semantics or pre-given cultural categories. To a rather considerable extent, they actively reproduce a socially institutionalized discourse in making sense of their professional engagement in the world of contemporary dance: *in narrating and interpreting their personal work experiences, dance artists say 'I', while simultaneously a rather anonymous 'one' or discourse is speaking.* Excavating the 'deep structures' or discursive stabilities informing the individual speech of artists comes with a hefty price tag, as it implies an operation of de-individualizing or de-authorizing, in the literal sense: the primary sources change into generic data. Interlocutors are bereft of their singular voices: their personal words represent a social discourse that is actually only observable in the always situational realizations it conditions. Hereafter I often slightly radicalize the standard academic practice to transform informants' views into anonymous assertions by treating the recorded statements as if they make up one corpus, thus willingly creating the false impression that only one person has been speaking, who is in fact the 'one' of the reconstructed social discourse. The resulting homogeneity sometimes flattens out important differences in sense making and does not do justice to individual nuances. Personal stories are made impersonal to such an extent that they silently evaporate into generalizing schemes or interpretations. The price paid for this particular kind of symbolic violence may only be compensated for by the kind of actively produced analytical clarity that deliberately obscures occasionally crucial shades of meaning.

Labouring/Becoming: Modes of Cooperation

Within contemporary dance, performers who work in a more or less permanent labour configuration for several consecutive years are the exception. Most productions are one-off projects; choreographers backed by a organizational structure usually prefer to selectively re-engage artistic collaborators and purposely hire new dancers in the light of the particular demands of an upcoming creation. This flexible regime of artistic accumulation pushes dance artists who assume the roles of both choreographer and performer in roughly two opposite directions when considering a collaboration in which they will play a subservient role. Indeed, a two-sided and rather predictable stance underlies the motivation to move into another dance maker's artistic world: 'As a dancer I do things because I am artistically interested or because I don't have work and must survive.' Entering a temporary project or signing a contract with an established company for predominantly instrumental reasons is almost always a negatively valued situation that is preferably avoided. Since there is no shared artistic interest, working for a choreographer out of sheer economic necessity is often not considered truly collaborative. The dismissive distinction between 'working for' and 'working with' partly reproduces the more general disavowal of monetary matters informing the functioning of artistic fields and the regime of singularity: a general semantic scheme opposing 'the economic' to 'the artistic', according to the value-logic of 'unworthy' and 'worthy', guides the self-observations within contemporary dance. Although this opposition as such does not exactly come as a surprise, it is striking that the contradistinction is so evident and yet only rarely addressed in a more reflexive mode.

When instrumentally 'working for' a choreographer, dancers tend towards a punctual and generally restricted personal engagement that is counter-balanced by the willingness to behave professionally. The performer tries to execute the dance maker's poetics and more specific directions as well as possible: 'I know what he wants and I'm used for it', 'I serve the proposition of that person, I will not question it. You have to accept it and find your place in it.' Although the artistic context is not always really satisfying, the dancer may still enjoy the work relationship when the choreographer behaves 'humanely' and demonstrates sufficient professional know-how. Clear communication on particular tasks or movements and the desired general outcome is greatly appreciated, since the performer primarily wants to understand and help materialize another's artistic vision. The classic sociological distinction between person and social role, or a bundle of general expectations regarding a social position, indeed applies here: the dancer effectively performs the role of a competent performer in a work relationship marked by an outspoken a-symmetry. One's aesthetic taste or individual view on dance is temporarily put 'on hold', although what the supervising artist actually demands or proposes may at times resonate with a problematic the dancer is also interested in. Nevertheless, the relationship is chiefly experienced as externally defined labour, inducing an attitude of reservation: 'the will to let myself be transformed by the work is limited.' Despite a personal detachment, the performer feels obliged, by an overall attitude indicating professionalism, to make an effort. As a rule, the dancer does not slack or count the hours but assumes a minimum of co-responsibility for both the work process and its final results. Positive criticism and constructive comments are regularly voiced in view of possible solutions, particularly when the choreographer is overtly contemplating various lines of possible action. The professional ethic of co-responsibility does not go that far that the performer will always defend the artistic value of the presented end product, were it to receive negative reviews or be greeted with public indifference. The choreographer is held accountable for the definitive performance's possible aesthetic shortcomings: the dancer only did the job reliably within a predefined configuration in which he or she had no direct personal or artistic stakes.

For the dance artist who assumes the role of performer, the ideal is a truly artistically motivated collaboration driven by two particular motives (which can both occur within a particular work relation). Whereas the first relates to the singular artistic vision of an esteemed dance maker, the second points to the furthering of one's personal capacities. A choreographer's creations may be so appealing that one wants to acquire a first-hand knowledge of the appreciated dance poetics through an active personal engagement with the artist: 'My collaboration with X had much to do with wanting to know how she works, how she "reads" people. You see the end product – and I value some of her projects very much – and you want to know how she arrives there. Essentially you want to get to know her as a choreographer.' In other words, *one wishes to become part of the working process because the final artistic work is strongly valued*. Also at play is the previously discussed quasi-magical logic of aura-contamination. One does not just enter a unique choreographic vision but becomes acquainted with its revered author, who as a rule already enjoys widespread recognition or is at least considered a promising dance maker. Hence an only rarely admitted strategic rationale might hide behind the initial wish for personal contact. For the aura of the renowned dance maker partly spills over to the performers: they gain in professional prestige, which may translate in increased market value. Indeed, working for prominent names serves one's CV or career portfolio rather well. The publicly professed desire to work for a personally appreciated choreographer can thus accord with, even warrant, the latent motive of raising one's professional capital.

The first reason seems to function as a necessary filter for the second. The idea that one assumes the role of performer mainly in view of an increased reputation is sometimes forcefully denied: 'I only do things I really believe in ... I would not want to work for someone whose work I don't really value positively.'

The pursuit of personal artistic development and possible growth predominates in the second motivation: dancers hope to sharpen already acquired skills and above all to explore performative possibilities as yet unknown. During a successful semi-directive collaboration they therefore regularly feel 'challenged' or stimulated 'to go beyond the limits of your comfort zone': the performer dares 'to take risks'. Accordingly, the work is at times experienced as an intense artistic self-confrontation. Personal limits shift and hitherto unimagined possibilities are effectively investigated on the suggestion of the choreographer: 'he gets you to do things that you thought you weren't capable of.' The dance maker acts as a quasi-demiurge who arouses previously unnoticed or unexplored capacities, because an established artistic identity formats – in a partly conscious, partly unconscious way – the dancer's activity. Provocative tasks or seemingly weird directions put to the test this imaginary self-image and the supporting *dance habitus* or the set of corporeal routines built up and stabilized through previous training and other activities. Or the choreographer just encourages the performer to engage in a novel practice such as acting and reciting text or soloing on a big stage. The dancer thus frequently enters – in Deleuzian parlance – into a process of becoming that momentarily de-segments or de-stratifies through a series of flight lines producing profound and often lasting cracks in the artistic self-image conditioning one's practice as a performer.

Self-transformation is a desired outcome: in sealing an artistically motivated collaboration, the dancer is often motivated by *the desire to go through a parallel process of artistic de- and re-subjectification*. The de-limitation regularly entails the discovery of new limitations: 'Being an artist is a rich experience because you bump into your own shit, into what you don't know, what you can't do...' However, some dancers – they represented a sizeable minority among my interlocutors – explicitly reject the logic of artistic self-discovery out of a negative association with the romantic vision of being an artist. They repudiate the idea of personal leaps or artistic growth, tending to view an artistically productive collaboration as a process of refining individual capacities in a thoughtful way. Personal artistic revolutions are dismissed in favour of a more modest evolution that a choreographer may further by inducing a thorough shift in perspective, one that teaches dancers to look at their own faculties through a different lens: 'It's less about the uncovering of a hidden dimension and more about a continual transformation of what I am able to do because this becomes something different through the way somebody else observes, whereupon you also do things differently. You pass via an external gaze in order to find internal solutions.'

Choreographers equally value the possibility of being profoundly challenged by the performers with whom they collaborate. A genuine desire to be positively irritated, forcing them to take a different view of the work-in-progress, invigorates their relationship with the dancers. Cognitive or informational irritation presupposes the existence of orienting anticipations that are subsequently refuted or contradicted. With every proposed task or verbalized feedback, the choreographer actually defines mostly implicit expectations about possible future movements, which loosely bind a performer's investigating activity and frame the dance maker's own inspection of the results. The ideally creative dancer personally appropriates and twists these expectations, thus suggesting new artistic possibilities to the choreographer: 'I like to work with people that do something other than what I tell them to do. I say "do this" and then I look and they are doing something else or slightly more, in the best case slightly more than what I imagined. That gives me other ideas and then it goes like magic.' The stimulating dancer generates variations that irritate the choreographer's expectations, without rejecting them. A thin line, however, separates the observation of a straightforward departure from a deviation that looks interesting and elicits new ideas. The distinction is in the eye of the beholder: the choreographer's gaze reigns. They have expectations, and anything that differs is valued either positively, as informative, or negatively, as merely noise.

Time is generally not on the side of those engaging in an artistic work relation: *a productive collaboration often exhausts itself through mutual habituation, inducing de-collaboration.* Thus the inspiring performer, whose surprising proposals once regularly opened up new horizons, over time transforms into a rather predictable resource that can no longer be provoked to act in a truly different way. In the gaze of the observing artist, repetition

begins to prevail over novelty: the 'magic' has waned. Choreographers in fact acknowledge that they regularly engage new
performers 'because after a while you lose interest in someone'.
Dancers often experience the non-intentional side effects of frequent interaction even more rapidly, particularly when working
with a renowned dance maker in the context of an established
company. One enters a semi-directive collaboration either in
view of a thorough first-hand knowledge of an esteemed choreographer's artistic universe or with the goal of personal development and artistic growth. In the first case, the effectively gathered
information already hollows out the initial motive after one or
two rehearsal periods; in the second case, the growing familiarity
with a specific mode of producing and choreographing material
results in a fading surplus: 'he no longer surprised me', 'There
was no longer a challenge'.

The self-destroying dynamic of creative collaborations can
be reflexively temporized by putting the work relation on hold after a first production or project, and possible re-activate it in the
future. The mutual habituation is thus spread out over a longer
period of time, yet in the end its negative consequences seem difficult to overcome. At stake is not only the increasing acquaintance
with a choreographer's poetics or a performer's artistic potential,
through reiterated interactions in which every action recursively
condenses into a next counter-action. As a social process, working
together also unavoidably produces, however vaguely, performative expectations about the other person's general individuality
– 'who she is' and 'who she can be'. These anticipations selectively frame observations, which in time tend to become self-
confirming, thus intensifying and accelerating the experience
that the other's new actions principally validate an already known
artistic identity. The self-produced deadlock of many artistic collaborations is the result of the awkward combination of, on the
one hand, socially generated and expected regularities, and on
the other, artistically desired and sought-after irregularities.

Intermezzo: Situating (Social) Structures
The word 'structure' connotes both temporal stability and the existence of a minimum of internal order or coherence. Indeed, over
a certain period of time a structure of whatever sort reduces the
virtual range of possibilities opened up by a particular potential.
The generic movement capacity of dancers becomes structured

through the many educational and self-training activities they engage in. The gradual emergence of a structured potential to dance amounts to the self-production of a set of stabilized corporeal routines. This is accompanied by an identification with a particular notion of the danceable, which strongly guides dancers' sense of legitimate and not so justifiable aesthetic possibilities. *A dancing subject's actual subjectivity* — once again, in the literal sense of the word *'subiectum'*: a 'bearing surface' or foundation — *resides precisely in the potentialities to move, think or feel that are structured by both a personal dance habitus and one's self-image as a dancer.* This double-sided identity can only be partially self-observed or consciously known and acts as an at once confining and abiding capacity. Within the opaque limits defined by their individual habitus and self-image, performers generate countless movements or poses and creatively interpret the tasks and comments given to them by a dance maker or peer, as well as the ones they themselves formulate. The same holds for the individuals affirming the status of choreographer: their subjectivity is also grounded in a structured potentiality, which informs their activity in a partly conscious, partly unconscious way.

A structure has a virtual nature and only exists through the continual iteration of the acts it simultaneously qualifies. The observable activity of moving, for instance, is the medium that the limiting structure both requires and orders: its sustenance hinges on that which it sustains. Through repeated variations and re-articulations of the supporting medial activity, a structure may be slightly altered or, on the contrary, undergo such a profound modification that the idea of structural change applies. Dance artists who emphatically reject the romantic myth of artistry tend to value and work within the horizon of aesthetic possibilities corresponding with their actual subjectivity. They do not feel the urge to radically transmute the underlying structure producing the difference between what they are momentarily able and unable to do. The opposite attitude, already hinted at, consists in actively searching for working contexts that advance processes of becoming that may renew the structured potentiality one actually is. The desire to transform one's artistic subjectivity equals a principally endless personal quest punctuated by temporary territorializations or re-subjectifications, and which may eventually come to a halt when a dancer feels that the subject-position he or she presently embodies fits their proper or 'real artistic self'. A plain paradox clearly distinguishes this journey: one acts on the basis of an organized potential in view of counter-acting, even re-arranging its limitations. Despite the notable differences in attitude they imply, both the 'gradualist' and the 'sudden conversion' approach presuppose the capacity to exercise self-discipline, through the deployment of various 'techniques of the self'. Michel Foucault, who coined the expression, gives this a specific meaning: a series of 'intentional and voluntary actions by which men not only set themselves rules of conduct, but also seek to transform themselves, to change themselves in their singular being'. A genuine rehearsal of human freedom is implied, one that does not invoke a mythical idea of individual autonomy, but points to a laborious work of re-creating the self through acts of self-empowerment, at once drawing on and addressing a structured potentiality.

'Social structures are expectational structures', Niklas Luhmann contends, in line with a long tradition of sociological thinking. 'Expectations come into being by constraining ranges of possibilities. Finally, they are this constraint itself.' A social structure reduces the scope of possible actions, including communications, within the relationships to which it pertains. The concomitant expectation or bundle of multiple anticipations may quasi-automatically emerge and fortify itself through the repeated implicit confirmation of all involved parties. Personal prospects thus change without much ado into shared expectations, structuring interaction by limiting the horizon of plausible individual activity. Take, for instance, the dancer who starts working with a choreographer and expects to be granted ample opportunities for co-creation. Without further conversational agreement, the choreographer meets this anticipation by allowing individual appropriations when proposing tasks or voicing feedback; consequently, a social structure regulating the interaction quickly stabilizes in the form of an implicit working consensus. Of course, the performer and the dance maker may opt for the alternative route and reflexively co-produce a set of mutually constraining expectations by explicitly discussing their respective views on artistic cooperation. Dancers and choreographers indeed frequently negotiate the overall terms of an envisaged collaboration before it actually starts. Yet whatever its nature, a social structure is mostly rather abstract: it points to a reduced potential of action still holding many possibilities. Social structures are in fact symbolic generalizations, guaranteeing situational adaptability but also requiring, again and again, a re-specification in the light of particular circumstances. A dancer and a choreographer, for instance, agree that they will cooperate in a truly semi-collaborative fashion: 'I expect to have a fair say in the creation process' (the dancer), 'I expect you to bring forth original material and to make innovative proposals' (the choreographer). The reflexively co-produced social structure framing their work relation significantly limits the possible actions of the two actors, yet it does not state what is appropriate in this or that specific situation. In other words, social structures are at once determinate and indeterminate: they only offer general guidelines and always open up a horizon of multiple alternatives of action and interaction. Even if they are explicitly discussed, shared anticipations therefore result in the possibility of inter-individual agreement and disagreement alike. General expectations are latently or manifestly agreed upon, with the risk of future disagreement on their contextual specification or interpretation: *no structured potentiality of collaboration without the possibility of disputes on its situational realization.*

The expectations that structure joint action essentially have a Janus face. Either they are related to a specific social position — regardless of the person he or she is dealing with, a dancer expects that a choreographer is professionally knowledgeable — or the anticipations are personal and address someone's individuality: on the basis of former interaction, a choreographer, for example, expects that a recently engaged performer will behave in a slightly reserved way but, despite 'her taciturn character', is highly willing to engage her artistic self. Both kinds of expectations may be confirmed or disproved by later actions or communications. The irritation generated by their non-fulfilment is by definition informative and creates a dual option: either the expectation holds or it is adjusted in light of the newly received information. When a performer observes that a choreographer is not that adept in reading movement material, he or she will probably not go so far as to conclude that it is inappropriate to expect interpretative deftness from a dance maker; the choreographer, on the contrary, repeatedly noticing over time that a dancer who was initially regarded as aloof begins to thrive and becomes more talkative, is likely to amend her person-directed expectations towards that individual. No easy middle-way exists between, on the one hand, a primarily cognitive processing of unfulfilled expectations, testifying of a readiness to learn and, on the other hand, their moral or normative defence against counter-factual evidence in the name of particular values or conceptions of what is desirable. Besides, when expectations are indeed based on values, the actual confirmation or non-fulfilment of those expectations generates esteem or non-esteem, respectively. Within the field of contemporary dance today, active co-creation is a rather influential ideal with corresponding strong normative expectations, which, if they actually are not met, may rapidly disqualify the sluggish or uninspired dancer and above all the overly directive choreographer. Seen through an ideal-typical lens, *the semi-directive mode of making dance together is nowadays a value-loaded or normative social structure and therefore an at once empirical and moral reality.*

One of the central normative expectations co-structuring participatory collaboration pertains to the general stance of choreographers. Despite their personal vision on contemporary dance, which may be greatly appreciated, they should be prepared to look for interesting qualities in movement material that may not completely fit their aesthetic taste. Performers therefore regularly invoke the moral semantic of openness that is one of the cornerstones of the broader legitimate culture which is nowadays regarded as self-evident by a considerable faction of the educated middle and upper classes. The open-minded person is able to handle irritations – again in the broad sense of ruptures between what one actually observes and quasi-spontaneously regards as right or wrong – without much visible effort and in a primarily cognitive mode. Accordingly, the choreographer must be willing to learn: this attitude – the word 'virtue' seems apt – preconditions the general possibility of discerning particular artistic possibilities in a collaborator's suggestions. Straightforward dismissals must therefore be avoided, as well as overtly valuating comments in terms of good or bad. In sum, the morality of openness asserts that it is wrong to plainly state that a performer's proposal is incorrect. Dancers find such a strong rebuttal rather uninformative, demotivating and see it as a sign of a complacent posture, going against the ethos of collaboration. Even for choreographers who fully embrace it, the value of openness frequently compels one to feign interest, to voice insincere feedback and to show enthusiasm when there is not really something to applaud. The communicative pretence is reflexively done, partly with an eye on one's moral status and particularly in view of a smooth cooperation: no shared morality without ritually paying lip service to its presupposed ethical validity.

Sharing Authorship: Saying 'I'

The making of a contemporary dance work equals the creation of new movements or poses and their final assemblage into a distinct choreographic plane of consistency that may convince the public. Overall, the regime of singularity reigns: whereas most dance makers aspire towards artistic originality, most performers join a choreographer with the hope of being truly creative during a rehearsal process. This shared personal yearning translates into the general expectation of being offered the possibility to co-create by the one commonly regarded as the principal creator. Given the agreed upon starting points or the initial problematic inspiring a collaboration, the dancer expects encouragement when putting forward personal artistic propositions, various opportunities to improvise or to probe tasks, as well as the chance to dialogue in an open way. The temporary work frames suggested by the choreographer should indeed not act as mandatory imperatives but rather contain an invitation for individual appropriation. In discussing collaboration, dancers therefore often call themselves 'interpreters'. The expression apparently involves a great deal of personal passivity: a performer obediently executes pre-given actions in the context of an already set choreography. Yet in relation to the preparation of a new dance work, the very same word points to the possibility of actively making sense of a choreographer's proposals. In sum, as interpreter the performer is granted a considerable amount of *interpretative flexibility* in dealing with assigned tasks or received feedback. Choreographers going for the semi-directive mode of collaboration widely endorse this idea: 'I want to work with makers and cooperate with – say – self-motivated, reflecting "movers" because that creates frictions and I have to convince them even harder. These are people that do not just move goody-goody in accordance with some little system but try to break out of it.'

'Research' is the, at once simple and – given its many connotations – complex, term that dance artists regularly invoke to describe the desired labour configuration. Stripped of its more rigorous scientific meaning, referring to exact methods, and disregarding the more specific practices of, for instance, preparatory investigations and autonomous movement research, the notion first and foremost points to a quasi-experimental social situation in which the dancer's propositions are not immediately assessed in terms of successes or failures. In a stimulating work relationship, the exploration of personal capacities nearly seamlessly

fuses with a collective research that is loosely animated but not too strongly guided by directing concepts, tentative phrases, or previously generated material. Artistic risk-taking is encouraged, which is incompatible with high production pressure and the envisioning of straightforward outcomes. Accordingly, making dance together in a research-like fashion is an open process from at least a double point of view. The choreographer and the dancers continually re-work material because they are looking for yet another interesting action or a fitting movement possibility still to surface. Indeed, during a creation, the 're-' in re-search points to a time-consuming search for possibly definitive options through a countless series of re-interpretative attempts. Moreover, the precise stakes of a particular sequence and the envisaged work as a whole are also collectively explored: both gradually take shape in the course of often unpredictable joint actions and countless conversations. A peculiar dialectic is involved, one that continually moves back and forth between the general and the particular. Momentary feedback and broad guidelines, perhaps inspired by underlying concepts, frame impromptu research activities that at once translate and exceed the communicated directions and concomitant expectations. These situated actions thus generate surprising results that urge the collaborating group to re-think the informing problematic, even to re-articulate leading ideas: 'so we're working on something in a certain direction, and then we find something very interesting that is not what I had thought before we started. For me the process is very often about that, about finding out what is the interest and where it comes together.'

No collaboration as co-creation without effective co-authorship, which essentially amounts to *the possibility of subjectification or saying 'I'*. Dancers desire to be given the opportunity to thoroughly individualize the overall work frame or particular tasks: they may transform both in keeping with their own interests and personal artistic potential. The performers can thus identify with what they are actually doing, as well as with the emerging creation, since the material they bring forth co-originates in 'them-selves'. 'I say I': an individual dancer ('I' or subjectivity in the generic sense) communicates individuality ('I' as subjectification) through the singularization of personal capacities. Collaboration temporarily loses this longed for creative dimension when the chances for subjectification are dim: 'then it's just work... It feels like gymnastics.' In situations not occasioning the possibility to inalienably effectuate – or at least partly actualize – individual artistic choices and possibilities, performers frequently switch to a detached mode of second order-observation, no longer engaging the self in a unifying way. The mind sees the body doing things out of obligation and simultaneously presses it to give lukewarm answers to the constraining external questions, whose artistic value is personally doubted. In these moments, artistic collaboration in the stricter sense starts to stagnate and changes into the mode of cooperation structuring the instrumental 'working for'-relationship, primarily entered into for financial reasons.

Dancers explicitly define work relationships against the backdrop of the normative social expectation that there will be a sufficient degree of artistic engagement, allowing for a real subjectification to occur. They therefore stick to this definition of the desirable when assessing a creation process: the choreographer has to meet the standard. Recurrent disappointments add up to the negative interpretation of an actual work context and are often given as a decisive reason to terminate the cooperation with a choreographer for good after a piece is finished. Overall, four scenarios may lead to a performer's decision to end a work relationship that is not economically motivated. Nourished by a growing number of less positive personal experiences, the performer may gradually realize that a cooperation, initially framed as semi-directive, in reality tends towards the directive mode. The discovery may be experienced, at times with a serious dose of moral anger when discussed retrospectively, as the breaking of an explicit engagement: 'She did not allow any point of view outside of her own frame of mind!' The resentment will be all the greater if a repeatedly voiced discontent regarding the impossibility to say 'I' is met by indifference or with a renewed promise of co-creation that is afterwards not fulfilled at all or only partially. In the second scenario, the dancer working in a company already for some time observes an increasing production pressure once the choreographer, who previously offered ample room for research, becomes more successful. A mostly tacit imperative to realize a specific aesthetic or a peculiar performing style begins to prevail over the chances to experiment. The dance maker now clearly goes for a predefined end result: 'The discussion on propositions happens much more in terms of "it works, it doesn't work".' All in all, 'the economic' seems to increasingly dominate 'the aesthetic', which also raises doubts as to a choreographer's artistic integrity and may arouse in the dancer the uncomfortable feeling that 'it's just work'. There is also the frequent side effect that growing success implies longer tours of the same piece. Although dancers greatly value being on stage, re-performing a work again and again often procures less physical or artistic pleasure over time. 'You become bored by doing the same kind of thing evening after evening': the enthusiastic applause at the end of the show no longer compensates for the individual energy that is required to stage a piece night after night.

The third implicit script directly involves the dancers themselves. Over time they feel more and more typecast because the choreographer increasingly directs them on the basis of a fixed image or a difficult to contest conception of their artistic abilities. 'The subject supposed to know' is now experienced as a powerful framer who lost curiosity in the dancer's non-charted potential: 'He no longer wanted to give me the time I needed for exploring other possibilities. I had the feeling that I was always playing the same role.' Typecasting often originates in a choreographer's observation that a dancer excels in a particular movement style or is highly proficient in relation to a defined set of technical demands. Yet a negatively inspired self-fulfilling prophecy can also confine performers to a stereotype of their artistic self. Upon noticing that a performer is not so good at producing a particular kind of desired movement material, a dance maker may infer that further investments are too time-consuming. The choreographer subsequently limits tasks and feedback to the dancer's presumably positive capacities and holds this line of action when the assumption is repeatedly confirmed. Non-intentional typecasting thus results from a choreographer's well-intentioned attempt to get the best possible performance out of a dancer in the light of available production time. Last but not least, performers who themselves regularly assume the counter-position of dance maker at times become discontent while collaborating because the choreographer looks unwilling or incapable of refining self-developed proposals. The option to switch roles and to self-direct the dismissed suggestions is mulled over and subsequently realized: 'You feel very uncomfortable, up to the point where you think "I can no longer complain, I have to do it myself, I have to test and see the material's potential myself, I have to find out if the questions I'm asking are answerable".' Proposals that are denied to have genuine value by a peer thus loop back into one's own artistic practice. However, the performer may also take along a rejected mode of moving the body or its underlying problematic to a different collaboration, in which it will be artistically re-contextualized. Due to the substantial labour mobility in the world of contemporary dance, this kind of transfer is actually happening all the time and not only includes materials or capacities momentarily deemed uninteresting. The flexible regime of artistic accumulation indeed advances a remarkable kind of implicit trafficking in the potentialities of movements and poses, general 'dance ideas' or singular performing bodies. They are selectively realized a first time in an always specific context and later on re-performed in one or more different work relations. Each singular collaboration thus indirectly contributes to the potential productivity of various others. *The continual nomadism of the artistic possibilities opened up by distinct dancing bodies, concepts or actions, and ways of collaborating perhaps defines contemporary dance's most crucial production force.*

Coda: Capitalizing Expressive Individualism

Around the mid-1970s, the American sociologist Talcott Parsons observed that the counter-culture and youth protest of the late-1960s signalled a deeper shift. A wider 'expressive revolution' was happening: various forms of authority and discipline, previously accepted as evident, were from then on contested in the name of personal self-development and the individual right 'to be oneself' or the value of authenticity. This profound cultural transformation has meanwhile shattered the once existing clear-cut hierarchical, command-based and vastly male controlled social order in institutional domains as diverse as education, health care, the family and politics. In the wake of the broader 'silent revolution' (Ronald Inglehart) which was only partially brought into the open during 'the roaring sixties', classic bourgeois materialism and its combined stress on private comfort and social standing was replaced by a post-materialist morality primarily privileging personal well-being through a preferably unmediated expression of individual capacities. The value change also affected contemporary dance: Judson Church was actually a seismographic forerunner of a much vaster tectonic shift. Already during the first half of the 1960s, this artistic movement emphatically rejected the authoritarian social functioning of the ballet world in favour of an informal cooperation based on social equality. It also deliberately turned down the disciplined ballet body in view of a much more freely moving and scenic performativity (Contact Improvisation would later partly re-codify this consequent search for 'democracy's body'). Yet several movements and artists preceded Judson Church's historical gesture, witness Isadora Duncan's early and firm rebuttal of classical ballet. Modern art's regime of singularity in general and its various romantic manifestations in particular are indeed the historical laboratory of contemporary 'expressivism'. This mode of self-caring has meanwhile supplemented the previously institutionalized forms of individualism. Whereas economic or instrumental individualism hails the calculative ego rationally pursuing self-interests, moral individualism primarily applauds human being's capability to be self-legislating and to gain in autonomy through a personally willed self-discipline consistently committed to the realization of an ethical ideal. Expressive individualism completes this cultural duo with a distinguished emphasis on the self as a potential that may be unearthed in such a way that there no longer seems to exist a gap between what one actually does or says and what one really is.

The current biopolitical economy, which thrives on generic capacities such as communication, imagining or feeling, has meanwhile selectively appropriated 'the expressive revolution' in the sphere of the creative economy (which is a partly ideological notion simultaneously pointing to a real change in the current production of economic value). Expressive individualism is indeed the solid cultural backdrop of the social expectations that frame, in various domains, so-called immaterial labour or, in the words of Michael Hardt and Antonio Negri, 'labour that produces an immaterial good, such as a service, a cultural product, knowledge, or communication'. Overall, the daily organization of immaterial labour greatly resembles the dominant mode of making dance together: *the semi-directive regime of participatory collaboration is, in today's 'creative capitalism', a widespread mode of generating economic value and surplus value.* In the various sectors involving creative work, ranging from ICT-innovation and scientific research to the many faces of the culture industry, labour has a direct social or cooperative nature that is aptly symbolized by both collective 'brainstorms' in the sphere of face-to-face sociality and the continuous, project-driven exchange of information through digital communication networks. Bosses have become coaches and lean organizations with relatively flat hierarchies are preferred over the numbing rigor of top-down bureaucracy and its many constraining rules. 'People managers' encourage workers to be co-creative and 'to give the best of themselves'. Realizing individual capacities is effectively furthered: one's personal 'human capital' is explicitly valued. In sum, being a productive immaterial worker equals self-development and vice versa: the maxim previously restricted to artistic labour nowadays underlies the social structures regulating diverse sorts of work. There is of course a proverbial dark side that puts the paradoxical nature of the heteronomous autonomy characterizing semi-directive collaboration in a different light. For the worker's prospect of actualizing a however structured potential to speak, think, imagine or feel fits the employer's desire to exploit it or to extract surplus value.

'The new spirit of capitalism' has partly incorporated 'the artistic critique' on self-estranging disciplines and bureaucratic hierarchies precluding personal creativity at the price of a growing social insecurity and inequality, as Luc Boltanski and Eve Chiapello have forcefully argued. This rather bleak diagnosis also holds for the world of contemporary dance. Economically and symbolically, the labour market for dance artists looks strikingly stratified nowadays and in fact seems to permanently gravitate towards a dual structure of over- and under-demand. Those in the small upper segment, who are held in high esteem and are always met with new interesting proposals, can be artistically selective and earn well (or even enjoy a considerable income, though this only holds true for choreographers). With notable differences between countries and possibly significant annual variations in work conditions and the related financial rewards, most dancers and choreographers belong to the creative 'precariat'. Their unenviable average labour conditions were already briefly alluded to: they hop from contract to project subsidy and cannot take pride in a widely validated artistic recognition or symbolic capital; consequently, they regularly have to accept less interesting jobs within or outside the arts and are already happy if they can earn a modest yearly income. Yet 'the new spirit of capitalism' has also pervaded the functioning of artistic fields through the by now widespread adoption of the neoliberal management logic and its concomitant market ethic. Partly under the pressure of funding agencies, a growing number of art organizations have first hesitantly copied and then fully endorsed the values of entrepreneurialism, turn-over growth and public or market-impact in their daily practices. The current field of contemporary dance is no exception to this general trend.

Indeed, a wider institutional context, not discussed in detail here, structurally informs dance artists' social-economic vulnerability under the regime of flexible artistic accumulation. Western-European performers unequally compete in an open transnational market for access to artistically furthering collaborations or for work opportunities merely enabling them to make a living. In turn, the dance companies and project choreographers channelling this over-demand vie for limited government subsidies and negotiate co-production money, mostly also indirectly stemming from official funding bodies with scarce means. Together with solo artists, they produce singular works for a whimsical dance market that constantly creates fads as well as foibles, because programmers are always looking for new talents who offer a symbolic profit that may be economically capitalized upon. Various gatekeepers, such as festival organizers or the artistic directors of theatres, act as firm mediators between the international market for contemporary dance performances and those trying to gain access to it. Due to the overproduction that has become more or less chronic after the 're-boot' of contemporary dance 'made in Europe' in the 1980s, the markets for both individual labour and artistic products are hypercompetitive. The crucial point, however, is that a growing number of contemporary dance actors effectively see themselves and their environment in neoliberal management and marketing terms. Despite the still reigning official disavowal of 'the economic', those keeping the books in artistic organizations today routinely take decisions on the premise that the various forms of flexible work are economically preferable over long-term contracts; moreover, they approach dance performances as distinctive products whose potential symbolic value must be adequately promoted by all communicative means in view of critical recognition and the ensuing economic gains securing new investments. The bottom line runs like this: a dance artist's potential is a distinctive human capital that must be managed as cost-efficiently and as labour-intensively as possible; and a choreography is a cultural commodity whose market value predominantly depends on a structurally contingent sign value that can be strategically framed.

Within contemporary dance and other art worlds, the seemingly contrasting logics of neoliberalism and personal creativity directly meet in the widely interiorized imperative of self-productivity. More and more artists are looking in 'the mirror of production', whose rather perverse imaginary effects Jean Baudrillard already noticed in the dominant tradition of critical theorizing. From Karl Marx to Gilles Deleuze, this influential line of thought celebrates the prospect of an unbound productiveness of labour or desire – or yet another dimension, considered crucial for the human condition, such as communication – against its constraining, if not outright repression by the powers that be. Without further qualifications, the argument risks to uncritically duplicate the capitalistic adage that a human being's worth is to be as productive as possible and therefore no chances of being active should be lost or overlooked. The ideal-typical artistic self nowadays frequently behaves accordingly, combining the ethos of self-productivity with a more or less explicit entrepreneurialism: it resembles, in more than one respect, a hyperactive 'Me, Inc.'. It bets on the possibility of actualizing, through successive work settings, singular capacities within the context of an overall neoliberal economic and cultural climate, which presents individual choices as determinant. For the majority of those populating the world of contemporary dance, artistic self-valorization does in fact equal economic self-exploitation (self-precarisation was the somewhat friendlier expression introduced earlier on). A general equation, whose empirical exactness is of the order of the sardonic over-statement, could be put forward as a tentative conclusion: to be personally creative = to further or transform a personal potentiality, functioning as an individual artistic capital, in a hypercompetitive market = to be continually self-productive or to say 'I', regardless of economic rewards = to initiate preferably artistically motivated participatory collaborations, characterized by heteronomous autonomy = co-producing externally appropriated (surplus) value = a statistically significant chance to lead the life of an underpaid flexible worker, continuously networking in view of more conducive opportunities to be creative. In the light of this series of equations a simple question arises: how can the aspiration to lead a creative life and the underlying expressive individualism be critically displaced and turned into oppositional forces again? How may the current entanglement of personal creativity and social productivity, self-precarisation and competitive exploitation be temporarily halted or at least minimally deconstructed? A possible answer, already alluded to in the third chapter, insists on the subversive potential of the impotentiality that every

structured potentiality by definition implies. *Within the neoliberal regime of flexible accumulation, criticality perhaps first and foremost amounts to the, however momentary, interruption of the (self-) capitalizing of expressive individualism through collective gestures that refuse economic productivity and affirm impotence.* Possibly this self-negating activity, positioning itself as a 'means without ends', delineates the primary critical horizon of artistic collaboration. At stake is the co-existence as a, in principle, creative capacity that does not realize itself or, in the words of Giorgio Agamben, 'a potentiality that has as its object potentiality itself, a *potentia potentiae*', 'a power that is capable of both power and impotence'.

Sources

Dance Capital Brussels
Somewhat dated empirical findings and general insights on the Brussels/Flemish contemporary dance world can be found in the collective publication *Canaries in the Coal Mine: Master Plan for Dance in Flanders and Brussels.* Brussels: Flemish Theatre Institute, 2007. The first decade of P.A.R.T.S. is recollected and put into perspective from various angles in Steven De Belder and Theo Van Rompay (eds.), *P.A.R.T.S. – Documenting Ten Years of Contemporary Dance Education.* Brussels: P.A.R.T.S., 2006. My brief characterization of the school's curriculum and overall functioning refers to the period preceding the introduction in 2013-14 of a 3+2 years bachelor-master structure. Elisabeth Currid discusses the social dynamic propelling creative scenes in *The Warhol Economy. How Fashion, Art and Music Drive New York City.* Princeton (NJ): Princeton University Press, 2007, quoted p. 110. The citation from Eleanor Bauer stems from her 2007 essay 'Becoming Room, Becoming Mac. New Artistic Identities in the Transnational Brussels Dance Community', which can be retrieved from www.b-kronieken.be. On the notion of transnationalism, see for instance Ulf Hannerz, *Transnational Connections: Culture, People, Places.* London: Routledge, 1996.

Intermezzo: Dance Artists' Precarity
The expression 'regime of flexible artistic accumulation' is inspired by Michel Aglietta's work on various historical regimes of capitalist accumulation; see for instance Michel Aglietta, *A Theory of Capitalist Regulation. The US Experience.* London: Verso, 1987. Guy Standing extensively analyses the current forms of precarious labour in *The Precariat. The New Dangerous Class.* London: Bloomsbury Academic, 2011. In-depth discussions of the precarious nature of artistic work can be found in Bernadette Loacker, *Kreativ Prekär. Künstlerische Arbeit und Subjektivität im Postfordismus.* Bielefeld: transcript Verlag, 2010 and Pierre-Michel Menger, *Portrait de l'artiste en travailleur. Métamorphoses du capitalisme.* Paris: Seuil, 2003. Isabell Lorey's quoted essay 'Virtuosos of Freedom. On the Implosion of Political Virtuosity and Productive Labour' was published in Gerald Raunig, Gene Ray and Ulf Wuggenig (eds.), *Critique of Creativity. Precarity, Subjectivity and Resistance.* London: Mayfly Books, 2011, pp. 79-90 (p. 87). Nathalie Heinich dissects the vocational regime in *L'élite artiste. Excellence et singularité en regime démocratique.* Paris: Gallimard, 2005, quoted p. 124 (italics in the original). Though it is much cited, the distinction that Max Weber makes between 'living for' and 'living from' politics, is evidently not the most substantial idea in this famous lecture 'The Profession and Vocation of Politics', reprinted in Max Weber, *Political Writings.* Cambridge: Cambridge University Press, 2010, pp. 309-369 (p. 318). The idea that making sacrifices belongs to 'the specific capital' artists may claim, is put forward by Gérard Mauger in 'Le capital spécifique', in Gérard Mauger (ed.), *L'accès à la vie d'artiste. Sélection et consecration artistiques.* Broisseux: Editions du Croquant, 2006, pp. 237-253 (p. 242). Hans Abbing spells out in detail how the vocational stance helps to explain the low income of most fine artists in his study *Why Are Artists Poor? The Exceptional Economy of the Arts.* Amsterdam: Amsterdam University Press, 2002.

Revisiting Rosas Anno 1995
Max Weber discusses the notion of the ideal type in the introductory chapter 'Basic Sociological Terms' of his posthumously published magnum opus *Economy and Society. An Outline of Interpretative Sociology.* Berkeley (CA): University of California Press, 1978, pp. 3-62. The strongly directive and hierarchical labour context in traditional ballet companies is well documented in Helena Wulff's anthropological study *Ballet Across Borders. Career and Culture in the World of Dancers.* Oxford: Berg, 1998 (which also includes perceptive observations on the much more participatory work style within the then Frankfurt Ballet, directed by William Forsythe).

The dancers who participated in the creation process of *Verklärte Nacht* were Marion Ballester, Iris Bouche, Misha Downey, Kosi Hidama, Suman Hsu, Osman Kassen Khelili, Oliver Koch, Brice Leroux, Marion Lévy, Cynthia Loemij, Mark Lorimer, Sarah Ludi, Anne Mousselet, Johanne

Saunier and Samantha Van Wissen. I am still very grateful to Anne Teresa De Keersmaeker for her permission to attend the production process and to the dancers for their hospitality toward the socially displaced 'intruder' wanting to study the company's labour sociality. With the exception of a couple of informal academic presentations, and one much later published article in Dutch, the collected material has not been translated into publicly available results. The decisive reason was that Rosas' public status made some of the gathered data and insights somewhat sensitive (the offered portrait is of course a historical snapshot and has therefore no principal validity for the current work context in the Rosas company). For the Dutch article summarizing the main results of the fieldwork, which is sometimes used verbatim in this and the next paragraph, see Rudi Laermans, 'De sociabiliteit van een danssstudio (een sociologische herinnering) [The sociability of a dance studio (a sociological recollection)]', in *De Witte Raaf*, (115), 2005, pp. 9–10.

The Choreographer's Gaze
The notion of peer coaching is borrowed from the chapter 'Work as Vocation' in Helena Wulff, *Ballet Across Borders*, pp. 59–88. My use of the expression 'attention regime' is loosely inspired by Dutch sociologist Abram de Swaan's acute observations on the importance of being noticed and given personal time in a very different social setting – the cancer department of a medical hospital – as reported in 'Affect Management in a Cancer Ward' in Abram de Swaan, *The Management of Normality. Critical Essays in Health and Welfare*. London: Routledge, 1990, pp. 31–56. Jacques Lacan introduced the notion of 'the subject supposed to know' in his 1967 essay 'The Mistaking of the Subject Supposed to Know', retrieved from http://web.missouri. edu/~stonej/mistak.pdf.

'Being Hurt' and the Logic of Symbolic Exchange
Pierre-Emmanuel Sorignet discusses the relation between the validating role of the renowned choreographer and dancers' insecurity about their legitimate belonging to the world of contemporary dance in *Danser. Enquête dans les coulisses d'une*

vocation. Paris: La Découverte, 2010, pp. 142–144 (p. 143). Judith Butler argues that human life equals precariousness in her essay 'Violence, Mourning, Politics', which is included in Judith Butler, *Precarious Life. The Powers of Mourning and Violence*. London: Verso, 2006, pp. 19–49 (p. 31). Moreover, reference is made to Karl Marx, *Capital. A Critique of Political Economy (Volume 1)*. Harmondsworth: Penguin, 1976 (the notion of surplus value); Marcel Mauss, *The Gift. Form and Functions of Exchange in Archaic Societies*. London: Cohen & West, 1966, p. 45 and p. 10; and David Graeber, *Toward An Anthropological Theory of Value. The False Coin of Our Own Dreams*. New York (NY): Palgrave, 2001, p. 220.

Talking Contemporary Dance
The twenty interviewed dancers-choreographers whose statements guide me in the remaining part of this chapter and the next one are: Alexander Baervoets, Varinia Canto Vila, Claire Croizé, Ugo Dehaes, Andy Deneys, Tale Dolven, Vincent Dunoyer, Alix Eynaudi, Davis Freeman, Nada Gambier, Domenico Giustino, Etienne Guilloteau, David Hernandez, Mette Ingvartsen, Heike Langsdorf, Agata Maszkiewicz, Lilia Mestre, Erna Omarsdottir, Salva Sanchis and Vincent Tirmarche. I owe them all many thanks for the time and often illuminating insights they shared with me.

Labouring/Becoming: Modes of Cooperation
Ralf Dahrendorf's *Homo Sociologicus* (London: Routledge, 1973) remains the locus classicus on the difference between social role and person. The distinction is put into perspective in the overall concept of social expectations loosely used throughout this paragraph; it is further clarified in the next one and is much indebted to the chapter 'Structure and Time' in Niklas Luhmann, *Social Systems*. Stanford (CA): Stanford University Press, 1995, pp. 278–356. Luhmann's work also inspires the deployed notion of irritation; see for instance the chapter 'Irritations and Values' in Niklas Luhmann, *Theory of Society. Volume 1*. Stanford (CA): Stanford University Press, 2013, pp. 115–123. The concept of dance habitus is grounded in Pierre Bourdieu's perceptive highlighting

of the conditioning nature of various sorts of corporeal routines, as it is for instance discussed in Pierre Bourdieu, *The Logic of Practice*. Cambridge: Polity Press, 1992. On becoming and the implied processes of de- and re-subjectification, see Gilles Deleuze and Félix Guattari, *A Thousand Plateaus. Capitalism and Schizophrenia*. London: Continuum, 2003.

Intermezzo: Situating (Social) Structures

The approach to structures in general and social structures in particular presented here draws heavily on the already mentioned chapter 'Structure and Time' in Niklas Luhmann, *Social Systems*, pp. 278–356 (p. 292). By contrast, the idea that a dancer's subjectivity primarily involves a particular self-image and habitus re-takes with markedly different, Bourdieu-inspired, accents the agency-model proposed by Anthony Giddens in the first two chapters of *The Constitution of Society. Outline of the Theory of Structuration*. Cambridge: Polity Press, 1984, pp. 1–109. Michel Foucault extensively discusses 'techniques of the self' in *The Use of Pleasure. The History of Sexuality Volume 2*. London: Penguin, 1992, quoted p. 10.

Sharing Authorship: Saying 'I'

The concept of interpretative flexibility originates in the field of Science & Technology Studies and was originally put forward by Trevor J. Pinch and Wiebe E. Bijker in 'The Social Construction of Facts and Artifacts: Or How the Sociology of Science and the Sociology of Technology Might Benefit Each Other', in Wiebe E. Bijker, Thomas P. Hughes and Trevor J. Pinch (eds.), *The Social Construction of Technological Systems. New Directions in the Sociology and History of Technology*. Cambridge (MA): MIT Press, 1987, pp. 17–50. Multiple viewpoints exist on the no longer novel but still much discussed notion of artistic research; for an interesting sample, see Annette Balkema and Henk Slager (eds.), *Artistic Research*. Amsterdam: Rodopi, 2004.

Coda: Capitalizing Expressive Individualism

Talcott Parsons situates 'the expressive revolution' against the backdrop of instrumental and moral individualism in the essay 'Individuality and Institutionalized Individualism', which is included in Talcott Parsons, *American Society. A Theory of the Societal Community*. Boulder (CO): Paradigm Publishers, 2007, pp. 424–510. The concomitant value-change is empirically documented in Ronald Inglehart, *The Silent Revolution. Changing Values and Political Styles Among Western Publics*. Princeton (NJ): Princeton University Press, 1977; for an update and further elaboration, see Ronald Inglehart and Christian Wenzel, *Modernization, Cultural Change and Democracy. The Human Development Sequence*. Cambridge: Cambridge University Press, 2005. Daniel Bell situates the artistic roots of expressive individualism in *The Cultural Contradictions of Capitalism*. New York (NY): Basic Books, 1976. The concepts of 'bio-political production' and 'immaterial labour' were coined within the Italian tradition of Autonomous Marxism and gained wider currency thanks to Michael Hardt and Antonio Negri, *Empire*. Cambridge (MA): Harvard University Press, 2000, quoted p. 290. Luc Boltanski and Eve Chiapello distinguish 'artistic critique' from 'social critique' and analyse 'the new spirit of capitalism' at length in *The New Spirit of Capitalism*. London: Verso, 2005. Pascal Gielen clarifies how this spirit has pervaded the arts and defines current practices within the creative economy in his inspiring and aptly titled book-essay, *Creativity and Other Fundamentalisms*. Amsterdam: Mondriaan Fund, 2013. Also referenced are Sally Banes, *Democracy's Body. Judson Dance Theater, 1962-1964*. Durham (NC): Duke University Press, 1993; Jean Baudrillard, *The Mirror of Production*. New York (NY): Telos Press, 1975; Giorgio Agamben, *Means without End. Notes on Politics*. Minneapolis (MN): University of Minnesota Press, 2000; and Agamben's short essay 'Bartleby' in Giorgio Agamben, *The Coming Community*. Minneapolis (MN): University of Minnesota Press, pp. 35–37 (p. 36).

The Social Choreographies of Collaboration
Tracing Conditions of Artistic Cooperation and 'Commoning'

First Movement: Qualifying Artistic Agency

Trusting/Distrusting 'the Artistic Subject Supposed to Know'

'Collaboration is about choosing the right people to work with, and then trusting them', dance maker Jonathan Burrows remarks in one of his many perspicacious thoughts collected in *A Choreographer's Handbook*. Mutual trust indeed greatly conditions the success of both collective live performing and the many hours of cooperative work it presupposes. No thriving artistic collaboration without reciprocal trust: whereas the dancer must have faith in the choreographer's vision and professional capacities, the dance maker must in turn have confidence in the performer. The dancer's trusted professional capital consists of a strictly artistic potential, including technical skills, the personal ability to eventually persevere when work becomes arduous, and the multi-layered social competence to behave politely, to be communicatively articulate and to dialogue with an open mind. There is also the trust that, in assembling a particular group, the future collaborators will reasonably relate to each other and a socially productive configuration is initiated: 'It's the most important decision in the preparation of a project. I think somebody said that 95% of the success of a project depends on the casting – while it's something that you do in the very beginning, when you know very little about the project. So you have 5% freedom in working with that constellation of people.' When engaging a new dancer, a choreographer can of course build on a loose combination of various observations: the performer enjoys a good professional reputation, is persuasive on stage or during an audition, was already experienced as highly stimulating during a workshop or informal conversations, and so on. However, even a fairly reliable knowledge of a dancer's capacities never offers complete certainty about their future behaviour in the singular context of the commenced cooperation.

To put one's confidence in someone is actually a particular way of dealing with the other's freedom as an autonomous subject. The trusting choreographer looks into the rearview mirror in order to have a minimal cognitive grip on a dancer's upcoming, contingent actions: he or she believes that in the future the other will behave more or less as in the past. In premising this personal consistency and temporal continuity, the performer's liberty to act differently, especially in a new work setting, is negated.

Moreover, an unavoidably incomplete picture of the collaborator's artistic potentiality and personality is magnified into a quasi-essence, a rather reductive and highly selective identity card. In the light of all disposable information, the choreographer presupposes that the dancer will show a genuine zest for work and be co-creative, act co-responsibly and communicate constructively. Yet trusting someone unavoidably involves a leap of faith. 'In the last resort, no decisive grounds can be offered for trusting: trust always extrapolates from the available evidence; it is ... a blending of knowledge and ignorance', Niklas Luhmann notes. Although many plausible reasons may be invoked, 'trust remains a risky undertaking': no future trust without the ever-present chance of being disappointed, even feeling betrayed. Nevertheless, cooperative work of the creative sort cannot do without a serious dose of reciprocal confidence: *the risk that a co-creation process may go wrong is exchanged for the risk of mutual trust.*

In line with the already highlighted symbolic logic of gift and counter-gift, the choreographer's visible trust in their individual capacities is met by the cooperating dancers' faith in the other's professional know-how and personal artistic vision, which may have motivated the cooperation in the first place. The choreographer is indeed 'the artistic subject supposed to know', the one assumed to have at least a vague idea of the principal stakes of the rehearsal process: he or she will be able to trace out a general artistic line informing specific tasks, personal feedback and collective discussions. This shared artistic faith greatly conditions the work relation's potential success and social productivity, since it creates a climate that fosters individual risk-taking: trust engages. Research activity may thus momentarily drift away from the initially agreed upon framing problematic. As long as the choreographer can formulate, however tentatively, reasons for encouraging inquisitiveness, diverse side roads can be explored without the dancers losing the belief that the developed material will serve the creation. In sum, artistic trust enables and stimulates the kind of guided experimenting most performers long for in a collaborative venture. Their confidence in the principal author enhances their self-confidence, which again furthers the personal appetite to explore hitherto unknown facets of their potentiality to dance and think dance.

The joint faith in a choreographer also significantly complements and even partly curtails the general expectation of

co-authorship or the possibility to say 'I'. The dancer's desire 'to have a fair share' in both a creation process and the final product is balanced by the personal trust that the dance maker effectively knows 'what the choreography needs' and how the artistic vision underlying a creation process must be implemented through all sorts of micro-decisions. Confirming once again the paradoxical nature of the semi-directive labour regime, *artistic trust generates both a general climate encouraging dancers' autonomy and a relatively non-disputed source of heteronomous authority*, legitimating the choreographer's directivity. Interim selections or decisive final cuts are therefore frequently regarded as artistically justified, particularly when the dance maker has amply demonstrated personal proficiency in rather difficult situations. Personal doubts on the actual usefulness of a task or the purpose of reworking a movement sequence are momentarily put on hold: 'When I have faith, I know that the choreographer knows better than I do what the piece is about, so I'm not going to contest.' Artistic confidence thus greatly facilitates the communication and acceptance of what could otherwise be viewed as negative decisions. The trusted choreographer can criticise personal propositions or choose not to include a performer's self-created movements in the final performance without immediately being regarded as a dictator. Perhaps dancers diplomatically defend their material or publicly voice a different opinion on the route taken, but in the end they acquiesce if they have confidence in 'the artistic subject supposed to know' and perform the choreographer's directions faithfully.

A genuine cycle of trust, which augments the amount of collective trust-capital invested in a project, characterizes the semi-directive collaboration experienced as prolific. Not unlike the logic of reinvesting gains in a profit-bringing asset, confirmed artistic trust enhances the confidence the dancers have already invested in a dance maker. Thus the joint faith grows substantially when the choreographer is recurrently able to detail his or her personal vision through appropriate tasks and articulated feedback. Displaying rather general competences, such as being encouraging, facilitating ordered dialogue and organizing work in an at once efficient and humane way, may supplement the otherwise relationally stabilized artistic confidence with professional trust. Both forms of trust commonly merge into a somewhat fuzzy notion of personal trust: the dancers have faith in the choreographer as such. However, even a self-propelling trust cycle remains highly vulnerable. At any moment, a relation of confidence can go wrong and quite abruptly transform into its opposite. Rather minimal gestures may produce maximal distrust. Not that many public signs of private vacillating are necessary for dancers to draw the conclusion that the dance maker lacks professional craftsmanship or a genuine personal vision. The choreographer who appeared trustworthy during several consecutive weeks thus suddenly raises collective doubts when he or she begins to utter inconsistent comments punctuated by long silences and is no longer able to provide convincing arguments during discussions. Several days with visible signs of not-knowing can effectively ruin a collaborators' faith: 'Once you start to doubt the choreographer, you are no longer there – you start to reflect, you become introspective, you observe yourself doing this or that.' The collective suspension of trust often produces less willingness to accept the dance maker's decisions unquestioningly. Directions, tasks and feedback are now repeatedly contested and discussed, which eventually results in long debates confirming the choreographers' perceived lack of decisiveness.

One either trusts or distrusts. From the moment when the collaborators first begin to question their confidence, the loss of faith can rapidly act as a self-fulfilling prophecy: selective observations only seem to corroborate the dancers' growing distrust. Initial actions that led to uncertainty now function as a possible bifurcation point or threshold creating 'an artificial discontinuity which levels out the area of experience before and after the threshold, and thus makes for simplification ... If there is a swing from trust to distrust – and the same is true in the rare reverse case – then the one who mistrusts adapts to this new pattern of expectation and thus makes this change of attitude socially apparent', writes Luhmann on the all-or-nothing logic structuring the interpersonal dynamics of giving and withdrawing confidence. Artistic distrust quickly intensifies when a choreographer is recurrently unable to indicate the desired direction the work should take and therefore postpones crucial interim decisions. 'The panic of a choreographer trying to get a piece together makes me anxious', says a dancer. Yet when that very same artist assumes the counterposition of dance maker, he or she in fact expects trust at those moments when 'the artistic subject supposed to know' does not really know: 'When the others trust you, they also trust you in your weakness.' Once again the semi-directive work relation implies a clear-cut paradox: *at the moments when a choreographer is visibly doubting or artistically indecisive, he or she trusts to still have the trust of the dancers – who actually begin at this moment to distrust.*

Collaboration's Quasi-Intimacy

Making dance together is mostly hard work, with rather indefinite outcomes. During a creation process, neither the choreographer nor the performers are certain that the material produced will start to cohere into a plausible result, a composition that holds and persuades. The long preparation period preceding a new performance therefore entails recurrent instances of personal stress, thorough self-doubt and even outright crisis. And when work goes well and one experiences a creative flow, the rehearsal process likewise engages to such an extent that it tends to overtake one's personal life, cancelling out the traditional difference between labour and leisure. This is the biopolitical nature of creative work: 'It imposes a new regime of time, with respect to both the working day and the working career, ... destroying the division between work time and non-work time, requiring workers not to work all the time but to be constantly available for work', according to Michael Hardt and Antonio Negri. A collaborating dance artist who feels engaged in a creation process, tests or muses over possible material at home or during weekends, thus actually doing a considerable amount of non-paid work. Time and again, work-related issues pervade the private sphere but the reverse is also true. Immaterial labour – indeed a somewhat awkward expression in relation to dance – directly involves the personalities of those collaborating, their 'being' and individual sense of existence: 'The thing with dance is that your private life is very close because it's about you, it's about your body.'

With the exception of a collaboration primarily instigated for economic reasons, the joint production of contemporary dance relies on highly ambivalent relationships that are at once relatively general and quasi-intimate, socially coded and personally animated. Intimacy arises when 'the complexity of a human being has significance for another human being and vice versa', Niklas Luhmann asserts. The other's subjectivity directly motivates and co-orders an interpersonal relation, in the strict sense: 'The "I", with special characteristics that can be attributed only to it, becomes an object of communication in which it is itself involved. It represents itself and is observed – and not only as fulfilling norms but also in its most personal characteristics.' Although it is strongly co-regulated by general expectations, shades of quasi-intimacy frequently colour the semi-directive regime of participatory collaboration. Filtered by the focus on the work as such, both the choreographer and the performer at times share the fascination for the other's irreducible otherness. In a fruitful cooperation, the latter recurrently guides, provokes, stimulates... and also beguiles, magnetizes, fascinates: 'Whether you are the dancer or the choreographer, you need to be intrigued or seduced by the person with whom you are working. There's a mystery, there's something that I look for in her...' The enigma in question is the other's subjectivity, that at once vast and ordered artistic potentiality, which engenders inspiring words, surprising movements or novel gestures.

'I think you have to fall in love with your performers', says a dance maker. 'I always work with people that have something that makes me want to look at them.' The 'something' alluded to is immanently interwoven with the fascination with the other's captivating artistic subjectivity but also implies the existence of a deeper psychosocial dynamic that simultaneously feeds and menaces a work relation comprised of many moments of direct physical contact. When dance artists try to make sense of the general conditions furthering creative collaboration the topic is mostly avoided or only hinted at through camouflaging expressions and the rather clumsy notion of 'love'. What it actually comes down to is difficult to put into words because the 'something' involves psychological processes that one undergoes in a necessarily passive mode: while they are actively experienced, these processes simultaneously point – in Freudian parlance – to 'the dark continent' of the unconscious. A Lacanian paraphrase, and somewhat bold hypothesis, may perhaps be risked here: the 'some-thing' in question is the uncanny Thing animating desire, 'the cause of the most fundamental human passion' (which Lacan later referred to as 'object petit a'). It can thus be premised that in an intense collaboration between dancer and choreographer, both frequently come to stand for the other's object of desire. However, all human desire signifies a never remediable lack and must be kept at a safe distance in view of its auto-reproduction: actually realizing desire amounts to the destruction of its very cause. When creating dance together, the necessary reserve is in part guaranteed by the social imperative to talk dance, to perform dance, to co-create dance. The mediating symbolic order co-structuring a rehearsal process thus obliges the collaborators to sublimate their unconscious libidinal investments: *the imaginary object 'Dance' substitutes the Thing of desire.* 'Real love' should not be shown, though this sometimes happens. Many dance artists have a partner who is also dancing and/or choreographing and whom they met through a work relation that was not as such intended to set the scene for a romantic personal encounter. The late-night gossip that socially holds together local dance scenes also includes various stories, often told with much indignation, about male choreographers harassing female performers (now and then one hears the reverse: a female dance maker consciously eroticizes the work relation with a male dancer). The unanimous moral dismissal of this intrusive behaviour confirms the general rule: 'real intimacy' is the work relation's no go area.

In qualifying the quasi-intimacy that drives creative collaboration, the ambiguous and somewhat tacky word 'love' can be given a meaning differing from the romantic idea commonly associated with the term: an erotically charged communication, eventually sealed by sexual interaction, between two persons who experience each other as mutually attractive enigmas. Baruch Spinoza is probably the most important thinker who has tried to approach affects from a truly naturalist point of view, doing away with sentimentality. He defines love simply as 'a joy, accompanied by the idea of an external cause'. We love the object that brings us joy through the enhancement of our life forces or that stimulates our primary desire to go on and to persevere, to expand the possibilities of Life or the virtuality one actually is. Hence *the productivity of an artistic cooperation arouses love, in the Spinozist sense, for the other whose inspiring presence makes the work prolific.* 'Love composes singularities, like themes in a musical score, not in unity but as a network of social relations', assert Michael Hardt and Antonio Negri in a sentence that fittingly describes the intensive heights of participatory collaboration. Once again a mostly varying distance is needed. The one providing joy may not come 'too near' in order to avoid that 'the Spinozist love' becomes over-signified by accidental gestures insinuating 'Romantic love'. The second corrupts the first: a romantically over-coded desire transforms the beneficial other into a Thing incrusted with imaginary identifications, blocking an open productivity. Moreover, a minimal aloofness is necessary to protect one's kernel of artistic autonomy, however fantasized, against the heteronomy of the external cause of love, whether real or imagined. This is perhaps the principal point: foreclosing how the 'greedy institution' that contemporary dance often is, metamorphoses into a singular personal relationship that, through an undeniable artistic productivity, swallows up an indefinable potentiality.

Directivity's Ambiguities

An already hinted at ambivalence is conspicuously present when dancers talk about collaboration. They long for the possibility to say 'I', yet this desire to be co-creative is mostly laced with *the imperative expectation that the choreographer formulates a sufficiently clear general artistic line*. Without minimal guidance and the suggestion of an overall vision, the cooperating performers may start to question the choreographer's artistic and professional competences, possibly resulting in a difficult to remediate relation of distrust. Also, an inconsistent work frame or hesitant feedback may hamper the urge to develop personal material and to engage in collective research. Working in an under-structured setting makes everyone insecure: the collaborator must repeatedly take artistic micro-decisions in the absence of agreed upon ideas or a general problematic. Research thus risks becoming a vacillating search for the actual object of the performed investigative action. Most dancers experience such a work situation as an aimless nomadic meandering that rapidly frustrates and often attenuates personal engagement: 'You are then producing something without knowing what someone expects; and this person obviously also doesn't know what she expects – that's very confusing.' A quasi-ruleless artistic context also creates a fuzzy collective focus, which complicates the verbal dialogue between dancer and choreographer. The viewpoints expressed by the dance maker look whimsical or erratic and lengthy discussions in which all collaborators start voicing their personal opinions may develop; they are usually not that productive and mostly aggravate the initial problem of artistic inconclusiveness.

A notable lack of direction also seriously blurs the difference between the role of co-creating dancer, only involving co-authorship, and the status of choreographic author. Many dance artists alternating both positions are reluctant to affirm the second identity during a work process initiated and overseen by another artist: 'When I work as a dancer for someone else and that person tells me "do whatever you want, improvise freely", without any further context, I can't do that because it confronts me anew with my position as choreographer.' In addition, under-directivity at times raises difficult to settle issues of authorship once a creation is near completion. Unguided dancers whose personal proposals end up almost unaltered in the final work mostly want to be given at least some credit for their individual achievements in the program leaflet. Sharp disputes can develop when the choreographer stubbornly refuses to honour this claim to public recognition. Not being granted the direct co-authorship one thinks one deserves, may over time result in deep feelings of personal anger and artistic exploitation: 'She sucked my blood dry!' However, under-directivity can also indirectly create problems of artistic authorship. For example, a young dancer freely generates a particular way of moving her body within the context of a messy collaboration and takes pride in the produced material's central role in the final choreography. Afterwards, when she makes a solo herself that further explores this self-developed corporeal style, she may be wrongly accused by peers and critics of not having a voice of her own: she is a copycat who only reproduces what she has learned from the dance maker she worked with previously.

The ambiguities in giving direction again highlight the paradoxical nature of semi-directive collaboration. Dancers wish to individualize their artistic self in line with the regime of singularity, while proceeding from and within the context of an articulated framework. The absence of a constantly re-specified general guideline blocks collective research and dampens individual engagement – but the demanded directivity should also not be too clear-cut, since this curtails the chances for interpretative flexibility and subjectification. A latent tension thus characterizes the work relation: the ideal level of artistic direction oscillates between an unwanted 'too much' and a likewise undesirable 'too little'. Both poles are subjective and point to the actual desirability of a well-balanced midpoint that can never be defined in advance. By and large, the collaborators' valuations of the offered guidance will momentarily shift, though a collectively validated definition of the work context as over- or under-directive may rather rapidly create a social reality that the choreographer cannot easily amend. The ambivalence also once more highlights the heteronomous autonomy pervading participatory collaboration. External directivity does in fact stimulate 'internal' decision-making: *in the*

semi-directive mode of making dance together, a performer's auton-
omy is partly effectuated through relational heteronomy. Indeed, a
productive collaboration that relies on a somewhat balanced guidance momentarily subverts the apparently unshakable binary logic suggested by the traditional opposition between subjectification
and subjection, artistic agency ('freedom') and aesthetic structure
('limitation'). At least to a certain extent, the performer's individual capacity to move and to not-move, and also to imagine and
explore new dancing possibilities, is a performative effect of the
general line supervised by 'the artistic subject supposed to know'.
In sum, the heteronomy symbolized by the overall authorship
of the dance maker at once constrains and enables the dancer's
co-authorship.

Dance makers are aware of their collaborators' desire for
an adequate degree of direction. When conceiving a new creation
or scheduling a working day, they anticipate the performers' wish
to have some grip or footing and their concomitant fear of an
artistic vacuum. A self-reflexive loop is often involved, since those
taking up the position of choreographer regularly alternate this
role with that of dancer. Expectations one entertains as a performer are reflexively expected when affirming the counter-position of
choreographer: 'I expect that you expect of me a passable general
work frame and well-articulated comments'. Meeting this expected expectation enhances the chances of a smooth cooperation,
without of course securing this outcome, and may put some personal pressure on the choreographer: 'Before the start of a collaboration I always have the image of the panicking choreographer.
There are five dancers looking at you and – that's where the panic
comes in – they ask: "What are we going to do?" That's the initial
image I have: will I appeal to them, shall I say interesting things
and will I be able to fill up their time... What will my discourse
be, what do I have to offer them? – while I simultaneously know
that I have to listen. I don't have to say everything – but how can
I initiate things, how do we come to a dialogue: I don't know yet.'

Choreographers making reflexive dance are keen to present an upcoming creation process as research that is thoroughly
based on a rather detailed and conceptually well-underpinned
problematic. 'Stating a problem isn't about uncovering an already
existing question or concern', Bojana Cvejić emphasizes with
regard to this mode of producing dance: 'On the contrary, to raise
a problem implies constructing terms in which it will be stated,

and conditions it will be solved in.' Hence the importance of preparatory activities such as the reading of theoretical texts and conversations with various kinds of relevant informants, including academics who have specialized knowledge. Collaboration may thus stretch out and include recurrent or even longer lasting non-artistic forms of cooperation with informational results that loop back into the creation process through basic concepts, general questions or specific movement material. Most reflexive dance artists actually uphold the idea that being well-prepared significantly heightens the success-ratio of a rehearsal period: 'You need to know when you start up a work process; if you don't know, there are plenty of things that you cannot do, that will not be possible — also time-wise! There are overall things that you must know, otherwise you will not be able to achieve them.' Going beyond the established practices of improvisation and formulating tasks, 'dance conceptualists' often also try to devise clear working procedures and semi-scores, which fix the basic parameters of the dancers' collaborative research. Engaging a dramaturge, perhaps only during certain phases in the work process, and inviting peers to comment on interim results are two other widespread strategies that may help a choreographer to clarify the stakes of newly developed material or an emerging choreographic plane of consistency.

Knowing that they are expected to behave as the 'artistic subject supposed to know' regularly confronts choreographers with a dilemma: 'Do I effectively expose to the dancers, even share with them, my personal hesitations? Or do I conceal my insecurity and simulate knowing while I am in fact in doubt?' Which line of action is chosen may have a profound impact on the work relation and the dancers' general trust in the dance maker, yet the momentary social climate condensing the always specific dynamic of a singular collaboration also vastly informs the stance taken by choreographers. When they feel much trust, bringing doubts out into the open seems more plausible than in a situation already marked by signs of distrust or frequent disputes. Confessing temporary artistic uncertainty does not necessarily generate paralyzing collective discussions. The choreographer can prefer to voice a shorter or longer variation on the sentence 'I really don't know for the moment' and subsequently give the dancers a longer break. The time-out zone allows for trying out possible solutions alone in the studio, to re-vision movement material registered on video, or to think through and meditate on the possible stakes of the piece in the making: 'When I'm blocked, I sometimes send the dancers home; and occasionally I say "Don't come in tomorrow, I will go walking for a day" – or whatever. A work process is a bit like a journey – and then you see where you arrive.'

On the Authority of the Choreographer

Within the semi-directive regime, processes of artistic de- and re-subjectification presuppose moments of a more or less self-reflexive subjection of the performer to the directing choreographer. The latter frequently takes the lead: with or without a visible display of social superiority, the dance maker wields power over the cooperating dancers. On the face of it, power has everything to do with 'the probability that one actor in a social relationship will be in the position to carry out his own will despite resistance' (this is Max Weber's famous definition). However, choreographers directing a performer in the context of a participatory collaboration only impose their proverbial aesthetic will at the beginning and the end of a creation process. Informed by a broader artistic poetics, they first define the basic axioms and problematic that underlie the cooperation. They may also already have fixed ideas about the music they want to use in the final choreography or about the end product's overall visual qualities. Even more defining is proposing a clear-cut series of movements as the creation's binding starting point. In the concluding phase choreographers mostly decide imperatively, possibly after consulting with the dancers, on the definitive material and its performative articulation. The dance maker's artistic power now manifestly comes into view: he or she effectively creates the dance that the public will witness. In doing so, 'the artistic subject supposed to know' now and then transforms into a commanding individual who is greatly convinced that he or she knows better. Some of the collaborators, if not all of them, may experience this direct affirmation of final authorship as a personal blow (this was already highlighted in the previous chapter): 'It was quite problematic when she started composing the piece because then your voice is kind of out ... She was surprisingly stubborn and did not make adjustments according to what we suggested. But this is where you realize that you are working for a choreographer – and it's her work of art.'

During the long period in between the start and end of a rehearsal process, the choreographer generally behaves like an at once inspiring and supervising coach who encourages the dancers to enter new terrain, to try out movements still unknown and to realize so far unexplored artistic possibilities. Power takes on a decidedly softer shape, one in which its actualization equals 'a set of actions on possible actions; it incites, it induces, it seduces, it makes easier or more difficult; it releases or contrives, makes more probable or less.' Practicing power, in the broad sense, involves 'a "conduct of conducts" and a management of possibilities. Basically, power is less a confrontation between two adversaries or their mutual engagement than a question of "government"' (this is Michel Foucault's well-known reformulation of the concept of power). The kind of governmentality that co-structures participatory collaboration is mostly genuinely semi-directive, yet in the often marked moments of downright directivity in the initial and the concluding phase the proverbial social core of the exercise of power, whether hard or soft, is visibly enacted. For all use of power involves decision-making, however reflexive, reducing the possible scope of action of one or more others (this is more or less Niklas Luhmann's view). Exercising power is indeed a functional equivalent to the collective building up and maintenance of social structures: both operations limit human potentiality to a certain extent. Managing the possibilities of others to perform in this or that way by definition requires the communication of decisions that will act as restricting premises for their potential activity. Taking socially binding decisions is indeed the hallmark of wielding power, but by relying on particular sources that legitimize power, which subsequently transform it into authority, this practice can be socially alleviated. The word itself says it all: authority authorizes the individual use of power through the deployment of one or more specific resources legitimating directivity, thereby justifying, for instance, both individual guidance ('you can perhaps do it this way') and the much more straightforward communication of obliging artistic instructions ('do it this way!').

Personal charisma is one possible cornerstone of an artist's legitimate exercise of power. Inspired by the persisting romantic myth of the highly gifted artist-genius, *charismatic authority* essentially implies a specific leap of faith from observed artistic achievements to the presupposed nature of their author. A dancer may think, usually because others share this belief, that a particular dance maker possesses unusually seminal artistic powers or anything but mundane qualities. The charismatic choreographer stands out, representing a creative state of exception: he or she embodies the value of artistic singularity in an exemplary mode. In an individual work relation, such anything but common faculties translate into the ability to inspire dancers in an extraordinary way. 'The power of charisma lies in the capacity to give the believer the feeling that he discloses himself through a pedagogical relationship that lends itself to an affective transfer', notes Pierre-Emmanuel Sorignet, adding that the charismatic choreographer knows how 'to reveal to the dancer his deeper personality by working on his movements, but also by provoking him and by defining himself sometimes as a "psychoanalyst of the body and the soul".' A sometimes strong emotionally toned relationship sustains the cooperation when the choreographer is experienced as the sort of demiurge whose tasks, suggestions and personal feedback push the performer, again and again, in novel directions, which are experienced as genuine manifestations of one's artistic self. Charged with the often unconscious libidinal investments already referred to earlier, the relationship resists symbolization and escapes verbalization. The dancer feels entrapped in a singular collaboration that altogether meets a longing for artistic self-transformation but simultaneously confuses because it brings into play other unclear desires as well. Vague anxieties about the possible outcome of the becoming-other may add to the overall experience of riding a rollercoaster, the exact nature of which is difficult to determine: 'where will this/I end up?' The feeling is sometimes confirmed by the observation that the choreographer no longer just boosts but also goes beyond the purely artistic, 'playing personal games', which partly undermines the charismatic authority. The intense and initially highly productive collaboration can therefore over time reverse into an uncomfortable, all too personal and stifling relationship. This explains one dancer's retrospective qualification, 'he is a monster', when speaking of a choreographer who was in fact responsible for greatly furthering her artistic capacities.

Although dancers sometimes speak of past collaborations with much respect and personal gratitude, the sketched portrait rarely resembles the ideal of the charismatic choreographer. Partly, this may have to do with the mostly retrospective nature of their observations, but of probably greater importance is the current cultural climate of the world of contemporary dance.

In line with the increasingly predominant collaborative work ethic, artistic heroism or an overly glorifying approach towards individual artists is generally dismissed as an out-dated remnant of modernism. Many dance artists also explicitly reject the romantic myth of the artist-genius as an ideological construct that usually conceals non-acknowledged influences and uncountable hours of hard work. Informality and an egalitarian spirit set the tone in today's field of contemporary dance: the idea of sharing a collective artistic condition transcending the existing divisions in choreographic vision prevails over the traditional focus on Great Creators that still informs the bulk of the media reports on art. Individual dance makers may of course still be admired for their conspicuous capacity to give an original twist to those parameters currently regarded as the most important variables defining dance works. Yet the reference to the crucial values informing the regime of singularity do not suffice to authorize a choreographer's actual decision-making during a participatory collaboration that was not initiated for economic reasons. Dancers' personal trust in an individual dance artist and their willingness to agree with the latter's opinions are primarily based on the observation that the choreographer is able to create innovative performances and can semi-direct in an at once proficient and stimulating way. This must be done in line with the morality of cooperation and visibly honour its defining notions of artistic participation and co-creation. *An always singular blend of personal artistic vision and general professional competence in genuinely collaborative directing nowadays seems to be the prime source of a choreographer's authority when creating dance together.*

The legitimating role of 'being collaborative' comes with two more specific expectations: the choreographer encourages critical dialogue with or among the dancers and sincerely takes into consideration its interim results; and 'the artistic subject supposed to know' discursively legitimates the socially binding selections he or she makes. 'Talking is really crucial; people must be able to discuss what they think, how they see the material or ideas... – otherwise it isn't collaboration': the ideal-typical semi-directive choreographer meets this moral rule, which actually points to a social reflexivity that may produce a surplus in common knowledge that exceeds the dance maker's individual artistic know-how. Yet encouraging and personally nurturing dialogue is a social competence that is not practised without risks.

Not unlike the general ambiguity that informs directing, choreographers should provide enough room for critical exchange and try to guarantee that every collaborator's voice is regularly heard — but at the same time they must watch over productivity: endless discussions only create confusion and eat away at the available work time, which is always scarce. By taking seriously the opinions of others or the relative consensus emerging during a group meeting, and perhaps also (partially) integrating both in artistic decisions, a choreographer not only demonstrates a professional commitment to the ethics of collaboration. In varying degrees, it communalizes the legitimacy of this personal exercise of artistic power during, for instance, the final phase of a creation: 'It's easier to accept the decisions to be made if prior to that there has been a kind of melting pot of ideas or exchange, so that you have the feeling that you could have had an impact on the work in the moment it was being made.' Making individual decision-making 'social' by 'talking dance' also happens when the choreographer fulfils the expectation to justify individual verdicts. Accounting for choices explicitly may significantly enhance their overall legitimacy and increase the chances that the dancers truly accept them or can at least 'live with' their effects. In other words, both the responsiveness to the cooperating dancers' ideas and the discursive justification of personal decisions corroborate a choreographer's artistic and professional legitimacy with a surplus of *dialogical authority*.

Founding or fortifying individual authority by giving it a social base accords with a wider historical trend. Accelerated by 'the expressive revolution' already put into perspective at the end of the previous chapter, the general outlook and functioning of diverse social relations rather drastically changed from the 1960s onward. In varying degrees and often specific normative framings, the interaction between parents and children, teachers and students, politicians and citizens or employers and employees became distinctly more egalitarian through the shift 'from management by command to management by negotiation' (according to Dutch sociologist Abram de Swaan). At least in the West, issuing unilateral orders is nowadays regarded as not done in most social spheres: the authoritarian style of leading or governing has been replaced by the imperative to dialogue and to look for possible consensus when wielding power (the change is actually mirrored by the differences in the cited views on power of Max Weber and Michel Foucault, respectively). Legitimate individual decision-making means to first meditate and then select possibilities that are socially acceptable because of previous communication with the very subjects who will be bound by the final verdicts. Dialogical authority co-founds the personal authority one may derive from other legitimizing resources, such as codified knowledge, official regulations or juridical norms. In sum, power and authority have become thoroughly democratized – and the labour settings in the different art worlds have followed this trend, though with notable exceptions in the spheres of, for instance, ballet and music (a conductor who is regarded as very talented may still behave as a quasi-general commanding a musical army). The prescriptive morality and empirical reality of creative co-production is the temporary end result of this broader shift in general society. To push the prospect of genuine democratic social arrangements beyond its current materializations is precisely the program of radical democracy advanced by political theorists such as Ernesto Laclau and Chantal Mouffe. The dominant forms of practicing equality within the context of dialogical authority indeed never fully realize democracy's promise or live up fully to the ethic of collaboration. We once again stumble over the Janus face of the semi-directive mode of participatory collaboration. As the expressions 'semi' and 'participatory' already suggest, this labour regime does not relinquish the principal power difference between a deciding subject and those subjected to its decisions. It regularly generates a severe contradiction in the experience of the involved workers between the various ways of soft governance and the usually short but intense moments of an outspoken individual exercise of power. 'So it's ambiguous', a dancer states. 'The more you contribute, the more you are fruitful and the more you will learn from the process – but then the greater the likelihood that you will feel blocked when it comes to the final composing of the piece.'

The Virtuality of 'Being an Artist'

Preparing a new creation can be hard: 'I'm generally confused', 'It sometimes already begins with the idea "I have to make a new work" – and suddenly I'm petrified and no longer know what "new" or "work" precisely mean.' Given the regime of singularity, the choreographer is expected to come up with something truly different that may translate into a broader set of notions, triggering a research or creation process: a handful of innovative ideas, an interesting mode of moving, a distinct way to theatricalize the body, a different view on the performativity of human and non-human actions, et cetera. Dance artists are not usually short of a potential problematic deserving to be addressed in depth, though there are evident exceptions. In dealing with several possibilities or just one Big Idea and the vistas it opens up, talking with peers, dramaturges and the like can help to diminish the personal uncertainty regarding their actual validity or potentiality. A principal difference distinguishes those dance artists who can rather rapidly decide on the basic outlines of the issues they will cooperatively explore from the choreographers who keep on going this way and that while attempting to circumscribe a possibly formative question. Whereas the prototypical 'conceptualists' – this is many dance artists' own categorization – quickly begin to document the selected topic systematically, the 'non-conceptualists' take their time to explore, in the studio, the various possibilities a particular notion or series of ideas suggests before definitively embracing or rejecting it. The first kind of artist generally rebuffs the second one as a somewhat naïve and old-fashioned believer in Romanticism, but there is a more pertinent feature, directly related to the definition of the legitimately danceable, underlying the indecisive attitude of the 'non-conceptualist'. Leaving aside exceptions, the seemingly vacillating dance makers are not devouring their artistic selves in search of an authentic action that is still to come. They simply regard physical movement as the ultimate test of an inspiring notion: 'I want to go beyond the initial idea. Surpassing the concept through physicality, that's what interests me.' A crucial difference co-structuring the self-observations in the field of contemporary dance is at stake: either corporeal movement performatively exemplifies an abstract concept, or a general notion is in the strict sense of the word embodied and 'given flesh'. Precisely the possibility of physically living out an idea, thereby also re-articulating it corporeally, is for most 'non-conceptualists' the decisive touchstone in the initial personal research.

Once a collaborative creation is underway, the choreographer must make countless artistic and other micro-decisions. Nothing is self-evident, every issue repeatedly confronts 'the artistic subject supposed to know' with the at times difficult to answer question: 'do I really know?' Even if they think they know, dance makers can by definition never anticipate the actual outcomes of possible aesthetic choices: they do not know which ones will effectively further, subvert or block the composing of a plausible

choreographic plane of consistency. That final phase is not only a dénouement for the collaborators but also for themselves as the artist they pretend to be. Or not: quite a few dance makers nowadays explicitly reject the notion of being an artist out of its presupposed association with the incurable Romanticist digging into their 'deep self'; they therefore prefer the supposedly more neutral label of choreographer, director, dancer or performer. Whatever the self-identification, the individual who claims the symbolic position of principal author time and time again faces *artistic precariousness*, or the most basic fact that making a potential work of art amounts to the constant reduction and selective actualization of aesthetic possibilities without knowing the future consequences of momentarily necessary decisions. Contingency reigns: the production and re-articulation of a structured potentiality always implies risks whose eventual perverse effects only reveal themselves later on. The choreographer never knows for sure if the particular movements selected for further exploration will really be fruitful. In being creative, the 'artistic subject supposed to know' observes and orders, through individual choices, a virtual realm of aesthetic alternatives – but this principal freedom comes with a lasting artistic precariousness that perhaps raises a hyperreflexive uncertainty that may spill over into a profound not-knowing. A not much publicly talked about fault line actually separates the frequently self-doubting dance maker from the rather self-confident artist. The first regularly confront their own self as a failing or non-informative potentiality and incidentally find themselves in a state of artistic crisis: 'I'm always frightened to cut off possibilities. Consequently I consider too many wrong possibilities: I conceive of too many possible improvisations or things that are not necessarily correct.' By contrast, the self-trusting choreographer can calmly say: 'I've never really doubted. In one way or another, it's always clear: this has to be in, this not, this we throw out. Once it is finished I may think "This or that could have been better".' Still others situate themselves halfway on the scale that runs from self-confidence to self-crisis in relation to artistic decision-making: 'My friends call me a comical drama. I have these moments of crisis, but at the same time I laugh about them.'

   To be often in artistic doubt, or not: this simple distinction tends to characterize the self-observations that dance artists have about their practice. The difference does not reproduce the more general division between, on the one hand, dance makers who subscribe to the inquisitive attitude that informs reflexive dance and, on the other hand, the few choreographers who self-consciously position themselves as Romanticists or the substantially broader contingent of dance artists hailing physical movement research and dismissing 'dry conceptualism'. The 'conceptualists', who seem to be always knowledgeable and never shy away from publicly voicing their personal opinion, may endlessly muse over aesthetic choices. Conversely, the choreographer who considers the body as a locus of artistic truth can sometimes take quick decisions after countless explorative detours when a deadline is near. Also, both types of dance makers are unable to discursively clarify the process of personal decision-making or the underlying sources of their artistic self-trust: 'Much of the work is unconscious, it's difficult to talk about.' 'Intuition' is the commonly invoked notion, which does not exactly clarify the issue and is sometimes related to other not so well-defined expressions such as 'skilfulness' and particularly 'experience'. By and large, choreographers make definitive choices on the basis of a black-boxed subjectivity they selectively affirm, without genuinely understanding the basis of their artistic preferences, which they alternately rely upon and then again doubt. The *subiectum* or bearing surface of 'the artistic subject supposed to know' is indeed largely non-transparent: *the artist knows and decides through the at times failing reliance on the structured potential that he or she is but never really grasps.*

'All artists have to realize themselves in the unknown', aptly states the subtitle of Pierre-Michel Menger's inspiring collection of essays on the artistic profession. This persisting uncertainty is essentially double-sided: artists make risky investments in both a competitive art world and in themselves. When entering an artistic field, debutants cannot estimate their chances of success; in turn, the mid-career artists, already fiddling around for some time, do not know if a sudden breakthrough is either imminent or will forever remain an imaginary, hoped for possibility. The momentarily successful artists seem much better off but must recurrently reckon with the possibility of an impromptu drop in the value of their symbolic and economic capital. With the exception of the ascending 'young wolves' who are given ample chances and a few *monstres sacrés*, the majority of artists indeed face a precarious future because contemporary art worlds are structurally unstable: trends come and go, creating aesthetic turbulence and abrupt market swings. Artists need the social recognition that they are doing something valuable in order to feel more secure, yet this collective esteem is mostly provisional. One has to earn it over and over again with every new production, upcoming personal exhibition or recently published novel. In addition, each artist engages in capital- and self-realization alike within a structurally indeterminate condition: not knowing who 'they really are' and what they precisely can or may express in their work. Without instructions for use, they handle an opaque artistic self, a series of faculties of which they only begin to get a limited idea by putting them to practice. Every exploration of one's personal capacities brings with it the risk of re-arranging, however minimally, the horizon of aesthetic possibilities they are working with and may generate a new appeal upon their unfathomable *potenza*. When artists ignore this call and stubbornly bet on the patient, auto-didactical deepening of a distinctive part of their virtual potentiality, thereby vastly self-structuring it, they do not know if this contingent selectivity will lead to something worthwhile. For a long time, the definitive outcomes of self-education remain totally unclear; it is even more dubious whether the uncertain results will also be socially recognized as artistically interesting.

Building on Aristotle, Hannah Arendt distinguishes labour from work. Whereas labour is marked by the demands of biological reproduction and therefore often involves routine action, work has a truly creative dimension. That is why making art is eminently work and why this activity is often considered as the true model for a non-estranged practice in which human beings can realize themselves. From an individual point of view, producing art permanently re-actualizes – in Aristotelian parlance – the difference between 'being as virtual potential' and 'being as act'. The continual transition from the first to the second state typifies 'being an artist' as a highly dynamic kind of work in which self-exploration and self-education, self-knowing and self-shaping are immanently entwined. 'The exercise of the profession transforms the individual', rightly emphasizes Pierre-Michel Menger. 'The temporal prolongation of the professional activity and work relationship gives previously non-present capacities and qualities the chance to manifest themselves and to break through: the accumulated experience and the exercise of the profession inform individuals on the capabilities that they possessed in a virtual state or provide them with additional competences that may significantly exceed the initial education.'

'Know thyself.' This Greek motto, commonly ascribed to Socrates, fits the activity of the individual art producer but also points to the unsurpassable limits in artistic self-understanding. 'The artist is the man without content, who has no other identity than a perpetual emerging out of the nothingness of expression and no other ground than this incomprehensible station on this side of himself', asserts Giorgio Agamben. The artists' self actually coincides with a strange quasi-substance consisting of personal possibilities that they often think is virtually present without having much certainty as to the truth value of this assumption: creative work at times bets on the future actualization of a perhaps non-existent capacity. In contrast to what Aristotle suggests, the recurrent passage from potential to act is not motivated by a quasi-automatic *dynamis*. Rather, the artist informing herself through self-activity follows a Spinozist logic: a *conatus* or 'drive' selectively realizes a *potenza* in an at once structured and contingent way. Structured — since self-exploration and self-education evidently make use of already developed capacities, of a professional experience condensed into more or less flexible habits that generate diverse intuitions, as well as of an often thorough knowledge of the actual tendencies in the art world one inhabits. Contingent — since auto-didactics involve incalculable strokes of luck and many unplanned encounters with inspiring peers or their works. All in all, the artistic self is a virtual potential — or a series of capacities — persistently singularizing, in an always singular medium, in a singular 'now, here'. Hence the word 'being' in the expression 'being an artist' should be crossed out: *artistry equals 'being an artist'*. Continually becoming is the artist's fate: they are a self-propelling process of learning and unlearning that uses the constant passage from structured potentiality to selective actualization as a prime medium.

Intermezzo: The Intimacy of the Dance Studio
It is a cold day in December 2004 when I visit a painter's atelier in the outskirts of Ghent. The location looks ordinary, even predictable: my first impressions totally fit the cliché image of the bohemian artist's studio. Dozens of unsold paintings, some hanging but most of them stacked upright in small rows against the white walls — as if they should not be looked at and valued; a couple of more than full ashtrays and an impressive collection of empty bottles that once contained strong liquor, neatly arranged on a

wooden table; a decrepit sofa, some magazines in seemingly hap-hazard piles; and of course brushes, paint tubes and turpentine: the indispensable tools of every painter. Art is undeniably pro-duced here, but the space is also used for various mundane ac-tivities such as making coffee, smoking and drinking or browsing through weeklies and particularly for just looking, thinking, doing nothing or daydreaming. Like all artists' ateliers, this workspace is also a place of constrained non-work — of patiently waiting for an idea, an intuition or a temper that may bring one to make a painterly gesture. What holds it all together, is the figure of *the artist as a particular zone of anonymous intimacy*, a non-localizable 'inner space' that is alternately occupied with emotions and con-scious images, impulses and moods, fascinations and phantasms, but that every once in a while also remains completely empty, transforming the self into an existential void. Everything in the atelier points to the intimate self-experiences of the painter that continually second his work and at times resonate in the final products (but how? — that is of course the true enigma). They just come to him: he actively appropriates or negates his inner-most states, which he experiences not as a subject or 'I' but in the mode of 'one': 'one feels', 'one thinks', 'one imagines'. The modern artist's freedom first and foremost concerns the way he deals with this anonymity of his intimacy. While working, paint may therefore alter itself in 'intimate matter' and become directly entwined with affects and intensities. Thus emerges the painterly pendant of 'the space of literature' evoked by Maurice Blanchot in his thoughtful book of the same title: language (paint, colour, canvas) changing into an intimate zone, a self that sinks into the unnameable materiality of the aesthetically deployed medium.

Flashback — it is May 2004 and I am coaching a P.A.R.T.S. student in one of the school's dance studios. The location is rela-tively big for a solo project and could easily house the preparation of a choreographed trio or quartet. In striking contrast with a per-sonal artistic workspace — not only a painter's studio but also for instance a writer's room — there are barely any traces of individu-ality. Along the back wall are the wooden barres on small wheels and the mirrors, which can be covered with a curtain, that one finds in many dance studios; a monotonously grey dance floor, with a handful of markings in black tape; a couple of chairs and a small table, two large loud speakers, a mobile stereo, a clock above the double-sided entry door. Only the sports bag and the sweater on one of the chairs plus the modest stack of paper and the laptop on the table lend a minimal individual touch to the overall setting. This is how a dance studio almost always looks: an empty box with the dance floor as its centre, populated by one or more bodies and perhaps a choreographer observing the dancers from a chair (which as a rule stands on the centre line). Not unlike the (in)famous white cube in the fine arts, the location is indeed not an individual but a generic dispositive. A dance studio does not bear a personal seal, it is not a semi-permanent residence in which an artist 'becomes present to herself' and simultaneously and without much thought, encrusts the space with various signs of a suggested individuality. This particular sort of work setting clearly misses character, even when the same company uses it for several years: the dance studio is an anonymous box, a garage in which bodies park themselves and find an only provisional abode. Generally, the bodies indeed come and go: studio time is often booked in advance, which helps to explain the presence of a clock in every dance studio. In line with the neoliberal regime of flexible artistic accumulation, dance work is done in this space today, and somewhere else next week. Indirectly confirming contemporary dance's social nature, the workspace is shared, actually or virtually. Even the soloists do not convert the studio into a 'room of one's own': they respect the location's identity as a collective generic site that is also used by others. At the same time, every dancing body immediately transforms the studio into a highly intimate space: one or more bodies explore physical possibilities, perhaps re-inventing themselves through movements that differ from the actions expected by the dancers themselves.

Modernity celebrates the individual artist as a strong-minded, volitional intimacy that does not languish in a mostly melancholic solitude. Successful artists — who are still the principal subject of the public discourse on art — know how to express themselves: they are able to give shape to the anonymous stream of emotions, ideas, sensory impressions, images, et cetera, in an at once personal and socially accessible language. The elusive and puzzling nature of a captivating poem or a fascinating choreography does not involve a completed self, a personal identity inventing fitting aesthetical forms. The art work's enigma is also that of the artist: both the artist and the work articulate a pre-individual intimacy, a non-localizable zone — perhaps a 'body without organs'? — in which volatile affects and fleeting ideas are not yet coupled with a stable subject self-attributing the constantly changing flow of various experiences. Every individual is familiar with this inner unfamiliarity, this no man's land of 'being just some-one' that a subject can neither claim nor possess. Within modernity, the artist − in the broad sense of the word − is given the right and the mandate to explore this zone. Artistry thus came to equal self-examination, or the meticulous self-observation of intense feelings (the romantic myth of authentic self-expression), of 'impure', provocative thoughts (the avant-garde and Conceptualism), or of the non-arguable preferences for already seen images, already heard sounds, already witnessed movements (the postmodern consciousness). All in all, the modern figure of the artistic author points to an exhausted, crossed-out subjectivity that does not subject itself to the seemingly evident rules of a medium but either cautiously redefines or recklessly deconstructs this very medium out of an allegiance to an opaque intimacy preceding the moment one says 'I think' or 'I want'. The artist's actual workspace − the location in which art happens − is indeed an indeterminate inner universe in which consciousness and corporeality are strangely linked and both are taken over by pre-subjective images, anonymous affects or quasi-generic near-thoughts. One does not encounter oneself there but an otherness that one truly is, Jean-François Lyotard writes in the short text 'The General Line' (1990), which is not by chance dedicated to Gilles Deleuze: 'But there is in this self another, this or that thing whose company we keep or seek to keep during our secret hours. This other exercises an absolute right over the self, a right that has never been the object of any contract and that knows nothing of reciprocity. It is completely other to other people. It demands our time and our space in secret, without giving us anything in return, not even the knowledge of what it is or of what we are. We have no rights over it, no recourse against it, and no guarantees of safety.'

Although the other that Lyotard alludes to undoubtedly maintains a close relationship to unconsciousness, it does not coincide with this 'dark continent'. To the improvising dancer exploring movement possibilities, alone or together with others and perhaps under the appraising gaze of a choreographer, the self's otherness shimmers through in motoric impulses, kinetic moods or whatever corporeal states that imply the affirmation of 'some-thing' one is but does not grasp. This danced intimacy has a genuine performative character, yet is anything but unmediated or spontaneous. Even the smallest micro-movement made by a professionally trained dancing body is thoroughly informed by an opaque physical memory, a corporeal archive condensing into a dance habitus allowing an articulated moving under the temporary exclusion of countless other possibilities. *Dancers enter 'the zone of intimacy' each time they explore, through the structured potentiality they are, the difference between structure and potentiality,* the demarcation line separating their own corporeal memory and the self-image grafted onto it from the possibilities they momentarily exclude. A hard limit is involved: the danced intimacy is often painful, in the literal but also especially the figurative sense, since the dancers repeatedly experience resistance from the side of their artistic self.

Most contemporary dance practitioners stay committed to an, in principle debatable, humanist self-understanding. However, current dance and choreography have also dissolved the human body into a general medium of movement and non-movement that is no longer regulated by strict cultural conventions or the kind of imperative aesthetic code underlying ballet practice. Dancers who, within the seclusion of the studio, investigate their artistic self thus probe the possibilities of 'the body in general' that is the danced counterpart of the 'art in general' put into perspective by Thierry de Duve in his perceptive discussion of post-Duchamp art. Contemporary dance in the humanist vein claims this generic physicality as a specific medium, which is re-specified each time dancers jeopardize 'them-selves' and contest with more or less vigour the structured potentiality they embody — on the basis of the very structures underlying their capacities. *The dance studio's generic identity mirrors the generality of contemporary dance's generic body.* However, dance is not just 'the art of the moving body'. The dancing body always couples movement and stillness with spatiality and through self-referential actions engenders an immaterial space within material space (and also an always particular temporality within linear time, as argued in the second chapter). This danced space appears and disappears with every new movement: the re-entry of space within space is constantly re-produced and re-articulated. Its readability requires that the material space in which the continually re-created 'own-space' literally takes place remains sufficiently abstract. The indeterminate dance studio precisely symbolizes this: it is an unmarked zone permitting an infinity of marks — a spatial potential abiding danced actualizations.

As a naked or empty space, this work setting shows the condition of possibility of every imaginable mode of dance, including the one contingently termed contemporary.

Second Movement: Composing Commonalities

(Not) Judging Art/Dance

Imagine you are witnessing a dancer silently trying out movements and poses. She improvises, though not freely but within the quite restricting confines of a self-defined task. Her action is actually two-sided: the dancer moves and regularly stands still or sits down on a chair in order to meditate the gestures she has just made. A particular self-dialogue thus unfolds over time, which at first sight coincides with a dialectical swing between doing and thinking, body and mind: corporeal action feeds conscious reflection, which generates new directions for physical movement. Yet a third operation, which is partly invisible to you, recurrently mediates between the two opposing poles. For the dancer also observes the produced movements either indirectly – she now and then looks to the sharp reflection of her agile body in the dance studio's mirror – or directly: her well-developed kinaesthetic sense provides her with a complex stream of information that is consciously processed and translated into mnemonic traces open to retrospective self-reflection or diverse afterthoughts and self-comments. Thus personal body knowledge substantially intervenes in the pendulum-like process that in reality does not oscillate between body and mind as such. Rather, the dynamic illustrates the kind of general self-conversation modelled by social psychologist George Herbert Mead: '*I* do', with more or less intentionality, and 'I observe *me* doing'. The dancing subject is indeed an internally divided, split subject for at least a double reason. There is the rationale already discussed at length: dancers know and do not know themselves because they realize a structured potential that can only be partially understood through its necessarily selective actualizations. At the same time, the dancing subject is both an 'I' and a 'Me': on the one hand a direct do-er possibly following non-premeditated, seemingly spontaneous impulses and, on the other hand, a partly conscious, partly embodied self-observer who objectifies his or her doings. Mead's trenchant formulae 'self = I + ME' indirectly re-positions the subject as both an action system and a multi-layered observation system, which effectively subverts the traditional humanistic semantic of body versus mind. However, the 'Me' is not just the 'I' selectively appearing as the apprehended object of bodily knowledge or conscious self-reflection. Through processes of identification, self-observations frequently refer to other-observations: one looks at oneself as others have done – one 'takes up the attitude of the other' (Mead). In trying to make sense of their actions, dancers indeed often implicitly quote the viewpoints of previous teachers, paraphrase remarks of performers or choreographers they have worked with or vary diverse comments of significant others. There is also the Big Other of language and discourse, the vast and collectively shared potential of words, categories and distinctions that structurally informs self-observations in mostly unnoticed ways. Even the soloing dancer is therefore never alone in the studio: in distancing the 'I' in a 'Me', a usually pluralized, polyphonic 'We' or series of general others is at work. The self-reflecting dancer is not a self-enclosed monad but a thoroughly socialized observation system operating according to complex software for which no user guide was written or could probably even have been envisaged.

When affirming the 'Me'-position, dancers basically do two things: they describe, analyse, and try to understand the action they are or were momentarily engaged in; and they assess, evaluate or discriminate between interesting and not so fruitful movements, ideas, incidences, et cetera. 'What am I doing, thinking, experiencing?' and 'is it worthwhile?': these two evident but sometimes notoriously hard to answer questions direct the dancer's self-observations. No dualism implied: the poles of reporting and valuing create a broad, even crucial intermediate zone in which the distinction between description and appreciation becomes blurred and hybrid accounts are the rule. Nevertheless, it makes sense to discern two general modes of sense-making that deploy distinct vocabularies or symbolic registers and which the modern differentiation between Science and Morality, Facts and Values has institutionalized with great effect (the capital letters indicate the social and epistemic importance of the distinction, especially from the point of view of science). Describing and valuating dance or choreography are indeed discursively mediated practices. Rather than making use of language, which already supposes the existence of an autonomous subject acting instrumentally, they literally happen *in* language. In becoming a contemporary dance artist, one actually does not just acquire a refined corporeal knowledge and a gradually built up, structured artistic potential through the laborious learning of ballet strides and the various techniques of steering the body associated with the names of, for instance, Graham, Limón or Cunningham. The aspiring performer or choreographer is also deeply socialized in *a common culture or discourse of 'talking dance' consisting of key descriptors and key values*, a lexicon to explain what one does and a vocabulary to justify the legitimately danceable. Such a culture functions as a *'sensus communis'*, a shared sense in personally dealing with the world at hand through a collective framework of various signifiers whose possible significations can be relatively taken for granted among those partaking in the same art world. Dance schools' public curricula do not always clearly state the promoted common culture, which teachers as a rule implicitly transmit in classes or during personal coaching. Their apparently personal communications continually reiterate, in a self-evident mode, the descriptive expressions and evaluative categories characterizing a specific common culture. In this way and without much ado, teachers transmit an always particular view on both the dancing body's presumably basic qualities and those of legitimate contemporary dance or choreography. Take, for instance, P.A.R.T.S. The Brussels-based dance school's founding documents frequently invoke the positively valued figure of 'the thinking dancer' as the prime goal inspiring the various learning activities. Student are therefore not only encouraged to discursively articulate and explicitly justify whatever kind of activity they engage in or to persist in a self-reflexive stance when 'just going with the flow' looks more promising. A rather overt curriculum actively promotes a quite consistent set of notions on the legitimately danceable that to a considerable extent retakes the main lines of Yvonne Rainer's famous 'No' manifesto: no to the direct expression of emotions or psychologism, no to spectacle and the aesthetically superfluous, no to romanticism and the belief in personal authenticity.

In matters of art, judging is probably the most pertinent mode of observation. Privately thinking or publicly communicating that a painting, poem or performance is beautiful amounts to the formulation of a reflexive judgment, Immanuel Kant posits in his classic *Critique of Judgment*. Whereas a determinate judgment is based on the application of a universal rule to a particular case, a reflexive judgment follows the reverse logic: the strictly personal enjoyment of a unique art work — Kant speaks of 'disinterested pleasure' — elicits a general verdict claiming universal consent through the appeal to a *'sensus communis'* transcending cultural differences or social barriers (in the eighteenth century, an undivided and transhistorical humanity — or rather: Humanity — was the emancipatory horizon considered evident by all pamphleteers or philosophers furthering the cause of Enlightenment). Actually, judging is of a markedly hybrid nature. A judgment of whatever sort indeed mixes facts and values: it simultaneously qualifies 'what is' and pronounces an evaluative verdict appealing to 'what must be'. 'Whether local or general, unusual or routine, the judgment expresses a particular point of view. It constructs the appropriate relationship between criteria of evaluation, whose relative composition and weighting are variable, as well as the way the situation is framed — in other words, the organization of the facts. *'Judgment combines value and knowledge'*, the French sociologist Lucien Karpik rightly stresses. The operation of judging again and again calls upon assumed facts or knowledge to corroborate appreciative statements — and vice versa: the gauged situation at hand is selectively portrayed as being this or that in light of particular normative axioms. Description supports valuation, but the latter also guides the first. Truth in the strict sense is therefore not the appropriate category: every judgment is a contestable opinion open to a principally interminable discussion that may refer to other relevant facts and/or different germane values.

Judging art implies the discriminating use of the categorical difference between art and non-art. To name or to not-name whatever artefact 'art' (or 'dance', 'literature', 'music') co-defines art's contemporaneity and the current condition of dance (this was already argued at length in the first chapter). However, in the active process of the collaborative production of contemporary dance, the semantic distinction art versus non-art is constantly varied, displaced and deferred and takes on so many guises that 'the name of art' no longer seems to matter. The more specific 'name of dance' by and large undergoes the very same treatment: it is overtly negated through the recurrent 'return of the repressed', in sublimated notions implicitly hinting at an obvious name not publicly nameable. The repeated act of judging individual propositions or collectively generated material — which is not just the choreographer's authorial privilege but also the mundane activity of every reflexively observing collaborator — thus makes use of a plethora of expressions to distinguish the worthy from the unworthy, that which is regarded as aesthetically interesting from possibilities to be negated. In sum, *in making contemporary dance together, using the name 'art' or 'dance' is mostly not done when passing judgment.* It is indeed an intriguing observation: dance artists quasi-systematically avoid framing and esteeming their own activity or that of others straightforwardly as art or non-art, dance or non-dance. Yet this explicit non-speech conceals an implicit dispute on the legitimately danceable that rapidly surfaces once the expression 'conceptual dance' is put on the table. Moreover, the striking multiplicity of notions substituting the words 'art' or 'dance' in 'talking dance' accords with the regime of singularity. Each collaboration within the context of an established company or every individual project asks for a suitable language, a proper vocabulary that adjusts the discursive potentiality to make and justify judgments to an always specific problematic and a particular social dynamic.

Revisiting 'Conceptual Dance'

'It's interesting to see how contemporary dance can survive its own paradoxes and tries not to be defined in precise terms, meaning that it can accommodate a broad range of forms', says a dancer-choreographer, adding: 'That is of course also the problem: the notion is vague.' In observing the art world that they at once passively undergo and however minimally co-define, dance artists agree on its strikingly plural, even heterogeneous character. This situation is accepted as a matter of fact and is not effectively valued or judged. Aesthetic tolerance appears to be the general norm, individual taste is the principal arbiter appealed to when appreciating singular works. Things slightly change when the word 'dance' is set apart and separated from the qualification 'contemporary'. Not that most dance artists have a clear-cut, readymade view on the actual stakes of their quasi-daily activity: the dance maker who can synthesize his or her personal approach into a coherent poetics is rather the exception, not to say a white raven. Presenting an artistic identity card is also avoided because most performers and choreographers alike wholeheartedly subscribe to the notion of research as an open, future-oriented process in the course of which new discoveries will hopefully be made. *Re-defining dance through research defines dance artists' sometimes explicit, often implicit basic view on their practice.*

Without much justification, many dancers and choreographers in fact still stick to the body humanism overtly questioned by 'dance/choreography in general' and also, though in different modes, by reflexive dance. In their opinion, dancing definitely equals moving — but a well-trained human body performs the action, thus simultaneously transforming the generic support of living corporeality into a particular aesthetic medium frequently associated with notions such as 'physicality' or 'expressivity'. Together with the concomitant idea that choreographing is synonymous with the temporal and spatial structuring or deliberate composition of human movements, this once highly evident approach to dance is already for some time now being critically contested and openly ironized or deconstructed: 'I think my frustration is how few works trust the organization of movement and the research of movement as a tool to make interesting contemporary work.' An ambiguity thus frequently surfaces in the self-observations of those dance artists who sincerely embrace the referential instability of 'the name of dance' and simultaneously favour a dance poetics that revolves around the central tenets of body humanism. Once again, a split is involved, this time between the positions of receiver and (co-)producer of contemporary dance: one is at once an aesthetic omnivore (as dance spectator) and an artistic univore (as dance artist).

Yet another dispute counteracts the apparently strong aesthetic tolerance within the world of contemporary dance. For the so-called conceptual wave that emerged during the 1990s not only largely subverted the premised essence of dance as bodily movement but also seconded this polemical gesture with a marked emphasis on the prime role of ideas against danced 'expressivism', particularly its emotionalist variant. The once heated debate on 'non-dance' has clearly abated, as the prevailing pluralist attitude partly indicates. Nevertheless, the relative normalization, even institutionalization of the reflexive approach within the European dance field did not undo the negatively perceived aspects of 'the moment of Conceptualism' or its lasting after-effects. Somewhat older dance artists who were already active around the recent turn of the century recount, often with anger, the strong-minded attitude with which some members of the first generation of 'conceptualists' rebutted the traditional framing of dance: 'A couple of years ago X told me "Today you can no longer dance". While it is simply legitimate if somebody desires to do so.

I really have a problem with everything that is of the order of doxa: "you may, you may not...".' Some proponents of reflexive dance apparently behaved with downright arrogance, publicly dismissing those choreographers and performers who stuck to emotional expression or movement research as blatant retards who had lost track of History. They deliberately violated the general rule of aesthetic tolerance, thus converting the otherwise rather easy-going interaction among dance artists into a discursive and moral battlefield. The impression that 'the conceptualists' conducted themselves as a closed clan willingly aspiring for power played a part as well, especially in France, where choreographers direct several important dance centres.

In the vocabulary of Pierre Bourdieu, the pioneers of reflexive dance actually initiated — and probably did win in several respects — a collective struggle against the reigning orthodox definition of the legitimately danceable in the name of a heterodoxy that partly rehearsed the principal lessons of the historical avant-garde, including its bitingly ironic style. Some dance artists take up the belated reiteration as a proper rationale to dismiss the conceptual trend accordingly: 'For me, it might have stopped with Duchamp's urinal because I understood the lesson. Perhaps Conceptualism is something for people who lack an academic education.' However, the aftermath of 'the conceptual wave' should not be underestimated. Articulating well-defined ideas through dance, bracketing the human body as a prime locus of artistic truth, questioning the critical relevance of emotionalism and the aesthetic legitimacy of the spectacular: for a significant group of dance artists, these and related articles of faith belonging to reflexive dance's catechism act as touchstones or gauges. Indeed, it sometimes seems as if Conceptualism functions as an artistic Super-Ego, a binding morality that has to be taken into account and to which one must relate, not the least when subscribing to another poetics. 'I feel the gaze of the Conceptualists on me', says a dancer-choreographer, 'with their eyes wide open.'

Talking and Judging Dance Together
Whatever the specificities informing a participatory collaboration, the cooperating choreographer and dancers collectively produce a work in process that gradually metamorphoses into a final product, a publicly witnessed performance. They thus regularly

engage in *'commoning', or the acting in common, which simultane-*
ously produces a common, a tangible collective good and/or a social
commonality. With the notable exception of truly flat or democratic
collaborations, which will be addressed later, the common action
is marked by a structural power difference: in line with the regime
of semi-directivity, choreographers have at times a (much) greater
say than the dancers. In general, they also successfully claim the
definitive authorship of the collectively created artefact, with or
without the public recognition of the performers' constitutive contributions through the ritual formulae 'made in collaboration with
the dancers' printed in the program booklet. At first sight, the
semi-directive regime of participatory collaboration reproduces
a crucial trait of current 'creative capitalism'. Nowadays, 'capital
expropriates cooperation', Michael Hardt and Antonio Negri observe, adding: 'Biopolitical exploitation involves the expropriation
of the common, in this way, at the level of social production and
social practice.' Choreographers may perhaps disprove the argument by contending that they actually initiate, greatly inspire and
daily supervise a creation process, for which they also take final
responsibility. In addition, they — or rather: the organization backing them — accumulate the necessary economic capital and put at
risk their symbolic capital: if the completed performance is not
exactly a success, the damage is first and foremost to them. This
line of thought only confirms the choreographer's principal status
as an artistic entrepreneur investing financial and other means
in a peculiar labour setting in view of primarily symbolic gains,
which may subsequently be converted into economic benefits (the
higher one's general artistic recognition, the bigger the chances
to assemble more subsidies and co-production money for a future production cycle). Nevertheless, both the active making of
the performance and its live (re-)enactment are chiefly a collective endeavour: a genuine social subject animates the rehearsal
process and its final outcome. Thus the (re)produced common is
effectively privatized through legal authorship; and the choreographer indeed seems to continually expropriate the various benefits
of cooperation and, more generally, the collaboratively co-created value. However, this apparently convincing critical analysis
is incomplete.

The disturbing factor is the notion of artistic value (and by
implication also the concept of artistic surplus value). The regime
of singularity culturally frames the production and reception of

art works, yet both processes in a paradigmatic way also exemplify the peculiarities of 'the economics of singularities' (Lucien Karpik). Like most cultural commodities of whatever nature, as well as various sorts of personal services, such as the ones provided by specialized lawyers or doctors, art works are traded on markets where quality competition prevails over price competition. Prices can therefore not be explained by supply and demand alone: neo-classical economics no longer directly applies because acts of symbolic appreciation decisively mediate the relationship between offer and consumer preferences. They are inherently risky, because quality uncertainty essentially marks every singularity. Thus dance lovers who are eagerly looking forward to an upcoming performance do not know if the show will please, annoy or alternately interest and irritate them. Hence the importance of diverse types of devices that assist art consumers in inspecting and provisionally evaluating the current offer. They range from publicly consultable critiques or essays in more specialized magazines to the shared appraisal of peers, friends or acquaintances who have already witnessed a performance or visited an exhibition. The devices must be trusted but never offer real certainty: just like the positive aura surrounding an artist, they can only slightly minimize the risk that the dance performance one plans to attend may lack quality, in the broad sense. What complicates matters even more is the complex, multidimensional nature of aesthetic artefacts and other economic singularities: they again and again generate utterly contrasting judgments. 'Am I worthy?', the object claiming the honorific title of art work anxiously asks. The answer performatively qualifying the artefact in question evidently varies with the applied standards and the specific hierarchy among the different criteria deemed relevant. Each recently published poem or every contemporary opera therefore not only raises the question of it being a genuine art work but also provokes a broader assessment addressing its assumingly basic features from both a more descriptive and a predominantly evaluative perspective. Yet judging the value, artistically or otherwise, of a singularity also continuously informs its actual production, the process through which the final artefact inviting judgment takes shape. Thus the young poet jotting down a still isolated sentence re-reads it over and over again, trying to determine its possible worth. The collaborative co-production of a work of contemporary dance — or rather: of an artefact claiming to be so — is no exception, quite the contrary. Cooperatively creating artistic value requires a common valuation activity, the collective negotiation of shared judgments that may contribute to a situated common culture or discourse. In sum, *producing artistic value together necessitates constantly valuing the active production together.*

The cooperating choreographer and performers act as a local interpretative community that repeatedly assesses individual or collective material, leading ideas, possible procedures or tasks, et cetera. The judging first and foremost brings into play various descriptors for interpreting, mostly in the realist first order-mode of observation, the features perceived through the senses of, for instance, a series of movements or a potential tableau vivant in the making. Publicly stating 'what is precisely involved?' intrinsically co-defines artistic collaboration: 'The talking part is really important because the articulation of what we do is important. We are constantly discussing what it means: we have to create the understanding of a work together because otherwise we can't perform it.' Various expressions or key signifiers borrowed from the broader common culture that frames contemporary dance activity inform the diverse individual reports. At once simple and telling notions such as 'presence', 'vivacity', 'flat' or 'physicality' are indeed widely shared and function in many rehearsal processes as a primary linguistic platform allowing mutual understanding or collectively meaningful agreements and disagreements. As a rule, they do not suffice to discursively singularize the specific stakes of a creation. Hence the step-by-step emergence of a more particular lexicon that has a thoroughly contextual nature: 'After a while, you really start speaking in the same way. You know that these specific words mean this and that; words become very precise but would not mean anything in another context: your vocabulary is attuned to this one production or even to a moment in the work process.'

By and large, the gradual building up and stabilizing of a common discourse seems to follow an evolutionary logic of variation, selection and retention filtered by both the social reflexivity and the self-referential nature that characterize communication. Different descriptive viewpoints are put forward in relation to this material or that task; some are explicitly criticized, others bluntly negated for being 'not interesting', but some signifiers start to circulate in the group because several members repeatedly take them up in their personal interpretations of the situation at hand.

An implicit descriptive consensus thus emerges through the sheer communicative reiteration of singular expressions or concepts. The agreement not only eases the collaboration's actual coordination but also performatively furthers both the individual and collective development of valuable material. Thus particular physical modes or bodily states, which may greatly define a creation, become fixed through the partly explicit, partly implicit production of a shared vocabulary. The generated *descriptive common* at once results from and frames the public exchange between the collaborators, yet without preventing private re-articulations in line with the logic of interpretative flexibility. It is indeed not at all unusual for a situated vocabulary to acquire distinctly individual accents. The same signifiers are thus coupled with different personal meanings: 'There is a code that you establish with the group that allows you to discuss the work, to be more precise about it and to define a common ground; and there is another kind of discourse going on as well, the one you establish with your own self in order to perform.' In sum, the publicly made and socially manifest 'text' generates various latent 'subtexts' not discussed but literally danced out within the context of the guiding descriptive common.

When passing judgment together, descriptive pluralism is seconded by normative multiplicity. Is, for instance, a proposed movement sequence worthy? Does it effectively possess potential qualities that can be built upon and further refined through a collaborative effort? Different answers will be voiced because of the deployment of various value registers or regimes of justification. The judged actions may be deemed original, conceptually interesting, testifying of a rare sort of physicality, containing promising links with other materials, and so on. At the same time, every valuation also indirectly appraises the work relation's general nature or productivity and often qualifies the contributions of one or more particular individuals. Without a clear-cut organizational shape, participatory collaboration actually functions as a so-called heterarchy marked by value dissonance or 'a form of distributed intelligence in which units are laterally accountable according to diverse principles of evaluation' (in the words of economic sociologist David Stark). The momentarily existing pluralism has to be trimmed down and turned away from the possible tendency to become magnified, in the direction of a possible congruity that not just flattens out but combines or blends at least some of the differences in individual viewpoints. An implicit working consensus has to be composed, which through repeated corroboration may subsequently generate a *value common*, however contextual or temporary. Yet when materials, tasks or underlying notions are inter-individually assessed in terms of their possible worth, pluralism is predictably harder to deal with than in situations focussing on the 'thick description' of their crucial characteristics. Dissonance is indeed often more outspoken, in the literal and figurative sense, when it comes to divergent or somewhat contrasting conceptions of the desirable or the discursive fine-tuning of a general value's 'real meaning'. Normative positions tend to be more personally engaging: what people find worthy directly implicates their self, that which they stand for as an artist – or even as a human being or individual – and identify with in a partly conscious, partly unconscious way. During a co-creation, differences in opinion on the worth of interim results therefore always risk hardening into difficult to settle disputes, if not into an open strife endangering the minimal social cohesion every productive collaboration must rely on. Avoiding the tipping point in which evaluative dissonance transforms into unproductive noise is perhaps the semi-directing choreographer's prime management task.

Collectively resolving questions regarding artistic, political, conceptual or whatever sort of value when incommensurable frameworks are at play, is a markedly difficult mode of 'commoning'. Polyphony has to metamorphose momentarily into a relative unison without having any solid ground to build up the necessary accord. Judging in the collective mode indeed usually creates a semi-public space in which divergent appraisals relate to each other. Differences are explicitly addressed, spelled out through an at times detailed argumentation and underpinned with various references to 'facts'. The actual conversational dynamic and its possible outcomes greatly depend on the very value that each party imputes to its value position since this strongly calibrates the effective chances to negotiate a middle ground judgment, to make 'an honest compromise' or to become convinced. Although the 'commoning' may commit itself explicitly to the ideal of a power-free dialogue only based on arguments or good reasons – which Jürgen Habermas regards as the quasi-immanent telos of discursively mediated communication – manifest and latent inequalities normally co-structure the exchange. Thus the authority of 'the artistic subject supposed to know' at times implicitly guides discussions. The choreographer's value stance then functions as a symbolic reference point having also social value: 'If I am not convinced, people will not push to go on.' In a word, the semi-directivity underlying a participatory collaboration also operates latently – read: without words, yet significantly framing the dancers' use of appreciative words or standards. Moreover, artistic work settings quite frequently display a peculiar form of communicative self-organization, not explicitly agreed on, that both codifies inequalities in linguistic ability and simplifies the social generalization of judgments. Three positions or roles actually stand out. The 'talkers' visibly enjoy the exchange of divergent viewpoints and are skilled language users: they excel in rhetoric and can relatively easily win over others (as a rule, the choreographer is one of them). The 'listeners' regularly voice an opinion, now and then raise clarifying questions and sometimes formulate an apt remark or argument – but they primarily take the time to sort out the pros and cons of the discussed judgments by listening silently before publicly taking sides with a singular value position. The third role also involves a primarily listening-directed attitude, yet the 'diplomats' overhear the different opinions in view of their possible mediation. Generalizing viewpoints is the diplomats' genuine standpoint: they verbally create building blocks for potential compromises, dampen heated discussions and have an overall well-developed sense for the possibly unifying melody resounding in a polyphony of judgments. Above all, diplomats know that a singular view never contains in itself generality – it is not of the order of truth – but this quality is exactly the task to be performed: the value common has to be constructed.

Collaboration's Multiple Micro-Politics

According to Hannah Arendt, sharing the world with others and trying to compose a common judgment of its most pertinent features constitutes the generic basis of political action and the public life in the polis. The thesis comes with some crucial qualifications. Judging is political insofar as it relates to other opinions in an essentially twofold way: one tries to persuade others of one's standpoint, and simultaneously one takes into account their judgments in view of a possible agreement. A judgment's validity indeed hinges on its possible social generalization or capacity to become shared, to define a collective discursive space in relation to the common world at hand. In a situation of value dissonance, this potential will be furthered when those involved act 'representatively': they openly acknowledge others' perspectives by representing them in individual thinking or speaking. Or, as Arendt writes: 'The more people's standpoints I have present in my mind while I am pondering a given issue, and the better I can imagine how I would feel and think if I were in their place, the stronger will be my capacity for representative thinking and the more valid my final conclusions, my opinion.' 'Talking dance' therefore acquires a political dimension on the condition that the various participants are willing to broaden their personal viewpoints through the mutual incorporation of those of the others present. Without this attitude, individual judgments remain only subjectively valid. Moreover, the public exchange of opinions then runs the risk of deteriorating into a pure auto-telic, if not narcissistic affirmation of individual standpoints, not directed toward the active communalization of judgment. Likewise, within the context of creative cooperation a genuine micro-politics only emerges when the different collaborators quasi-ethically unite in a shared willingness to think and communicate 'representatively', to construct a value common through the discursive interlacing of a plurality of opinions, thus at once condensing and superseding the initial pluralism. An even broader relevance or social validity comes into view when the variety of standpoints presented is linked to the multiplicity of possible opinions in the still absent public with whom the final product will be shared. Using a vocabulary pointedly similar to Arendt's, a dance artist explains: 'Different perceptions are important: in a way, we together as performers can represent the audience. My view as choreographer is one view, but it's much better to have ten views. Although multiple views are not really representative of the public, chances are higher that this comes closer to what an audience could perhaps understand.'

'The progressive composition of the common world ... is the name I give to politics', Bruno Latour contends. The statement may be given a broader twist: *'commoning', or the collective production of a common (a commonality, a common good), is the essential practice through which 'the social' instantiates 'the political'*, be it on the macro or micro level. When collaborating, dance artists develop in common a singular movement vocabulary (in the broadest sense) that is performatively linked to the co-creation of a specific discursive vocabulary, a partly self-developed and shared mode of 'talking dance'. The social generalization of judgments not only frames or co-conditions but immanently defines this situated micro-politics. In dealing with value dissonance, those collaborating may negotiate, compromise and/or rhetorically convince, thus in fact exemplifying an established cliché image of politics. However, making dance together also rests on two decidedly particular modes of overcoming individual differences in both descriptive interpretation and normative appreciation. *Work-oriented 'commoning'* is the first one: the piece in the making and the varied activity it demands function as the primary locus of collective attention, and this also when discussing together the actual value of a particular proposition or the potential worth of an unusual idea for a possible task. A distinct ethos is involved, one that does not systematically attribute sometimes vast differences in opinion to a self or subject but assumes that proficient collaboration requires a distanced, rather impersonal orientation to work. In this way, disagreements are thoroughly de-individualized. 'My viewpoint' is not counter-acting or buttressing 'your opinion' because we both first and foremost address an external referent, including at once work (labour) and the work (the envisaged final piece, the task at hand contributing to that object's coming into existence). 'It's important to locate problems in the work and not in the relation: the work has to be primary', states a choreographer. 'We have different relationships to the piece because we all have different affinities, feelings or responsibilities towards it — but it's also something we can discuss. The work is to make an object that we can somehow agree upon to present.'

Being centred on work frequently spills over into the kind of pragmatist 'commoning' that truly defines the immanent micro-politics of collaboration. Pragmatism is the loose denominator for the philosophical stance that consistently substitutes the metaphysical desire to attain representative accuracy for the mundane idea that the actual value of any action or thought primarily resides in its empirically testable capacity to solve a particular problem or to further new practicable possibilities. In artistic collaborations, this ethos underlies the marked attitude to cut short discussions animated by difficult to reconcile judgments with an appeal to action: 'I try to create a space of experimentation in which everything seems possible. Most of the times I say "OK, let's try it".' The individual opinion repeatedly defended by one collaborator or the singular viewpoint backed by several dancers but criticized by the choreographer thus changes into a hypothesis whose possible value or generalizability is no longer only a discursive matter but should be assessed in the light of the visible outcomes of its however empirical translation. Confirming the notion of performing research together, the question 'what is it worth?' is displaced from the realm of language to the domain of doing and observing, yet the pragmatic test predictably in turn elicits various descriptions and divergent appraisals. This brings about the distinctive dynamic and self-propelling cycle that characterizes the pragmatist politics of 'commoning', which also helps to settle value disputes and significantly re-articulates their stakes. Inspired by the overall problematic that frames the collaboration, a particular proposition is, for instance, first tried out and then collectively judged and discussed. This contextual debate generates differences in individual or collective judgment, which are pragmatically rendered into new proposals to examine this and to explore that. Experimentation rules: a judgment is neither true nor untrue but opens up a potential to move, speak or otherwise re-activate the work — again in the double sense of labour and artefact — that may be beneficial and create a relatively complex common world asking once again to be reduced through selective assessment.

Imagine that in debating material, a choreographer says X and two dancers voice Y — and consequently both X and Y are put to the test. In judging the empirical results, the dance maker immediately formulates positive comments on Y and dismisses X: 'Now I see!' The situation may look quasi-banal but is also somewhat extraordinary: in light of the visible outcomes of the experiment, 'the artistic subject supposed to know' explicitly affirms that the dancers knew better. Such a marked switch in position, de-authorizing the one presumed to have authority, frequently occurs when making dance together. A particular dialectics indeed repeatedly shifts the semi-directive regime of participatory collaboration in the direction of a more balanced governmentality, blurring the apparently fixed positional differences between the one who presumably leads and those expected to follow. For both parties again and again take the initiative by making proposals, developing material or judging the results of tasks, with always uncertain, unpredictable outcomes. Initiatives are often counter-initiatives in response to an already created situation or previous activity. Within this dynamic, the leader is merely the one creating an opening 'now, here', through the contextual definition of a promising potential to further the work at hand. The temporary leader produces an event in the course of the joint action that one or more of the others will actively appropriate and re-articulate, discuss and value. They can relate to it, or rather: a singular relation asking for social confirmation and continuation is brought forth within the overall labour setting. Subsequently, and regardless of its distinct status, a second collaborator may take the lead by responding to the proposition with a counter-movement, re-creating the temporal horizon of virtual possibilities which all those partaking are collectively sustaining and individually assessing. In a word, a genuine inter-action unfolds in which the operations of leading and following are constantly re-distributed. Thus the collaboration instantiates, in a micro-context, *the peculiar political configuration of an a-personal 'leadingfollowing' (or 'followingleading')* that provisionally displaces and de-segments the general line of inequality informing a semi-directive work relationship. The expression 'leadingfollowing' is André Lepecki's, who in turn uses Erin Manning's perceptive analysis of walking or dancing tango together as a principal source of inspiration. 'I am leading. But that does not mean I am deciding. Leading is more like initiating an opening, entering a gap, then following her response. ... I am not moving her, nor is she simply responding to me: we are beginning to move relationally, creating an interval that we move together', Manning writes.

Cooperating in the mode of 'leadingfollowing' brackets the question of both legitimate authority and personal authorship because the collaborators are truly moving together, thus creating an enigmatic kind of social subject. For each collaborator's actions are now grounded in an interpersonal dynamic, not reducible to only individually accountable initiatives or proposals and also superseding the exchange logic of attributable gifts and counter-gifts. Nobody commands or really has authority: there is just the constant altering of leading and following, in which leading also includes following and the latter activity permanently passes over into the first. This Gordian knot functions as a 'choreopolitical plane of composition', Lepecki observes, adding that 'following-as-leading-as-following requires a kind of *a-personal agreement*', 'a kind of shifting adherence, an immanent yet precarious, always renegotiated a-personal suturing'. The work, in the already emphasized double meaning, must be the activity's direct focus, particularly in the always somewhat dreadful moments that it seems to be lacking sharpness. Subjectivity has to be bent or curved, away from the personal self and in the direction of the anonymous one-ness underlying the singularization of any potential whatsoever: 'one acts, 'one thinks', 'one experiences', 'one speaks', 'one judges'. And also: 'one moves' — one is literally *in* movement because one is moved, inhabits a conjunctive state in which the bifurcating difference between activity and passivity, leading and following, no longer applies. Actually, the issue of de-personalization and a concomitant suspension of subjectivity seems crucial in artistic collaboration, and this despite the participants' desire to say 'I' or their longing for genuine de- and re-subjectifications, which also greatly informs the co-creating. Whether 'commoning' or 'leadingfollowing', a distinctive ethos is demanded that relativizes the self in favour of various doses and different forms of anonymity. Impartiality, non-moralizing and being reasonable (in dealing with one's own viewpoints and the opinions of others), responsibility and loyalty (in relation to the work), openness and the readiness to test individual proposals pragmatically (with the risk of being refuted), humbleness and the ability to lose both authority and authorship (in regard to 'leadingfollowing'): these and related stances vastly underlie the multiple micro-politics of collaboration. Most of them indeed sound decidedly modern, even downright modernist...

The Non-Directive or Flat Mode of Collaborating

Nowadays, making dance together is a much discussed mode of collaboration that risks to push other important forms of mutual cooperation to the background and make them somewhat invisible. Within the European dance community there is a more rhizomatic way of 'commoning' that essentially focuses on the social exchange of various sorts of valuable competences or knowledge, ranging from the specific results or materials of individual or collective research to scores, working procedures or in-depth information on more specialized topics. The deployed media are quite diverse: personal blogs (although they seem less popular these days), open-source platforms, online magazines, or the formats borrowed from educational practice, such as lectures, workshops or seminars. Active collaboration within the frame of longer lasting projects or creations is replaced by temporary convergences, an incidental sharing by dance artists, critics, dramaturges or theoreticians who first and foremost follow their own trajectories.

The short-lived digital crossing or face-to-face meeting is indeed generally motivated by personal interest: collaboration takes on the shape of a truly cooperative individualism. 'Commoning' through the mutualizing of divergent sorts of knowledge, in the broad sense, is also a noteworthy 'flat' practice partially overlapping with the much vaster, worldwide peer-to-peer movement and its stress on use value (against exchange value) and collective intelligence.

Flat collaboration also exists in the spheres of autonomous dance research and co-creating dance. For example, in 1999 Xavier Le Roy, mostly associated with the so-called conceptual wave, initiated the three-year-long project E.X.T.E.N.T.I.O.N.S. In different places, workshops with varying groups of participants addressed the central parameters determining the contemporary production of dance, in a primarily non-directive way. The exploratory journey made use of game and play procedures, which also informed *Project*, the 2003 piece retaking principal outcomes of the research within the set format of a public performance. A distinctive problematic co-defined the work: how to represent or perform on stage artistic collaboration or, in more general terms, 'the collaboratory'? Reflexively looping back the process of making dance together into the dance work itself, thus explicitly resisting artistic fetishism, also framed, for instance, several pieces of artist twin deufert&plischke and the 2012 performance *Tentative Assembly (the tent piece)*. The public announcements credited the latter to Eleanor Bauer but it was actually co-created in an overall egalitarian labour setting. The work critically joins the issue of staging collaboration, thus partly continuing this practice in the relation with the public and linking it to the wider question of how current society can still be or may be transformed into a social space of genuine togetherness: one that does justice – in the vocabulary of Jean-Luc Nancy – to the ontological 'being with', the fact that existence is essentially co-existence in the mode of the 'being singular plural'.

In a truly flat collaboration there is initially often only the shared desire of some artists to work together, mainly because they appreciate each other's ideas, practices or previous performances and therefore guess that joining forces in a predominantly research-driven collective project may perhaps generate something valuable. At the beginning, a general line or even a vague topic may not yet exist. Consequently, those involved have to find out what they actually and potentially share and where they do not agree. It costs quite some time and a lot of discussion to create mutual understanding or to collectively frame a problematic that might produce the necessary working consensus. The sought-after common only slowly emerges through verbal exchange and by collectively trying things out in an improvisational spirit marked by the shared wish to discover, quasi-experimentally, what may eventually structure the collaboration beyond the sheer fact of togetherness. 'Commonalizing' thus takes on a markedly reflexive form: 'talking dance' now visibly equals a discursive micro-politics that includes the joint search for plausible ways of organizing the work, for potential modes of shared decision-making and for procedures that may ease the settling of inter-individual disagreements. In the absence of even a minimal hierarchy and relatively clear-cut social positions or roles, the relationships among the collaborators often also become a central conversational topic. Time and again, social self-observation brings with it the risk of appropriating the work setting and diverting attention too much from collective research as such. Talking about the effectively existing and the hoped-for work relation then begins to form the relationship's primary substance. The dangers are evident: 'It is a waste of time', 'You can get hooked on details that are not really interesting.'

Collaboration's quasi-intimacy always looms in the background, but distinctively more pronounced than in a semi-directive cooperation. The artistic journey that tries to live up to democracy's general promises in a micro-setting always verges on that rather uncanny border where inter-individual closeness significantly animates the co-activity. The sociality therefore threatens to change into the kind of hyper-personal bond that cancels out the minimal mutual distance necessary to entertain a work relation. Avoiding the dynamics of quasi-familial fusion that characterizes small communities is therefore the prime collective task of flat collaboration. One possible solution is to frame the dense social contacts by the institutionalized notion of friendship, which implies personal openness, may even include a sublimated eroticism, but decidedly bars overt hints of sexuality. Yet artistic collaborations of the equal sort do not only over-activate the quasi-intimacy that feeds every somewhat intense work relation in the domain of the arts or 'creative capitalism'. Also, negatively toned personal features that latently undermine the setting's potential productivity frequently come to the fore, such as recurrent individual passivity, lack of personal preparedness, the notable unwillingness to think and talk in the 'representative' mode, or not assuming sufficient responsibility for the collective work. Moreover, a hard to control narcissism may be at play, or the 'mixed' desire to be positively valued by others and not to be repeatedly outdone by their actions: 'You therefore have these strange situations like "it is actually true what the other one says" — but because he is already right for the third time, you try to make it a bit problematic to get the point through. It's totally irrational: you don't want it, but you need it for your ego.' This and related behaviour generates irritations that from a certain moment onward must be brought out into the open, with the evident risk of over-heated moralizing disputes and still more conversations not 'talking dance' but 'discussing us'. In a word, *the personal' is at once the positive attractor and negative vanishing point of non-directive collaboration.*

How to establish, reproduce and incidentally renew a lasting flat cooperation, a genuine artistic collective whose individual members also deliberately use this very term, knowing all too well that it is open to misunderstandings? A balanced mix of mutual personal love, in the already mentioned Spinozist sense, and a shared work-oriented ethos that de-personalizes possible contentions seems to be a crucial success factor: 'Long-term collaboration is very much connected to friendship and love, that's for sure. If it works with us, it's because I do admire all the others: I am sure they are the best! And the admiration primarily regards the work they do, not the person.' Someone's individual behaviour may at times be seriously doubted and even profoundly questioned, but their artistic and professional capacities are trusted because their productive actualization has been repeatedly witnessed, not the least in those difficult moments when a plausible way out looked impossible to achieve but was nevertheless delivered by the person in question. In addition, a common culture or discourse informing both description and evaluation has been effectively established over time: 'Everybody speaks in the same way'. In dealing with this or that task or movement sequence, many possible questions are then no longer raised since a stabilized working consensus exists. Situations demanding generalized judgments are relatively rapidly co-defined and sorted out because they have already been collectively settled before in similar contexts. Yet a possible and reflexively observed hazard shimmers through: 'You risk to reproduce yourself: there are many questions that you no longer ask anymore.'

The trust in both the others and the collective's lasting productivity relies on the frequent experience of personal enjoyment and the social surplus value received. Doing research and creating performances together is experienced as a common wealth — in the multi-layered meaning Michael Hardt and Antonio Negri give to this expression — that greatly furthers individual capacities: 'The work we make together is more than what each of us could achieve alone. The basic thing is that we are going to get more in being together than in being divided.' The cooperatively engendered and sustained common wealth keeps the collaboration going, despite moments of interpersonal crisis or conjectural difficulties in maintaining a somewhat sane balance between the group's intense demands and the desire to have a personal life. Within this particular context, the issue of personal authorship metamorphoses into a contingently individualized social matter. *This is flat collaboration's distinctive micro-politics: 'one' happens to accidentally represent and publicly voice the possible accord virtually insisting among 'the many'*, the constitutive multiplicity impregnating the artistic collective's not being — not wishing to be — a community. The lucid and self-confidently uttered words that put a long-lasting collaboration in the flat mode into perspective, deserve to be quoted extensively because they draw out their possible conceptualization: 'We speak a lot, we talk a lot, we discuss a lot of things. And at one point, there is crystallization: "Oh, that is the idea!" At one point, somebody is able to name what is at stake. For sure, it is often the same people who do this — but the idea does not only come from them. It emerges from the group, from what we speak about, from the discussions we have. The crystallization can happen because the others nourish you. So being a collective means that the one who has an idea does not get this idea because he's a genius but because he's part of a collaborative way of working. It's like people involved in writing software: there's a federation of people and now and then there's one who is collecting the energy. Does this person have such a big ego that the others disappear? — that's the question. None of us is actually pretending to be a genius, or an artist who has a revelation. Moreover, those who listen are as important as the one who speaks. If you speak and nobody is listening, your speech is meaningless. This is exactly the point in a collective: the one who is listening can say "yes" or "mmm..." — and the "mmm..." is very important.'

The decisive social test of a non-directive collaboration is the actual organization of decision-making. Multiple choices have to be considered, communicated and trimmed to a final selection binding all those partaking. A robust common culture greatly helps to settle issues through collective discussions in which one person may voice the sought-after decision that already potentially exists within the group. Yet two additional, deliberately opted for procedures may facilitate the unavoidable exercise of power within the context of a collective, thus contributing to performatively displace – not: to resolve – the noteworthy paradox of combining the absence of a general asymmetry with hierarchical decision-making. Leadership can rotate over several projects in accordance with someone's effective share in a creation, their contribution to the principal building blocks framing the work, or the specific competences deemed crucial in a rehearsal process. Differences in skills also directly inform the second reflexively deployed method: the overall decision potential is divided into individual niches of authority based on a distinctive ability or know-how. Task differentiation then goes hand in hand with the fragmentation of legitimate power. The collaborator who excels in writing has the final say in matters of text; and the one who knows best when it comes to technicalities takes the lead when the final lighting dramaturgy has to be composed. Once the partly collectively discussed, partly implicitly generated constellation of functional authority has arisen, its overall outline must be accepted. This requirement is not always easy to live up to but must be honoured tacitly: 'Each of us has specific responsibilities, which means that you have to forget about your ego: critical thoughts do not vanish, but they are not expressed.'

A final observation: dance artists clearly communicate in different discursive registers when talking of semi-directive and flat collaborations. Not only are the specific stakes and dynamics of both frequently very different, which is rather self-evident, but the speaking subjects also position themselves in a different way in relation to the work, again in the double sense of labour and artefact. When focussing on participatory cooperation, the discourse tends to highlight the principal asymmetry between performer and choreographer, which results in a dualistic speech: there is 'I', and there is 'him/her'. The artistic and social distance informing the work relation is thus emphasized, along with the existence of a conditioning hierarchical division in authority and decision-making. Notwithstanding the many chances 'to have a fair share' in the work process and the final artefact, a rather under-nuanced social duality is recurrently affirmed and corroborated through multiple references to various 'facts'. By contrast, a flat collaboration quasi-automatically invites to speak in terms of 'we', also when the work relation is reported to be sometimes difficult because of interpersonal rivalry or others' lacking engagement. According to dance artists' self-observations, a productive democratic labour setting is definitely of the order of a polyphonic togetherness whose description continually provokes the perhaps conscious, perhaps not that reflexive use of the simple word 'we', although the speaker usually also firmly dismisses the communitarian idea of social fusion. 'I' versus 'him/her' on the one hand, 'we' on the other — but also implicitly structuring the discursive difference in 'talking collaboration' is the reference to two different modes of engagement. In discussing the semi-directive regime, work and 'the artistic' regularly blend for the dancer, but overall an observable split dominates his or her discourse because 'the artistic subject supposed to know' appropriates both labour and the produced artefact through a supposedly prime authorship also acknowledged by law, critics or the public. Conversely, both dimensions appear much more entwined in the speech on flat collaborations. Work and 'the artistic' tend to coincide, not in an 'I' but precisely in the 'we' to which the 'I' belongs in a non-identifying mode, without coinciding with the enigmatic social matter making up collaboration.

Coda: Defining 'the Collaboratory'

Creating together, within and outside the arts, deserves its Hegelian moment, so to speak: we are in need of a genuine theory of *the collaboratory', or the always contextually embedded, at once partially realized and still virtual potential to co-create.* By way of conclusion, some tentative ideas for such a theory, which will by definition be a collaborative effort, may be suggested. In line with already presented notions, *commonalism* appears to be the appropriate name to single out the primary stakes and principal contours of creative co-operation. All in all, three sorts of commons are involved, Antonio Negri rightly asserts. There is 'the common as a base for accumulation, constituted by material and immaterial forces', which consequently allows 'the common as production, along a retreated border and ever renewed values' (this second form was indeed previously termed 'commoning'). The joint action in turns brings forth diverse commonalities within the context of the collaboration and final products whose eventual status as common goods principally depends on their general accessibility. Are the jointly created end-objects, in the broad sense, capitalistically captured, commodified and privatized through the laws of copyright and authorship? Or do they indeed land in the commons, or the domain of free use transcending the traditional distinction between private and public that affords artefacts' collective re-employment as gratis resources in future processes of 'commoning'? De-commodification, or the various struggles pro the protection and particularly the extension of common goods, distinctively marks all politics inspired by the social reality of commonalism.

'The collaboratory' actually presumes the pre-existence of an always already common. Co-creation cannot take off without a divergent set of heterogeneous competences, ideas, interests and attitudes that must be presupposed as being shared. The principally assumed capacities have a generic nature: the abilities to think, to communicate, to feel or to imagine that co-defines humaneness. Together with the human body's faculty to move or to stand still in a reflexive way, these general potentials are mostly taken up, without much further notice, as constituent elements in collaborative dance practices. The active collaborator is usually regarded as an autonomous subject formulating ideas, speaking out, having conscious emotions, inventing future lines of action or engendering physical gestures. Yet in doing so, they always actualize common abilities uniting human kind. Paolo Virno therefore contends that in creative immaterial labour, 'the one is not a promise, it is a *premise*.' This 'one' or *generic common* of course enters collaboration in a structured or individualized mode. Due to differential backgrounds and training trajectories, the networked general capacities have a personal nature. *One* for instance speaks or moves: this is the common quality of communicating or dancing that can never be undone or negated. And at the same time there is this and not that *I* saying something or gesturing in a singular mode: this is the structured potentiality that individually translates the generic common that the implied subject only partly knows. The promise of a true social productivity animating collaboration wagers itself on possibilities yet to come — yet to discover, produce and actualize — that at once activate and deconstruct each dancer's personal practicing of shared capacities. The other collaborators' otherness is a principal, if not crucial guiding instance. Hence the mostly implicit ethics underlying the sometimes smooth, at other moments disharmonious and faltering functioning of 'the collaboratory', which Krassimira Krushchkova aptly summarizes in one line: 'The thinking of the collaborative ... has a weakness, a weakness [in the sense of a preference — RL] *for* the potentiality of the other and otherness.'

The continual activation of the (individualized) generic common is driven by a *common cause* framed by a collaboration's initial problematic, which in the course of the joint action will be further refined and re-interpreted or complemented with other notions. 'The collaboratory qua collaboratory works on problems', states anthropologist Paul Rabinow: 'Common problems should be a factor of both cohesion and individuation.' They act as shared matters of concern and prompt the personal commitment of those taking part. The collaborators invest in the collectively done artistic labour, and this also in the libidinal sense: they are individually attached to the project's stakes and feel responsible for it. Moreover, the common cause produces a collective focus that works, rather paradoxically, as a uniting producer of a multiple set of differences. For both the general line informing a creation and its recurrent re-specifications elicit descriptive disputes, value dissonance, disagreements on power or authority and perhaps even strife. The common cause both mingles and pluralizes the collaboration, up to the tipping point that the 'dissensus in consensus' may start to threaten the minimum of solidarity every collaborative undertaking presupposes. All engendered relational activity contributes to the processes of 'commoning' and the produced *social common*, which is perpetually renewed through the vast flow of verbal or non-verbal communication and pushes every collaboration 'now, here' in the direction of unknown futures.

'The collaboratory' defies and repeatedly subverts 'the subjective'. Through cooperation, those partaking become other: they experience processes of de- and re-subjectification. Yet the enacted social common operates as the principal *'subiectum'* or bearing surface of joint action. Time and again, it provokes every collaborator's individualized potential to communicate, think, feel or move and to go beyond, even deconstruct its subjective encapsulation. This is *the operation of singularization*, which in most collaborations has a genuinely paradoxical form: at once un-realizing the personal proclivities associated with one's subjectivity and realizing anew the generic common shared with others in a way that is nevertheless still indirectly marked by the suspended self. A collaborating group is therefore 'an ensemble of productive singularities set to work and — as such — productive' (Negri again). Repeatedly, new improbable thoughts or divergent series of hitherto never executed actions instantiate the state of becoming, the transition from 'being in common virtually' to 'commonly being in actuality'. They are event-like actualizations of the shared generic potentials that both by-pass and temporarily redefine the collaborators' subjectivity. Their unplanned emergence also produces flexible lines of flight within the entertained social common that momentary de-stratify and intensify the conditioning relational dynamic. The corresponding 'microwaves' are by definition unstable and do not survive the momentary rhizome eliciting their provisional existence. Creative collaboration thus 'produces massively from within itself singularities that are no longer characterized either by any social identity or by any real condition of belonging, singularities that are truly *whatever* singularities', Giorgio Agamben observes. A-personality reigns: the social common does not assemble the activities of autonomous subjects but resembles a network of various singularities that appear and disappear according to an undecipherable, uncontrollable and prolific logic of co-creation. This rhizomatic reality draws its force from the connected capacities, yet the singularities that selectively realize the virtuality of 'the collaboratory' also gain their momentarily becoming thanks to the continually shifting relations within the network. The singular actualizations of shared human faculties occur 'now, here' because of a sociality happening in the nowhere zone defining the contemporaneity of acting together. Their contingent surfacing immanently hinges on the untameable interplay of the generic common in which all collaborators participate and the momentary commonality it allows. The singularities are neither 'mine' nor 'ours': a distinctive anonymity is at work. Commonalism indeed honours the multidimensional one-ness that exhausts unity. 'Whereas "we" is posited a priori, "one" exists during the time of an incarnation by X or Y; it reconfigures, one can enter and exist in it', says choreographer Boris Charmatz in one of his recorded conversations with Isabelle Launay.

'The collaboratory' is a constantly renewed, never drying up *potenza* that individually empowers and socially connects in the absence of any substantial collectiveness. Yet every creative cooperation not only brings forth a common wealth made up of mutually induced singularizations but also resembles a self-organizing commonwealth or a self-deciding republic. Collectively binding selections have to be formulated 'beyond representation', so without representatives or delegates. How to organize work? What has value? How to go on with topic X or issue Y? And how to agree when disagreeing? These and related questions at times urgently necessitate answers. How they are addressed co-defines collaboration's mode of directivity, which ranges from the multiple forms of semi-governmentality to the truly flatly operating collective. Deciding on daily organization of the work setting, the possible worth of interim results or the potential value of self-generated creativity is however realizing the intrinsic relationship between 'the collaboratory' and 'the political'. The possibility of non-agreement and opposition, not to mention the prospect of an individual's departure, structurally informs *the politics of commonalism, whose principal stake is the furthering of the common, in all existent meanings, through an in principle common decision-making* that will take on various forms. Every discord, no matter its theme, is a crucial test of the micro-politics underlying collaborative practices. The momentary dispute must be resolved, yet it can usually not be disentangled without a minimum of harm being done. According to Carl Schmitt, 'the political' therefore tends to bring forth an unbridgeable rift between friends and enemies. The politics of commonalism bets on the potential to avoid this antagonism and to re-articulate disagreements between agonists into agreements among commonalists. How this local working consensus may be effectively produced, is a contextual matter and varies with the specificities of each singular collaboration and the performative political imagination of those involved. A principal prospect is at stake: the effective possibility to practice collaboration as a contingent experiment in *democratizing democracy*. The programmatic contours of the implied social-political horizon have meanwhile become amply visible: advancing by all possible means the chances of self-organizing commons, whatever their nature or concrete manifestations. Or as Jean-Luc Nancy notes: 'How can we think about society, government, law, not with the aim of achieving ... the common, but only in the hope of letting it come and taking its own chance, its own possibility of making sense?' This is indeed the main political question raised by cooperative labour. It should not be answered timidly, and probably

also not by morally contrasting the various ways of collaborating: they ask for distinctive modes of micro-politics informed by the general perspective defining the politics of commonalism.

Sources

Trusting/Distrusting 'the Artistic Subject Supposed to Know'
The chapter's main title implicitly refers to Andrew Hewitt, *Social Choreography: Ideology as Performance in Dance and Everyday Movement*. Durham (NC): Duke University Press, 2005. The expression 'the artistic subject supposed to know' paraphrases Jacques Lacan's characterization of both the psychoanalyst and unconsciousness as 'the subject supposed to know' in his 1967 essay 'The Mistaking of the Subject Supposed to Know', retrieved from http://web.missouri.edu/~stonej/ mistak.pdf. With both wit and acumen, Jonathan Burrows comments collaboration and various other issues in his *A Choreographer's Handbook*. London: Routledge, 2010, quoted p. 59. The presented view on trust owns much to Niklas Luhmann, 'Trust', in Niklas Luhmann, *Trust and Power*. Chichester: John Wiley & Sons, 1979, pp. 1–106 (p. 26 and p. 73) and Piotr Sztompka, *Trust. A Sociological Theory*. Cambridge: Cambridge University Press, 1999.

Collaboration's Quasi-Intimacy
Michael Hardt and Antonio Negri outline the effects of biopolitical economy and the role of love within immaterial labour in their joint work *Commonwealth*. Cambridge (MA): Harvard University Press, 2009, quoted p. 146 and p. 184 respectively. Luhmann extensively discusses intimate communication from a systems-theoretical point of view in the chapter 'Interpenetration' in Niklas Luhmann, *Social Systems*. Stanford (CA): Stanford University Press, 1995, pp. 210–254 (p. 223 and p. 225). In *Love as Passion: The Codification of Intimacy* (Stanford (CA): Stanford University Press, 1986), he offers an even vaster and historically underpinned analysis. Sigmund Freud infamously asserted that 'the sexual life of adult women is a "dark continent" for psychology' in this 1926 essay 'The Question of Lay Analysis', which can be found in Anna Freud (ed.), *The Essentials of Psycho-Analysis*. London: Vintage, 2005, pp. 7–65 (p. 32). The notion of the 'Thing' as the cause of desire, later replaced by the concept of 'objet petit a', was elaborated by Jacques Lacan in one of his famous seminars: *The Ethics of Psychoanalysis: The Seminar of Jacques Lacan Book VII*. London: Routledge, 1992, quoted p. 97. Baruch Spinoza defines love in his *Ethics*. Oxford: Oxford University Press, 2000, part III, VI: proposition 13S.

Directivity's Ambiguities
The remark on the entwinement of agency and structure in participatory collaboration is partly inspired by Anthony Giddens, *The Constitution of Society. Outline of the Theory of Structuration*. Cambridge: Polity Press, 1984. Bojana Cvejić situates the delineation of a problematic in artistic research in her essay 'A Few Remarks about Research in Dance and Performance or – The Production of Problems', in Gabriele Brandstetter and Gabriele Klein (eds.), *Dance [and] Theory*. Bielefeld: transcript Verlag, 2013, pp. 45–50 (p. 46).

On the Authority of the Choreographer
Max Weber defines power and subsequently differentiates between three sources of legitimate power or authority (charisma, tradition and juridical rules) in the introductory chapter 'Basic Sociological Terms' of his *Economy and Society. An Outline of Interpretative Sociology*. Berkeley (CA): University of California Press, 1978, pp. 3–62 (p. 53). For a brief statement of Michel Foucault's re-articulation of the notion of power, see Michel Foucault, 'The Subject and Power', in Michel Foucault, *Essential Works 3: Power*. London: Penguin, 2002, pp. 326–348 (p. 341). Niklas Luhmann summarizes his view on power in the essay 'Power', included in the already quoted volume *Trust and Power*, pp. 107–184. Inspired by Weber's famous remarks on the charismatic prophet and political leader, Pierre-Emmanuel Sorignet aptly typifies the charismatic choreographer in *Danser. Enquête dans les coulisses d'une vocation*. Paris: La Découverte, 2010, quoted p. 143 and p. 144 respectively. Reference is further made to Abram de Swaan, 'The Politics of Agoraphobia', in Abram de Swaan, *The Management of Normality. Critical Essays in Health and Welfare*. London:

Routledge, 1990, pp. 139-167; and the chapter 'Hegemony and Radical Democracy', in Ernesto Laclau and Chantal Mouffe, *Hegemony & Socialist Strategy. Towards a Radical Democratic Politics*. London: Verso, 1985, pp. 149-194.

The Virtuality of 'Being an Artist'
Pierre-Michel Menger has collected his various articles on artistic labour in *Le travail créateur. S'accomplir dans l'incertain*. Paris: Gallimard/ Seuil, 2009, quoted p. 102. Hannah Arendt discusses the distinction between work and labour at length in her by-now classic study *The Human Condition*. Chicago (IL): Chicago University Press, 1998. For an inspiring portrait of the modern artist that deviates from the one presented here, see Giorgio Agamben, *The Man Without Content*. Stanford (CA): Stanford University Press, 1999, quoted p. 55. Indirectly referenced are Aristotle, *The Nicomachean Ethics*. London: Penguin, 2004; Spinoza, *Ethics*; and Gilles Deleuze and Félix Guattari, *A Thousand Plateaus. Capitalism and Schizophrenia*. London: Continuum, 2003 (the notion of becoming).

Intermezzo: The Intimacy of the Dance Studio
This paragraph is a slightly reworked version of a short essay previously published in Dutch; see Rudi Laermans, 'De intimiteit van de dansstudio (een essayistische speculatie) [*The Intimacy of the Dance Studio (An Essayistic Speculation)*]', in *De Witte Raaf*, (115), 2005, p 8. The general emphasis on the anonymous nature of the described kind of intimacy is loosely inspired by the analysis of affects in Deleuze and Guattari, *A Thousand Plateaus*; see particularly the chapter 'November 28, 1948: How Do You Make Yourself a Body Without Organs?', pp. 149-166. Other important sources of inspiration are Maurice Blanchot, *The Space of Literature*. Lincoln (NE): University of Nebraska Press, 1989; Jean-François Lyotard's essay 'The General Line (for Gilles Deleuze)', in Jean-François Lyotard, *Postmodern Fables*. Minneapolis (MN): University of Minnesota Press, 2003, pp. 115-122 (p. 121); and Thierry de Duve, who analyses the Duchamp-effect and the idea of 'art in general' –

which inspires the notion of 'the body in general' – at length in *Kant after Duchamp*. Cambridge (MA): MIT Press, 1997.

(Not) Judging Art/Dance
The insights referred to and the model of the self of social psychologist George Herbert Mead, which partly laid the foundations for so-called symbolic interactionism, are rather unknown outside sociology; see especially the posthumously published lecture notes of some of his students collected in George Herbert Mead, *Mind, Self, and Society (from the Standpoint of a Social Behaviorist)*. Chicago (IL): Chicago University Press, 1967. Mead's view is loosely combined with cyberneticist Heinz von Foerster's ideas on observation systems as formulated in his collection of essays *Observing Systems*. Seaside (CA): Intersystems Publications, 1981. Also referenced are Yvonne Rainer, '"No" to Spectacle...', reprinted in Alexandra Carter (ed.), *The Routledge Dance Studies Reader*. London: Routledge, 1998, p. 35; Immanuel Kant, *Critique of Judgment*. Oxford: Oxford University Press, 2007; and Lucien Karpik, *Valuing the Unique: The Economics of Singularities*. Princeton (NJ): Princeton University Press, 2010, quoted p. 41 (italics in the original).

Revisiting 'Conceptual Dance'
The link between Conceptualism and contemporary dance has already been discussed at length in the fourth chapter. This paragraph focuses on dance artists' views on the issue, but also contains an explicit reference to Pierre Bourdieu's sociological approach of artistic fields, already introduced in the fifth chapter, and an implicit one to Freud's notion of the Super-Ego as the locus of moral consciousness; see Pierre Bourdieu, *The Rules of Art: Genesis and Structure of the Literary Field*. Stanford (CA): Stanford University Press, 1996; and Sigmund Freud, 'The Dissection of the Psychic Personality', in Anna Freud (ed.), *The Essentials of Psycho-Analysis*, pp. 484-504.

Talking and Judging Dance Together
Michael Hardt and Antonio Negri discuss the specificities of biopolitical

exploitation in the chapter 'Capital (and the Struggles over Common Wealth)', in Michael Hardt and Antonio Negri, *Commonwealth,* pp. 130-188 (pp. 140-141; italics in the original); the same book also vastly inspires the used notion of the common in this paragraph and the next ones. Another important source of inspiration, in which also the verb 'commoning' is put forward, is Peter Linebaugh's *The Magna Charta Manifesto: Liberties and Commons for All.* Berkeley (CA): University of California Press, 2008. The presented analysis of singularities, in the economic meaning, paraphrases some of the main arguments in Lucien Karpik's already quoted study *Valuing the Unique.* The metaphor of value dissonance and the concept of heterarchy are borrowed from David Stark, *The Sense of Dissonance: Accounts of Worth in Economic Life.* Princeton (NJ): Princeton University Press, 2009, quoted p. 19. Implicit reference is made to Jürgen Habermas, *The Theory of Communicative Action.* Boston (MA): Beacon Press, 1989, 2 volumes.

Collaboration's Multiple Micro-Politics
Gilles Deleuze and Félix Guattari greatly contributed to the institutionalization of the notion of micropolitics; see particularly the chapter '1933: Micropolitics and Segmentarity' in Deleuze and Guattari, *A Thousand Plateaus,* pp. 208-231. Hannah Arendt discusses the relationships between politics, judging and the 'representative' mode of thinking and communicating in the essay 'Truth and Politics', in Hannah Arendt, *Between Past and Future.* London: Penguin, 2006, pp. 223-260 (p. 241). The Latour quote on politics' intrinsic relation with the building up of a common stems from Bruno Latour, *War of the Worlds: What about Peace?* Chicago (IL): Prickly Paradigm Press, 2002, pp. 8-9. For a more elaborate development of the argument that takes into account the existence of non-human actors as elements of commons, see Bruno Latour, *Politics of Nature: How to Bring the Sciences into Democracy.* Cambridge (MA): Harvard University Press, 2004. Pragmatism's *locus classicus* remains

William James' *Pragmatism: A New Name For Some Old Ways of Thinking.* Cambridge (MA): Harvard University Press, 1975. Erin Manning discusses the entwinement of leading and following in her essay 'The Elasticity of the Almost', in Erin Manning, *Relationscapes: Movement, Art, Philosophy.* Cambridge (MA): MIT Press, 2009, pp. 29-42 (p. 30). Building on this text's suggestions, André Lepecki crucially gives them a political twist in his 'From Partaking to Initiating: Leadingfollowing as Dance's (a-personal) Political Singularity', published in the already quoted collection edited by Gabriele Brandstetter and Gabriele Klein, *Dance [and] Theory,* pp. 21-38 (p. 34; italics in the original).

The Non-Directive or Flat Mode of Collaborating
Xavier Le Roy's *E.X.T.E.N.S.I.O.N.S* and the ensuing performance *Project* are analysed at length from the point of view of collaborative dance production in Pirkko Husemann, *Choreographie als kritische Praxis. Arbeitsweisen bei Xavier Le Roy und Thomas Lehmen.* Bielefeld: transcript Verlag, 2009; and Martina Ruhsam, *Kollaborative Praxis: Choreographie. Die Inszenierung der Zusammenarbeit und ihre Aufführung.* Wien: Verlag Turia + Kant, 2010 (this book also puts into perspective some works of the artist twin deufert&plischke). In their conceptualization of collaboration both studies primarily rely on the work of Jean-Luc Nancy, which is mentioned in passing; see especially Jean-Luc Nancy, *Being Singular Plural.* Stanford (CA): Stanford University Press, 2009. The parenthetically referred to idea of common wealth is again the one advanced by Hardt and Negri in *Commonwealth.*

Coda: Defining 'the Collaboratory'
This paragraph is a revised version of an already published text; see Rudi Laermans, '"Being in common": Theorizing Artistic Collaboration', in *Performance Research: A Journal of Performing Arts,* 17 (6), 2012, pp. 94-102. For broader statements on the politics of commonalism, see Rudi Laermans, 'The Promises of Commonalism', in Lieven De Cauter, Ruben De Roo and Karel

Vanhaesebrouck (eds.), *Art and Activism in the Age of Globalisation*. Rotterdam: NAi Publishers, 2011, pp. 240-249; and Pierre Dardot and Christian Laval, *Commun. Essai sur la revolution du XXIe sciècle*. Paris: La Découverte, 2014. With the exception of the implicit references to *A Thousand Plateaus* by Deleuze and Guattari (which underlies the presented view on singularization), *Commonwealth* by Hardt and Negri (the realm of the collaborative production of common wealth as a possible political commonwealth), and Carl Schmitt's *The Concept of the Political* (Chicago (IL): Chicago University Press, 2007) the following sources of inspiration are quoted directly: Antonio Negri, *The Porcelain Workshop. For a New Grammar of Politics*. Los Angeles (CA): Semiotext(e), 2008, p. 65; Paolo Virno, *A Grammar of the Multitude. For an Analysis of Contemporary Forms of Life*. Los Angeles (CA): Semiotext(e), 2004, p. 25 (italics in the original); Krassimira Kruschkova, 'Mit-Sein, Kollaboration, Respons. Zur Ethik der Performance', the foreword in Martina Ruhsam's already referenced *Kollaborative Praxis*, pp. 9-16 (p. 13); Paul Rabinow, 'Collaboration, Concepts, and Assemblages', in Paul Rabinow, *The Accompaniment. Assembling the Contemporary*. Chicago (IL): University of Chicago Press, 2011, pp. 113-126 (p. 125); Antonio Negri, 'An Axiomatics for Empire', in Antonio Negri, *Empire and Beyond*. Cambridge: Polity Press, pp. 8-13 (p. 12); Giorgio Agamben, 'Marginal Notes on *Commentaries on the Society of the Spectacle*', in Giorgio Agamben, *Means without End. Notes on Politics*. Minneapolis (MN): University of Minnesota Press, 2000, pp. 73-90 (p. 87); Boris Charmatz and Isabelle Launay, *Entretenir. A propos d'une danse contemporaine*. Dijon: les presses du réel, 2003, p. 110; and Jean-Luc Nancy, 'Communism, the Word', in Costas Douzinas and Slavoj Žižek (eds.), *The Idea of Communism*. London: Verso, 2011, pp. 145-154 (p. 150).

On the Author

Rudi Laermans is Professor of Social Theory at the University of Leuven (Belgium) and a regular guest teacher at P.A.R.T.S., the Brussels-based international school for contemporary dance headed by Anne Teresa De Keersmaeker. As an academic, he has published widely in both national and international journals and books within the areas of social theory, cultural sociology and the sociology of the arts. For several years, he was the director of the Centre for Cultural Sociology at the University of Leuven and was involved in empirical studies on cultural and arts policy, cultural participation and the fields of performing arts, cultural heritage and the visual arts. Also active as a critic and essayist, he published numerous articles on contemporary dance and is one of the leading voices on, and partly also within, the Flemish dance field.

Arts in Society Series

Moving Together: Theorizing and Making Contemporary Dance is the 18th publication in a series of books that map the interaction between changes in society and cultural practices. Inspired by art and critical theory, the series Arts in Society studies the possibilities of a repositioning of the arts and culture in society. The series is open for publishing proposals in the form of essays, theoretical explanations, practice-oriented research in the arts, and research studies.

Editor-in-chief
Pascal Gielen
p.j.d.gielen@rug.nl

Index

I/II/III/IIII 229
3Abschied 131, 210

A

Abbing, Hans 333
Acconci, Vito 171
Actor-Network Theory (ANT) 81, 232
Adorno, Theodor W. 257
Agamben, Giorgio 23, 30, 38, 53, 55, 79, 81, 160, 161, 187, 332, 335, 359, 390
Aglietta, Michel 333
Aka Moon 108
Alberro, Alexander 239
Alibi 180
Alperson, Philip 80
Amperdans 240
Arendt, Hannah 36, 358, 376, 377, 394, 395
Aristotle 53, 54, 358, 359, 394
Armitage, Karol 205
Art & Language 198
Artaud, Antonin 170, 188
Articificial Nature Project, The 229
Aslan, Odette 241
Aughterlony, Simone 161, 166, 167, 169, 170, 186, 188
Auslander, Philip 187
Austin, John 68, 80
Avdal, Heine 161, 226, 227

B

Bach, Johann Sebastian 105
Bacon, Francis 139
Baecker, Dirk 250, 281
Baehr, Antonia 206
Baervoets, Alexander 40, 334
Balanchine, George 126, 204, 225
Balkema, Annette 335
Ballester, Marion 41, 333
Ballet of the Twentieth Century 13
Balsamine, Brussels 97
Banes, Sally 61, 80, 95, 126, 130, 132, 204, 225, 239, 241, 335

Colophon

Colophon

Moving Together
*Theorizing and Making
Contemporary Dance*

Author
Rudi Laermans

Antennae Series N° 18
by Valiz, Amsterdam

Part of the Series
'Arts *in* Society'

Proofreading and editing
Ula Sickle

Copy editing
Leo Reijnen

Proof check
Els Brinkman

Index
Elke Stevens

Production
Pia Pol

Design
Metahaven

Paper inside
Munken Print 100 gr 1.5,

Paper cover
Bioset 240 gr

Printing and binding
Ten Brink, Meppel

Publisher
Valiz, Amsterdam, 2015
www.valiz.nl

ISBN 978-90-78088-52-3

This publication was made possible
through the generous support of

Fontys School of Fine
and Performing Arts, Tilburg

The author and the publisher have
made every effort to secure
permission to reproduce the listed
material. We apologise for any
inadvert errors or omissions. Parties
who nevertheless believe they can
claim specific legal rights are invited
to contact the publisher.

Distribution:
USA /Canada/Latin America: D.A.P.,
www.artbook.com
GB/IE: Anagram Books,
www.anagrambooks.com
NL/BE/LU: Coen Sligting,
www.coensligtingbookimport.nl
Europe/Asia/Australia: Idea Books,
www.ideabooks.nl

ISBN 978-90-78088-52-3
NUR 675

Printed and bound in the Netherlands

Antennae

Antennae Series

Antennae N° 1
The Fall of the Studio
Artists at Work
edited by Wouter Davidts
& Kim Paice
Amsterdam: Valiz, 2009
(2nd ed.: 2010),
ISBN 978-90-78088-29-5

Antennae N° 2
Take Place
*Photography and Place
from Multiple Perspectives*
edited by Helen Westgeest
Amsterdam: Valiz, 2009,
ISBN 978-90-78088-35-6

Antennae N° 3
**The Murmuring of the
Artistic Multitude**
Global Art, Memory and Post-Fordism
Pascal Gielen (author)
Arts *in* Society
Amsterdam: Valiz, 2009
(2nd ed.: 2011),
ISBN 978-90-78088-34-9

Antennae N° 4
Locating the Producers
Durational Approaches to Public Art
edited by Paul O'Neill
& Claire Doherty
Amsterdam: Valiz, 2011,
ISBN 978-90-78088-51-6

Antennae N° 5
Community Art
The Politics of Trespassing
edited by Paul De Bruyne &
Pascal Gielen
Arts *in* Society
Amsterdam: Valiz, 2011 (2nd ed.: 2013),
ISBN 978-90-78088-50-9

Antennae N° 6
See it Again, Say it Again
The Artist as Researcher
edited by Janneke Wesseling
Amsterdam: Valiz, 2011,
ISBN 978-90-78088-53-0

Antennae N° 7
**Teaching Art in the
Neoliberal Realm**
Realism versus Cynicism
edited by Pascal Gielen &
Paul De Bruyne
Arts *in* Society
Amsterdam: Valiz, 2012
(2nd ed.: 2013),
ISBN 978-90-78088-57-8

Antennae N° 8
Institutional Attitudes
Instituting Art in a Flat World
edited by Pascal Gielen
Arts *in* Society
Amsterdam: Valiz, 2013,
ISBN 978-90-78088-68-4

Antennae N° 9
Dread
The Dizziness of Freedom
edited by Juha van 't Zelfde
Amsterdam: Valiz, 2013,
ISBN 978-90-78088-81-3

Antennae N° 10
Participation Is Risky
Approaches to Joint Creative Processes
edited by Liesbeth Huybrechts
Amsterdam: Valiz, 2014,
ISBN 978-90-78088-77-6

Antennae N° 11
The Ethics of Art
Ecological Turns in the Performing Arts
edited by Guy Cools & Pascal Gielen
Arts *in* Society
Amsterdam: Valiz, 2014,
ISBN 978-90-78088-87-5

Antennae N° 12
Alternative Mainstream
Making Choices in Pop Music
Gert Keunen (author)
Arts *in* Society
Amsterdam: Valiz, 2014,
ISBN 978-90-78088-95-0

Antennae N° 13
The Murmuring of the Artistic Multitude
Global Art, Politics and Post-Fordism
Pascal Gielen (author)
Completely revised and enlarged
edition of Antennae N° 3
Arts *in* Society
Amsterdam: Valiz, 2015,
ISBN 978-94-92095-04-6

Antennae N° 14
Aesthetic Justice
Intersecting Artistic and Moral Perspectives
edited by Pascal Gielen &
Niels Van Tomme
Arts *in* Society
Amsterdam: Valiz, 2015,
ISBN 978-90-78088-86-8

Antennae N° 15
No Culture, No Europe
On the Foundation of Politics
edited by Pascal Gielen
Arts *in* Society
Amsterdam: Valiz, 2015,
ISBN 978-94-92095-03-9

Antennae N° 16
Arts Education Beyond Art
Teaching Art in Times of Change
edited by Pascal Gielen & Barend van Heusden
Arts *in* Society
Amsterdam: Valiz, 2015,
ISBN 978-90-78088-85-1

Antennae N° 17
Mobile Autonomy
Exercises in Artists' Self-Organization
edited by Nico Dockx & Pascal Gielen
Arts *in* Society
Amsterdam: Valiz, 2015,
ISBN 978-94-92095-10-7

Colophon

429